Josep

S

MW01258883

...ue, Apartment 2109
Oakland, California 94611

THE CULT
OF PURE
CRYSTAL
MOUNTAIN

THE CULT OF PURE CRYSTAL MOUNTAIN

✦ ✦ ✦ ✦

Popular Pilgrimage

and Visionary Landscape

in Southeast Tibet

✦ ✦

TONI HUBER

New York Oxford
Oxford University Press
1999

Oxford University Press

Oxford New York
Athens Auckland Bangkok Bogotá Buenos Aires Calcutta
Cape Town Chennai Dar es Salaam Delhi Florence Hong Kong Istanbul
Karachi Kuala Lumpur Madrid Melbourne Mexico City Mumbai
Nairobi Paris São Paulo Singapore Taipei Tokyo Toronto Warsaw

and associated companies in
Berlin Ibadan

Copyright © 1999 by Toni Huber

Published by Oxford University Press, Inc.
198 Madison Avenue, New York, New York 10016

Oxford is a registered trademark of Oxford University Press

All rights reserved. No part of this publication may be reproduced, stored in a retrieval system, or transmitted, in any form or by any means, electronic, mechanical, photocopying, recording or otherwise, without the prior permission of Oxford University Press.

Library of Congress Cataloging-in-Publication Data
Huber, Toni, 1956–
The cult of Pure Crystal Mountain : popular pilgrimage and visionary landscape in southeast Tibet / Toni Huber.
p. cm.
Based on the author's thesis (doctoral)—University of Canterbury.
Includes bibliographical references and index.
ISBN 0-19-512007-8
1. Tibet (China)—Religious life and customs.
2. Mountain worship—China—Tibet.
3. Buddhism—China—Tibet—
Customs and practices. I. Title
BL1945.T5H83 1998
294.3'923'09515—dc21 97-35716

1 3 5 7 9 8 6 4 2

Printed in the United States of America
on acid-free paper

For

Tara,

Shanti,

and Nima

Preface

From where did the snow lion come?
It came forth from the glaciers of Tsari.
It brings joy to the world just by coming
To show off its turquoise mane.

Seng ge ga nas phebs pa//tsa ri'i gangs nas phebs byung//
'dzam gling g.yu ral ngom par// phebs pa tsam gyis dga' byung.

Proud white snow lions with turquoise manes are mythical beasts believed to dwell on the great snowy ranges of Tibet. The snow lion and the mountain are also the contemporary emblems used by exiled Tibetans to represent themselves to the world as an independent people. Snow lion is a poetic epithet, as well, for Tibet's most well-known type of religious practitioners and saints—the hermits and yogins who meditate in solitary caves and retreats in areas of high mountain wilderness. The subject of this book, the Tibetan district of Tsari and its sacred snow-covered peak, Pure Crystal Mountain, is one such abode of snow lions, of both the mythical and the human kind. This remote part of southeast Tibet has long been a place of symbolic and ritual significance for Tibetan peoples. It has served as a center for Tantric meditation and yoga, a site of mountain deity worship, and, not least, as one of Tibet's outstanding natural venues for popular pilgrimage.

This work provides the first comprehensive account of Tibetan life at Tsari, the cult of its Pure Crystal Mountain, and both the esoteric and popular traditions of ritual there. It is my primary aim to present a very detailed and multifaceted study of a major Tibetan pilgrimage tradition, which has not been done before. In addition to this documentation, I have tried to contribute to our knowledge of the construction and meaning of certain Tibetan cultural categories of space, place, and person and the practice of ritual and organization of traditional society in relation to them. I have written with the intent of presenting this material to a wider readership than the specialized field of Tibetan studies and have thus adopted conventions appropriate to that aim.

This study takes the form of an ethnohistorical reconstruction that makes extensive use of Tibetan oral and written sources. While devoting attention throughout to a longer historical perspective, my main focus is the period of the 1940s and 1950s, ending at 1959, the year during which one of the most crucial events in modern Tibetan history took place—the Lhasa uprising against Chinese occupation and the ensuing Tibetan diaspora into South Asia and further afield. All Tibetan life has changed dramatically since then. I selected this particular period for two main reasons. First, I wished to thoroughly document Tibetan social patterns and cultural traditions at Tsari, which largely disappeared after 1959, while it was still possible to do so with informants possessing firsthand knowledge and experience of conditions there. Second, the revival of the site and revitalization of its ritual traditions that has recently begun to take place, following a ban of over two decades on all religious activity in the area, deserves to be the subject of a separate book-length study, which I have already begun.

Although in most of its content this work covers completely new ground, I must stress that it represents only a preliminary study at best. In particular, further careful historical work with Tibetan sources will no doubt yield further insights into many details of the complex mountain cult I have attempted to describe. Further research access to materials from the government archives of the premodern Central Tibetan polity, now in collections administered by the People's Republic of China, may also reveal more details about the nature of state involvements and interests in this cult.

The general terms "Tibet" and "Tibetan" used throughout this book mean many things to different people. They are problematic for two main reasons. First, they evoke the existence of stable or unitary social and geopolitical entities that readily gloss over an enormous actual complexity and fluidity both past and present. Second, they are also contested in various contemporary discourses. Herein I intend the use of "Tibet" in a broad ethnographic sense, as the general area throughout which are found populations sharing a manifestly high degree of linguistic similarity, cultural and social patterns, and historical experience, that is, the "Tibetans." Tsering Shakya (1993) has rightly pointed out that there is in fact no indigenous term that includes all the populations often denoted by the use of the word "Tibetan" in Western literature; discussions of the utility and justification of broad ethnographic definitions of Tibet can be found in the work of Melvyn Goldstein (1994), Hugh Richardson (1984), and Geoffrey Samuel (1993). The site and local population under study in this work were part of the premodern Central Tibetan polity, based on Lhasa. However, I specifically choose to employ a very broad definition because the ritual users of Pure Crystal Mountain, who regularly far outnumbered the local inhabitants, came from areas throughout the higher altitude Himalayan zone, including parts of present-day Bhutan, India, Nepal, and areas currently administered by the People's Republic of China encompassing the central and western Tibetan plateau and the eastern sections of it generally referred to as Kham and Amdo. Some of the actual complexity of premodern "Tibetan" identities will be considered in the course of this study.

Between 1987 and 1995 my Tibetan informants in India, Nepal, central Tibet, and Switzerland provided the bulk of the material on which this book is based, with additional help from others living in Bhutan. The data was collected in the form of extended interviews (conducted variously in Tibetan, English, or in a few cases in Chinese using a translator), hand-drawn maps, songs and oral ritual texts, and so on. My informants also supplied me with important written sources and access to iconographic representations, photographs, videotapes, and other materials. Due to publication restrictions on manuscript length, and also due to the problems of converting tape-recorded colloquial interviews with many dialect words and expressions into accurate written texts, I have supplied Tibetan text in my notes only for unpublished oral sources where written versions were also provided by my informants. These are primarily song texts. Concerning the Tibetan literary sources referred to and translated throughout this book, in all but a very few cases interested specialists will be able to consult the published originals in major libraries and archives with well-stocked Tibetan collections.

Often ethnohistorical research relies as much on insights gained from field work experiences as it does on interviews, textual scholarship, and archival work. My own participation in and observation of a wide variety of contemporary popular pilgrimages undertaken by Tibetans and Tibetan-speaking peoples at many sites during the last fifteen years was of great value in interpreting and elaborating much of the data relating to concepts and ritual practices discussed in this work. For the record, these sites include ones in central and western Tibet (Ganden, Samyé, the greater Lhasa area, the Yarlung valley, Namtso, Dzamling Chisang Kora at Tashi Lhunpo, and to the Panchen Lama in Shigatse, Tsibri, and Labchi), Southern Amdo (Shadur and Shar Dungri), Nepal (Solu-Khumbu, Kathmandu valley, and Chumig Gyatsa), Bhutan (Paro Tagtsang and Chumphu), and North India (Bodh Gaya, Sarnarth, and to the Dalai Lama in MacLeod Ganj).

On occasions throughout the main text and notes where a specific oral source is indicated, either the initials of the informant given in parentless after their names are used (see also the acknowledgments) or one of the following pseudonyms is supplied: "Apha," a male layperson aged 84; "Dorje," a male cleric in his early fifties; "Drolma," a female layperson in her late sixties; "Nawang," a male cleric aged 35; "Ngödrup," a male layperson aged 59; "Pema," a male cleric aged 56; "Tashi," a female layperson in her early forties. I know that some of my informants will not agree with various interpretations of the data that I have tended, and I take full responsibility for the presentation of the material, along with any errors that may remain.

Charlottesville, Virginia T. H.
May 1997

Acknowledgments

At all times my work on the cult of Pure Crystal Mountain and Tibetan pilgrimages benefited from the inspiration, collaboration, and assistance generously offered to me by many people around the world. They range from my intimate companions at home to anonymous pilgrims I met on the back of Chinese trucks as I hitchhiked in rural Tibet. I wish to thank them all sincerely, though I am unable to mention them all here by name. I owe a special debt of gratitude to Umdze Shérab Gyatso (SG) of Darjeeling, whose knowledge of Tsari is second to none. He openly transmitted it to me without prejudice or concern for the "cultural correctness" often encountered nowadays among many educated Tibetan refugees. While I remain grateful to all the peoples of Tsari who helped me, my special thanks go to Thupten Nyamtsur (NT) and his family for greatly facilitating my later work and offering their kind hospitality.

Much of the material presented in this book was initially part of my doctoral dissertation defended in 1993 at the University of Canterbury, New Zealand. My special thanks are due in particular to Paul Harrison and Bo (William) Sax who supervised my dissertation research and who acted in many professional capacities and as good friends to assist me throughout the project. Their thoughtful guidance and constructive criticism has always served me well. I read some of the important Tibetan primary sources together with Paul Harrison, and his critical eye helped solve many of the difficulties of translation I encountered. The original idea for this research was stimulated by discussions with the late Christoph von Fürer-Haimendorf concerning the Indo-Tibetan cultural interface in the eastern Himalaya. My work on ritual and politics, but especially on pilgrimages, has always been greatly inspired by the keen scholarship and kind encouragements of Alexander Macdonald. And it was R. A. Stein's erudite studies of architecture and landscape in Asia that stimulated my own interests in those topics in Tibet. As preliminary readers, Larry Epstein, Geoffrey Samuel, Cathy Cantwell, Paul Harrison, Jens-Uwe Hartmann, Robert Mayer, and Alexander Macdonald all offered useful suggestions on earlier drafts of the material used in this book. Another scholar of Tibetan pilgrimage and friend, Katia

Buffetrille, has always generously shared and discussed her research findings with me, for which I remain grateful.

I also wish to thank the following people who provided all types of assistance and materials during my research: Michael Aris, Gordon Aston, Joachim Baader, Michael Balk, Martin Brauen, Chimed Yudron, Chödrup, Christoph Cüppers, Dochung Tsering Dhondup, Drigung Chetsang Rinpoche, Franz-Karl Ehrhard, Richard Ernst, Elena De Rossi Filibeck, Flip Ketch, Frances Garrett, Geshé Ngawang Dargyey, Paul Hackett, Richard Huber, Karma Phödzo, Khatagpa Tashi, Khenpo Könchog Gyaltsen (KG), Khenpo Puntshog Tashi (KPT), Kunzang Tengye, Per Kværne, Losang Dawa, Dan Martin, Gary McCue, Colin Monteath, Mynak Tulku, Ngawang Tenzin, Ngawang Tsering, Norbu Dorje (ND), Nyima Gyeltsen, Pemala, Charles Ramble, Matthieu Ricard, Hugh Richardson, Rongpo Drolma (RD), Hamid Sardar-Afkhami, Shakya Palzang, Singye Dorji, Sonam Paldrön, Sonam Palgye (SP), Sonam Tenzin (Martin Daellenbach), Wim van Spengen, Tashi Dolma (TD), Tashi Namgyal, Tashi Tsering, David and Sharon Templeman, Tenzin Wangchuk (TW), Tsering Dolkar, Jack Whittemore, and Heinz Zumbühl. I apologize to anyone I may have carelessly overlooked.

Finally, my heartfelt thanks go to both the Huber and Daellenbach families of Christchurch, New Zealand, for their many years of unconditional support of my scholarship. And to Mona Schrempf for her generous assistance, encouragement, and useful suggestions during the final stages of the research and writing.

Contents

Note on Tibetan Words

It is difficult in many cases for nonspecialists to pronounce Tibetan words rendered in transcription according to their proper spellings. For example, the term for "meditation place" is spelled *sgrub gnas* but pronounced something like *drupné* in many dialects. In the absence of any standard or widely accepted system for representing Tibetan pronounciation, I have used my own simple phonetic equivalents for Tibetan words throughout the main body of the text and notes. The pronunciation generally follows that of Central Tibetan dialects, although it is not entirely consistent with any one area. Correct written forms of Tibetan words, using the common Wylie (1959) system of romanization, are given for each phonetic equivalent in the Tibetan word list at the end of the book. Not all spellings are regular or found in lexicons, as some words, mainly in place names, are known only from oral sources and local spellings. Cited portions of Tibetan text in the notes are written according to the Wylie system. Sanskrit, Chinese, and Japanese names and terms are romanized according to the standard systems.

Part I

✦

PILGRIMAGE

1

✦ ✦ ✦ ✦

Introduction

In 1812 a Tibetan yogin named Shabkar sang his reflections upon a grueling mountain pilgrimage procession he had just performed and the vicissitudes of life in cyclic existence according to the Tibetan Buddhist worldview:

When progressing with difficult passage on the
Narrow paths, rivers, and bridges of the Land of Savages,
It occurred to me that it must be like this
When treading the perilous paths leading between one's death and rebirth.

When I saw the cheerful progress
Of all those who were able-bodied and well equipped,
It occurred to me that it must be like this
When going to the next life possessing the Buddha's teachings.

When I saw the painful progress
Of all those who were feeble and ill-equipped,
It occurred to me that it must be like this
When going to the next life without the Buddha's teachings.

When I saw the progress of those
Leaving their ailing friends behind,
It occurred to me this is just what one means
When talking of friends who lack a sense of shame.

When I saw the progress of those
Carrying their ailing friends upon their backs,
It occurred to me this is just what one means
When talking of friends who have a keen sense of shame.

When I saw some giving food and supporting
Those bereft of everything,
It occurred to me that this is just what one means
By those one talks of as aspiring to Buddhahood.

When I saw many pilgrims
Dying of starvation and illness,
It occurred to me that they
Had truly given their bodies and lives for Buddhist religion.

When I saw pilgrims by the tens of thousands
Parting to go their separate ways,
It occurred to me that this is just what one means
When talking of the impermanence of all phenomena.[1]

Shabkar's poignant metaphorical song captured the intense human experience of ritual journeys around one of Tibet's most venerated natural holy places—the Pure Crystal Mountain of Tsari. His words remained a valid characterization of a major Tibetan pilgrimage tradition as long as it was vital, until 1959. Like all phenomena, rituals too are impermanent, and the great Tsari pilgrimages now survive only in a much-reduced and modified form under present-day Chinese administration. But before traditional Tibet's brutal encounter with the forces of modernity, Tibetan-speaking peoples—ordinary men and women—regularly gathered in tens of thousands around this remote and wild mountain to undertake pilgrimages they knew would be fraught with hardships and even great personal dangers. The story of their visits to the holy place of Tsari and the cult of Pure Crystal Mountain that inspired them are the subject of this book.

The high snow peak named Pure Crystal Mountain, or Dakpa Sheri in Tibetan, the sought-after goal of pilgrims, is located in the remote Himalayan border district of Tsari, in southeastern Tibet (see figure 1.1). According to many Tibetans, it is considered not only one of the most important sites at which to perform pilgrimage during one's life but also the most challenging and dangerous of all Tibet's numerous holy places. While visiting it, the ordinary pilgrim had to contend with a rugged and often harsh environment of high mountains and deep ravines, as well as hostile tribal peoples with a penchant for ambush in the dense local forests to the south using lethal poison-tipped arrows. Ritual itineraries of the mountain, made on the basis of a complex set of beliefs about it, were and still are undertakings that require a significant investment of time, stamina, and—not least of all—faith and courage. The various pilgrimage circuits around the mountain enjoyed the patronage of a wide range of Tibetan and neighboring Tibetan-speaking peoples until 1959. Some events regularly staged at Pure Crystal Mountain attracted over twenty thousand pilgrims at a time (a number equivalent to the entire population of premodern Lhasa city), making them by far the most popular ritual of mountain worship in Tibet as well as, it would appear, the largest Buddhist processions staged throughout the high Himalayan zone. The mountain was a cult place of leading Tibetan protective deities, and thus attracted the attention of both the state and the laity. It was famous as a region where powerful alchemical and medicinal herbs and substances employed in ritual could be obtained. In addition, the sacred peak has long been regarded and used by an élite group of Tantric Buddhist yogins as a site par excellence for the performance of specialized forms of yoga and meditation relating to the powerful deities believed to dwell there. And besides being a holy sanctuary, the mountain was also the common and at times contested territory for the domestic life of a mixed group of borderland peoples.

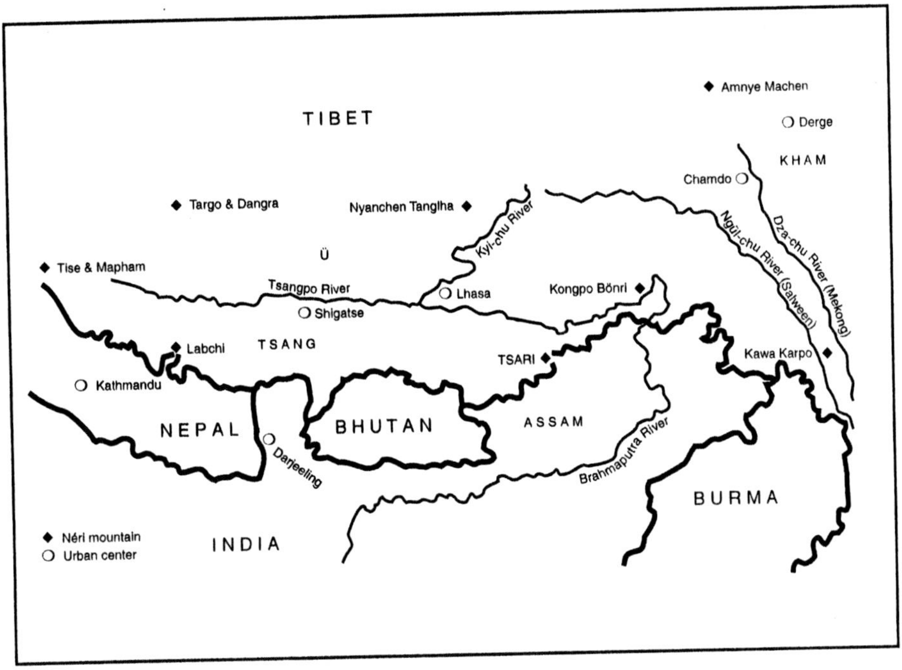

Figure 1.1. Location of Tsari and the principal Tibetan *néri* mountains.

In contrast to other important Tibetan cult mountains of its kind, the Tsari area maintained a sizable settled population, comprising both upland Tibetans to the north and Tibeto-Burman-speaking highland tribal groups from the upper Subansiri River basin of present-day Arunachal Pradesh to the south. Prior to 1959, life at Tsari was not like that found in other better known parts of Tibet. Although the area was apparently fertile, with good rainfall and excellent game habitat, all cultivation and hunting was forbidden around the mountain; thus its environs formed something akin to a traditional Tibetan "national park" or nature preserve. Apart from the practice of small-scale pastoralism, there existed virtually no other food production. The local Tibetan inhabitants, the Tsariwa ("Ones from Tsari") lived in a fairly sophisticated rural economy combining harvesting of natural products, craft work, trading, begging, and, in particular, some specialized forms of service labor relating to the popular pilgrimages performed there. Considered together, Pure Crystal Mountain, its cult, and its transient ritual and settled domestic populations constitute the complex unit for investigation herein.

Outline of the Book

The specific purpose of my study is to document and analyze the set of representations, ritual practices, and peoples centered around this important Tibetan holy mountain. I will also be concerned throughout with two further general frames of inquiry: first, that of investigating a fundamental relationship between forms of high and popular religion in premodern Tibetan society; second, that of appreciating the social and cultural features of large-scale Tibetan pilgrimages and one common type of site around which they focus. By "high" and "popular" religion here I refer, respectively, to an exclusive and esoteric system of Tantric or Vajrayāna Buddhist ritual and cult and the widespread and, in contrast, "public" practices of pilgrimage and mountain worship. These very different types of religious expression were combined in particular ways in Tibet into a syncretic cult of sacred mountain sites known as the *néri* or "mountain abodes." Such a development epitomizes the type of broad cultural transformations that occurred in Tibetan society following the systematized introduction of certain forms of late Indian Buddhism onto the high plateau. Pilgrimages to the *néri* mountains became an extremely popular and enduring feature of Tibetan religious life, having ongoing implications for social structures and processes. One of the defining features of pilgrimage as a social practice is that it requires travel to holy places remote from the pilgrim's home or natal place. Thus in recent centuries this particular form of Tibetan ritual and some of its premier events and sites maintained a social significance that far exceeded the limited horizons of specific localities and the parochial concerns of individual communities. Precisely for this reason, the cult of Pure Crystal Mountain at Tsari is worthy of detailed investigation.

The content of this book falls into four interrelated thematic parts. Part I concerns perspectives on Tibetan pilgrimages, the cult of sacred mountains in Tibet, and their study (chapters 1–3). Part II presents various Tibetan representations of Pure Crystal Mountain (chapters.4–5). Part III describes major Tibetan Buddhist ritual institutions at the mountain (chapters 6–9). Finally, Part IV deals with local identity, cult maintenance, and social organization (chapters 10–11). In chapter 2 pilgrimage is considered as a specific form of ritual practice in Tibetan society. Such pilgrimage is much more broadly considered as a cultural and social phenomena in chapter 3, where I review the origins, development, and characteristics of the *néri* class of cult mountains, of which Pure Crystal Mountain is a premier example. Such mountains served as the most important type of natural pilgrimage places in Tibet over the last three or four centuries.

In chapters 4 and 5 I discuss the principal Tibetan representations associated with Pure Crystal Mountain and its environs. A creation narrative and different Tantric visionary interpretations of the site are analyzed in chapter 4 to show how systems of spatial classification of the landscape and perceptions of the local environment are derived from them. Chapter 5 introduces two important types of ritual literature, both "narrative maps," which are discussed in terms of how Tibetans construct their historical consciousness of the area as ritual users; the ways in which they interpret and navigate its landscape during pilgrimages; and how the site's powers are traditionally presented.

In chapters 6 through 9, I give accounts and analysis of the three main types of ritual institutions that existed at the site up to the 1950s and attracted the participation of practitioners from outside the region. These include Tantric meditation and yoga (chapter 6), a cycle of popular annual pilgrimages (chapter 7), and large twelve-yearly processions and tribute ceremonies (chapters 8 and 9). The presentation of these different institutions follows the order of their establishment around the mountain, which in part accounts for their characteristics and successive development.

In chapter 10 I consider specific local and annual cycles of ritual that mainly relate to the identity of the Tibetan communities inhabiting the environs of Tsari and their role in maintaining the cult of the mountain. Chapter 11 is concerned with the social organization and livelihood of the Tsari peoples, and how these related to the mountain's cult and the existence of popular pilgrimages there.

The Study of Tibetan Pilgrimage

While I was developing this research, it became clear that the existing scholarship on the topic of Tibetan pilgrimages and their sites was limited in some fundamental respects. It provided no adequate point of departure for appreciating a major pilgrimage tradition and cult place, such as Pure Crystal Mountain, from a Tibetan point of view. Nor did it suggest any explicit theoretical frameworks within which, or against which, to discuss the materials I will present here.

Various overviews and remarks on Tibetan and Tibetan Buddhist pilgrimage have been produced, along with ethnographies, historical studies, and translations and analyses of guidebooks and ritual manuals.[2] Research interest in pilgrimage rituals and their sites has also grown rapidly within the last few years.[3] Much of this research is of great interest and value, being the result of decades of careful scholarship. Much of it has, however, followed three distinct trends that work together to narrow rather than broaden one's perspectives on the topic. Briefly, these trends are first, a tendency to place too much explanatory emphasis on Buddhist doctrines and models rather than viewing pilgrimage in terms of an overall Tibetan worldview, a complex syncretistic religious history, and the observable characteristics of its practice; second, an approach to the topic through many small-scale traditions and localized events. This approach has left the major Tibetan sites and events and their very popular traditions of mass ritual journeys—to the holy city of Lhasa; around sacred mountains like Tise (Mount Kailash), Tsari, and Kawa Karpo; to ceremonies such as the Drigung Phowa Chenmo or the Dukhor Wangchen (pre- and post-1959), and to the Dalai Lama and Panchen Lama, for instance—largely unstudied in any detailed and critical manner, in spite of the availability of materials and access; third, a failure to produce either a convincing synthesis of the wealth of available empirical data or any consideration of the theoretical issues, debates, and comparative perspectives common in other pilgrimage studies. All future research will have to work against these trends if any significant advances in our understanding of this particularly rich aspect of Tibetan social and cultural life are to develop.[4] One of the aims of this study is to begin, in a modest way, to shift the direction and style of research into Tibetan pilgrimages and their sites.

The rising scholarly interest in the topic of Tibetan pilgrimage has occurred in the wake of a more general elevation of pilgrimage studies in different branches of the social sciences. In this wider frame, the stimulus given by Victor Turner's work on pilgrimage and ritual theory within cultural anthropology has been of seminal importance.[5] Turner suggested that by their very nature as journeys to distant and powerful sites, pilgrimages as collective rituals tend to enjoin a temporary suspension of regular social status and hierarchy, thus bringing about a state of free and equal affiliation between pilgrims not possible within the structure of the everyday social world. Moreover, attaining this experience is one of the main driving forces behind the pilgrim's ritual undertaking. Since Turner's well-known and humanistic appeal to universal categories—such as "communitas" and "structure/antistructure"—operative during pilgrimage, most major studies of pilgrimage have positioned themselves in relation to his model, challenged it theoretically or tested it in the field, and found it wanting.[6]

As a "post-Turnerian," I too have found little to support his general thesis in relation to Tibetan pilgrimages, in both this ethnohistorical study of Tsari and in fieldwork at various Tibetan Buddhist sites in northern Nepal, Bhutan, and Tibet. Pure Crystal Mountain of Tsari, a powerful yet peripheral site attracting the ritual attention of a whole spectrum of pilgrims, is quite typical of that suggested in Turner's model. The material on its pilgrimages presented throughout this book shows that, on the one hand, there were possibilities for a more egalitarian ethic to prevail, or for certain types of horizontal (as opposed to hierarchal) relations to develop. On the other hand, many of the annual pilgrimages and mass processions around the mountain clearly worked to maintain the status quo of social order, even at times to graphically reiterate and reinforce a whole range of established identities, hierarchies, and social boundaries. These pilgrimages at Tsari also appear to be related to the naturalization of social inequalities and asymmetries in various ways, as well as the legitimation of a particular hegemonic order within a specific historical and cultural context.

But beyond such perspectives, the study of the Tsari pilgrimages and the cult of the mountain itself also provide examples of resistance, conflict, and a range of competing discourses circulating among all those who gathered around the site and engaged in its worship. It appears that identities were actively negotiated and symbolic resources continually appropriated during the rituals. As Eberhard Berg recently pointed out in a review of Himalayan pilgrimages, these and other similar Tibetan pilgrimages might better be seen as "both 'functionally integrative' and 'structurally disintegrative'. In real life the pilgrimage process can constitute an arena for the staging and playing out of conflicts, and also a context in which those conflicts—at least temporarily—can be dissolved."[7] Exactly how this might be the case in one major tradition of Tibetan pilgrimage is the subject of the later chapters of this book.

The ethnohistorical material presented herein, on the traditional cult life of one of the most important Tibetan pilgrimage places of the mid-twentieth century, can be seen to have many continuities with and parallels to contemporary Tibetan contexts, experiences, and events. It was, after all, a time within living memory. I must stress here, however, that much of what happened at Tsari in the 1950s can not be too easily projected onto the ritual life of the present day. While contemporary Tibetans still exhibit a great interest in performing pilgrimages, as they did in times past; the context of their ritual activities has been rapidly and radically transformed since the Chinese occupation of 1959 and the ensuing flow of Tibetan refugees into South Asia. It has now become apparent that since 1959 two quite different although related Tibetan societies, one in South Asian exile and the other under Chinese administration, have begun to emerge as a result.

Furthermore, the post-1959 context of Tibetan religious life has witnessed a number of distinctive trends, including: the linking of Tibetan Buddhism in different ways with secular modernity in the changing contexts of both the exile community and the policies and practices of the Chinese state; attempts to formulate a new national identity on the basis of a former religious one; the extensive missionary activities of Tibetan religious sects and lamas and their interaction with a global audience; the reification of varieties of "Tibetan culture" and its traditional sites as objects of consumption in a global market economy (e.g., Chinese-controlled international tourism and Tibetan exiles' fund raising) and as vehicles, venues, and media for self-conscious political expression and contestation. During this period all Tibetans as pilgrims have increasingly had to share and compete for the same pilgrimage sites with other ethnic, religious, and secular groups whom they rarely, if ever, had contact with only three or four decades ago. Under these changing circumstances one would expect the emergence of a greater diversity of discourses and of competing interpretations and identities, the invention of traditions, a shifting of geographical focus for ritual activity, and so on, in relation to the pilgrimage process. Attention to such developments must be a central concern of all research on contemporary Tibetan pilgrimage.

While the foregoing comments apply to the comparison of specific social contexts over time, there exists nevertheless a set of conceptions and ritual practices characteristic of Tibetan pilgrimage that are durable and of long standing. They appear to hold true as much for contemporary pilgrimages by the majority of Tibetans as they did for the known traditions of fifty years or even several centuries ago. Such conceptions and practices are worthy of an extended treatment here, as it has not been attempted before and as they inform a great deal of the ritual to be described throughout the rest of the book. The review of them that follows in chapter 2 is based on a wide reading of indigenous sources, my own fieldwork observations, and the published scholarly accounts.

2

✦ ✦ ✦ ✦

Tibetan Pilgrimage

Concepts and Practice

Approaching Tibetan Ritual

The practice of pilgrimage by Tibetans has to be viewed as a part of the whole field of their ritual life and the worldview that informs the actions that constitute it. Both historical records and contemporary observations reveal an extraordinarily rich range of Tibetan practices that can be classed as "rituals" or "rites" of one form or another.[1] Research on Tibetan ritual has to recognize this great diversity and the fact that Tibetan religious life has long been characterized by a high degree of syncretism, with processes of mutual assimilation and influence resulting in a complex historical and social field.

Earlier scholarship tended to divide the material on ritual into that which was either manifestly Buddhist or Bön—the two dominant, textually mediated, historical religious systems in the region—or belonging to the so-called folk religion or local tradition. Another division stressed was that between the monastic cult and lay practices. Appeals were often made to various canonical, polemical, and universal distinctions in so doing. The more recent trend has been to cut across these familiar categories by, for example, analyzing the variety of terminology that Tibetans themselves have used, isolating the underlying logics or structures apparent in a single, complex cult apparatus, or distinguishing a set of important orientations that are articulated within a shared (albeit complex) cosmology and system of values.[2] Taken together, such recent approaches begin to demonstrate that although Tibetan ritual life may be highly multiplistic, it is governed by a common and long-circulating pool of symbols, categories, metaphors, strategies, and goals. Ethnography has shown that Tibetan practitioners themselves draw from this pool largely *according to context* and are not apt to isolate or abstract its features, as these are implicit aspects of a general worldview. It is here that the productive ground is to be found for understanding how Tibetans attach meaning to the ritual actions they perform. While it is useful to classify, and important to recognize where certain ideas, beliefs, and practices may have originated in time and space, an equally important question is:

What is assumed to make any particular ritual activity worthy of performance according to its specific method; in what terms is it considered to operate and be efficacious by the participants themselves?

Turning to the bulk of ethnographic and historical studies, one finds a more or less universally accepted system of underlying ideas in Tibetan culture that both justify ritual behavior and explain its effects. For Tibetans the meaning of ritual practice is constructed in terms of an extensive set of beliefs about the world and about the person as a psychophysical and moral entity, as well as the powers, vital forces, and laws that animate, sustain, are embodied in, and determine them. The Tibetan vocabulary of ritual's operation and efficacy more commonly invoked in oral explanations and written texts includes notions such as "action" or "karma" (**lé**), "auspiciousness/good luck" (**tashi**), "causal connections" (**tendrel**), "defilement/pollution" (**drib**), "good fortune" (**lungta**), "honor" (**uphang**), "life-energy" (**sog**), "longevity" (**tse**), "merit" (**sönam**), "personal power" (**wangtang**), "purity" (**dakpa**), "sacred power/energy" (**chinlab**), "sin/transgression" (**dik**), "soul/vitality principle" (**la**), and so on. For the most part, these forces, powers and properties are assumed to be contingent, embodied, and contagious, or related in some way to the activity or disposition of nonhuman beings. Nonetheless, they each have their own discrete range of meanings and usages subject to both social location of interpreters and historical and regional variation. Despite the fact that they originally derive from various distinct cosmologies (Indic, ancient Tibetan, and probably Chinese, among others) that sometimes stand in contradiction (e.g., classical Buddhism does not admit the notion of a "soul"), in Tibetan religious life they are not treated as being mutually exclusive. Different ideas and principles have been theologically accommodated by the élite, while in popular expression they can at times be freely compounded, interchanged, and elaborated in relation to one another, even when there is an explicit knowledge of the possible divergences between them.

Similarly, empirical studies also reveal a common set of themes, often expressed in the narratives that accompany rituals, that explain and justify ritual practice. These include, in particular, certain "models" (**pé**) of concern with: defilement and purification; illness and healing; influencing the course and processes of physical life, death, and future life (e.g., rebirth and final liberation from it); gaining efficacy in the phenomenal world or powers to influence its operation; the extension of perception beyond the mundane limits of space and time; the coercion and conversion or destruction of that which is perceived as an obstruction or a threat; and maintaining advantageous contacts and identifications with nonhuman forces in both the local and universal cosmos. These themes and the forces believed to be attendant on the ritual activity they enjoin are what gives meaning to and coordinates the application of the huge array of different practices in circulation in Tibetan religious life. They also frequently become compounded such that a ritual tradition can not be understood in terms of a discrete liturgy. Especially in the case of popular cults, one is often witnessing not one ritual but a complex combination or ensemble of different ones accommodated by tradition. This is certainly the case with Tibetan forms of pilgrimage.

Tibetan Pilgrimage

Almost all Tibetans undertake pilgrimages at some time during their lives. Yet these popular ritual journeys are in no way an obligatory aspect of either Tibetan-style Buddhism or the Bön religion. In addition to their high frequency and wide distribution, pilgrimage rituals in Tibet can also be thought of as being "popular" in other senses. For instance, they lack a fixed canonical status and even in many cases any textual expression whatsoever, while their performance does not require the presence or participation of any type of officiant or priest. Like many examples of Tibetan popular ritual, they are in fact often combinations of different acts and rites. Their possible constituent practices are of great variety, as are the specific sites, objects, and persons around which they focus and the range of motivations and circumstances that inspire and contextualize them. As such, Tibetan pilgrimages can encompass mundane material concerns, complex social agendas, and both proximate and ultimate soteriological orientations and goals. Thus, as a general class of ritual activity they are not amenable to either simple description and analysis or rigid classification.[3]

Orthodox Representations

As noted in chapter 1, much of the general literature on Tibetan pilgrimage has tended to discuss it in terms of Indic Buddhist origins and doctrines and Sanskrit terminology, particularly classical metaphysical imperatives involving the well-known concepts of karma and merit (*punya*). The classical ideal is that such ritual journeys result in the accumulation of merit—which in turn leads to future rebirth of the person on higher levels of cyclic existence (*saṃsāra*)—and also function as a necessary preparatory stage toward ultimate liberation (*nirvāṇa*).[4] On the one hand, there are certain good reasons for this tendency. There is no convincing evidence in the earliest records of Tibetan culture, such as epigraphic texts and the Dunhuang manuscripts, to suggest that any ancient ritual form resembling pilgrimage as we know it existed before the systematic introduction of Indian Buddhism. Furthermore, many Tibetans themselves tend to explain what they do as pilgrims in these same doctrinal terms. On the other hand, the tendency to interpret pilgrimages (and other aspects of Tibetan life) too exclusively in this way has also been reinforced by pervasive Buddhist religious orthodoxy, the historical dominance of textually focused Indological and Buddhological approaches in Tibetan studies, and a lack of access for field studies—many scholars only very recently began to visit the sites and observe and perform the rituals they were writing about.

I have hardly met a Tibetan pilgrim who did not mention "merit accumulation" (*sönamki tsog* in Tibetan) as a reason for performing a ritual journey. While there is no doubt about such motivations or their sincerity, the explicit use of Buddhist language in relation to pilgrimage is often little more than a superficial (and socially acceptable) gloss over other complex assumptions, and bears no immediately obvious relationship to observed practices.[5] Approaches to pilgrimage via Buddhist formulations hardly do justice to the richness of the Tibetan traditions, and result in both implicit Tibetan understandings of the world and the embodied experience of pilgrims being largely overlooked, as well as in neglect of their social significations. Perhaps a better approach to pilgrimage as a distinctive class of Tibetan ritual is, as suggested earlier, one that focuses on the common concepts and vocabulary of efficacy that pilgrims associate with their own ritual acts and objects and that also imply a set of assumed categories and qualities of place and/or space, substance, and person and their complex articulation during ritual.[6]

Relations between Persons and Places

The common Tibetan expressions for the ritual activity that the English word "pilgrimage" describes are *nékor* and *néjel*. They can be translated respectively as "going around (*kor*) a *né*" and "meeting a *né*." I will discuss the meaning of *né* shortly. The idea of circumambulation (*korwa*) conveyed here is related to that of *pradakṣiṇā* (literally, "moving clockwise") as prescribed for Buddhist pilgrimage in classical Sanskrit sources. However, the explicit Tibetan notions of *né* and *jel* are missing from the classical term, and although the cliché about ritual circumambulation in Tibetan religions is "clockwise for Buddhists, counterclockwise for Bönpo," in practice at important and popular sites this is not necessarily the case. For instance, at the pilgrimage mountains of Shar Dungri in Amdo or Kongpo Bönri in southern central Tibet, Buddhists circumambulate counterclockwise, while at Pure Crystal Mountain of Tsari Bönpo circumambulate clockwise, and all women do half a circuit in each direction. In addition, circumambulation direction can be a flexible symbolic indicator that is employed for identity manipulation in Tibetan ritual and in the constitution of essential identity distinctions in other cultural contexts.[7] Circumambulation of a holy site, object, or person is the act that generates merit for the pilgrim. In common with ideas of merit accumulation in other ritual contexts, Tibetans believe that one can redirect the merits of pilgrimage to other persons who do not take part directly. This is the basis for the practice of substitution pilgrimages in the form of circumambulations of various holy places by hired proxies. It must be realized, however, that the somewhat abstract idea of accumulating merit is only one of many diverse aspects involved in walking a circumambulation path on pilgrimage. Although circumambulation is important to the concept of pilgrimage, for Tibetans it is rather the notion of *né* as the object of circumambulation and a host of other ritual activity that is central.

In the context of pilgrimage, the word *né* basically means "abode" signifying the temporary or permanent residence of a deity. Such an abiding (*né*) can be within apparently "empty" three-dimensional space, at a fixed geographical location, or within a specific structure or object. In this aspect, *né* are attributed a subtle level of reality, claimed to be apparent only to the most spiritually refined persons. But the deity or spirit of a *né* is also commonly thought of as embodied, and therefore apparent, in the actual form of physical landscapes and objects, or their substances and materials. Thus, *né* may be externally "read" by all interpreters, and a range of direct physical contacts with them are possible and desirable. The most important objects of pilgrimage are termed *néchen* and *néchok* (sometimes *nédampa*, *né tsachenpo*, or *nézang* in colloquial speech), which can be translated as "great abode" or "principal abode," respectively, and *néri* as "mountain abode." Such terms are regularly applied to particular natural landscapes, urban areas (e.g., Lhasa), religious structures and icons, the places of residence or "seats" (*densa*) of living incarnate lamas, as well as their postmortem remains, and the sites (e.g., caves) of Tantric practice by yogins and meditators. In the case of persons and their bodies, they are *né* by virtue of either being considered human incarnations of deities (e.g., the Dalai Lama) or having a deity temporarily in residence during specific ritual operations, such as advanced forms of Tantric meditation or yoga. Icons, shrines, buildings, and so on, generally defined as "supports" (*ten*), become *né* by having a deity projected onto them or invited to take up residence (*né*) in the consecration ceremony termed *rabné*. The concept of *ten* as a "support" or "representation" of a deity is closely related to, and interchangeable with, that of *né* in many instances in pilgrimage.

The designation of any space, site, object, or even organism as a *né* implies various other categories and qualities. It also implies specific types of relationships between *né* and persons, as well as between the persons who relate to them in the form of rituals such as pilgrimage. The main implication of the *né* principle for ritual is that places so designated are ascribed a very high or positive ontological value. They are, quite simply, the best parts of the phenomenal world, and the logic of much Tibetan pilgrimage ritual is founded on this idea. Therefore, the imperative of much ritual action on pilgrimages is all about constructing certain types of relationships between persons and *né*. This relationship can take various forms of mental identifications with, physical contacts with, and orientations toward these highly valued sites.

Underlying this ritual logic is the important and common Tibetan assumption that persons and places are involved in various degrees of mutually determinate relationships. This assumption about *né* resonates strongly with other ancient and popular ways of thinking about the ritual relationship between persons and aspects of the physical world that are, apparently, external to and discrete from them. Here one could specifically mention the assimilation of the early monarchs (*tsenpo*) of the seventh to ninth centuries to both mountains and their earth mound tombs via their guardian deities (*kula*);[8] the mobility of the individual and collective "soul" or "vitality" force (*la*) and its embodiment (*la né*) in the external world (e.g., in mountains, lakes, stones, etc.);[9] and the dual residence of the personal protective gods (*drablha*, *pholha*, and *molha/phuglha*) both within the human body and the domestic environment.[10] In general the great variety of beliefs and practices in Tibetan folk culture (concerning illness and cures, purification, agriculture, building, childbirth, magical practices, weather-making, fertility, good and bad fortune, and so on) assume a complex ontological continuity between persons, places, substances, and nonhuman beings.

Transcendent Power and Its Effects

Tibetan pilgrimage has to been seen in the context of this worldview, yet it constitutes a distinctive expression of it which is informed by Buddhism. Aside from the orthodox formulae describing a ritual relationship with *né* (e.g., prostrations, offerings, and circumambulations), there is a specific Tibetan vocabulary of efficacy and style of ritual practice associated with pilgrimages and *né*. Most commonly featured among these are the notions of "sacred energy" or "empowerment" (*chinlab*), "defilement" (*drib*), "sin" (*dik*), relative "purity" (*dakpa*), and gradual transformation through "cleansing" (*jhang*). Taken together in the context of ritual, they enjoin certain types of behavior, styles of representation, and systems of spacial organization and social ranking with which merit, karma and circumambulation have little to do.

Né, of course, are sites where the pilgrim goes for a direct meeting (*jel*) with the deity or deities in residence. At *né* the pilgrim may make the standard petitions, prayers, offerings, and so on that are commonly found in other forms of regular worship and not particular to pilgrimage. But as parts of the phenomenal world, *né* have the primary quality of being potential sources of "sacred energy" or "empowerment" (*chinlab*), a quality that is associated with the presence of the highest classes of deity, and *né* are often represented as such by pilgrimage guides and interested parties such as lamas and clerics. Outside of the technical vocabulary of Tibetan Tantra, *chinlab* is popularly understood in a substantial sense as a "field of power" in place and space; translated literally it means "wave of *chin*," where *chin* is the deity's positive power or energy. The term in full is *chingyilab*, literally "flooded by power," hence "empowerment."[11] *Chinlab* is often conceived of as being essentially atemporal;[12] spacially distributed outward from the ideal center of a *né*—the seat of the deity; and affecting anything within its range. Recently invoked Tibetan metaphors for *chinlab* and its action include those of an electric field or fluid saturation, and these relate to what is often for Tibetans important ritual behavior at *né*.[13]

> All objects at great *né* have the empowerment (*chingyilab*) of the deities and great practitioners associated with that place. It is like [the effects of] water soaking into things, so it includes rocks, dirt, water, plants, trees. This is also called "empowerment of *né*" (*néki chinlab*). Thus, this empowerment can be collected in the form of rocks, dirt, plant parts, and so on, and due to the Tibetans' great faith in the power of these things they do collect them.[14]

The collection of stones, pinches of soil or dust (often called *nédo*, "*né* stones," and *nésa*, "*né* earth," etc.), plants, the drinking of water, and so on in the physical environment of a *né* are all common, though subtle and thus often unnoticed, forms of ritual activity on pilgrimages. Such *chinlab* "harvests" thus procure portable sources of a site's power to be directly consumed, or carried off for later use and further distribution.[15] At its most formalized level, this collection of residual empowerment takes the form of an exchange economy in which individual lamas and the operators of monasteries and shrines distribute a whole range of empowered items (cloth strips, strings, pills, clay seals, etc.) to pilgrims in return for "donations" and "offerings." Such exchanges are of great importance to most pilgrims and provide yet another concrete support for the vague but normative concept of merit accumulation. In all cases the importance attributed to *chinlab* is based on the view of it as a type of transformative power of transcendent origins with generative, revitalizing, purifying, or preservative aspects. As such, *chinlab* can be compared with many similar concepts of sacred, transcendent power evoked in other popular pilgrimage cultures, such as that of *ling* or "magical power/efficacy" in Chinese traditions. In common with these other notions of sacred power associated with pilgrimage traditions, *chin-*

lab, as a productive power conceived of as outside society, can also be regarded as an ideological mystification or misrecognition of society's own productive power as it is manifest in collective ritual action like pilgrimage.[16]

Chinlab often implies social relations. The value placed on it is one of the factors that motivates mass gatherings, interactions, and exchanges on pilgrimages, and that value also conditions the ritual priority given to physical contacts and contiguity during their performance. A good example is found in recent Dukhor Wangchen or "Great Kālacakra Initiation" ceremonies. The larger of these now frequently held mass initiations constitute the single biggest contemporary pilgrimage events for Tibetans, attracting up to several hundred thousand persons from all parts of Asia. During the staging of Dukhor Wangchen, the ritual site itself becomes transformed into a great *né* through the production there of a maṇḍala, a sublime divine palace, while the Dalai Lama, who presides over the ceremony, is himself also an important human *né*, being the incarnation of a deity. Many pilgrims state explicitly that they attend the ceremonies mainly because of the *chinlab* that is generated, and following the close of the ritual they will flock by the thousands to get as close to the center of the site as possible and touch the Dalai Lama's empty chair, which is believed to be saturated with *chinlab*.[17]

In opposition to *né* and their *chinlab* power, Tibetans view the body of the pilgrim as the site of accumulated physical and mental "contamination" or "defilement" (*drib*, literally, "shadow" or "stain") as well as embodied "sin" (*dik*). In common thinking *drib* is generally conceived as a form of both physical and social pollution that is associated with various substances and proscribed social practices and relations, as well as with deities inhabiting both the body and the external world. In Tibetan Buddhism and Bön the term *drib* is also used in a more precise way to describe both gross and fine grades of physical and cognitive "defilement" associated with the three levels of the psychophysical person. The notion of *drib* is further compounded with formal Buddhist ethical concerns in terms of the "sins" (*dik*) that the person accumulates and carries as an entity, both together being denoted by the compound *dik-drib*. In all social contexts *drib* and *dik* are viewed as negative, obstructive, unlucky, and even threatening (to health, longevity, fertility, prosperity, etc.) aspects of ordinary human social and material existence. Soteriologically they are considered an impediment to all forms of spiritual progress. *Drib* is associated with decrease and is thus opposite to the productive connotations ascribed to *chinlab*. Much popular ritual activity is devoted to concerns about such ritual pollution and its negative effects, and indeed it is one of the most ancient of Tibetan ritual concerns. The same concerns are prevalent in Tibetan "high" religion, and the foundational process of Tibetan Tantric practice involves the removal of *drib* from the person in four progressive stages.

Pilgrimage is seen by Tibetans as a fundamental method of removing, purifying, or cleansing embodied *drib* and *dik* and is thus a ritual of relevance to a wide range of general material, social, and salvational concerns, from which all levels of practitioner can benefit. Technically it is the gross level of embodied sin and the defilement resulting from certain actions (*léki drib*) that are removed by way of pilgrimage, although most pilgrims do not bother with such discriminations and view their practice as generally cleansing the psychophysical person. *Drib* and *dik* are popularly thought of as being removed in two ways: by the actual physical work or action the pilgrim's body has to perform; and by the general transformative effect of contact with empowerment and empowered substances at *né*, which runs counter to the effects of *drib*.

Concerning the actual physicality of practice, it is a very common formulation of Tibetan ritual texts that "Defilements of the body (*luki drib*) will be cleansed through prostration and circumambulation."[18] And in addition to the basic act of circumambulation, one finds logical extensions of this general principle. Tibetan pilgrimages are well known for a combination ritual in which circumambulations (*korwa*) of a *né* are made by measuring out full-length body prostrations (*chagtse*) around the site. Such a practice, which is not uncommon, is explicitly called a "cleansing defilement prostration circumambulation" (*chagkor dribjhong*). This can further be seen in terms of the importance of maximum contiguity with the empowered substance of a great *né*. The Fourteenth Dalai Lama recently made this observation about the practice of prostration circumambulation at the famous *néri* of Tise or Mount Kailash in western Tibet: "When you walk a circular pilgrimage route, such as this one around Mount Kailash, your feet touch the earth with big spaces between them, but when you prostrate, *your whole body connects with the sacred ground* to close the circle."[19]

Such physical acts on pilgrimage are conceived of as effecting gradual embodied transformations. In common with many other pilgrimage traditions, the changing status of the ritual body is often linked by Tibetans to hardships and suffering that must be faced on the ritual journey.[20] In the context of many Tibetan pilgrimage rituals, the language of such gradual transformation often alludes to or invokes the image of water or liquid and its washing and flowing action within the body. Tibetans talk of having their defilements and sins "washed off" (*trü* or *dak*) and "cleansed" (*jhang*) through both the action of making the ritual journey around a *né* and by the consumption of various empowered substances (water, earth, plants, etc.) from its environs. Thereby the ritual body may attain a state of higher "purity" (*dakpa*).

This common Tibetan ritual transformation imagery of washing, and of water purifying the pollution resulting from improper actions, is an ancient one.[21] In contrast to the ubiquitous Hindu pilgrimage practice of ritual bathing in rivers, lakes, and tanks, most Tibetans rarely (if ever) bathe as pilgrims. Notwithstanding actual Hindu beliefs about ritual bathing, Tibetans distinguish their own practice and notions of inner cleansing from those of Hindus in colloquial expressions, such as "Hindus clean on the outside, Buddhists clean on the inside."[22] The essentially "cool" and liquid Tibetan conception of internal transformation, especially when linked to ritual hardships, is exactly opposite to that of "ascetic heat" (*tapas*) and its burning transformative power found in the language of Indian pilgrimage to the south of the Tibetan plateau. Thus, in contrast to Tibetan thinking, the ritual process of *tapasyā*, "the production of ascetic 'heat' through actions of self-denial and austerity," is central to the conception of embodied transformation in present-day North Indian Hindu pilgrimages.[23]

Whether conceived of as washed, purified, or flooded by power in various ways, the ritually transformed body of the pilgrim attains a different status. Most often this is simply a matter of personal acknowledgment, in terms of considering one's prospects of a better rebirth to be higher, illnesses to have been cured, general prosperity and luck increased, and so on. It may also figure as a post facto explanation for various positive outcomes later in life. Much less frequently, it can also be socially and publicly attested. A dramatic example of such social recognition, in which the conventional social order is inverted, is found in the welcoming ritual for pilgrims who finished their circuit of the great Rongkor Chenmo procession around the *néri* of Pure Crystal Mountain in 1956. The local monks laid their shawls on the ground like a carpet for the now "purified" (*dakpa*) pilgrims to walk on in order that they might collect empowerment from their feet. One can compare here an account of the present Dalai Lama (who is considered a *né*) recently visiting village communities in North India: "As His Holiness approached, people covered the path with their own clothes . . . and monks laid down their shawls (*Zen*) for him to step on and bless."[24] Similar examples of the social recognition of transformed pilgrims are found in other Asian Buddhist contexts.[25]

Embodied Qualities and Social Distinctions

While some Tibetan pilgrimages may offer the rare possibility of status increase being temporarily attested, for the most part they serve as a ritual context in which existing social distinctions and hierarchies based on birth, wealth, gender, and so on, become explicit, are reproduced, and are reinforced. Much of this ritual context focuses on the notion that relative degrees of defilement or purity (*dakpa*) characterize the embodied physical and moral state of the pilgrim in relation to the pure and empowered object of pilgrimage. This is hardly surprising, as the conception of *drib* has been shown to have wide-ranging implications for social relations in Tibetan-speaking societies.[26] In general, concerns about *drib* become socially manifest in the spatial ordering between persons and in the ranking of persons and substances by degree of presence/absence of "impurity" (*mitsangpa*). In pilgrimage rituals this ordering is often expressed in terms of graded access to the ritual space of a *né*, where relative height and proximity to an ideal center are the dominant indicators. In subsequent chapters I give comprehensive examples of how such a spatial ordering and social ranking was conceived of and practiced in pilgrimage rituals around the *né* of Pure Crystal Mountain.

In addition to the definition and use of ritual space, other aspects of pilgrimage relate to the ascription of social, moral, and cognitive status or ranking. Further examples are found in the traditional usage of language in relation to pilgrims and *né*, as well as types of "testing" rituals frequently encountered at Tibetan pilgrimage places. The Tibetan language, like many others, has various levels of common and honorific speech, plus other markers that indicate rank and status. Some are applied in written and spoken text to persons and places specifically in the context of pilgrimage. In general there are two interrelated representations that are applied to persons; they are based on levels of purity/absence of pollution and levels of facility of cognition. Most persons who visit *né* as pilgrims are described as falling into two main classes, that is, "ordinary persons" (*sokyewo*) and "excellent persons" or "saints" (*kyébu dampa*). For example, incarnate lamas, advanced Tantric meditators, and senior clerics might fall into the second category. All pilgrims can be ranked as to whether they are "pure" (*dakpa*) or "impure beings/defiled persons" (*madakdro/mitsangpa*), referring to the status of their *drib* and *dik*. Their cognitive abilities are ranked according to their level of purity (which also relates to karmic status) with the "highest" (*chokrab*) described as those with "pure vision" (*daknang*), followed by the "middling" (*tringpo*) and the "lowest" (*thama*). Such designations become important in relation to Tibetan cognitive claims about the various levels of subtle and gross reality of *né*, of who can perceive them, and so forth. They become socially expressed on pilgrimage in a class of landscape interpretation rituals, for example. Places, too, are ranked, and as I have shown, terms such as *néchen*, *néri*, and so forth indicate sites of relatively high ontological value. Those *né* with the highest deities in residence are called "pure abodes" (*nédakpa*) or "fields of purity" (*dakshing*), the latter term being a common synonym for the field of power or world-system of a Buddha.

Many aspects of the Tibetan understanding of pilgrimage strongly imply a conception of embodied morality. This concept is not limited to the body of the pilgrim as a carrier of degrees of accumulated *dik* and *drib*; it also applies to the physical *né* site itself. The Buddhas and other top-ranking deities are the highest expression of moral being for Tibetans, and so, by extension, are the *né* they occupy or the human bodies they are incarnate as—they are all designated as highly *dakpa*. In Tibetan, "purity" as *dakpa* indicates moral purity and carries with it the senses of "authenticity" or "correctness," and its compounds denote legal correctness, "proof," and "testimony." The perceived embodied moral quality of *né* is made explicit on Tibetan pilgrimages in a ritual of moral testing or measurement involving a type of physical transaction between the "pure" local landscape and pilgrims who embody sins and contamination. A common practice around popular *né* is for pilgrims to attempt to fit their bodies between cleft boulders or pass through narrow holes and passages in rocks.[27] Regardless of the actual size and shape of the pilgrim's physical body, they will not be able to complete the exercise if they have high levels of accumulated sins. The pure moral substance of the *né* reads the embodied moral status of the pilgrim on contact, and it is believed the clefts and passages change size automatically to allow any morally suitable candidate to pass through, regardless of their actual body shape and size. The particular rock sites often have names such as "sins black and white" (*dikpa karnak*), indicating the comparative moral test they involve.[28] These ritual tests work to reaffirm the moral and ontological—and by extension cognitive and social—hierarchies the pilgrims locate themselves within.

While Tibetan pilgrimage has its share of particular characteristics, when discussed in terms of sacred powers and sites, the pilgrim's ritual body, contacts and exchanges with the transcendent, and embodied transformations, it immediately appears less unique and invites comparison with the panhuman phenomena of "pilgrimage" in world historical or universal religions in general. It also invites comparison with neighboring cultural systems. For instance, it appears that Tibetan pilgrimage shares traditional South Asian concerns about mutually determinate relations between place and person, and has analogies with general models of a "transactional culture" proposed recently for Indic South Asia.[29] The difference is perhaps that Tibetans do not have the same types of formal theories as Hindu South Asians do to explain why, for instance, contiguity is so important to them in many contexts and how it relates to the social order. The social context of Tibetan pilgrimage ritual is of interest as it is one site at which ideas about the qualities of and relationships between place and person are articulated and can become explicit on occasion, or at least can be more easily inferred from the wide range of interrelated representations and actions that are brought into play.

The preceding introduction to Tibetan understandings of pilgrimage and its practice is admittedly both abstract and biased, but necessarily so. It needs to be elaborated in relation to specific studies. As a result, certain familiar features of Tibetan pilgrimage, such as landscape interpretation exercises and the role of oral and written texts, have only been alluded to here. Furthermore, while the highly specialized Tantric visionary approach to pilgrimage is important because of its role in the establishment of Tibetan cult sites and networks, it is in reality a practice tradition restricted to only a tiny minority of pilgrims. I have been concerned more with explicating a range of common or popular assumptions and practices, which normally remain implicit or obscure, rather than with reiterating orthodox, formalized, or textualized statements and representations. Such a treatment has also largely avoided dealing with diversity of perspectives, as there is, of course, no single Tibetan discourse about pilgrimage. The high lama and the illiterate nomad will have very different experiences and even competing interpretations of the same *né* and pilgrimage rituals. However, their mutual presence at a site or event will itself be based on the shared assumptions that I have discussed about the power of *né* and the transformative effects they are believed to have on the person. The range of possible approaches to pilgrimages and their cult places can best be drawn out in context, and throughout the book I will be attempting to do so in relation to Pure Crystal Mountain and its ritual traditions.

3

✦ ✦ ✦ ✦

The Cult of Pilgrimage Mountains in Tibet

Mountains have, without a doubt, been the most venerated and culturally significant feature of the Tibetan landscape throughout space and time. Tibetans have considered various mountains to possess a special status or to be powerful or sacred in different ways for the entire period of their recorded history. Yet this has never been a static phenomenon. It can be demonstrated that the sacred mountains Tibetans themselves came to take for granted are the cultural products of long and particular processes of social construction. Certain ancient forms of Tibetan mountain worship have long been extinct, declining and dying out along with the defunct social orders with which they were associated. Some have persisted over the *long durée* while still others have come into being and risen to popularity more recently. Despite this variety and change, mountains have remained symbolically and ritually important for successive Tibetan societies, for whom they have come to function as one significant form of organizing principle. Common cultural understandings of the mountain have been shared by, and perhaps at times served to unite, an otherwise quite diverse set of peoples separated by geography, dialect, forms of production and social organization, customs, and so on.

In this chapter I will consider general historical and social aspects of the cult of Tibet's most important class of pilgrimage mountains, the *néri*.[1] As Pure Crystal Mountain of Tsari is considered a premier example of this type of mountain by Tibetans, the following discussion will serve as a context within which to situate the detailed material of the later chapters. The origins of the *néri* mountain cult can be identified with a definite milieu of religious and social change on the Tibetan plateau. One must ask why, during a certain period, a new and sophisticated way of defining such mountains arose and what the social and cultural conditions attendant on this process were, and one must consider the implications of this innovation as well as the enduring popularity of these sites and their rituals.

Here I will show that the *néri* cult appeared in connection with concerted Tibetan élite attempts to convert their culture thoroughly to a Buddhist one. By using a comparative perspective at times, it can be seen that the development of the *néri* mountain cult in Tibet is analogous in many respects to social and cultural processes associated with the systematic integration of Buddhism in other regions of Asia. The *néri* tradition should be regarded as a complex product of the syncretism stimulated by the agency of so-called universal religions. Although the *néri* mountains represent only one specific type of Tibetan pilgrimage site, I would argue that the features that characterize their development and traditions are of wider relevance for understanding all Tibetan pilgrimages and holy places.

The Category of *Néri* Mountains

The site of Dakpa Sheri or Pure Crystal Mountain at Tsari is generally classified as a *néri*, a term that can be translated literally as "mountain abode." For most Tibetans, such mountains are "abodes" (*né*) in the sense explained in chapter 2, being considered the places of residence and activity of certain important deities. This can mean that not only is the deity thought to dwell in the vicinity as a separate entity, but also that it is identified or equivalent with the actual mountain, the physical form of which can be regarded as a divine embodiment. In a secondary and more specialized sense, usually acknowledged only by scholars and associated with specific sites, the Tibetan word *né* translates the Sanskrit term *pīṭha*. This refers to a type of Tantric cult place featured in the Indic texts and traditions that were utilized in the creation of the Tibetan *néri* cult. In common Tibetan usage, the classifying reference *néri* is often incorporated into the full proper names of this category of mountain to distinguish them from other types of sites. For example, the great *néri* mountain named Kawa Karpo rising between the Mekong and Salween gorges in southeastern Tibet is often called Néri Kawa Karpo by Tibetans, and Pure Crystal Mountain is commonly referred to as Né Dakpa Sheri.

Although a great many mountains throughout Tibetan areas are considered to have resident deities, most peaks are not classified as *néri*. In his classic work on the cult of Tibetan protective deities, René de Nebesky-Wojkowitz described *néri* as mountains that are the residence or embodiment specifically of the *chökyong*, or "defenders of Buddhist religion," a class of deities that constitute a large section of the rich Tibetan pantheon.[2] While this description is correct in many cases, the main Tibetan *néri* are in fact far more complex, being identified as abodes for different classes of deities simultaneously, often arranged in a complex hierarchy. These nonhuman beings can range from quite low-ranking local spirits right up to the *yidam*, the highest "chosen meditational deities" involved in the most advanced forms of Tantric ritual. Thus, major Tibetan *néri* mountains can often be the focus of complex cults that encompass a wide range of ritual practices and orientations.

The *néri* class of mountains should not be identified only with Tibetan Buddhism, for *néri* have also been an aspect of the systematized Tibetan Bön religion for as long as they have been important to Buddhists in Tibet. Concerning this point, there is a good case for identifying the *néri* mountain cult as "Lamaist," in the specific sense suggested by Per Kværne, due to the common centrality of the Tantric lama as ritual specialist in the development and cult of both Buddhist and Bönpo *néri* sites.[3] Thus, in common with their Buddhist counterparts, Bönpo *néri* also tend to combine the ritual and representation of Tantrism with that of the cult of the *bönkyong*, "defenders of Bön religion," and other minor or local deities. According to my recent textual and field investigations, and aside from a few variations on certain themes, I regard the cults of both Buddhist and Bönpo *néri* as conforming to exactly the same cultural pattern.

In addition to *néri* mountains in Tibet, there exists a widespread cult mountain type identified more exclusively with the *yüllha* ("god of the locale") and *shidak* ("owner of the base") deities. These genii are generally understood as local and regional territorial gods and godesses, whose worship apparently predates the intensive introduction of Indian religious systems into Tibet.[4] Despite a recent increase in research efforts, this cult mountain type as it exists in many parts of Tibet remains poorly understood. While one should be careful not to oversystematize differences, it is worthwhile to briefly compare these two main types.

Two Types of Cult Mountain

Attempts have been made to draw a clear distinction between *néri* and *yüllha* type mountains in terms of ritual orientation. The former can be viewed as the focus of systematic Buddhist or Bönpo religious worship and spiritual exercises, like circumambulation and meditation, and the latter seen as the object of "secular" worship (no circumambulations, etc., are performed around them) that seeks success in purely mundane activities as well as to increase "glory, honour, fame, prosperity, power and progeny."[5] In these terms, it could be said that *néri* ritual, being more soteriological, tends to have its ultimate focus on death and future life (as either rebirth or liberation), while local mountain cult ritual tends to be focused on present life and this world. There are other differences one could point to, but it is worth emphasizing the local and specific nature of *yüllha* type mountain worship as opposed to the more universal character of *néri* cult and ritual, and the fact that while the former is essentially a nonliterate tradition, the latter originated and is embedded in extensive textual traditions.

When considered in terms of social identity and power in Tibetan society during the last millennium, it appears that the *yüllha* type mountain cult may have been an important ritual basis for the constitution and vitality of local communities, as well as part of their political self-definition. Each Tibetan rural community is usually based around a local sacred mountain to which they perform collective worship. In contrast, the major *néri* mountain cults, like that of Pure Crystal Mountain, were often a focus for more extensive pan-Tibetan religiopolitical and sectarian identities and interests. As such, they were sites around which sectarian disputes, large-scale rituals, missionary activities, and the involvement of the state were often centered. Given these distinctions, one would expect the ritual and social life around *néri* to be more diverse and complex compared with that of the local mountain cult.

Although on one hand there are clear differences between the *néri* and *yüllha* types of mountain cults, on the other hand there are certain points of similarity and blurred boundaries between local mountain worship and the major Tibetan *néri* that must be acknowledged. For example, Tibetans on pilgrimage to *néri* very often anticipate and seek many of the forms of "secular" advantages and success that are associated specifically with the *yüllha* type cults. They also at certain times and on certain *néri* perform some of the same rituals as the local mountain cult, such as *sang*, or "fumigation offerings," the deployment of *lungta*, or "wind-horse," images, prayers for good luck and fortune, and the deposit of imitation weapons. The great majority of pilgrims at *néri* are, after all, the same people who worship the *yüllha* type mountain at home, just in a different ritual setting with additional frames of reference. It has been pointed out that local mountain deities can withdraw their favor because of "internal conflict and disunity . . . which will affect the power and prosperity of the community."[6] Indeed, it is well known among Tibetans that such deities are very sensitive to disruptions in the order of things and the breaching of ritual limits, and that in general they are quite capricious and even dangerous. Yet, one finds all the same concerns and consequences associated with *néri* and their divine residents as well, with regard to whom it is also the religious sect or even the state itself that must take care to cultivate the deities' favor by regulating conflict and disturbances and maintaining consistent petitioning through correct ritual. Finally, in relation to the active building of "national identity" it has been said that the tradition of local mountain cults "is deeply rooted and more marked among Tibetan communities in the border areas . . . where encounters with people of different cultures who display their own national aggressivity are a daily experience."[7] The same comments could equally apply to Tibet's most popular *néri* sites before 1959: Tise (or Mount Kailash), Tsari, Kawa Karpo, Kongpo Bönri, and Labchi are all in border areas (see fig. 1.1), sometimes themselves actually marking the border, and most of them lie within zones of contact with a variety of non-Tibetan cultures, some of whom have for long been regularly aggressive toward Tibetans. As the study of Pure Crystal Mountain will show, the definition of larger scale (i.e., nonlocal) forms of "Tibetan" identity was certainly an active feature of ritual life at borderland *néri* sites up until 1959.

Given the complex syncretism that characterizes Tibetan religious life in general, it would be disingenuous to argue categorically for fixed distinctions between the two kinds of mountains just discussed. Indeed, the ethnographic and historical materials on Tibetan cult mountains reveal a collection of exceptions to any rules one might like to formulate, various special cases, and an overall ambivalence. One can only consider all Tibet's cult mountains in terms of a gradient along which they vary, from the "model" *néri* at one extreme to the "typical" local cult mountain at the other, with most falling somewhere in between. What must be recognized is that historically most of the major *néri* areas were in fact once *yüllha* type mountain cults, or that they have assimilated many of their features and built on them.

Certain mountains were appropriated and converted during a particular era in the context of new religious ideas and social forces that formed on the Tibetan plateau. As was the case, for instance, with cult mountains in neighboring China, certain Tibetan mountains and their gods changed identities with changing times, being assimilated into larger cults and networks within the context of expanding, centralized religiopolitical interests and powers.[8] Yet, despite centuries of alternative developments and ritual innovations at these sites, many of their users continue to reproduce the features of the local mountain cult at them, albeit often projected onto a different scale and set of logics. At *néri* one finds archaic beliefs and purely mundane orientations combined with proximate and ultimate salvational goals in a complex ritual and symbolic field. *Néri* can be interpreted as vital points on the actual Tibetan landscape where old powers gave ground to new ones, and where the existing Tibetan cultural patterns of a certain period were successfully combined with new and foreign ones. It is precisely because of the success in assimilating new cultural patterns to old ones that the *néri* cult commanded and continued to attract so much literary, administrative, and ritual attention from sects, states, and all classes of practitioners alike. The *néri* are an enduring and vital product of Tibetan religious syncretism.

Historical and Religious Developments

There is clear historical evidence that very early Tibetan interest in sacred Buddhist pilgrimage mountains was first directed toward China. This took the form of eighth century AD Tibetan visits to Wu-t'ai Shan and later, in 824, a formal Tibetan request to the T'ang dynasty administration for a map of the same holy mountain, which the Chinese duly provided.[9] The Tibetan state of the period had its own indigenous mountain cult which focused on the monarch or Tsenpo. But by this time, the Tibetans had already adopted Buddhism as the state religion and it is not surprising that there was official interest in sites such as Wu-t'ai Shan. Since there are virtually no reliable, contemporary historical sources for the period following the collapse of the Tibetan empire during the mid-ninth century until the eleventh century, any discussion of the beginnings of the *néri* cult in that period would be mere speculation.

The great Tibetan *néri* tradition has its main roots in the period from about the twelfth to the fifteenth century AD. During that time, Tibetan society and its cultural landscape were in the process of transformations on a scale not seen again until Tibet's difficult confrontation with modernity following the fall of the Lhasa-based state in the 1950s. These earlier changes were both stimulated and, to a certain extent, determined by new religious influences and cultural models passing northward from India across the Himalayan divide into Tibet. Notable among these changes, for our present purposes, are three related innovations: (1) In the "new Tantra" (*sangnag sarma*) period, for the first time on a wide scale the "supreme yoga" (*anuttarayoga*) class of Indian Tantric rituals and narratives were being systematically translated, practiced, and developed in a fully Tibetan social and cultural context. (2) New sects of Buddhists and Bönpos were establishing themselves on the basis of monastic communities both as centers of scholasticism and as sites of articulation with patronage and political power. (3) While monastically based scholars studied, taught, and cultivated their connections with the laity, certain adherents of the new sects followed the method of practicing as yogins and hermits in the Tantric tradition. They went (or were sent) into the mountains of Tibet to perform solitary meditation retreats and wander as mendicants outside the normal limits of monastic institutions and mainstream social life. Some of these figures attained the status of saints in popular tradition, and it is mainly within this context that one finds them associated, often retrospectively, with the *néri* cult.

Although the written and oral traditions about the origins of *néri* invariably appeal to earlier precedents (e.g., back to ancient cosmodramas, or enlightened masters such as the historically sketchy figures of Guru Rinpoché or Tönpa Shenrab), it is specifically the wandering hermit type of Tantric lamas from the twelfth to fifteenth century who are historically credited with "opening the doors" (*négo chewa*) to what later became the most popular pilgrimage routes for circumambulation around the great Tibetan *néri*. The narratives describing the openings of these main pilgrimage places and routes all conform to a general pattern. In it the central lamaistic hero figures, such as Gyelwa Götsangpa (1189–1258), Riwa Drukse (b. 1290), or Tsangpa Gyare (1161–1211), visit the *néri* so as to practice and attain realizations. In order to do so, they must not only encounter and deal with the local spirit forces residing there but also compete with the interests of other religious sects to become masters of the sites. At all stages in the openings of *néri* sites as they are depicted in the narratives, one witnesses a dramatic struggle to gain power on multiple but connected levels, that is, power over outer unruly autochthonous forces, over present religious and political rivals, and, not least, over the practitioner's own inner weaknesses, doubts, and impurities. The Tantric lama (from a particular sect) always emerges as ritually superior here. The opening hero's technologies of power for gaining access to, taking control of, and ordering these mountains as places of ritual performance all derived from Indian Tantric traditions. These included an array of minor rituals, paranormal abilities, and meditative states. But the most important was the method and skill to perceive and locally realize there within the very terrain of the place itself the maṇḍala, a type of three-dimensional cryptogram or psycho cosmogram, complete with its array of divine inhabitants (see figures 4.1 and 4.2).

Mandalization

The maṇḍala is one of the most significant hierarchical and replicative spacial organizing principles to be introduced into Tibet and the rest of Asia from India. In various forms and applications throughout Asia, maṇḍala have served as archetypes of the ideal city, models of the cosmos, blueprints for centers of royal power, templates for the operation of polities, networks for the distribution of resources, plans for sacred architecture, representations of the divine mansion or palace, and schemes for the distribution of vital energies within the human body.[10] In Tibet already from the twelfth century on one finds maṇḍala used to order and represent large-scale geographical schema;[11] it is likely that the influence of the maṇḍala model in Tibet was felt even earlier. It was this ordering principle of the maṇḍala that was most often projected onto and embodied within the specific topography of the new category of cult mountains. Thus, during their establishment, Tibet's major *néri* had a system of representation applied to them that could be identified with the governing forces located and operative within the individual, at the place of worship, in the centers of worldly and otherworldly power, and across cosmic space and time.

As I have intimated, mountains were not arbitrarily chosen as the new foci of a universal Tantric ritual order that was being imposed on the landscape. They were already defined as powerful features of the Tibetan environment before the systematic uptake of Indian religious traditions. Certain mountains had long been centers of local and regional cult activity on the Tibetan plateau. During the era of imperial Tibet (seventh–ninth centuries) they featured prominently in origin myths, notions of descent, the constitution of community identities, conceptions of the source and legitimation of religiopolitical power and prestige, and as abodes of some of the most powerful deities that the Tibetans shared their world space with.[12] The opening and consequent transformation of the natural landscape of *néri* by way of mandalization or the "practice of 'mandalizing' geographical areas," was also carried out at sites that had, or could be claimed to have, some older cultural status or importance.[13] These older associations often added legitimation but eventually became merely submerged within a new lamaistic representational agenda. Good cases in point here are the mountains of Tise and Kongpo Bönri with their earlier associations to areas of religiopolitical power and community during the period of the Tibetan empire, or the *néri* of Labchi and Tsari as the sites of ancient mountain goddess cults like the Tenma Chunyi. Many *néri* opened in later times were also claimed to be the ancient sites where "hidden treasure" (*terma*) texts were once deposited. Such claims are common in both Bön and Nyingmapa Buddhist *néri* traditions.

The various conversions of such powerful regional and local spirit powers into the services of new sects of Buddhism and Bön also occurred in relation to mandalization. The older mountain gods and goddesses were incorporated into the expanding pantheons on two, frequently overlapping, levels: into higher Tantric initiatory capacities as chosen meditational deities or as members of their retinues (e.g., the "sky-goers," or *khandroma*); and into service roles as "defenders of religion" or their local minions. Good examples of these different assimilations and transformations of identity associated with *néri* are the Bönpo meditational deity Gekhod of Tise, the Buddhist sky-goer Dorje Yüdrönma of Tsari, and the popular god and mountain of Nyanchen Tanglha.[14] In some cases this assimilation process came to designate *néri* as sites for Tantric practice, for worship of the defenders of religion, and for their local cults simultaneously. At *néri* held to be ancient repositories of hidden treasure texts, the local deities were converted to become guardians of such treasures. But despite these formal, textualized redefinitions, most ordinary Tibetans still regard and ritually approach (with the exception of animal sacrifice) the divine inhabitants of *néri* mountains in various ways that certainly parallel characteristics of the local mountain cults and the practices of the folk religion.

It is hard to imagine that the creation of *néri* and their mandalization was ever a straightforward or rapidly executed process, particularly in its early phases. It involved the deployment of a great deal of local and imported (mainly from India) ritual and narrative resources, as well as the need for claims to be put forward and accepted. It is known that already by the early thirteenth century many claims about geographical and cultic identity were made in order to begin assimilating existing Tibetan cult mountains as *néri* sites by certain emerging Tibetan Buddhist sects, and that these claims were strongly contested by scholars of rival schools.[15] The narrative sophistication of the *néri* cult seems to have developed only slowly compared to other contemporary examples of Indic-inspired assimilation and conversion traditions in Tibet. One can think here of those concerned with legitimating divine kingship in Buddhist terms or promoting the ritual superiority of the Tantric lama as represented by the works of the early Tibetan Buddhist historians, the *Mani Kambum* and the biographies of Guru Rinpoché, all well in progress in the twelfth to thirteenth centuries. In comparison, the early visionary descriptions of the Tsari area as a maṇḍala palace date from the fourteenth century, while the full narrative of its mandalization, including its cosmic framing with the important story of Rudra's subjugation by Heruka, dates, as we will see, from about 1570. The later sources often claim to be (and quite possibly are) based on earlier ones.

In the context of discussing the conversion of Buddhist *néri* sites, Alexander Macdonald has considered whether the mythic and ideological schema employed were intentionally exported from India and spread in Tibet because they suited the purposes of the Buddhist élite involved in the processes he terms "Buddha-isation" and "Lama-isation."[16] Whatever the case, the success the mandalization process attained at *néri* was also due to a certain amount of congruence between local and imported schema. Here one can recall Stanley Tambiah's general observations on the prevalence of the maṇḍala as a form of "cosmological topography" in Asia:

> It is possible to see Indian and Chinese precedents, Hindu and Buddhist sources, for these ideas, but one thing is clear: They could have taken root . . . only because indigenous conditions and social practices favored their incorporation or because they represented a "literate" culture's formalization of images already experienced and emergent in local conditions.[17]

Regarding Tibetan *néri*, there is at least one important case of symbolic congruency one can point to as an example of Tambiah's point. Just as the ancient Tibetan sacred mountain lay at the center of conceptions of divine origins, power, and the source of human moral order in both the old royal religion and local mountain cults, so, too, each Indian Tantric maṇḍala cosmos possesses its own great central mountain of Sumeru on top of which the chosen meditational deities dwell in their divine palaces, radiating their power and new moral order outward to lower orders of beings. Such schemes fit well with the general cultural significance accorded to height or elevation and centrality existing since ancient times in Tibet and probably reinforced by these Buddhist ideas. In the old royal religion, the mountain's height metaphorically modeled the divine origins of kingship and authority, while in later Buddhist times it modeled the transcendence implied in the rituals that focused on it. The combination of such fundamental conceptions made the innovation of *néri* not only possible but also eventually popular among a much wider section of the Tibetan population.

Once the *néri* mountain sites were established according to the new Indo-Tibetan model, they certainly did not remain the static, immutable holy places with fixed institutions that indigenous literature is apt to portray them as. On the contrary, they continued to be transformed, their popularity changing and their specific patronage shifting over the centuries. They were constantly subject to declines and revivals or innovations linked to large processes of historical and social change as well as to the agency of specific individuals.[18] To briefly take the example of Pure Crystal Mountain detailed in the chapters to follow: Established in the late twelfth century, it developed during a phase of Buddhist sectarian expansion, being initially patronized by Tantrists as both meditators and pilgrims. Popular lay pilgrimage began much later, with its regular pilgrimage routes fixed by the sixteenth century. The mountain's largest pilgrimage ritual was only created in the eighteenth century in conjunction with the rise of a new hierocratic state in Central Tibet, while its meditation traditions had virtually died out by the nineteenth century, only to be revived again in the early twentieth century. All rituals ceased in 1959 or soon after under Chinese administration but were recreated again in modified form by the mid-1980s during a period of social liberalization and local revitalization, fueled in part by a specific generation of the exile community.

Stepping back from Tibetan specifics for a moment, it is instructive to consider what happened in other Asian societies at points in their histories during which introduced Indian Mahāyāna and Tantric forms of Buddhism began to gain both cultural sophistication and social ground. Looking to China and Japan, for example, one finds that neither the development of Buddhist pilgrimage centers at earlier mountain cult sites nor the use of Indian and Tantric representations like the maṇn-ḍala for their appropriation and organization are unique to Tibet during the period of the establishment of the great *néri*. In neighboring Chinese society the central mountain of the Buddhist maṇḍala cosmos, Sumeru, was already being identified with the great sacred mountain of K'un-lun around 500 AD.[19] From the T'ang (618–907) onward, the Chinese began to focus much attention, under Buddhist influence, on mountains as major pilgrimage centers, particularly places like Wu-t'ai Shan and Omei Shan. Such sites often received their legitimation and impetus for development by way of sūtra traditions such as the *Hua yen ching*, and the cults of the great celestial bodhisattvas Mañjuśrī, Avalokiteśvara, and Samantabhadra, who were thought to abide and manifest on such peaks. Yet, using the imagery of Buddhist pure lands, the Chinese drew on the same symbolism as the Tantric maṇḍala cosmos in order to fit with the designated terrestrial mountain sites. The common Chinese phrase used to describe the performance of pilgrimages, "journey to a mountain to present incense" (*ch'ao-shan chin-hsiang*), indicates the central ritual status of mountain pilgrimage found in Chinese religious consciousness.[20] In Japan during the Heian period (793–1185), the conversion of sacred cult mountains by ascetics who were inspired by Tantric or so-called esoteric Buddhism and who employed the theory, symbolism, and practice of the maṇḍala preceded the same type of process that occurred in Tibet.[21]

In general, the creation of new orders of place and space in the natural environment accompanied the development of an introduced Buddhism throughout Asia. While each transformation of indigenous mountain cults occurred differently in relation to existing local historical and social contexts, the cultural resources for stimulating and effecting such changes often derived from the wealth of Indic ritual and narrative complexes that had been carefully translated and imported for centuries by Buddhist missionaries, traders, pilgrims, scholars, and rulers alike.

Organized Religion and Nature

Historically the establishment of major *néri* throughout Tibet marked a consolidation of newly formed, monastically based sectarian interests and territory. Symbolically this process also legitimated the superior powers of Tantric lamas and their systems of Buddhism or Bön by claiming control of apparently ancient Tibetan places of power and a conversion of their divine residents in the natural landscape. In general, the *néri* cult appears to have become much more widespread and popular by the sixteenth and seventeenth centuries. By that time it was a concrete expression of a number of important transformations that had become widespread in Tibetan society and worldview, including: the role and power of the lama in relation to local communities and cults; the existence of alternative conceptions of the natural world; and the formation of ritual and social networks based on new orders of space and time.

The Lama

In relation to the rising importance of both the ritual and social roles of the lama in Tibetan society, the new control over space that the conversion of *néri* represented was one of several indicators of changes in ritual orientation and consequently in various forms of social relations throughout the Tibetan cultural sphere. In this respect the development of a system of *néri* mountains can be compared to the historical banning of animal sacrifice in Buddhist Tibet, upon which Geoffrey Samuel has recently remarked:

> The Tibetan emphasis on this point is not only, or even primarily, because of the Buddhist prohibition on taking life. The banning of animal sacrifices was historically in Tibet the sign of Tibetan Buddhist dominance over local pre-Buddhist deity cults. Animals as offerings are replaced by dough images, and the lama approaches the local deities through the universalistic procedures of Tantric ritual. . . . This change, however, can only weaken ties to the local community and its locally based ritual practices.[22]

The development of the great *néri* marked a point at which the lama entered as the new ritual specialist of Tibetan mountain sites and cults. This change did not immediately contradict the continued existence of community-based rituals directed toward mountains. However, over time the change no doubt played a role in their gradual erosion in many areas as individual and group pilgrimages to the *néri* continued to build in popularity and the cultural model of the *néri* was spread by lamas to convert an increasing number of local sites.[23] While the local mountain cult was closely tied to discrete units of territory and exclusive notions of descent and social boundaries, the *néri* model was mobile and socially unrestricted. The relative versatility of the two types of mountain cults is clear from the fact that while local populations might only with difficulty relocate their own mountain cults intact during migrations (e.g., with a few exceptions, many did not survive the 1959 exile), an individual lama with sufficient ritual status could move with the *néri* model and promote and install it in a wide variety of local contexts.

New Conceptions of Nature

An increasing amount of research has shown that there are multiple but often interrelated notions about the natural environment as sacred geography or landscape in Tibetan societies. Within this diversity one can view the conversion of *néri* mountains as one particular type of "place creation" during the last millennium of Tibetan cultural history. It is one in which Tantric Buddhism was particularly instrumental by way of the agency of the lama, who provided sophisticated visionary representations of the world. Other widespread or popular Tibetan schemes for reordering and appropriating space or defining categories of place often utilized the actual building and strategic placement of a range of structures across the surface of the landscape. Examples of this ritual architecture abound in Tibet, and more obvious ones can be found, for instance, in the network of "suppressing" and "taming" temples attributed to the early king Songtsen Gampo, the development of grand palaces and regional monastic complexes of leading incarnate lamas, and the occurrence of *chöten*, or reliquary shrines, at key geographical locations. Most such forms are also instantiated at the village or local level.

However, the *néri* tradition redefined nature, the wild or uncultivated environment, in a compelling new manner without recourse to physically altering or constructing any actual edifice on the land. At great *néri* sites, actual ritual architecture was preceded by the Tantric lama's visionary representation and imaging of landscapes with a "subtle" architecture of the grandest and most elaborate kind—the maṇḍala palace—and then later surpassed by large-scale popular ritual movements of people across the terrain.[24] One could argue here that due to their remoteness, great altitudes, and extreme environments, *néri* mountains could never have been redefined by the building of ritual architecture. Unlike the situation in China, where pilgrimage mountains with environments more conducive to human activity were conceptually and spatially redefined through the often extensive construction of monasteries, temples, shrines, elaborate trail networks, and so on—under imperial patronage—no state or religious school in Tibetan history could have marshaled the resources necessary to achieve the same on *néri* mountains. But other sociocultural factors are also involved.

One can distinguish two broadly different traditions of sacred geography in many societies, two ways to attach meaning to the natural environment. One tradition is that of preliterate and stateless populations who assume (rather than impose) chthonic or telluric sacredness within the features of the natural landscape, such as mountains and lakes. The other is that of the imposition of meaning on the environment—the embodiment of historical discourse—mainly through building activity within the context of the centralized order of the state and organized salvational religions. These two different approaches to sacred place and space are often closely combined in pilgrimage cults that have been historically constituted through the introduction of universal religions into local contexts, as found, for example, in the cults and shrines of Andean pilgrimage.[25] Tibetan societies also have aspects of both approaches, sometimes referred to as shamanic versus clerical or ontic versus epistemic modes.[26] In terms of such a discussion, the *néri* as a category of sacred place or ritual space combine aspects of these two approaches or modes; there are no significant buildings, but a meaningful, albeit visionary, architecture of landscape is generated and imposed on the natural environment of the earlier sacred mountain sites. Ritual and other forms of representation ensure that this subtle and naturally embodied architecture is regularly redefined at *néri* sites. Alongside such clearly Indic- or Chinese-derived notions of the sacred mountain as elaborate, sublime palace or mansion, many of the ideal conceptions of space and place (e.g., paired, gendered mountains and lakes, linking of height with status, purity and divinity, vertical tripartite divisions, dwelling of the vitality principle [*la*], etc.) found in both early textual sources and the so-called folk religion, as well as the concerns usually focused around them, are still very evident in the *néri* cult, although often redefined and developed in a number of ways.[27]

A new order of representation and utilization of space comes into being during the establishment of a *néri*. The interesting idea that this process marks a "passage from nature to culture," a "taming of nature" or a process of "cultivation" or "civilization," as recently discussed in relation to Tibetan views of nature and sacred places, requires qualification.[28] Certainly, it may appear to be represented in these terms in élite textual sources whose purpose is to advance the moral and ritual supremacy of organized religions. "Nature," however, was never empty of meaning for Tibetan peoples, and any notions of a "civilization" process are totalizing attempts to deny former social constructions of the environment that existed before Buddhist and Bönpo orthodoxy begun their massive programs of culturally editing the Tibetan world.

However, such notions exist as part of an ideal world that evaporates in the face of lived experience. For the majority of ordinary visitors to *néri*, who do indeed consider these sites as divine abodes or embodiments, the actual experience of their ritual journeys is definitely a move away from civilization toward a wild and unpredictable nature. There have always been, *in fact*, considerable hardship, danger, and risk involved in pilgrimages at various *néri*. One faces on the one hand cold, rain, snow storms, avalanches, dangerous cliffs, and rivers, as well as various privations, and on the other the unpredictable and often wrathful character of the resident deities, especially if ritual limits are somehow breached; and these two aspects are closely associated, in any case, in the minds of many Tibetans. As traditionally represented by the élite, the *néri* do resemble perfect Buddhist or Bönpo maṇḍala worlds, yet the frequent hostility of their actual environments gives rise to a graphic contradiction. In the face of this contradiction, the brute forces of nature continue to be explained and related to by most pilgrims in terms of the personalities of the ambivalent local spirits inhabiting the world, just as they were before any Indic paradise came down to earth in Tibet. Just where "civilization" and "taming" of the environment fits in here, outside of certain idealized narrative schemes, is not readily apparent from the Tibetan point of view of actual experience. Moreover, the boundary between the wild and the civilized (in the sense of *dulwa*, "tamed" or "conquered") is not permanently established in Tibetan thought and cultural models, being merely provisional at a mythic level and thus requiring constant reconstitution and maintenance in the everyday order of ritual life.[29]

Space-time Networks and Society

The innovation of the *néri* through the agency of the Tantric lama should be understood as a process in which orders of space become more abstract and by which conceptions of space start to become delinked from those of locality and redefined in relation to it. The Tibetan case is one of many such encounters between the cultural features of small-scale, preliterate societies and the forces set in motion by universal, soteriologically oriented, textual-historical religious systems, such as Indian Buddhism.[30] In relation specifically to pilgrimage, evidence of the proliferation and miniaturization of pilgrimage sites and their traditions of ritual and representation is an important crosscultural type of indicator of these processes developing. Therefore, what happened, for example, in terms of proliferation and miniaturization in the development of pilgrimage sites in Buddhist Japan is true of the Tibetan world also. In the Tibetan case, miniaturization and proliferation in local pilgrimage contexts has been based on the model of the great *néri*.[31] The resulting formation of networks based on a model also implies the creation of a moral hierarchy of space, in which the unconverted local ritual site is subordinate in various respects to those places redefined by the *néri* model.

Just as notions of space became more universal with the development of the *néri* mountain cult, so, too, did those of time to which they were linked. This shift is particularly evident in terms of the timing of ritual in relation to the idea of *néri* being the mountain abodes of important deities and their retinues. Judging from recent ethnographic evidence, the main ritual life of local Tibetan mountain cults has been in the form of annual community celebrations, usually involving a ritual journey to the nearby sacred mountain to perform various ceremonies. These regular visits to the mountain gods permanently dwelling at the sites are occasions for annual purification and reconstitution of the relationship between divinity, individual, and community. They are also often associated with the annual domestic production cycles, seasonal access to resources, human movements, and so on, of specific communities.

In the ritual calendar of the *néri* cult, in contrast, time (like space) became delinked from locality to a certain extent. The specific annual and seasonally based sense of timing in local mountain worship gave way to a more universal one aligned instead with a standardized twelve-year calendrical cycle along with new ideas about the regular mobility and congregation of mountain deities. Thus, most *néri* have a "great pilgrimage festival" (*kor duchenmo*) that occurs once every twelve years, being identified with one of the twelve animal years that recur regularly in the standard Tibetan calendrical cycle (e.g., Nyanchen Tanglha is associated with the sheep year, Tsari with the monkey year, Tise with the horse year, and so on).[32] The designated animal year can be a time for the staging of major mountain pilgrimages, such as processions, or be regarded as the most auspicious period during which to visit a particular *néri*. Apart from the often multiple narrative justifications that fix the Tibetan animal year for any one site, the *kor duchenmo* traditions are often based on a notion of regular and localized gatherings of deities (*lhatsogdu*)—such as Tantric initiatory goddesses, protective deities, or regional collectives of mountain gods—at the *néri*, as well as their circulation.[33] This understanding and systematization of *néri* as cyclic gathering places for both deities and practitioners appears to have some parallels with Tibetan interpretations of the earlier Indian Tantric *pīṭha* cult which influenced the early Tibetan formulation of the *néri* cult and in which initiatory goddesses congregate periodically in a network of sites.

The reordering of *néri* ritual time into larger cycles that both enable and reflect the establishment of wider networks of sites and orders of ritual space in Tibet is typical of what occurred elsewhere in Buddhist Asia.[34] In the case of Tibet, the long-term development of such pilgrimage systems can be associated with changes that occurred together with the spread of organized Buddhism in general: a trend to horizontal integration, as local cults were linked to regional or panregional networks that promoted the wider circulation of persons and symbols, the sharing of values and goals, and so on; and an opposite but related trend toward differentiation, as new orders of ritual space and time generated hierarchies in which local cults, specifically those not converted, became morally subordinate as they lacked the cosmological underpinning and legitimation of those conforming to the model. What social effects did these developments have, particularly in terms of the relationships between new pan-Tibetan pilgrimages, their cult systems and networks, and the development of economics, trading, and the polity? How did such relationships actually manifest and operate in specific social and historical contexts and at particular sites?

Discussion of these important issues has barely been raised in the literature on Tibetan pilgrimage. This neglect is in part due to narrow focus, in that a large number of studies are devoted only to localized and smaller scale events and traditions. The substantial exception is provided by Robert Ekvall and James Downs, who began discussing pilgrimage in terms of the large-scale dynamics of Tibetan society and polity. They describe it working as a "unifying mechanism" over the vast geographical and ethnic extent of Tibet, circulating people within the territory to foster a common identity, and promoting an egalitarian social ethic "by the assumption, and expectation, that social differences would be set aside on pilgrimage and all pilgrims be equal," and so on.[35] One finds similar general, but unsubstantiated, assumptions echoed in many studies of Tibetan pilgrimage. Ekvall and Downs's analysis, like other studies of Tibetan pilgrimage and ritual life in general, is based on the assumption of an unproblematic functionalist perspective of social integration and unification. It provides a good example of the problems involved in uncritically treating major Tibetan ritual institutions simply as "local cults writ large."[36]

From the point of view of this case study of Pure Crystal Mountain *néri*, I, too, will contend that certain pilgrimages did play a significant role in the ways a larger Tibetan social order was regularly defined and organized at various levels. This reconstitution occurred precisely because of the large-scale ritual and social networking and gathering pilgrimages engendered. Examples of how this was so in relation to the active constitution of the premodern polity, as well as of ethnic, interethnic, and regional identities and of gender construction in the 1940s and 1950s are discussed in chapters 7 to 10. Unlike Ekvall and Downs, I argue that major Tibetan pilgrimages and their cult places and networks did not simply or even necessarily promote social integration, egalitarian values, and so on. Many settings that may have allowed for this were also characterized by the reinforcement of strong social divisions, boundaries, and identities, as well as by resistance to them, competition for access to and appropriation of symbolic and material resources, and the presence and mediation of competing discourses.

In much of the preceding discussion I have compared a generalized acount of the *néri* type of cult mountains to that of the *yüllha* type commonly worshipped by local Tibetan communities. While the two are quite distinct in many important respects, there are undeniable continuities and parallels between them. From the analyst's point of view, one of the key differences lies in the far more complex social life focused around *néri* and engendered by the ritual and cultic networks they participate in and help to constitute. From the Tibetan pilgrim's point of view, it is rather the narratives of their conversion to powerful maṇḍala landscapes populated with divine beings, their openings by heroic Tantric lamas, and the rituals that these events define that make the *néri* essentially different and especially worthy of ritually journeying long distances to. To these Tibetan interests, and their particular representations in relation to Pure Crystal Mountain, I shall now turn.

Part II

✦

REPRESENTATIONS

4

✦ ✦ ✦ ✦

Cosmodrama and Architectonics of Landscape

Wheel of great bliss and perfect cognition
Called glorious Tsari, shining upon everything,
Maṇḍala of gods and goddesses of the three bodies,
Shrine of the triple world-space, I bow down to you!

This short prayer forms the opening lines of an early-nineteenth-century Tibetan pilgrim's guidebook to the famous *néri* of Tsari, a guidebook still in use today.[1] To non-Tibetans it may appear to be simply another devotional verse. Yet these four lines contain the essence of an entire complex representational system. It is a system that Tibetans have applied for centuries to a mountain topos that modern observers have more recently described in essence as the 5,735-meter Himlayan peak Takpa Shiri at latitude 28° 37' and longitude 93° 15', using their own alternative representational system.[2] Anyone who reads or hears this short verse is given the cues, line by line, that the place encompasses sublime human knowledge and happiness, that it is all-pervasive in its effects, and that it has two architectonic forms, the maṇḍala palace and the offering shrine, which constitute at once an abode of many classes of beings and a hierarchized ordering of space and the physical environment.

The representational system that is used to define Pure Crystal Mountain and that enjoins the basic logic of all ritual performed there has an origin in cosmic space and time for Tibetans. Accordingly, as does any developed indigenous account of the mountain, I will begin by considering its origin narratives and then detail the set of referents they help determine. This set of referents—the sublime, cosmic reality of the mountain—was first realized in the visionary experiences of Tantric yogins and then "brought down to earth" and projected onto the local landscape, where it came to form the boundaries for the social life of the mountain cult, as I will show in later chapters.

It is a general feature of classification systems of premodern societies that they make use of narratives, such as etiological myths, that always point back to the origin or "zero point" of the world, the social group, and its practices. Zygmunt Bauman recently commented that "What the fables of (pre-modern) yore set to do was to 'explain' and 'legitimize' the being by its birth. After birth, there was nothing left to explain. The birth was the unique, the *only* 'moment in time', after which time has stopped, ground to a halt."[3] One finds that the narrative components of many Tibetan rituals conform in general to such a description. In an important sense, much Tibetan ritual practice is a reenactment or repetition of the essential moments in time portrayed in such myths, and the perceived identifications of present actors and actions with the "original" ones is regarded as fundamental to the efficacy of the ritual itself.[4] This is true also of the ritual-narrative complexes of the *néri* cult, for which one can usually distinguish two overlapping stages: the cosmic foundation, and the historical human foundation. One finds the first stage replayed within the ritual practice of Tantric yogins and meditators. They visit *néri* to internally reenact the original event of mandalization by identifying themselves with the main chosen meditational deities and their actions. The second stage is recreated by the ritual itineraries of ordinary pilgrims. In making their circumambulations of *néri*, they repeat the original circuits initially performed by the Tantric superheroes or saints of the past when they opened these sites for human use, and thus first defined the external boundaries of the maṇḍala within local landscapes.

Just how such ritual reenactments were actually practiced in recent times around Pure Crystal Mountain is the subject of the chapters that follow. In this chapter I will consider the stage of cosmic foundation that generates the whole system of representations and how it serves to classify and contextualize the site into several levels of reality and fundamental orders of spatial reference. One can identify these as the Buddhist cosmic space of the world-system, the Tibetan geographic space of the trans-Himalayan zone, and the local topographic space with its specific architectonics of maṇḍala landscape. None of the representations I will present is exclusive to any one social group, and various traces of the system are found in all Tibetan discourse expressing cultural understandings of social organization and practice in the area. However, in the texts and words of Buddhist lamas and yogins one often find the fullest and most sophisticated expression of these ideas. Their extended accounts constitute the big picture, of which smaller vignettes appear in the accounts of other Tibetans, often according to their own particular social positions and interests.

A Cosmodrama Comes down to Earth

The origin myth of Pure Crystal Mountain as a sacred place and maṇḍala landscape derives from Indian Tantric narratives of the subjugation of Maheśvara (alias Rudra or Bhairava) by Vajrapāṇi, or Jigjay's subjugation by Heruka as it is recast in the later Tibetan versions. A developing line of research has recently demonstrated the importance and popularity in northern Buddhist traditions of these narratives.[5] Working from Sanskrit, Tibetan, and Chinese textual sources, scholars have considered the development, "travels," and possible significance of these influential stories. Despite this extensive scholarship, the ethnologist is still left to pose the question: If this narrative or mythic scheme was, and perhaps still is, so influential and popular in northern Buddhism, how has it affected the actual social lives of Buddhists? What really did "fall down to earth" as this lofty cosmodrama unfolded, multiplied, and traveled through Asian time and space?

In Tibetan areas, various local versions of the story of the subjugation of Jigjay by Heruka have probably enjoyed at least an eight-hundred-year residence. They have been continually adapted and deployed by Buddhist authors throughout that period in order mainly to legitimate and authenticate the practice of originally Indian Tantric ritual systems in a new Tibetan context. This legitimation process includes the frequent use of these stories in relation to the development of the cult of *néri* mountains and other pilgrimage sites. Versions of the narrative are associated with all the major Buddhist *néri* in Tibet, and at Tsari this association had already taken place by the sixteenth century; most probably, it occurred even earlier. The myth's specific application to the site of Tsari has local representational implications.

Ferocious Jigjay's Subjugation at Tsari

For Tibetans the story of the Tsari area and Pure Crystal Mountain begins with important events in the history of our world-system. The spatial setting for the story is the recently formed universe itself, but more specifically our southern cosmic continent of Dzambuling (Jambudvīpa), as it is conceived in Indic Buddhist cosmologies that have long been known in Tibet. The events unfold in the context of cosmic time, over the countless millions of years of the four cosmic ages. It was at the beginning of the fourth (and present) cosmic age of disharmony that a cosmodrama unfolded in which two sets of divine forces competed for hegemonic power, and the control of the world changed hands.

According to our Tibetan versions of the story at Tsari, at that time our world-system came to be occupied and dominated by the powers of an obnoxious divine couple, Jigjay (Bhairava) and Dütsenma (Kālī) and their ferocious emanations as localized spirits. On one level these characters represent the influences of heterodox systems, such as Śaivism, and on another they can be read as the negative predispositions that need to be overcome by the Tantric yogin in practice. This divine couple and their representatives were then subjugated by a "father-mother union" (*yabyum*) of Buddhist chosen meditational deities, namely the Heruka emanation Khorlo Dompa/Demchok (Cakrasaṃvara/Saṃvara), his consort Dorje Pagmo (Vajravārāhī), and their own retinue. They represent not only the system of Buddhism but also the yogin's own overcoming of tendencies toward defilement and ignorance. The action of the story takes place at twenty-four main sites and eight secondary sites, the latter set being identified as charnel grounds. These places are frequently mentioned in Tantric literature as being the abodes of initiatory goddesses and meditation venues for advanced practitioners who have entered into the *caryā* or "action" phase of yoga in the Khorlo Dompa (Cakrasaṃvara) Tantra practice system. It should be noted that Tibetan translators and later purveyors of these narratives employed the word *né* to translate the Sanskrit term *pītha* and thereby represent the concept of the "action sites." Many of these main and subsidiary action sites are identifiable in the ancient religious geography of the Indian subcontinent. In the logic of the Khorlo Dompa Tantra system, where macrocosm and microcosm are equated and integrated, these twenty-four action sites and the powers active at them are represented not only in the geography of the external world but also as being arrayed around an internal network within the psychic body of the yogin, throughout which vital energies flow during ritual. In terms of this equation, the external world is thus also represented as a cosmic and geographical body, the action sites of which are each assimilated to body parts, and the circulatory interconnections between them as the routes of ritual journeys. This so-called adamantine body (*vajra-kāya*) system of correspondences, clearly a development of earlier themes in Indic cosmic dismemberment myths and introduced into late Indian Buddhism by way of extensive borrowings from Śaiva literature, came to serve as the basis for a Tibetan pilgrimage network based on certain of the *néri* mountains and associated sites.[6]

What is most significant in Tibetan sources is the longstanding identification of certain of these twenty-four (or thirty-two) essentially Indic sites with a series of places in the actual landscape of Tibet and the high Himalayas. In the process of assimilating the Tantric culture of late, North Indian Buddhism during the course of the last millennium, Tibetans relocated this India-wide scheme of sacred geography into their own world-space and in terms of their own cultural discourse. (I have discussed Tibetan interpretations of this scheme in detail elsewhere and will not dwell on them here.)[7] Pure Crystal Mountain at Tsari, along with other *néri* locations like Tise and Labchi, form an important part of this system and its development. For Tibetans the process of Jigjay's subjugation in the Tantric cosmodrama myth establishes the fundamental identity and nature of these sites as great Buddhist power places or empowered landscapes in terms of the cult of the *néri*.

All the available Tibetan written and oral sources that locate Tsari in this cosmodrama scheme do so by employing greatly abbreviated versions of the much longer subjugation narrative detailed in other sources. The short sixteenth-century version given here is commonly recycled in various oral and written accounts of Tsari. In the full text, the author first sets cosmic and geographical space in order by describing the general arrangement of the universe and the position, class, and names of the twenty-four main and eight subsidiary action sites. He then relates Tsari to the system of action sites, and picks up the narrative:

> This [place, Tsari] is said to be the great charnel ground to the south of them, according to the explanation brought forth by the Buddha in the [Tantras]. In the past, shortly after the time this world-system came into existence, these abodes (*né*) were seized by eight couples of powerful male and female gods and antigods, bestowers of harm and ogres, and serpent deities and horseheaded men. As a result they were called the *né* of action in the [three world-space realms of] celestial action (*khachö*), action on the earth (*sachö*), and underground (*saog*), and were famous as the eight great charnel grounds. And at that time, as the ferocious couple Jigjay and Dütsenma, alias the god Wangchuk Chenpo (Maheśvara) and the great goddess Umā who have their divine palace on snowy mount Tise, were regarded as the rulers of the world, those denizens made offerings to these two. As they were addicted to sexual intercourse, that couple could not go to these sites when invited by those denizens. Therefore, they bestowed on those twenty-four or thirty-two sites stone megaliths (*liṅga*) representing [Wangchuk Chenpo's] head, and so forth. Those denizens made offerings to them as well.
>
> As a consequence, the world fell into a period of establishment in the paths of evil and conversion to unbounded suffering. So, seeing that the time had come to subjugate them, from the highest heaven that Heruka whose substance is perfected experience established there a Heruka that was an emanation-body, having a blue-colored body, four faces, twelve arms, together with a Dorje Pagmo which he had himself emanated, performing a clockwise dance. As a result these emanations appeared on the summit of the central cosmic mountain, and the Buddhas of the five lineages, having emanated a divine palace and a troupe of offering goddesses, presented these to them as gifts,

> thus completing the great maṇḍala of the assembled lineages there. After the subjugation of ferocious Jigjay and his retinue by means of the absorption of their wealth and power, at the time that the great *Root Tantra of Demchok*, the "Ocean of Knowledge," was preached [by the Buddha], This place was one of the eight great charnel grounds, that to the south of the maṇḍala.[8]

And at this point a nineteenth-century version adds:

> And in accordance with that, all the *né* of action in the realms of celestial action (*khachö*), action on the earth (*sachö*), and underground (*saog*) that had been seized by the ferocious one and his retinue were reempowered in their very essence as the sphere of action of divine heroes and their consorts, and were conquered.[9]

Spatial Representations from the Narratives

By equating the Tsari area with the Indian Tantric charnel ground of Cāritra (or Tsāritra in Tibetan) the Tibetan accounts link it into a complex cosmic and terrestrial network of sites. Detailed Tibetan versions of the subjugation story divide the space of the great world-system maṇḍala into a three-tiered organization around which the main sites are arrayed and which is referred to briefly in our accounts.[10] The *tribhuvana* (*sasum*), or "three levels," system is an earlier Indian cosmological scheme found in the Sanskrit sources from which the Tibetans derived their narratives, and which appears to be analogous to indigenous Tibetan tripartite ordering of the phenomenal world.[11] Regardless of its origins, such a three-level organization of space is completely pervasive in Tibetan thinking about the world, whether in a vast and more abstract cosmological sense or in terms of the perceivable physical environment on any scale. Its implications for the representation of Tsari are multiple.

In cosmic space Tsari can be visualized as lying on the southern edge of the great world-system maṇḍala, whose center is the great cosmic mountain, Meru, somewhere to the north. This picture accords with the location of the eight great Tantric charnel grounds depicted around the perimeter of the maṇḍala of the Heruka form of Khorlo Dompa (see figure 4.1).[12] The twenty-four main action sites and associated charnel grounds in the scheme are divided into three sets of eight, each set being located on one of the levels of the three-tiered world-system. Tibetan sources describe these as the "eight *né* of celestial action (*khachö*)," "the eight *né* of action on the earth (*sachö*)," and "the eight *né* of action underground (*saogchö*)."[13] Each set is further characterized in terms of the three aspects of the enlightened being of the wrathful Heruka form of Khorlo Dompa, as represented by the vanquishing emanations he manifested in those places. This entails a hierarchy from the sublime to the gross material, with the upper level *khachö* abodes associated with mind (or "heart," *thug*), the middle *sachö* with speech (*sung*), and the lower *saogchö* with body (*ku*).[14] In these terms, the identification of Tsari as a charnel ground surrounding the world-system maṇḍala included it in the *khachö* set of abodes, as a place of Heruka's mind. This is why Tsari is commonly referred to by Tibetans as "the *né* of Khorlo Dompa's mind."[15]

Related social and geographical implications arise from these notions. When asked to describe Tsari as a part of Tibet, my informants invoked a well-known, and

Figure 4.1. Nepalese scroll painting of the sixty-two deity Khorlo Dompa *maṇḍala*. (Courtesy Private Collection R. R. E.)

perhaps antiquated, threefold scheme that related the site with two other *néri* in Tibetan geography.[16] When Tsari is described as the *né* of Khorlo Dompa's mind, Labchi is called the *né* of Khorlo Dompa's speech, and Tise or Mount Kailash the *né* of Khorlo Dompa's body.[17] Sometimes other related *néri*, such as Kawa Karpo, will be added as well. Tibetans not only think these three main sites in a geographical network, they use it as a ritual network for pilgrimage as well. Many pilgrims I met had visited several of these sites, and it was their common aim, often constructed in terms of a vow, to visit all three during their lifetime. This ritual network of recent popular pilgrimage was done by the serious Tantric practitioners of the past as a matter of course.[18] A contemporary ritual text divides up the Tibetan world-space and its peoples on the basis of this network:

> There is a proverb that states: "In the three districts of Ngari up in the west, they are guided by their own *né* (i.e., Tise). In the four horns of Ü and Tsang in the centre,

they are guided by their religion (i.e., Buddhism). In the six ranges of Amdo and Kham down in the east, they are guided by their lamas." And in accord with that, from among the many important *néri* that exist within Tibet, they always perform circumambulations and prostrations in connection with the great *né* of glorious Khorlo Dompa: In the west the very famous "King of White Snows" Tise, *né* of the body of the white lion-faced [goddess]; in the center the excellent Labchi, *né* of the speech of the striped tiger-faced [goddess]; and in the east the peerless Tsari, *né* of the mind of the black sow-faced [goddess].[19]

Being a charnel ground in the Tantric scheme, Tsari is located in the upper level of the triple world-space, in the celestial action zone of *khachö*—literally "sky-going" or "active in space" in Tibetan—and also is structured like a maṇḍala, palace (see figure 4.2). The triple division of the world-system implies a strong vertical ontological gradient from gross at the bottom to more refined or pure above. This gradient applies equally to the quality of existence of the physical environment and to the beings and other forms of life that inhabit it. While the underground action zone is populated mainly by serpent deities, we humans, the animals, and a collection of earthbound spirits live in the zone of action on the earth's surface. Sites in the celestial or sky zone of the three-layered maṇḍala world-system are described as "pure abodes" (*nédakpa*) in the Tibetan sources, resembling something like a heaven or paradise. And their inhabitants are purified beings, principally heroic gods and initiatory goddesses and other grades of enlightened sentient existence. These residents of *khachö* are called "sky-goers" (male/female: *khandro/ma* or *khachöpa/ma*).[20] Thus one finds that Khorlo Dompa's female consort Dorje Pagmo, principle resident sky-goer at Pure Crystal Mountain, is given the epithet Khachö Wangmo, or "Chieftainess of Khachö," by Tibetans (see figure 4.2).[21]

While the *khachö* zone may be the abode of sky-goers, Tibetans believe that at Tsari, under the right circumstances, humans may perceive it or enter it as well. The famous yogin Shabkar once characterized the site as "Tsaritra the glorious *né*, a great Buddhafield . . . which is equal to the actual pure *khachö* when seen by those endowed with good fortune, purified perception, and karma."[22] Tsariwa tell a story, found in various textual versions also, of an Indian Tantric master named Lawapa, who meditated near the summit of Pure Crystal Mountain and is said to have "passed into the *khachö* zone after going on to the peak." What is important to the storytellers is that Lawapa entered the *khachö* zone while still in a human body. A song about those who worship at Tsari states: "At the time of death they will be lead to the field of pure *khachö* by divine heroes and sky-goers."[23]

Here one must be careful not to build the *khachö* zone at Tsari into a kind of Luftschloss, merely afloat in space. While the designation "*khachö* pure abode" (*nedakpa khachö*), which is so frequently applied to Tsari, involves the space around and above the mountain, it also applies to the actual landscape of its uppermost slopes.[24] Elements of this designation are coded into the different place names for the mountain's high altitude topography, such as the main summit of Pure Crystal Mountain (Dakpa Sheri), the eastern peak of Khachöri ("Khachö Mountain"), the four high peaks collectively called Dakpa Khachörishi ("Four Pure Khachö Mountains"), and the former high point of the Rongkor Chenmo, the great procession route around the mountain, called Dakpa Tsari Thugpa ("Heart/Mind of Pure Tsari").[25] In later

Figure 4.2. Tibetan scroll painting of the *khachö* pure abode. (Schoettle Collection, Courtesy Joachim Baader.)

chapters I will show how the intense purity of this upper landscape and the space around the mountain is taken account of in the structure of rituals and in general Tibetan life practice at the site. I will also show that the pure beings, like the sky-goers and others, who abide in the *khachö* zone do not just fly around remotely in space but, as far as Tibetans are concerned, are active on the ground of the mountain as well.

Fluid Spaces and Schematic Repetition

There are further considerations of space at Tsari that relate to its status as a site in the narratives of Jigjay's subjugation. These features are less well known to most people, being more of interest to Tantric practitioners, although I note them here because enough yogins and ordinary folk do mention them for it to be significant. I have just stated that the Khorlo Dompa system posits the correspondence of macrocosmic and microcosmic space. This correspondence is usually represented in terms of the arrangement of all the external "*né* of action" being present in miniature in the yogin's body. If a yogin reports, "When I was practising at place X, all the twenty-four *né* were present there," such a statement is often interpreted by Western commentators as symbolic or intentional language to describe an inner psychic experience of space.[26] This may be so, but it is only one possible interpretation.

For many Tibetans, both lamas and laypersons, the whole set of action *né* are considered to be physically, not merely symbolically, contained in the local environment of any one of the external locations, such as Tsari. The lama Dilgo Khyentse has said that "within any single valley one can identify the entire set of the twenty-four sacred places."[27] During my own fieldwork at Labchi and Pawongkha, two places in Tibet considered to be among the twenty-four Tantric action *né*, I was shown other versions of the twenty-four *né* in the local geography by practitioners. A Tibetan guidebook to Tsari asserts that the twenty-four are present there also and lists sources that classify them.[28] One informant from Chikchar at Tsari said that they were present in that area but have probably all but disappeared now due to the violation of the site by the occupying Chinese army since 1960.[29] On this phenomenon Dünjom Rinpoché maintains that existing power places such as Uḍḍiyāna, one of the twenty-four *né*, can shrink in surface and even disappear from an area when the conditions are no longer conducive to spiritual practice.[30]

At Tsari one finds the same large-scale representational themes that are established through the subjugation narrative being applied to the vertical and horizontal organization of space at all levels. For example, written and oral accounts of the site image the regional geography as a gigantic ritual scepter or *dorje* laid on its side.[31] The western tip of this *dorje* is formed by Pure Crystal Mountain, the so-called Ancient Tsari (Tsari Nyingma); its spiral center is the adjacent lake of Tsari Tsokar, or "White Lake," to the east, and the easternmost tip is formed by the related sites of Tsari Sarma and Tashijong, or "New Tsari" and "Auspicious Valley," some seventy kilometers away along the Himalayan divide to the east (see figure 8.1).[32] All three are recognized as *né* of the chosen meditational deity couple Khorlo Dompa and Dorje Pagmo and have a threefold ranking applied to them with Pure Crystal mountain being the *né* of speech, White Lake the *né* of mind, and New Tsari the *né* of body.

In another example, concerning the site of Chikchar, the location of Tsari's most important temple and meditation retreat centre, one finds the three-level world-space scheme repeated in small scale. When the temple of Dorje Pagmo ("Adamantine Sow") was founded there between 1567 and 1574 by the Tantric scholar Pema Karpo, he began construction on receiving the prophecy of a local sky-goer: "You should labor zealously because the time has arrived for a pig-faced one to be self-produced underground (*saog*) and for the appearance of a sow active in the sky (*khachö*) above and a sow active on the earth (*sachö*) between these!"[33] Correspondingly, contemporary Tibetan accounts of the site describe its appearance precisely in terms of these three divisions of the local world-space.[34] One could even say that this threefold organization of space is repeated again in miniature within the body of the Tantric yogin who meditates at the site according to practices of the Khorlo Dompa system.[35]

Such examples are taken from many threefold divisions of space that Tibetans use at Tsari. This pattern is strongly reinforced by the repetition there of another representational element from the narratives of Jigjay's subjugation, the architectonic form of the divine mansion of the chosen meditational deities, the maṇḍala palace.

Reading the Architecture of Landscape

In the core narratives of the subjugation drama just presented, the world-system becomes constituted as a great maṇḍala palace of Khorlo Dompa and his consort, radiating out from the summit of the cosmic mountain, with sites such as Tsari distributed around its perimeter. The Tibetan commentators extended this idea, perhaps following implicit Tantric themes of equating the organization of macrocosm and microcosm, and went on to represent *néri* as complete maṇḍala palaces in their own right. While Tibetans applied this representational form to their mountains, as well as to various other local sites during the course of many centuries, it appears that at Tsari this practice of mandalizing geographical areas was most systematically both applied to landscape and actualized socially in ritual and domestic behavior. Landscape first became realized as maṇḍala in the visionary experiences of Tantric meditators who practiced at the site and recorded their perceptions of the mountain's sublime reality.

Most non-Tibetans who have seen Tibetan Buddhist maṇḍala will relate to them as flat, two-dimensional images such as those represented in painted scrolls (see figure 4.1), woodblock prints, drawings, and ritual arrangements of colored sand. Yet for Tibetans these are just the diagrams or ground plans for what is always conceived of as a three-dimensional structure, in which the vertical orientation is the most dominant (see figure 4.2). The true three-dimensional form of maṇḍala is reproduced constantly in Tibetan cultural life. This reproduction takes place in multiple ephemeral constructions, such as ritual hand gestures, the positioning and movement of persons in certain ceremonial and performative events, the heaped arrangement of offering substances in regular rituals, or the sustained and highly detailed mental productions generated in advanced forms of Tantric meditation. More permanent constructions are instantiated in architectural forms ranging from entire temple complexes—for example, the great Samyé temple—to reliquaries (*chö-ten*) and other shrines of all sizes and ritual structures fashioned from metal, clay, thread, wood, or dough, and nowadays even generated with computer-assisted drafting programs and stored as electronic media. In some of these forms, particularly the architecturally elaborate buildings and visualized mental constructions, one can appreciate that in three dimensions a maṇḍala as a built-up palace or mansion is more than just an ornate and impressive facade. Such maṇḍala have an even more complex interior of halls, chambers, galleries, archways, thrones, and so on, populated by a highly ordered group of divine residents. Thus, both the entire structure itself and its inhabitants constitute a specific pantheon, in the fullest sense of the word.

In order for non-Tibetans to begin to appreciate the process of the mandalization of landscape at a place such as Tsari, one must start by imagining both a sophisticated, three-dimensional exterior and interior of the mountain. If such a vision of the landscape, or at least its possibility, is not borne constantly in mind, one will miss the fuller significance that such representations have for Tibetans when they encounter Pure Crystal Mountain. One runs the risk of reducing this particular way of thinking about place to the mode of two-dimensional diagrams or to the mere facade or surface of three-dimensional forms only. Such cautions not only apply to non-Tibetan analysts and readers of conceptions of the architecture of landscape, but also are invoked in Tibetan debates about ranked cognitive abilities that determine who gains access to the various dimensions of reality that are admitted by the Tibetan worldview.

Maṇḍala Palace Geography and Topography

Referring to the Tantric visionary interpretation of the mountain's landscape, the standard guidebooks for Tsari generally indicate that "Pure Crystal mountain . . . has an arrangement of peaks, lakes, and regions with the innate nature of a maṇḍala";[36] that it is "a great, naturally produced maṇḍala of Adamantine Secret Mantra";[37] and that when circumambulating up on the mountain one is said to "have entered into the maṇḍala of the Great Secret."[38] Some Tibetans describe Pure Crystal Mountain and its environs in great detail as a maṇḍala palace of the chosen meditational deities Khorlo Dompa and Dorje Pagmo. The lists of deities, their qualities, and their locations given in such accounts are describing the interior structure of this maṇḍala palace as it lies behind the covering of the mountain's exterior landscape features. Buddhists recognize the level of reality of this interior structure as the form realm of *saṃbhoga-kāya*, the "enjoyment body" of enlightened Buddhahood. This particular form realm is only accessible or conceivable for those persons practicing at advanced levels of Tantric meditation, with a refinement of cognition equivalent to the upper stages of the bodhisattva path.

When heard or read these esoteric accounts of landscape may seem fantastic to the uninitiated; however, they are not entirely unique, as they conform to the maṇḍala liturgies found in texts, and the painted and sculpted representations depicting these liturgies. What is unique, however, are the Tibetan interpretations of geographical space and topographical form based on the conception of the actual maṇḍala palace being within the mountain itself. It is mainly these interpretations that I will detail here.

The maṇḍala palace manifest as Pure Crystal Mountain is identical to the three-tiered cosmic maṇḍala palace already outlined in relation to the subjugation drama just presented, although it is reduced in extent to fit the topos of the mountain. Thus the same triple division and hierarchy applied to space, being, and environment are found once again but discussed here mainly with reference to architectural forms. The foundations (*mangshi*) of the structure—what one would term the geological root of the mountain—are laid in the underworld deep within the ground. The divine palace (*phodrang*) sits upon a gigantic lotus flower base (*péden*) rising out of the center of an underground lake. The structure occupies the triple world-space at all three levels. And as for the section that exists above the level of the ground, the mountain itself:

> It is a maṇḍala that is made in the form of a mountain.
> This Crystal Mountain, which is a superior symbol,
> Is made from precious crystal substance,
> With the shape of a great *chöten*.
> On its apex dwell the lamas and the chosen meditational deities,
> About its middle dwell the Buddhas of the three times,
> And at its base dwell the defenders of religion and guardians.
> Round about it dwell divine heroes and sky-goers;
> Its environs comprise a heavenly palace.[39]

One finds in these statements both vertical and horizontal referents for imaging the mountain's topography as a maṇḍala palace. Summarizing from many oral and written sources, one can briefly outline the architecture of the maṇḍala palace in the landscape. (I defer for later discussion the *chöten* or "reliquary shrine," shape and crystal substance mentioned here.)

First, the central summit of Pure Crystal Mountain is the highest chamber of the palace in which Khorlo Dompa and Dorje Pagmo, and one's lama (who is equal to the chosen meditational deities), dwell. It is equivalent to the pericarp of the lotus at the very center of the maṇḍala (see figure 4.1). It is here inside the topmost mountain peak/palace that the raison d'être of this sublime architecture, the original cosmic subjugation drama, continues; its chosen meditational deity inhabitants are described as still "dancing on the corpse of ferocious Jigjay and the breast of Dütsenma."[40] The interior of the great palace is, therefore, to be understood as an atemporal reality that can be ritually accessed and used by the qualified.

The area of high altitude terrain below the summit, circumscribed by the series of high passes that surround it, has its landscape features divided horizontally into sets of four. This division is based on the layout of this terrain being like a *svastika* cross or that of a five-pointed ritual sceptre, in which the fifth point projects vertically from the center to form the main peak. The intermediate levels of the maṇḍala palace, between the central pericarp chamber above and the four doors below on the four outer walls, are divided into four quadrants of different colors (see figure 4.1). Here the various chambers housing divine occupants, the ritual decorations, such as vases and white conch shells, and the outer petals of the pericarp are all divided into sets of four along both the cardinal axes and the intermediate points of the horizontal plane. Thus, correspondingly, one finds this landscape zone contains the summits of four peaks around the center; then, further out, four main passes; four ravines with four rivers that flow down from the summit of Pure Crystal Mountain in the four directions and carrying water of four different colors; four caves and four stone thrones on the mountain side; and four important lakes.[41]

The four doors on the outer walls of the palace are identified with main mountain passes, valleys, and ravines in the cardinal directions. These were the sites where humans first entered the palace landscape, when Tantric yogins "opened the doors to the place" in times past, as I will show in the following chapter. In this lowest zone the point of entry to the great maṇḍala, where one must initially encounter the guardian and protector deities, is said to be in the main valley of the Tsari River due north of the central peak. Certain of the charnel grounds that are found arranged around the palace, outside the doors, are also identified as sites in the outer environs of the mountain. The whole maṇḍala is enclosed by a circular girdle or fencelike enclosure of ritual scepters (*dorje rawa*), which forms the divine threshold of the arrangement. There are places on the ground that the great girdle of ritual scepters is thought to traverse, marking the boundary of the maṇḍala.

In addition, there are many other references to the maṇḍala structure and its divine occupants in Tibetan descriptions of Tsari. In fact, the detail in such accounts of the place will make little sense to the hearer or reader who is not versed in the maṇḍala liturgy or who is unused to imaging landscape according to such representations. All these important features of the maṇḍala palace precinct are found cataloged and described in Tibetan oral and written accounts. I will not reproduce all this material here but will have occasion to refer to certain features selectively in later chapters as their interpretation dictates the pattern of specific aspects of ritual and domestic life in the region.

Sublime Aquatic Architecture

As I have shown, the maṇḍala and *tribhuvana* systems have very closely related ways of ordering space. The maṇḍala, in addition, develops a horizontal pattern of order at the site. Just as the *tribhuvana* system is repeated at various levels to interpret the phenomenal world, so, too, is the process of mandalization. Tsari is located on the cosmic maṇḍala, and the mountain is a maṇḍala, but also on the mountain itself a group of the most important individual sites are described as maṇḍala: the alpine lakes that are found around the high summit. In the ancient Tibetan worldview and the folk tradition, lakes—along with mountain peaks—are the most significant type of landscape feature, and the two are often considered together as a gendered pair (commonly male mountain, female lake) forming an ideal unit of sacred geography. They are a dwelling place of both the collective and personal vitality or life force principle (*la*), and their waters produce and provide both visionary and physical access to other dimensions of space and time. In line with these themes, the Buddhist maṇḍala lakes on the slopes of Pure Crystal Mountain are permeable zones, windows or portals in the hard rock and earth walls of the great palace, through which one can see or enter into the chambers of the divine residence.

Although the main summit is the most powerful place in the great landscape maṇḍala, it is physically (though not meditatively) unreachable. The various maṇḍala lakes are all accessible—they can be circumambulated at close quarters; their waters can be consumed or collected; offerings can be placed in them; and they can be ritually entered through bathing or meditation. The Tibetan guidebooks catalog these maṇḍala lakes, the specific deity abodes they contain, and the powers they can offer the practitioner. Their depth provides the vertical dimension of the palace architecture; but their surface tension is also said to mirror this divine reality. And like the rest of the high altitude environment on the mountain, they are close to, or within, the *khachö* purity zone; thus the water and other substances they contain have a high ritual status.

The most important maṇḍala lake is Great Palace Turquoise Lake (Phodrang Chenpo Yumtso), located to the south of the main summit; the term *phodrang* refers to the maṇḍala palace it contains. This lake itself is described as "[c]hief of all the lakes, origin place for all paranormal powers, and the complete maṇḍala palace of glorious Khorlo Dompa."[42] When famous yogins visit the spot, they are said to "see this lake itself as the maṇḍala of glorious Khorlo Dompa, and enter within it."[43] Such maṇḍala lakes at Tsari are the initiatory sites par excellence in the local landscape.

Mandalization is repeated on an even smaller scale at Tsari. The smallest and most intimate level of its application is within the human body of the practitioner. Once again, patterns for conceiving space and place are reproduced and reinforced.

One more major aspect of the representational system applied to Tsari remains to be outlined, which further amplifies all that has been detailed so far: the conception that the mountain has the architectural form of a *chöten* reliquary shrine (sometimes called *chödong*).

Nature's Enormous Crystal Reliquary

The conceptions of the mountain as maṇḍala palace and *khachö* zone were developed out of the subjugation narratives relating to the supreme yoga class of Tantra traditions in Tibet. By designating Tsari as a charnel ground, these conceptions also pave the way for its landscape to be imaged as a Buddhist reliquary shrine or *chöten*. In Tantric liturgies and icons the charnel grounds that surround the Khorlo Dompa maṇḍala are portrayed as each containing a white *chöten*. Each charnel ground also has a mountain and a tree associated with it. Tibetan commentators use all these features to argue for the identity of sites like Tsari with those described in Tantric sources. Later Tibetan works recycle this Indian imagery in detail in accounts of the great charnel grounds. They often mention great *chöten*, sometimes the size of mountains, which are "self-arisen" or "naturally produced" and made out of pure crystal as their central feature. The twelfth chapter of the important fourteenth-century Tibetan "revealed treasure" (*terma*) text *Pema Khatang*, for instance, gives a detailed account of one such *chöten*, which forms the central palace of the land of Uḍḍiyāna in northwest India.[44] It is said to be a great abode of Heruka or Khorlo Dompa, which reflects the status of the site of Uḍḍiyāna as it is mentioned in the subjugation narratives. All the same images turn up in later revealed treasure guidebooks to Pure Crystal Mountain of Tsari, as I will show. Once again, Tibetans have reworked a developed Indian representational scheme and applied it in detail to their own local landscape.

Tibetan sources represent Pure Crystal Mountain as a *chöten* or shrine in a number of ways, emphasizing different aspects of its form and meaning. It can be seen as an enormous natural monument to the victory of Buddhist teachings, referred to in terms of the *dharma-kāya*, or "absolute body" aspect of the Buddha. At the same time, this monument is both identified with, and contains within itself, the *saṃbhoga-kāya* aspect of the chosen meditational deities, who embody the victory of Buddhism over both cosmic negativities (the subjugation of Jigjay) and personal negativities (the cleansing of the "twin defilements," or *dribnyi*). For example:

> The divine hero Heruka—whose soles are coated
> With the red blood that pours from the slain Jigjay—
> Together with the sky-goer [Dorje Pagmo], who both purify the twin defilements,
> Constitute the evil-conquering Crystal Mountain, a shrine of the *dharma-kāya*.[45]

Other descriptions detail the monument's form as manifest on three relatively different levels of reality—the outward (*chi*), inward (*nang*), and esoteric (*sang*). For example:

> Esoterically (*sang*) [this] Snow Mountain of Pure Crystal arose naturally in the shape of a ritual vase (*bumpa*). Thus, it has been said to be an empowered *chöten* that is naturally produced and self-manifested.[46]

The ritual vase (Sanskrit: *kalaśa*) referred to here has the esoteric meaning of representing a maṇḍala. In maṇḍala rituals practiced by Tibetans, one or several vases contain the deities and form the "palace." The vases themselves become the central initiatory structure in processes such as the "vase consecration" (*kalaśābhiṣeka*). In Tibetan the same term, *bumpa*, is used for the dome or vaselike receptacle of the Tibetan-style *chöten*, which houses the deities or their representations in the same arrangement as a maṇḍala palace.

Although its architectural details differ, the ubiquitous Buddhist reliquary shrine or *chöten* is equal to a maṇḍala palace. For Tibetans the two are functionally similar as ritual structures, as they both contain either Buddhas or the substantial and symbolic equivalents of Buddhas in the form of relics, texts, or images. By virtue of this content, both possess a similar ambiance of empowerment (*chinlab*). In actual structures built in Tibet, the architectural forms of both are conspicuously combined to the point where the distinction between them collapses. In sculptural representations the summit or crown of Sumeru, the central cosmic mountain of the world-system maṇḍala palace, is a *chöten*, and the top of any Khorlo Dompa maṇḍala palace is itself equivalent to the Sumeru.[47] The unity of the two representations becomes even more apparent as further details are given of the "outward" and "inward" reality of the mountain: "Pure Crystal Mountain is a great *dharma-kāya* shrine, and this itself resembles a heart-shaped snow mountain outwardly (*chi*), [and] inwardly (*nang*) contains a great celestial palace of pure, divine hosts in the naturally produced and self-manifested form of an auspicious many-doored *chöten*."[48] In addition:

> It is the great edifice of an auspicious [many-doored] *chöten*, which if seen from the outside (*chi*) exists in the form of a three-peaked snow mountain, and if seen from the inside (*nang*) is a luminous, auspicious [many-doored] *chöten* made out of a crystal jewel material. Its summit is established as the abode of the gods.[49]

The architecture of this type of *chöten*, which Tibetans refer to as *trashi gomang*, or "auspicious many-doored," is more like a maṇḍala palace than any other *chöten* style found in the Tibetan world.[50] The revealed treasure guidebooks of the Nyingmapa sect, for example, describe the mountain's exterior in great detail as an auspicious many-doored *chöten*.[51] The interior complexity of this style is elaborated on in the traditions of other Buddhist sects interested in the mountain, such as the Kagyüpa. When visiting the Great Palace Turquoise Lake at Tsari, the founder of the Drigungpa lineage, Jigten Gönpo (1143–1217), perceived the mountain as an auspicious many-doored *chöten* housing two thousand eight hundred deities. Kagyüpa written and oral guides to the mountain have continued to represent it according to this elaborate architectural scheme:

> [I]t is the heart of hearts of the place of Tsari. It arose in the center of that place, and previously the accomplished ones perceived it directly as a great auspicious many-doored [*chöten*], which they perceived as containing: the four great kings and the other seventy-two glorious protectors at the seventy-two doors to the lion's throne of the *chöten* ; in the center of that the glorious four-armed protector and other defenders of religion and guardians; on the four steps possessing great faces eight hundred shrines on [each] great face; in each and every one of the two thousand six hundred doors on the steps the divine assemblies of the four classes of Tantras; in the dome the divine assembly of the maṇḍala of the lord Heruka Dorje Sempa alias Khorlo Dompa in father-mother union; on the capital and parasol Dorje Chang encircled by the Kagyüpa lamas. In terms of its true state, it is said to be a great palace that is essentially a vast ocean of maṇḍala. However, even in terms of its external appearance, this towering and beautifully shaped snow peak clearly resembles the form of a many-doored *chöten*.[52]

According to historical sources, this particular *chöten* architecture of Pure Crystal Mountain has long existed in Tibet in the form of smaller humanmade "visible representations" (*ten*). During Jigten Gönpo's lifetime multiple replicas of the Pure Crystal Mountain many-doored *chöten* were built at Drigungthel monastery in Central Tibet to conform with his vision.[53] They are still being rebuilt today.[54] Another form of portable *ten* of Pure Crystal Mountain is a painted-scroll image, with the sublime architecture of a *tashi gomang* or auspicious many-doored *chöten* housing the chosen meditational deities in its central dome (see figure 4.3).

These materials are very important. The representational system I am describing here is known to have had a long public life in the form of oral and written guidebook, eulogy, and prayer texts. But it has also long been available for visual consumption in Tibet in material forms, some of which are portable, such as the painted scroll. Although the differences between maṇḍala palaces and auspicious many-doored *chöten* (and, for that matter, representations of Buddhafields) are often only

Figure 4.3. Tibetan scroll painting of Pure Crystal Mountain as a *tashi gomang* shrine with pilgrims. (Courtesy Heinz Zumbühl.)

subtle, the fact that these public forms are of the *chöten* and not explicitly of the maṇḍala is significant. There may well be esoteric restrictions on the public display or reproduction of the Khorlo Dompa maṇḍala, but other more down-to-earth explanations are possible. An elderly southern Tibetan once described Pure Crystal Mountain to me as a huge crystal *chöten*; when I asked if he understood it as a maṇḍala, he replied, "Of course we [laypeople] know about maṇḍala, but the lamas know everything [about them]. Well, if you go to Tsari and see the mountain in front of you, it just looks like it's a big *chöten* of white crystal!"[55]

Such a statement is not isolated, nor does it merely reflect contemporary sentiment about how Tibetans regard mountains. A Tibetan layman who visited the mountain in 1794 recorded in his biography: "From the summit of the Drölma Pass I directly encountered (*jel*) the snow mountain of Dakpashri, palace of glorious Khorlo Dompa, that resembles a mountain of crystal."[56] General references to the geography of Tibet found in earlier Tibetan literature often use descriptive phrases like "mountains that resemble *chöten* of spotless crystal."[57] Talking and thinking of mountains as *chöten* has had a long history in the Tibetan world. In general it could be said that *chöten*, like mountains, are everywhere in the traditional Tibetan world-space. They are the most common and accessible religious edifices in the Tibetan environment (or used to be before their mass destruction during the Cultural Revolution), and most journeys in public space involve circumambulating one sooner or later. Popular pilgrimage journeys to mountains represented as *chöten*, as I will show, also involve the same fundamental ritual performances.

The dual representational system of maṇḍala palace and *chöten* applied to the mountain tends to present a vision of the site that is more esoteric in the first case, and more popular and public in the second, although the distinction between them is never hard and fast. It is a system within which the visionary reality of the Tantric cult and popular worship and imagery have become closely combined.

Several scholars have noted longstanding Tibetan beliefs about the powerful geomantic and physical effects that the location of *ten*, such as images, temples, and especially *chöten*, can have on the environment.[58] Their placement for the purpose of subjugation of non-Buddhist spirit forces and their auspicious and empowering effects on the substance of the landscape are common themes in Tibetan narrative and ritual discourse. The mandalization of landscape at Tsari in the Tibetan accounts of the subjugation of Jigjay and the mountain's representation as a *chöten* are these same themes being played out again. This time no actual physical construction has taken place, yet the resultant mentally constructed edifice is many thousands of times larger than anything humans could possibly build. Throughout the remainder of this study I will show that although these monuments are not physically built at the site by people, they are continually being socially, and in some cases, meditatively reconstructed or reconstituted at Tsari through the performance of a wide range of rituals.

Recapitulation

To summarize briefly, and at the risk of laboring the point, I must reiterate a point that Westerners, habituated in dualistic forms of thinking the world, might easily miss, or misconceive. The organization of space at Tsari in its representations as a *khachö* field, a maṇḍala, and a gigantic *chöten* is based on notions of continuity for Tibetans. The fixed and dualistic dichotomy of sacred versus profane space found in so much Western thinking and writing is an inappropriate model in this context. In the scholarly literature one often reads that pilgrimage sites or "sacred" places are a "bridge to the other side," a link between heaven and earth, between humans and divinity, the two separate dimensions of reality, the sacred and profane. While all these notions may at least be partially true of Tsari (e.g., there are certain thresholds), they lead one away from the basic Tibetan understanding that the other side is actually present right here, that heaven and earth interpenetrate on the mountain, and that divine and other nonhuman beings live with and even within us. And Tibetan Buddhist philosophy provides ample underpinning for such popular belief. There is a continuity of being between the environmental qualities and inhabitants of the sublime and the gross material dimensions of the three-level world. This grading together can be, and does become, a phenomenal reality. Experience, and the quality of the environment, changes for Tibetans as they ascend or descend through it.

5

✦ ✦ ✦ ✦

History and Prayer as Map

If they abandon the oral guide to Tsari,
The pilgrims are liable to turn into sightseers.
Without the eulogies of the Tsari pilgrimage circuit,
They just gossip about the theft of the monastery's yak.

As this local proverb reminds us, it is important for pilgrims to have certain forms of explanation and glorification of a site in order for them to negotiate it, meaningfully interpret it, and remain focused on its virtues during their ritual journeys.[1] In fact, the notion of pilgrimage in the traditional Tibetan understanding would be meaningless without such forms. For example, the most common ritual act at *néri*, the walking of a main circumambulation path, is essentially the pilgrim's reenactment of the well-known narratives of the first such circuits performed there by the original heroes who opened these places. Research on Tibetan pilgrimages continues to show that oral and written texts of all sorts are constantly in play during their stagings. These texts support ritual activities not only by providing inspiring models (*pé*, which themselves are directly related to the perceived efficacy of the actions they define) but also by acting as aids for negotiating both the gross and sublime dimensions of any site. In the case of *néri*, which often have rich cultic histories, both the phenomenal and the subtle levels requiring ritual attention on the part of the practitioner can be very complex and thus require a variety of ritual texts to manage. Quite a number of these are still available for the site of Pure Crystal Mountain.

I will present two pieces of such material: one, from a guidebook, is written and old, but continually being recycled up to the present day; the other, a prayer or eulogy, is oral and of unknown age, and remains in use today as well. They are excellent representatives of two important forms that are constantly invoked in Tibetan ritual relationships between persons and places. Although short, both texts contain a large amount of information about the cult of Pure Crystal Mountain. For these reasons alone they are worthy of inclusion in translation here. However, my main purpose for including them at this point is to discuss their styles of representation of the site and some of the implications of these styles for the interpretation of landscape and the ritual relationship with place at Tsari. These materials show, as just discussed in the previous chapter, how the conception of landscape and organization of space in the form of divine residence, as maṇḍala or elaborate reliquary shrine (*chöten*), are more than just cosmically determined. For Tibetans they are also historically constituted and reproduced by the activities of particular human beings at the site. As a prelude to understanding all ritual and domestic life around the mountain, these materials begin to show the extent to which the representations of landscape at Tsari are recognized "on the ground" by Tibetans.

Alternative Maps

In the last few decades a large Western literature has developed on the concept of "map." Our notion of map has been extended from the paper maps of classical Western cartography, which represent the earth's surface, to include, among others, cognitive and social maps, the complex electronic maps of computer systems, and mathematical maps for navigating the multiple dimensions of hyperspace. Like many other cultures, Tibetans have used a variety of mapping systems for navigating their "world-space" (*shingkham*).

There have long been graphic painted maps in Tibet, closer to what we usually think of today as maps. These can be called *shingikӧpa*, or "arrangement of a region/field," and they most often represent the other possible world-systems or Buddhafields of Mahāyāna Buddhism, maṇḍala and other cosmograms, and the paradisiacal landscapes of alternative realities, such as the "hidden land" of Shambhala or of Zangdok Pelri, Padmasambhava's "Glorious Copper-colored Mountain." Actual Tibetan landscapes came to be represented in this style of map when the Buddhafields that Tibetans recognized on earth, such as the Potala palace and its environs or the great *néri*, were portrayed in paintings. The places important in the lives of great saints also appeared as the background landscapes of their portraits. This style of representing landscape only became fully developed quite recently (post–eighteenth century) in the history of Tibetan art and owes much to the influences of Chinese landscape painting. But in virtually all cases these works are not maps that Tibetans could use to negotiate their own countryside, although their representation inspired a certain way of relating to the landscape as Buddhafield, maṇḍala, *néri*, and so on. Also, as objects they did not have a mundane status but were considered as *ten*, representations of the Buddha and his reality to be used as supports for meditation, considered as *tongdrӧl* (able to "liberate by sight" of them), and worshipped and treated with respect for the empowerment with which they were charged.[2]

There are a few more recent (nineteenth–twentieth century) examples of maps usually called *sabtra*, literally "variegated countryside," with the syllable *tra* here signifying a blending together of many colors, forms, and textures of various landscape features. It can also mean "register," "index," or "a framed window" in other compounds, and indicates a certain perspectival approach to representing landscape. As this etymology suggests, these maps resemble the style of Western cartography a little more and do not appear to have a particular ritual status, although they retain a unique Tibetan system of projection and spacial reference.[3] Even more recently one finds Tibetan maps heavily influenced by exposure to Western-style cartography and worldview.[4]

While the history of Tibetan cartography is interesting, my point here is that maps in the way we think of them, as portable graphic representations, have not had a long history in Tibet, were often accorded special status, and were rare. Instead, most Tibetans have relied heavily on oral and written textual maps or guides to navigate and interpret particular physical landscapes. These forms are much more intensive and immediate ways of relating to landscapes and places, as they can simultaneously invoke history, myth, cosmology, theories of substance, place, and person, social relations, and much more, besides just geography and topography. They are carriers of multiple systems of representation and signification, and they have a certain fluidity as well.

Textual maps come in many forms, and it is undesirable to define a genre for which there is no Tibetan equivalent. My task is somewhat easier here as I am only interested in those forms that describe landscapes of the greatest significance for Tibetans themselves, such as *néri* like Pure Crystal Mountain. Pilgrimage sites, whether as humanmade complexes or natural landscape features, have several types of text devoted to them. There are guidebooks of widely differing lengths and styles, eulogies, and prayers or petitions. The limited Western notion of text as written or printed book must be greatly expanded, or even abandoned, when working in this context. All these forms are interchangeably oral and written in whole or part, and many are versified specifically for mnemonic purposes. In pre-1959 Tibet, many people—such as laypersons with no written literacy—could hear, memorize, and recite these types of texts accurately without ever having contact with a written or printed version. With few exceptions they are nonexclusive, public forms. When considering them as maps, as I am about to do, one could call these fluid forms narrative maps or oral/textual maps with a translation of what Tibetans call *néki logyü* ("narratives of *né*") and *néshé* ("oral explanations of *né*") in mind.

Good Stories Travel Far

The following chapter from a sixteenth-century text will no doubt be read and used as a "medieval" history of Tsari and the saintly figures and religious institutions that gathered around it. I would argue that for Tibetans it is far more than that; certain narratives one might call history are also sophisticated textual maps that can enjoy long periods of currency in a variety of written, oral, or even performative expressions.

This first text can be classed as a "narrative of *né*" (*néki logyü*), and forms the fourth and longest chapter of a written guide to Tsari. Its author, Pema Karpo (1527–1592), has been renowned in the Tibetan world since his own day, earning the title "polymath" (*kunkhyen*) for his vast and often inspired scholarship.[5] Although there are earlier surviving guides, more detailed guides, and still shorter guides to Tsari, Pema Karpo's text, particularly the chapter translated here, became and remained the seminal work on the mountain. Portions of it are used in many different contexts relating to Tsari. For example, sections of the text can be found as the performance narrative for a ritual dance still current in Bhutan;[6] quoted in biography;[7] employed extensively to construct other later oral and written guides;[8] recycled in prayers and eulogies;[9] and slipped into contemporary speech when people talk of Tsari.[10] Why? Surely in part because of Pema Karpo's great prestige in certain circles, but mainly because his text *works*, as far as its Tibetan users are concerned—the polymath was a good storyteller, and good stories travel far. To construct it he wove together a whole series of short pieces, at times inspiring, dramatic, and entertaining (there is little sex, but much magic and violence), yet always informative. Quite simply the work is consumable and memorable, and for the Tibetan hearers or readers who might or do go to Tsari, it is more than just a good story.

Reading a Tibetan Narrative Map

Reading the following narrative carefully, one can see that it functions on many related levels at once for the pilgrim. I will discuss but a few here. It is general knowledge that the mountain is a special type of place, one that is "self-produced" (*rangchung*) and "spontaneous" (*lhungidrup*), thus possessing an innate, natural power or "empowerment" (*chinlab*) from which it gains its high status. The central theme of the narrative is this power of place, the power of certain human and nonhuman beings, and the different exchanges that occur between them. It tells how the great, natural maṇḍala palace is ritually accessed, its landscape doors successively "opened," and its powers obtained in the form of various types of paranormal abilities, realizations and prophecies, and cleansings of defilements by a lineup of some of Tibet's most important yogins and lamas. Even for many of these Tantric superheroes, the task is extremely challenging, as the place itself is so powerful; throughout the narrative any disrespect or doubt regarding the *néri* (e.g., the stories of Gampopa, Lawapa's disciple, and Tsongkhapa) creates instant problems; ritual impropriety there (e.g., the story of Nyö, Gar, and Chö) leads to failures; human jealousy at the site (e.g., the story of Drukpa and Tselpa yogins) unleashes natural disasters elsewhere; failure to heed local omens and signs (e.g., the story of Drigung Lingpa's disciples) results in bad fortune and tragedy; and so on. The message to human visitors is clear—this place is supercharged with power, handle it with care!

The narrative also reveals that the mountain is not an anonymous powerhouse. It is inhabited by all manner of nonhuman beings whose individual powers humans must either subdue and convert or pay great respect to, depending on the ranking of such beings in the maṇḍala palace hierarchy. Nothing about the mountain's environment can be taken for granted—not the local weather, lakes, or animal life, or even minerals, herbs, or water. Although it is inherently powerful, the mountain also continues to accumulate even more status by having such a prestigious cast of saintly persons associated with it.[11] Power in various forms is exchanged. For Tibetans the exchange is not just symbolic but substantial, as *chinlab* is transferred from enlightened bodies to spots in the physical environment, and vice versa. This subtle transformation is not the only change in the landscape registered in the narrative. Imprinting of one kind or other is occurring constantly as the historical events become physically incorporated as landscape features or as existing features are stamped with marks or shaped, and a whole collection of significant toponyms are generated. These first human actions also establish the ritual dimensions of the whole empowered landscape. Everything that happens in the narrative becomes ritually significant for later human visitors to the mountain, often by way of imitation and reenactment, as I will show in the following chapters.

The following translation of the fourth chapter of Pema Karpo's guidebook to Tsari, entitled *How the Doors to the Né Were Opened*, successively recounts the stages of initial human ritual access to the mountain through the doors of its sublime architecture, which are embodied in the local landscape.[12]

[*Part 1: The Early Indian Masters—The Southern and Eastern Doors*]

[18a] At the time of the early diffusion of Buddhism to the land of Tibet the ritual formula-holder and accomplished one Padma[sambhava] came through the southern door, the Jowo Thempa La (Lord's Threshold Pass) of Char.[13] He performed meditation for an interval of seven years, seven months, and seven days in the Zilchen Sangwé Phuk (Cave of Secret Great Brilliance).[14] He systematized a complete vision of this great *né* [in his meditation]. [18b] He concealed innumerable, profound religious treasures there, and shortly after that Vimalamitra arrived there by way of his magical powers. After dwelling in the divine palace [of Khorlo Dompa], he taught Buddhism to the nonhuman beings.

Then, there was one known as meditation master Lawapa, and from among the many so-called this Lawapa was the one from the east [of India], who was a teacher of the lord Atiśa.[15] Because his disciple named Bhusuku had said that he wanted to go to the actual *né* of Demochok in Uḍḍiyāna [in northwest India], he told him, "There is a *né* that has greater power than Uḍḍiyāna, in the barbarous border-country to the north [of Bengal], go there!"[16] He went, but did not locate it. He returned, and [Lawapa] told him, "I will help you," and they entered via the eastern door and came through Parparong (Poisonous Worm Ravine).[17] At first they went to Chikchar (Simultaneous Realization), and then to the Machen Lawa Phuk (Lawapa's Chef Cave). Then, when they stayed in the Dorje Phuk (Adamantine Cave) on the side of Khachöri (Khachö Mountain) [Lawapa told his disciple], "You go down below; there are some dancing virgins, so bring me the one in the middle!" After seizing a bowl of incense he recited the ritual formula of *The Pure Nature of Reality*, and went. Thus he met with the twenty-one virgins living there. After leading off the one in the middle, he departed. A minute passed, and when his concentration lapsed for an instant, the virgin vanished, and he found a radish in his hand. Thinking that the virgin had turned into the radish, he questioned the meditation master, who said, "Wash the radish," [19a] and, "After you have washed it, chop it up and cook it [into a broth]." When [Bhusuku] said, "It's cooked," he was told, "Bring a full bowl to me. You should drink it as well!" He handed the meditation master a full bowl. But, thinking it was human flesh, he was unable to drink it himself. He swilled it around and threw it out to a dog that was there, and it followed after them. As a result, later the meditation master and the dog both went to the summit of Khachö Mountain where they departed to the Khachö paradise. [Bhusuku] was left behind and so, uttering lamentations, he pleaded with the meditation master. Because of this the meditation master came back, and peeling aside the skin from his body, he bestowed upon him a [vision of] a self-manifested sixty-two deity Demchok [*maṇḍala*] assembly. Thus, he returned to India, and his impediments ceased. It was prophesied that he would obtain the mundane level of paranormal powers. The meditation master himself disappeared into a rainbow light. The meditation master was offered the paranormal powers by a sky-goer named Laghi.

Therefore, in accordance with that story, it is not right to have doubts about anything at this *né*. Even when the great Tsongkhapa went there on pilgrimage, he thought it improper for a cleric to drink beer and so he did not partake of it [during a local ritual], and as a result a pain like bamboo splinters in his feet nearly killed him. Nothing others could do for him was to any avail. Realizing that it was a kind of retribution for his having discursive thoughts about beer at that great *né*, he consumed some consecrated substances, and because of that he recovered. This is as it appears in his own biography.[18]

Later on [19b] [Lawapa's] disciple returned there and then obtained the mundane paranormal powers as a result. His name was [Prajñā]rakṣita. He was one of the hundred and eight teachers of the master Marpa the Translator, and some of the precepts of his school are found in the lineage stemming from Pagmo Drupa.[19] After a prayer to [Lawapa] by the teacher from Nyö, the great Traorpa Chöwar Trakpa, who was a personal pupil of the master Rechungpa, the skin [that Lawapa had peeled off] of his body was brought to Nyel by the master's magical powers, to the village of Nangtra.[20] At present it is said to be found in the heart of the reliquary shrine of Traor. And when Atiśa traveled to Tibet, he made a request to the meditation master Lawapa to show him the *maṇḍala*, and so he explained the directions to him, saying, "Go to that spot in the barbarous border-country to the north [of Bengal] where there exists a meditation place." Although the Lord [Atiśa] did not go there in person, from the summit of the pass of Sangphu he had a vision of the glorious Khorlo Dompa *maṇḍala* of Lūhipā at this *né*, and then composed a eulogy.[21]

[*Part 2: The First Tibetan Meditators—The Western Door*]

The king of religion Gampopa, who was extolled as the eradicator of the disease of moral and cognitive obscurations, and also known as Dakpo Lhaje ("The Physician of Dakpo") in the three worlds, was prophesied to be like a Buddha by the Buddha himself in his own teaching, as "The monk-physician in the later diffusion [of Buddhism to Tibet]."[22] After many days on the religious-throne of Zanglung, [20a] the mountain that symbolizes the great *né* of Gampo, [Gampopa preached]:[23]

> In this place yonder where the sun is refracted into the rosy clouds, mists, and rainbows of the southeast, there is a directly manifest divine assembly of glorious Khorlo Dompa, a great palace that is spontaneously arisen, the one called Tsari Tsagong Parvata (Tsari Superior Herb Mountain).[24] It is a *né* at which to make offerings of meat and beer to Dorje Pagmo, where all the paranormal powers are realized as desired by those with the appropriate karma and fortune, and where those without fortune are annihilated by the worldly sky-goers who rejoice in flesh and blood. The entry path of the noxious demons is frequented by such things as tigers and leopards, savage bears, wildmen, horse-flies, and hornets. The ground in all directions is covered by an inconceivable variety of flowers. There is a constant stream of fragrant incense. It has a place that continuously emits harmonious music.

Because the time had arrived to open the door of that *né*, he pointed his finger at it and asked [his disciples], "Which of you is able to do it?" And because it was a fierce *né*, seven boils erupted on his finger [due to his disrespect of pointing directly at it]. Then the following day he stuck [his finger] out straight, and even though he asked for three more days, no one came forth who was up to the task. A day later, when he looked directly at Kyewo Yeshé Dorje, that great ascetic Kyewo thought, "What? Is my precious lama talking to me?" [20b] and then asked, "Can I have permission to go [and open it]?"[25] To this [Gampopa] was very willing, and so the eleven, Kyewo Yeshé Dorje the master and his [ten] disciples, first went up through the Druma valley.[26] When they did so the path was obstructed by the protective deity Trigugchen. That is, after midday, mist and cloud closed in, and they lost their way. Sometimes [the protector] rolled around like a langur monkey, at others he rang out like a bell, and sometimes he poked at them as if he were a ritual scepter, and leaped into the air.

They presented him with a ritual cake and implored him, "Don't come here! Go elsewhere," and so that protector disappeared into a rock. Even now, on that rock's surface there is a distinct body [imprint]

They turned back, and arrived in Lawagyal. After seeking lodgings with a nun there, they rested. They asked her, "Is there a spot where people can get through farther on from this valley? What is the valley like? Have you been there?" So the woman replied, "I have never been there. I have no knowledge of the valley that you mention. However, I have a daughter who has gone to give a circular feast offering at Tsāritra. She goes to all the festivals. She left already yesterday. You go, too, you can meet her on the way and ask her."

After that, Kyewo the master and his disciples proceeded. At the foot of the pass they heard the daughter's distant, whispering song, and having realized that she was a sky-goer [21a], they presented her with a circular feast offering. After questioning her, they crossed the pass and came to the small white cave of Phölung (Tibet Mid valley). Mist and cloud closed in. Innumerable demonic apparitions appeared. [Kyewo] dispatched his disciples to another cave. He himself remained there, meditating in the demon-conquering concentration for seven days, and as a result the omens and magical deceptions abated of their own accord. There, in Phölung, smoke rose in the day and fire blazed at night. Because they went there, the [sky-goers of the five Buddha families] appeared: the buddha sky-goer in a space matrix-triangle, the adamantine sky-goer in a rock matrix-triangle, the jewel sky-goer in an earth matrix-triangle, the lotus sky-goer in a water matrix-triangle, and the action sky-goer in a wood matrix-triangle. In particular, labia of white alchemical stone appeared there in that rock matrix-triangle or vulva.[27] The following morning the sky-goer Senge Dongchen and sisters, all three, appeared to them in person and said, "Kyewo and company, don't sleep, get up! Get up and act like you were taking refuge! Get up and meditate like you would on the arising of thoughts!

> If you don't shed your human life like [old] skin and hair,
> There is a danger your constituents of existence will hang upon you like an animal's pelt.
> If you don't sever your attachments like a rotten rope,
> There is a danger your Karmic imprints will pursue you like a separated foal.
> If you don't cast off your worldly desires like phlegm,
> There is a danger your thirst will increase as when drinking salt water.
> If you don't defend your vows as if they were a fortress for your life,
> There is a danger your delusions will overwhelm you like an army."

And then they said:

> Yogins, your perseverance is great. But because you have no regard for life and limb, and wear these [monks'] garments, neither will you realize the wishes of your lama nor will you delight the mother goddesses and sky-goers, nor will you open the door to the *né* of Tsari, nor will you see the divine faces that appear within or attain the supreme and the mundane paranormal powers. Therefore, if you wish to open the door to the *né* of Tsari, come [properly prepared] at about this time next year, having put a rain hat on your head, rain boots on your feet, and a walking stick in your hand! While continually carrying an unceasing stream of incense smoke and the twin requisites of means and wisdom, come in singing nonstop from the peaks of the three mountains! Come in dancing nonstop from the junction of the three valleys! Offer an unending flow of libations and ritual cakes, and pray fiercely. If you do that now, we, too, will help you to open the door to that *né*!

Having said that, they were absorbed into the stone vulva there. After that, the [master and his disciples] all went back. About a year later, acting in accordance with the teachings that were imparted to him, [Kyewo] went there. He petitioned his gracious root-lama [Gampopa] seated on the sun-moon throne on the crown of his head[22a]:[28]

Lead the way to open what was commanded.
Reveal the divine faces that manifest within.
Empower the self-liberated, luminous mind.

I pray that inner and outer impediments do not arise,
And that I be granted the supreme and mundane paranormal power.
I petition the Phö Domtsenchen (Sexed Rocks of Tibet),
And beseech the Düdgön Nakpo.

Through his petitioning with [the words "Lead the way to open] what was commanded," and so on, he saw into the western door of the girdle of ritual scepters [encircling the maṇḍala palace]. After that, he passed through the sites of Domtsang (Bear's Den) and Kalā [Dungtso] (Conch-shell Conduit Lake). At first, he came upon the Ömbartso (Blazing Light Lake). Thinking he had encountered the Yumtso (Turquoise Lake), he returned, but the lord Gampopa said, "It was not the Yumtso, search still further."[29] The second time, he performed a lefthanded circumambulation. He came upon the Phodrang Kyomo[tso] (Long-handled Ladle Lake Palace).[30] Having thought this was the Yumtso, he returned, but it was not the Yumtso and he continued on. The third time he performed a righthanded circumambulation and thus he saw the Phodrang Yumtso (Turquoise Lake Palace). He met directly with the internally manifest divine assembly of Pure Crystal Mountain and their retinue. Because he was given some *lingchen* herb[31] by the field-protector sky-goer and her two sisters, he obtained the mundane paranormal powers, beginning with the power of levitation. He consolidated his understanding of Great Seal (Mahāmudrā) yoga. After taking hold of the *lingchen* herb in his right hand and a walking stick in his left, he performed a dance, and he sang:

This supreme *né*, glorious Tsari,
Is not wandered by all and sundry [22b].
I have abandoned worldly activities,
I have self-luminosity of mind itself.

It's a place to fling down life and limb.
It's a place to remove hindrances whose causes are outer and inner.
It's a place to make an analysis of cyclic existence.
It's a place to weigh ascetics [and their accomplishments] in the balance.

It's a place for thoroughly understanding the mind.
It's a place to preserve the clear light with the mind.
It's a place to receive the two levels of paranormal powers.

This supreme *né*, glorious Tsari,
Is not some minor monastery up behind a village.
This *lingchen* herb, which is a paranormal power [producing] substance,
Is not the spittle for smashing demons and demonesses.[32]

The clerical siblings of this assembled religious family,
Are not [the type of] ascetics who roam around the marketplace.

Then he made those words resonate in his mind. He struck his walking stick on a rock and it went in as if being pushed into mud. Even nowadays the imprint of that is still found there.

[*Part 3: Establishing Sectarian Interests—The Northwestern Door*]

One generation after that, Kyopa Jigten Sumgi Gönpo established his eastern monastic seat of Daklha Gampo. From the summit of Riwo Shānti (Tranquillity Mountain), he saw directly all the characteristics of the outer, inner, and secret *né* of Tsari, and with that he dispatched his three best disciples, Nyöchenpo Gyelwa Lhanangpa, Gardampa, and Pelchen Chöyé.[33] They went, passing through the Druma Valley of Dakpo. Because they followed the tracks left by three white grouse, they found the Kongmo La (White Grouse Pass). They went to Phökhasum (Facing Tibet Three Ways).[34] And [at the same time], when Tsangpa Gyare [23a] was sitting in meditation at the mountain of Jomo Kharak, the following morning the sky-goer Senge Dongchen appeared to him on three different occasions and prophesied, "Gyare, the time has come to open the door to the *né* of Tsari, therefore go there!"[35] He thought, "Is this really necessary?" and as a result, during his stay there at about sunrise on the mountain peak of Kharak, [a vision of] the great accomplished one Ling Repa appeared before him in a dwelling tent of five kinds of rainbows and [said]:[36]

Gyare, my son, hurry your meditation without delay!
In the maṇḍala that is manifested as Tsari,
There is the Khandro Doénying Phuk (Sky-goer's Stone Heart Cave).

There is *lingchen* herb, which bestows paranormal powers when eaten.
There is the empowerment of the mother-goddesses and sky-goers.
The Buddha that requires no cultivation is in that *né*.

And the apparition disappeared on the instant of giving that advice. After that took place, he announced his intention of going to Tsari. Gradually he went as far as Drigung. His companions returned each to their own provinces. By means of his own understanding of his lama's yoga, he held his breath for one meditation session, and in that way he got to Phökhasum on that very day and met with Nyö, Gar, and Chö. They asked him, "Who are you?" He answered, "I am Gyare the big-eyed one, disciple of Ling Repa the big-bellied one." So they asked, "Well, where are you going at present?" Thus he said, "I am going to open the door to the *né* of Tsari." [23b] So they replied, "As we need the substances that are the means and wisdom materials for a circular feast offering there, we must travel accompanied by many servants, otherwise we can't go." However, he understood that the means and wisdom substances are nothing other than meat and beer, and said, "You do it that way yourselves! That is not the way I see it!"

As they went on their way together, a small young boy appeared riding on a horse that had lumps of gold and turquoise decorating it. He requested them: "Lamas, you ascend through here, since there is nothing other than one hermit there," and because they proceeded in accord with that ever since it has been called the Ribpa La (Hermit Pass).

This was the northwest door. From there they went below Khadingdrak (Garuḍa Crag). They halted there, and because Nyö arrived, saying over and over, "This resting place of our friend Gyare is pleasant" [Gyare] offered, "If it pleases you, keep it yourself, friend!" Again, they descended together. When they came to the Bepa Yumtso (Frog Turquoise Lake), the path was blocked by a terrible frog as strong as a yak, and it would not let them pass. At this Nyö meditated in concentration, Gardampa meditated on the generation-stage of Dorje Jigjay, and Pelchen Chöyé deployed ritual cakes, and when they were all thinking, "Oh! Be pacified," the religious lord Gyare leapt onto its back without hesitation, and so Nyö [24a] called out, "Brave friend, don't do that! Not only will the life and limb of our honored friend be devoured by this malicious serpent deity, but it will also do harm to following generations."

To this the lord Gyare replied, "Whether long or short, my life span will be fifty-one years. In the future a spring will emerge from beneath this threshold. At that time, my followers will migrate from this *né* and may have to take some action, otherwise nothing will happen."

After saying that he trampled that frog violently, and in consequence it was turned into a boulder and remained like that. Many extremely clear footprints appeared on it. The magical deceptions abated. After that, when they went to Yümé (Lower Country), one hundred thousand sky-goers who were made from wisdom and action appeared in ranked assembly. When they had taken up their seats there, after Gardampa arrived, he said, "This resting place of our friend is pleasant," so [Gyare] offered, "If it pleases you, keep it yourself, noble friend!"[37] After that, descending from the Kyobchen La (Great Assistance Pass) the religious lord Gyare arrived in Chikchar, and at that time the path was blocked by the nonhumans manifesting as a multitude of vulvas. Then, having made his penis suitable for the deed he inserted it into them, and as a result they turned into rock and the imprint of them stood out clearly. He found the Doényying Cave. There he bound the field-protector sky-goer Dorje Yudrönma by oath.[38] [24b] To that she responded, "I will be your religious-protector." So he replied, "A female religious-protector is no use to me," and she promised, "Although I am of no use to the master himself, in the future your descendents will occupy this place, and at that time I would be happy just to look after the yaks."[39] That great goddess acted as his Tantric ritual consort. The field-protector Senge Dongchen also promised to do all he commanded.

After that he descended. When he sat in a seat that had magically self-manifested, the directional guardian Shinje Gyelpo came before him in the pleasing form of an eight-year-old boy, received ordination, and took the name Chikchar Marpo.[40] He left by way of the same pass as before, and as a consequence [the three, Nyö, Gar, and Chö] met him on the summit of the Shakam La (Dried Meat Pass). They requested of him: "Today, friend Gyare, you must make the preparations for an offering!" and so he promised, "I will do that." Therefore, after he had held his breath for one meditation session as before, he left, and so saw the field-protector's nomad tent. As a result of his begging there, butter and cheese inconceivable in extent appeared. The friends arrived and gave an extensive circular feast offering with it. Because the leftovers were heaped up in that place, it is called Kardogtang (Dairy Food Scraps Plateau), that is, nowadays it is a great heap [25a], which turned into and remained as white mineral stone.[41]

They proceeded as far as Shibmo Tratrig (Billion Fragments). After that, darkness fell at noon, and with the appearance of a billion stars the three—Nyö, Gar, and Chö—delayed their departure. The religious lord Gyare then said:

> Here there is *lingchen* herb, which bestows paranormal powers when eaten.
> Here there is the empowerment of the mother-goddesses and sky-goers.
> It's a place for weighing ascetics in the balance.
> It's a place to gauge the measure of a monk.
> It's a place for the journey of myself, the yogin Gyare.

He departed without hesitation. He penetrated to [the lake of] Marnag Rakta (Blackish-red Blood). The face of the goddess Ekajaṭī, together with her retinue, was revealed. [She said], "Because you have received the [Tantric] vows, there's no doubt that we are equals." When the vow-holding lineage of Drukpa disciples arrive here a single, clear, hot sun that dries cotton garments will very surely appear. And because one can know of the vicissitudes of the Drukpa lineage teachings through the rising and falling of that lake, it is called the Drukpaé Lamtso (Drukpa's Vitality Lake). After that he arrived at Phodrang [Yumtso]. [In his meditation] he directly encountered an internally manifested divine assembly. It was prophesied by the Blessed One, glorious Khorlo Dompa, that in this happy aeon he would become the Buddha Sangye Möpa, and by the Blessed Lady Dorje Pagmo, the Adamantine Queen, that his teachings would spread as far as a vulture can fly in eighteen days. There, in the religious lord's own uppermost cave [25b], he prophesied the future arrival of Gyelwa Götsangpa, saying, "A disciple of mine who has reached the tenth bodhisattva stage will come." After that Gyare traveled along a precipitous path, and as he dwelt [in a cave] in front of the Lake of Sindhura, a sky-goer brought water along a diamond conduit and offered it to him. Then the perfect-cognition sky-goer [Dorje Pagmo] emerged from that Lake of Sindhura like a bursting bubble. She offered him a pair of eye-shades that were woven out of her own hair, and so after that the name Gyare Mikra Phuk (Gyare's Eye-shades Cave) was given to that great cave.

Later, on returning to Yütö (Upper Country), behind there [he found] a mountain resembling Dorje Pagmo, and he constructed a bamboo hut beneath a tree like a yogin's trident and then dwelt there for three months. As a result, one dawn, sounds, lights, and the sweet fragrances of incense that were beyond the reach of the imagination were emitted, and at that very moment the seventh superior Buddha manifested before him. He bestowed upon him the entire doctrine of causality. With an unimpeded knowledge of all things that can be known, he became accomplished as a Buddha with perfect dual knowledge.

At that time, the three—Nyö, Gar, and Chö—intended to circumambulate Tsari. They went before Kyopa [Jigten Sumgi Gönpo], and thus he dispatched them with instructions, stating, "You could not circumambulate Tsari because you did not encounter the face of Marnag [i.e., Ekajaṭī]. Return once more." On the second occasion he said, "Once again, you could not circumambulate [to] Chikchar. [26a] There you did not meet the four gods that are special to me." He dispatched them a third time, sending them to the Druma Valley. On that occasion Nyöchenpo entered into the ranks of those who had given all the divine heroes and sky-goers in Chikchar a circular feast offering. After he dwelt in that place it was known as Nyöki Dochel (Nyö's Paving Stone). In this place I, Pema Karpo, built the temple of Dorje Pagmo Denyishel (Two Truths Face Dorje Pagmo) through the inducement of the field-protector sky-goer's words: "You should labor zealously, because the time has arrived for a pig-faced one to be self-produced underground, and the appearance of a sow (*pagmo*) active in the sky above, and a sow active on the earth between these![42]

On that occasion also, in this region an inconceivably extensive garland of divine heroes and sky-goers singing and dancing came as nectar for the ears of all those assembled there.

On that third occasion, the three—Nyö, Gar, and Chö—had a vision just like a divine host manifested within.

Of the eighteen functionaries, the servants of the four superior lamas [of the Kagyüpa sect lineages] who moved to Yütö, six were of the Drukpa lineage, one was of the Shang

Tselpa lineage, two were Densatilpa lineage, and the remainder were Drigungpa lineage.

At the time they arrived there [26b], a personal disciple of the glorious Pagmo Drupa, the yogin possessing a ritual consort, who was known as Gyergom Shigpo, was already dwelling there in Yütö.[43] Thinking it improper that this power place was occupied by a yogin with a female partner, they told him so, and therefore Gyergom rode off on a white mare; and so later on that pass that he rode across was named Takar La (White Horse Pass).[44] He dwelt in the cave of Kyudo (Kyu Down Valley).[45] In that place there can still be seen the reliquary shrine containing the relics of his final liberation from the cycle of rebirths. When he departed, he left behind his fire flint there and thus said, "In my wake there will probably be nothing but continuous smoke [i.e., my lineage will continue here]." Later, hermits of the Shugseb order at Nyepu were sent out by the Tselpa lineage.[46] These are the Chöd practitioners of the present. After that, having been accepted by Tsangnag Phukpa Thukje Senge, they adopted the Drukpa lineage.[47]

When Gyelwa Götsangpa dwelt at Phoma Lhakhab, he was afflicted by leprosy.[48] Although he went to other power places, such as Tise and Jālandhara, he could not rid himself of it. Later he arrived at this place. Because of his great physical strength, he took care of all those at Tsari who were sick and weak. As he used to fetch and carry [sacks of flour], his back became covered with sores. Then the others said of him, "Can I borrow that old, red donkey of you Drukpas?" At that time he dreamed that his entrails all fell out [symbolizing the removal of his defilements]. Because he wondered, "Will they go back inside me?" a white man told him, [27a] "If your diligence [in practice] is small, they will return." At that time all his defilements were purified, the basis of his illness disappeared, and he gained incomparable advantages in his meditation.

He practiced in the many mountain hollows of Tsari and remained one-pointed. The Drölma La (Goddess Drölma Pass) of upper Chikchar was also opened by him. As one out of about every hundred pilgrims who passed the extremely fierce bird-face [rock formation] of Gönporong (Protector Ravine) died there, he turned back the face such that this stopped happening. In the great Ömbartso [lake] there was a large chunk of turquoise. Because the master [Götsangpa] said, "May it stick to this pine staff!" on account of his truth utterance it stuck to that staff, and he grasped it in the palm of his hand. The [eighteen] functionaries wrangled over it, and so, thinking it bad that it had become the object of a dispute, he told them, "You go to the shore of the Ömbartso, and I will throw the turquoise chunk back in there." They said, "We will do that," and they gathered on the lake shore, and from Yütö he threw the turquoise chunk. It went splashing back into the lake, and so the matter was resolved.

After that he went to Phodrang Ütse (Pinnacle Palace). When he bound the god Brahma by oath in the Namkha Phuk (Sky Cave), he saw a face in the great maṇḍala palace there. A crow-faced goddess asked him, "Do you want the mundane paranormal powers?"[49] He replied, "The mundane paranormal powers are of no use to me, I am striving for the supreme ones," [27b] and announced his intention of offering a gemstone ladle full of gold and turquoise as a present to the chief [deities of the maṇḍala], and because of that he met with the chief father-mother union [of Khorlo Dompa and Dorje Pagmo]. They prophesied that he would obtain the supreme paranormal powers during his life, and so he said:

When I meditated in the forests of Tsari,
The divine faces manifest within appeared as human beings.

As I have attained the mundane [paranormal powers] I am sufficiently cultivated, thus
I am a yogin who is dedicated to the supreme [paranormal powers].

Then, a short time after this, because the nephew of Üri[pa] excelled in the midst of an assembly of about eight hundred accomplished ones, he received the name Tsari Rechen.[50] When they were performing such things as offerings, he arrived there by flying through the air. The spot where that happened was named Chaphurgang (Bird Flight Ridge).

After a generation had passed, the so-called eight assistants, who were disciples of the lord Chena [Trakpa Chungné] and Drigung Lingpa, arrived there. They opened the door to Sarma Yangdzö (New Innermost Treasury). After that, around this part of Tsari, many inauspicious omens appeared to most of the people. When the Mongol army overran Drigung monastery [in 1290] at the instigation of the Sakyapa sect, that incredible miracle, the many-doored reliquary shrine that possessed the layout of Pure Crystal Mountain and contained two thousand eight hundred deities was destroyed. Eighteen thousand monks were burnt in the fire, and as a result, one hundred people who had attained magical powers flew through the air from that spot and later landed in Ngari and Lowo. [28a] It is said, "The great damage done to the teachings of the precious Kagyüpa sect at that time was unprecedented and never to be repeated."

[*Part 4: The Final Opening—The Northern Door*]

After that, when another generation had passed, the functionaries of the Drukpa lineage became much too powerful. As those of the Tselpa lineage could not tolerate this, they felled the tree resembling a yogin's trident [which was the Drukpa's vitality-tree (*lashing*)], breached the lake shaped like a blood-filled skullcap [which was the Drukpa's vitality-lake (*lamtso*)], and smashed the boulder that was like the nipple of [Dorje Pagmo's] body [which was the Drukpa's vitality-stone (*lado*)], and a spring gushed forth from beneath the threshold of the large meadow, where there arose a clay mound, as had been prophesied previously by the religious lord Tsangpa Gyare.

Due to all these events, it happened that the Drukpa officials had to leave the area. As a result of that conflict, many people and cattle died through being infected by the plague of a wrathful mother-goddess. This caused thirteen human bodhisattvas, such as the king of Kyem[dong], Tag Dorje, to visit the great, glorious seat of Ralungthel.[51] At that time the religious lord Pökyapa was the throne-holder, and so they petitioned that lord directly and asserted, "There is no need to stop meditators going to *né* that give rise to emotions."[52] With that, king Tag Dorje drew out a knife from his waistband and made an appeal that went straight to the point: "If you won't allow meditators there the only way I will return home is dead, I'll commit suicide! Going back now will be no better than dying anyway because of the mother-goddess's plague." So the religious lord told him, "If it is that important to you, I promise to let the meditators go back. You should select a protector of living beings yourself." [28b] And due to that decree the king pointed his finger saying, "Although the protector of living beings Sönam Gyeltsen is the youngest from among the great ones, he will be good."

And so, [King Tag Dorje's] request was granted. For the protection of the hermits within this *né* he invited about thirty monks from Druk Ralung, and from the central area the lama servants of Tranre, and the master Chöku Dewa Chenpo and his students, as the external sponsor, and different functionaries from Chuwori and Lakha eastward, Changüri northward, Zangzang-Nering westward, and so on, as the attendants of the hermits, and thus the dispatch was completed. Furthermore, the lord [Pökyapa] had said, "There is a *né* called Chikchar Pelgi Nakjong (Simultaneous Realization Glorious Woodlands), which was given to me by one possessing a mane of flesh with the color of blood, named Chikchar Marpo, the field-protector's younger brother, so go there." The [dispatch party] asked, "How do we get there?" and so they went according to these directions: "When you have passed the thirteen waterfalls as far as Chösamdong (Religious Bridge Face), there is a three-tiered meadow resembling a turquoise maṇḍala, so enter that."

They proceeded to follow the waterfalls as far as Chösamdong and thereby descended to Senmogong. They arrived there, the sun shone at its zenith on the morning of their stay, and a sky-blue woman mounted on a mule came up from the river bank. The protector of living beings [Sönam Gyeltsen] followed after her, and with that the woman disappeared into the rock of Samdong. Because he waited for a moment in that very spot, [29a] a boy about eight years old, who was red, with a disheveled mane of flesh, appeared, after which he said, "Come with me, as the path to your *né* is the one that is found above here!" and, taking hold of the protector of living beings' garment, he led him off. Then the protector of living beings said, "I could pass through, but what about the baggage-yaks?" so [Chikchar Marpo] directed the yaks further down, saying, "It is enough that they came as far as this." In that spot where the protector of living beings passed, a bridge was later constructed, and thus was named Lhamo Samdong (Goddess Bridge Face). From there, when they all descended to the mountain pastures of Chikchar, the protector of living beings told the king, "Shoot an arrow," so the king shot an arrow, and seven animals, a mother and her offspring, appeared.

Because the protector of living beings asked the king three times there what they were, the king also replied three times, by offering the explanation, "They are antelope (*gya*)," it was established that this was the Serpangma (Golden Meadow) that was prophesied [by Tsangpa Gyare] with the words, "It is a good omen that the tracks of one *gya* are followed by another.[53]

This was the northern door. On that day, the final door to the pilgrimage circuit of Tsari was opened. This was of great benefit to everyone, and this protector of living beings is that great person who is mentioned in exactly the same way in the *Guidebook of Padmasambhava* as well.

Reading or hearing all or part of this narrative provides Tibetan pilgrim visitors to the mountain with a sophisticated map of the very landscape they must travel over and directly encounter. It is a map that offers dimensions of both space and time, of both gross visible and sublime unseen substances, powers and life forms, and all this is related to actual named sites and routes around the mountain at the same time. It is a rich map indeed, and becomes even more so when one understands that all it contains is further elaborated on by other written, oral, and performative narratives. The pilgrims who visit the mountain with this narrative map can potentially live out all that it presents; they will face the same powers, walk the same routes, perform the same rituals, and perhaps have the same purificatory, meditational, and initiatory experiences.

If this narrative is a history, it is one of powerful places and powerful beings and the interrelationship of their powers over time. If it is a map, it is a complex spaciotemporal coordinate system indicating all dimensions of that power, and how and where one can ritually interface with it in a positive manner. In either case, such narratives of *né* and the pilgrimage rituals they are related to were important and popular vehicles for the creation and maintenance of a specific magical view of reality in traditional Tibetan society.

How Is a Prayer a Map?

Pema Karpo's text provides one example of a traditional narrative map of Pure Crystal Mountain, and one that gives the core narratives on which the later ritual institutions of Tantric meditation and popular pilgrimage circumambulation are based. Another type takes the form of a prayer or petition. In Tibet, as in other parts of the world, people often pray to mountains. This has been a practice since before the introduction of Buddhism, but prayers to mountains have not always meant the same thing, because the conception of what or who a mountain is has changed. In the past Tibetans might have worshiped Pure Crystal Mountain as a clan ancestor god, a monarch assimilated to the mountain via his personal guardian deity, a warrior god, a regional territorial god, and as the seat of the vitality or soul principle of a community or single person. However, since the conversion of the mountain at Tsari to a Buddhist *néri* site, all these possibilities have become more or less redundant, having been incorporated into or erased by the conception and architectonics of the maṇḍala palace, which are altogether far more grand in scale and detail. There still existed clear distinctions between different types of divine forces—the chosen meditational deities and their retinues, the powerful and wrathful protectors, the minor local spirits, and the ways they were approached—but they had all become enmeshed and ranked in an overarching symbolic system.

Tibetans praying or conducting other rituals at the Buddhist Tsari have a vast landscape palace inhabited all over by literally thousands of deities of all descriptions and ranks whom they must address. As the just quoted text shows, different deities may have their own fixed abodes at the site, may move between several, or may be in all places simultaneously. Their residential locations are as ritually important as they are themselves—not only because one must address or visit certain spots in the landscape to encounter them directly and make contact with them, but because the beings themselves are not ontologically distinguished from the physical environments that constitute their abodes. The great saints and meditators of the past who are mentioned are also thought of as still present at the sites of their former dwellings. The empowerment (*chinlab*) they generated through identification with chosen meditational deities during the practice of deity yoga there long ago has saturated the spots they had physical contact with and remains energized.

How does the worshiper keep track of this complex divine residential landscape? With another type of oral map, or landscape index, in the form of a prayer. The text of the *The Great Oath Prayer to Tsari* provides an example of one such prayer map.[54] The entire prayer is comprised of 185 lines of verse, and like many oral texts it is fluid. The opening sections of the prayer can be chanted separately. The first six lines form a well-known short invocation to Tsari, attributed to the famous Gelukpa reformer Tsongkhapa, and are used in various other contexts.[55] A version of the following seven lines is found in Pema Karpo's narrative (f. 22a), where it is attributed to the yogin Kyewo Yeshé Dorje, who opened the mountain, and it, too, is employed separately in various rituals.[56] These two early verse sections appear to constitute the core of the prayer, in particular the second one, which in its original form begins to sequentially address specific deities and their local abodes on the mountain's slopes. To illustrate the style of the prayer here are the opening section, a few lines of the main body and closing appeal:

The Great Oath Prayer of Tsari

Lamas of the Kagyü lineages, chosen meditational deities, gods, sky-goers, and defenders of religion at glorious Tsāritra, pure *né* of Khachö, I entreat you! Grant me the empowerment to purify bad deeds and obscurations, to dispel adversities and dangers, and bestow both the supreme and mundane paranormal powers.

Oh! Lead the way to open the door!
Draw back the veil of both cloud and mist!
Reveal the divine assembly that is manifest within!
Oh! If those who pray and the Tantric kin,
Make earnest petitions, produce empowerment for them!

I pray to my gracious root-lama,
Seated on the sun-moon throne atop my head.
I pray to the fathers, the Kagyü lineage lamas,
Whose abode is the palace of the radiant absolute body of the Buddha.
I pray to the Buddhas, the protectors of the three families,
Whose abode is the palace of body, speech, and mind.
I pray to the five families of victorious Buddhas,
Whose abode is the palace that thoroughly cleanses the five poisons.
I pray to the mothers, the five types of sky-goers,
Whose abode is the palace of the five types of cognition.
I pray to the divine assembly of inner, secret Tantra,
Whose abode is the palace of the Tsari maṇḍala.
I pray to the twenty-eight hundred deities,
Whose visible representation is the palace of Dakpa Sheri (Pure Crystal Mountain).
I pray to the white-bodied sky-goer,
Whose abode is the palace of Kalā Dungtso (Conch-shell Conduit Lake).
I pray to the four-armed protector,
Whose abode is the palace of Düdgön Lamtso (Demon Lord Vitality Lake).
I pray to the master Chöki Gönpo,
Whose abode is in Chikchar Pelgi Naktrod (Simultaneous Realization Glorious Woodlands).
I pray to the accomplished one, Shawa Ripa,
Whose abode is the palace of Chakberong (Iron Frog Ravine).
I pray to the sky-goers who bathe secretly,
Whose abode is the palace of Khandro Trütso (Sky-goer's Bathing Lake).
I pray to the accomplished one, Lawapa,
Whose abode is the palace of Lawa Phuk (Lawapa's Cave).
I pray to the twenty-one Drölma goddesses,
Whose abode is the palace of Drölma Lamtso (Drölma Vitality Lake). . . .

I request empowerment with these prayers, and that my stream be matured and brought to deliverance. I pray that inner and outer impediments do not arise, and that I be granted the supreme and mundane paranormal powers."[57]

The style is repetitious—intentionally so for mnemonic purposes—and in the past, the prayer was remembered word perfect and transmitted orally. The general form of this type of Tibetan Buddhist ritual text is not unique, and examples exist for other important *né* sites.[58] Some texts relating to the ubiquitous incense offering (*sang*) ritual practiced in the folk religion and local mountain cult worship also contain analogous lists of local deities and their geographical locations or abodes. Mental ritual journeys undertaken by priests to a sequence of places listed in an oral text are also known from neighboring Himalayan peoples. It is possible that such traditions provided the model for this later type of popular Buddhist *néri* prayer.

The Great Oath Prayer to Tsari is remarkable in that it extends this pattern to form the most extensive surviving index of the mountain's powerful beings, both divine and human, and the main individual abodes (*né*) where they or their empowerment are locally situated. As an oral map it describes and catalogs over sixty toponyms of major landscape features, including mountain peaks, hills, and ridges, passes, ravines, lakes, plateaux, caves, charnel grounds, meditation retreat sites, alpine pastures, paths, and even meditative states that one can travel to at particular sites. It is at once both a map of the vast array of spirit forces that occupy the mountain and an earnest petition for entry into their realm and access to the power that is situated there.

The Ongoing Interpretation of Landscape

How, exactly, are these types of texts used by Tibetans? At least one common way is in the interpretation of actual landscape features. This interpreting is a common ritual activity in Tibet—it is done in specific contexts of space and time; it requires, and can be a test of, faith and other personal qualities of the performers; it involves much more than merely looking at a site or feature and has a strongly developed performative dimension for Tibetans, as particular landscapes and bodies must be fitted together at times in prescribed ways; it can involve mental activity in the form of visualizations; and it is directed by a set of oral and written ritual manuals, some forms of which I have presented in this and the previous chapter.

Such landscape interpreting happens on both a very large and a small scale; in its meditative dimension it is an individual act, but as perceptual looking, and as physical performance, it is frequently a group activity. In fact, on many of the shorter Tibetan pilgrimages I have attended, the gathering-together of persons at sites that required the ritual interpretation of landscape were often the most socially significant moments. It is in relation to these sites that certain representations of social order, of persons, and of their relationship to the physical world can be made explicit and contested. I have not yet visited Tsari myself and can provide no firsthand account, as I have elsewhere, to support the investigation of landscape interpretation at the site.[59] However, a great many written and oral accounts are available that illustrate aspects of the practice. The following selection of these relates to just one fairly small but very significant locality that every person performing circumambulation of the mountain must pass by.

Looking for Sexed Rocks

Divine body parts, come down out of the skies to earth and turned into stone, are representational elements that have traveled great distances from their origins in the cosmic dismemberment narratives of ancient India. The division and organization of Indian Tantric cult places was based on the tradition of distribution of the body parts from the dismembered goddess throughout the landscape of the Indian subcontinent. Being partly derivative of this tradition, certain major Tibetan *néri* sites, such as Tsari, are also associated with divine body parts in various ways. As Pema Karpo's account of the cosmic subjugation drama and narrative map both show, some of these body parts are claimed to be located in the valley of the Tsari River. These particular body parts are a set of stone genitals—a vulva and a phallus—which Tibetans call the "Sexed Rocks of Tibet" (Phö Domtsenchen). The discrete rock formation constituting this site in the Tsari valley is doubly significant. It is held to be the Tibetan one (hence the name Phö, or "Tibet," for the area) of the megaliths or stone phallic symbols (*liṅga*) representing the god Maheśvara (alias Jigjay), and which he himself installed at the twenty-four action sites before his downfall at the hands of Heruka. It is also the place where the first Tibetan to open Tsari had a magical encounter with the leading sky-goer goddess, at which time a rock vulva with labia of alchemical stone was manifested there. A standard guidebook for the area describes the site in the following terms:

> Here are clearly visible a vulva and a mark of Īśvara (i.e., Maheśvara's phallus), which are made of stone, called the Sexed Rocks, and which have water that is self-produced flowing out of the center of the vulva. This immutable power place, so marked, is the site for perfectly obtaining the paranormal powers of psychic breath and mind. At this site Kyewo Yeshé Dorje had a personal vision of the five sky-goer families and the sky-goer Sengdongma; and the sky-goer Sengdongma herself is said to have been absorbed into the genitals of stone once again.[60]

The site is clearly presented as being of significance to Tantra practitioners, those in a position to cultivate and obtain paranormal powers, for instance. But in general its powers were important to not only yogins but also lay pilgrims, as twentieth-century accounts point out. An aristocratic women pilgrim whose pilgrimage party visited the site in about 1930 with a local guide states:

> [W]e halted for the night at a sacred place called Do Tsen. Do Tsen translated literally means sex organs of the male and female, and in this place there were natural forms of the male and female organs in the rocks. Since these forms were not manmade, they bestowed special powers of procreation, enabling any childless couple who prayed to them to be blessed with children.[61]

A leading meditation master at Tsari in the 1950s adds:

> At that place there are miraculous rocks, and to understand them you have to go around them bit by bit and have them explained, but there was nobody who could really do that completely. The Sexed Rocks were in the shape of genitalia, and from the stone vulva there the pilgrims used to drink the waters of a spring. Yogins can see this as a

né of the sky-goers, and there is empowerment to aid you in gaining realisations. . . . Famous lamas like Dzokchen Pema Rigdzin [1625–1697] came to this place to meditate, and they attained realization there.[62]

Both of these accounts are by elite persons (senior cleric and aristocrat) who had access to the narrative maps of the site, to the oral and written guides. They show that laypeople and Tantric practitioners did interpret the site's powers and their benefits in very different ways. They did different rituals there; some prayed and consumed while the others meditated and visualized. But there are other important differences, already hinted at. In their interpretations higher level practitioners claimed to actually perceive the site differently from laypersons. How this might be so is explained in another guide:

There are the Sexed Rocks of Tibet, and . . . in the space between three smooth, white mounds there exists a town of the sky-goers, and it is this rock formation that is said to be seen by those with pure vision (*daknang*) as a great city with four open streets, by those who are middling as a small hut which is of sapphire, and by those who are lowest as a few rocks and plants.[63]

As I have discussed Tibetan notions of the graded perception of sacred landscapes elsewhere, I will limit my remarks here.[64] Regardless of the élite clerical theories that are invoked, relating karma, fortune, and purity of vision to cognitive ability, all levels of person ranked according to such systems in the Tibetan world can and do find landscape interpretation an ongoing challenge. Two accounts by pilgrims who visited Sexed Rocks several hundred years apart from each other show as much. The first, by one of the most highly ranked Bhutanese Drukpa clerics of the eighteenth century, who had access to esoteric written sources on the site, states:

On the eleventh day of the ninth month of the water-male-tiger year (1782), I arrived at the Sexed Rocks of Tibet within the *né* of Tsāritra, the powerful Khachö. Previously, when Kyewo Yeshé Dorje came to first open the door to this *né*, he was met here by the five long life sisters. In the middle of a mixed thicket of *sang* plants there was a flat rock with a chequered pattern. . . . I expected to see the Sexed Rocks as a phallus or a vulva, but instead they appeared to resemble thighs pressed together. I knew there were symbols which look like thighs, explained as the twenty-four symbols, including the symbol that looks like thighs and the symbol that looks like a phallus, in [Tantric] commentaries about the twenty-four countries. Today anyone, the wise and the foolish, going to see the site will all agree it resembles thighs pressed together, no matter how much time you spend above it. From another position it suddenly seems to be placed exactly like a stone phallus. There, it appeared recognizable as Sexed Rocks, and it is only this view that accounts for it as [one of] the twenty-four Sexed Rocks.[65]

My informant "Ngödrup," an uneducated peasant from Kongpo who visited the site in about 1958, when in his twenties, had this to say:

When my brother and I went to Tsari, our village neighbors had explained the route beforehand; they told us of the Sexed Rocks, saying it was an important place where a lama opened Tsari, the only rocks like this in Tibet, where you made prayers and could get empowerment, and drink the fertility water. When we got there we were disappointed, as we thought the genital shapes would be bigger and more obvious; we couldn't make them out really. My brother thought he found them, but we didn't

> know if it was correct. Lamas can see them, but none was present. So we left, and went on to Chikchar.

Both pilgrims were prepared with a narrative map of the site before they got there, but nevertheless both high lama and farm-boy had to put a conscious effort into their acts of interpretation to make the site fit with what was expected. Needless to say, perhaps, not one of the Western expeditions that visited Tsari mentions this site, although some spent considerable time in close proximity to it, and all noted various other "holy places" in the Tsari area. They had no narrative map with which to distinguish this one rock from any of the others along the valley.

The numerous pilgrim visitors who used the site always required maps of some kind to negotiate its significant landscape features and powerful environment. But there was another category of ritual users of the mountain who were intimately familiar with it, since they resided there, often for long periods of time, performing meditation and various other specialized activities around its slopes. These were the meditators and yogins who were either lineage descendants of, or inspired by, the Tantric superheroes of the past who had opened the doors to the great *néri* and reputedly attained powerful insights into the nature of reality there. To these practitioners and their activities at Tsari, and to the other major ritual institutions on the mountain that developed in their wake, I will now turn.

Part III

✦

RITUAL INSTITUTIONS

6

A Tantric Environment

In the chapters 6–9 I will introduce and discuss the principal institutions that define the most common ritual relationships between person and place at Pure Crystal Mountain. By a Tibetan reckoning, these fall approximately into three categories: Tantric meditation and specialized circumambulation; three non-Tantric annual circumambulation pilgrimages, all with differing itineraries; and one large twelve-yearly procession and associated tribute ceremony. In dealing with each of these ritual relationships, I shall also investigate their social implications, as well as the connections and continuities between the two cults of esoteric Tantric Buddhism and popular Buddhist worship at the site.

Written Tibetan sources portray Pure Crystal Mountain as having been first and foremost a place par excellence for serious Tantric practitioners. There seems no reason to doubt this picture. Only in much later times, from about the sixteenth or seventeenth century on, did this *néri* begin to attract very large numbers of lay and non-Tantric clerical pilgrims from many parts of the Tibetan cultural sphere. Tantric yogins, as a small group of either permanently wandering or temporarily nonmonastic practitioners, and their lama teachers (many of whom did lead monastery-based lives in later life) were more the heirs of an Indian Vajrayāna heritage than any other class of Buddhist practitioner in Tibet. The genealogy of all the Tibetan material that I presented earlier in chapter 4 is originally Indic. Its ancestral Buddhist representational systems were intentionally imported to Tibet and modified and applied to local landscapes by an élite of Tantric practitioners, many of whom were both religiously and politically active and influential in the society of their day. Not all aspects of this introduction process were always unanimously accepted, even within this élite itself, but the process went on regardless and attained a high degree of sophistication.[1] It was Tantric yogins who introduced and established the foundations of all the social practices found on the mountain in later times. Over time their actual population and activity at the site seem to have drastically declined, while popular pilgrimage increased. However, the institutions they created to serve their own specialized needs have endured, and shaped the way all other categories of practitioners use the mountain's environment. I want not only to outline the Tantric rituals in the cult of Pure Crystal Mountain here, but also to show that far from being just exclusive and esoteric activities, as they are often presented, they can have significant social and public dimensions as well.

What's In a Name?

What's in a name? In the present context the answer to this question is: Everything! Names are a form of representation. They are social documents. Names for particular landscapes, as I have already begun to show, act as the cues for longer implicit narratives and are loaded with conceptions about the place and space they are applied to. An entire landscape can be condensed into a place name. In chapter 4 I analyzed the Tibetan name for "Pure Crystal Mountain," Dakpa Sheri, and contextualized it within systems of cosmic and architectonic space. As an introduction to Tantric cult at the mountain, I will now turn to the *néri*'s other common name, Tsari. (By discussing its Tibetan etymologies here, I want to make a social and historical, rather than philological point.)[2]

The name Tsari has been applied to both Pure Crystal Mountain itself and the general geographical area surrounding it for at least eight hundred years.[3] During that period the name has been spelt in various ways. These variants, given below in transliteration using their proper Tibetan spellings, are quite closely related and all still in use today.

1. *Tsa-ri*: the spelling found in the modern Tibetan lexicons. It is the most basic form of the name, reducible simply to *tsa*, the seventeenth consonant of the alphabet, and ri, meaning "mountain." But in premodern sources *Tsa-ri* serves as an abbreviated form of version 4 that follows.

2. r*Tsa*-ri (or r*Tsā*-ri): r*Tsa* means "channel" or "vein," and in Tibetan Tantric texts it translates the Sanskrit technical term *nāḍī*. The *nāḍī* are vital energy channels running throughout the subtle body of the Tantric meditator, with a complex, radiating network of them built around a central channel running up the axis of the spinal cord and two main side branches to the left and right sides. The spelling r*Tsa*-ri thus means "Psychic Energy Channel Mountain." When conceived of as vital points within the yogin's body, the twenty-four Tantric action sites (*pīṭha*/*né*) of the Khorlo Dompa meditation system are arrayed at points around this subtle channel network.[4] Together, the sites and channels constitute the body maṇḍala, which is a microcosmic version of the larger Pure Crystal Mountain maṇḍala and cosmic world-system maṇḍala. It is not uncommon in Tibetan Tantric geographical traditions that actual landscapes are represented in terms of the subtle body structure.[5] The name r*Tsa-ba* can also mean "root," "foundation," "primary," or "origin," and in relation to it being a naturally arisen maṇḍala, some Tibetans explain r*Tsa*-ri as "Foundation Mountain."

3. *Tswa*-ri or r*Tswa*-ri and *Tsa*-ri r*Tswa*-*gong* (or *Tsa*-ri *Tsa*-*gong*): r*Tswa* (or *tswa*) means "herb," yielding "Herb Mountain." This etymology is explicitly given in Tibetan texts, and often the related compound form, *Tsa*-ri r*Tswa*-*gong*, is used in older texts, where *gong* means "superior," yielding in full "Superior Herb *Tsa* Mountain" or "Superior Herb Psychic Energy Channel Mountain" or "Superior Herb Tsari[tra]" (see version 4 that follows). In Tibetan sources, *rtswa-gong* (sometimes *rtswa-mchog* or

rtsa-mchog) identifies one of several Tantric alchemical herbs for which Pure Crystal Mountain is famous as a natural habitat. The understanding of Tsari as Herb Mountain is also a popular one. For instance, we find that in an episode of the Tibetan Gesar epic entitled *Tsari Mendzong* ("Tsari Medicinal Herb Dispatch"), the hero must gather powerful herbs from the Tsari area in order to save Tibet.[6] Tsari thus fits into the common Tibetan place designation of *menjong* or "lands of medicinal herbs," applied particularly to wetter regions of the Himalayan zone along the southern fringes of Tibet which possess rich botanical diversity.

4. *Tsa-ri-tra* (abbreviated as *Tsa-ri*), *Tsā-ri-tra* (abbreviated as *Tsā-ri*), and *Tsa-ri-ṭra*: All these are transliterations of the Sanskrit proper name Cāritra. In the ancient geography of India, the site of Cāritra was a southern port city on the Orissan (Uḍra) coast. In Indian Tantric literature and Tibetan commentaries it is variously identified as one of the twenty-four action sites or eight great Tantric charnel grounds. The notions of "action" and "movement" are foremost here. Monier Monier-Williams (*Sanskrit-English Dictionary*, 393), gives *cārita* ("set in motion"), and *cāritra* ("moving," "proceeding," "manner of acting," "conduct") from the root *car* (see *cāra*) ("wandering about," "proceeding," "motion," "going," etc.). *Car/cāra* in various forms is translated by Tibetans as the verb *spyod-pa* (pron. *chöpa*), meaning "to do," "to act," and, substantively, "action," "activity," "way of acting," "conduct." Some Tibetan etymologies of *Tsa-ri-tra* relate this form to *spyod-pa la gshegs-pa* (pron. *chöpa la shegpa*), the "entering into the action (*caryā*)" phase of Tantric practice, an advanced stage of yoga, which practitioners who "wander" to places like Pure Crystal Mountain are expected to be in. Such etymologies are intended both to denote the site as one for Tantric yogic "action" and to legitimate its identity as Cāritra in the Tantric geographical schemes.

These Tibetan etymologies make clear that every known variant of the name Tsari is derived from the historical, representational, and ritual concerns of Tibetan Tantra, its institutions, and its élite yoga practitioners. Tsari was, and to a limited extent still is, a Tantric mountain. And the multiple but related meanings encoded into the mountain's name were all expressed through human activity in the Tantric ritual institutions of Pure Crystal Mountain.

Tantric Meditation Communities

From the twelfth and thirteenth centuries on, when the mountain was colonized in particular by various sub-branches of the Kagyü sect, a style of Tantric asceticism involving homeless wandering and remote mountain retreats in caves and small huts by yogins (*neljorpa*) and solitary meditators (*gomchen*) was common in Tibet. At the personal retreat places of famous practitioners, often the founders of sects or lineages, small meditation communities (*drupde*) developed in many mountainous and isolated areas throughout Tibet. Tsari was no exception to this pattern. Such communities did not just develop by themselves but were produced out of a specific combination of social practices.

Patronage has been a central theme throughout the entire history of institutionalized Buddhism. Despite popular Western notions about Tibetan yogins living completely independently from society, subsisting on thin air and wild herbs, in reality all practitioners and their meditation communities required reliable and committed sponsors or patrons for their establishment and maintenance. Their fortunes were directly linked to the economic, political, and religious vicissitudes of these supporters. Sponsorship was offered to yogins by persons and institutions for a variety of reasons, ranging from the generation of personal merit (in a soteriological sense) and the personal accumulation of public prestige through the desire of a sect and its aristocratic patrons to lay claim to a certain territory for political reasons. Although often physically isolated from society, Tantric meditation communities were also an integral part of it in Tibet.

In the early centuries of Pure Crystal Mountain's colonization, the retreat communities there probably remained physically remote from the rest of the social world, for Tsari is a very isolated spot. This physical isolation did not last, however. Tantric meditation communities were nonproductive in a material sense, but in another sense of "economy" they were productive by generating for the practitioners and their sponsors what one could call, following Pierre Bourdieu, symbolic capital.[7] They produced status or prestige as well as, and by virtue of, spiritual cultivation. In various forms this phenomenon was to remain a feature of Tibetan society until 1959 and still exists in exile communities today. Status, as we know in the West, accrues not only to persons but also to institutions and to names (a c.v. with "Harvard" or "Oxford" on it opens many more doors than one with "Hicksville College"). But in Tibet, in line with certain aspects of the Tibetan worldview, status also accrues directly to place, and not just in name only, but in a substantial, physical manner. I have shown how generations of great Indian and Tibetan yogins were associated with the mountain by those writing about it already in the sixteenth century. Not only were these saints and "masters of reality" believed to have gained enlightenment experiences due to the power of the place, but according to Tibetan thinking, their own empowerment (*chinlab*), generated at the peak of their yogic performance, fused into the physical substance of the mountain's already very potent natural environment.

As a result of the accumulation of status by social reputation and physical empowerment, Tsari became one of *the* places to visit in Tibet for certain types of ritual interaction with place. In short, Tsari ceased to be physically isolated from the social world. If the Tibetan historical accounts are to be credited, many hundreds of yogins began to go there to perform retreats and pilgrimages, and following them, over the centuries, very large numbers of lay and non-Tantric clerical pilgrims as well. That this happened, and that it was a constantly changing process over the centuries, is established in general. However, it is not my intention to fill in the many details of the religious history of the Tsari area here.[8] My present interest is only in tracing the establishment and maintenance of the major ritual institutions (particular Tantric practice communities, pilgrimages, processions, etc.) that endured around Pure Crystal Mountain up until the 1950s.

With regard to meditation communities, there is an account of one early community in the biography of Tselpa Samten Pelwa (1291–1366), recorded only a century or so after his activity at the mountain. Although the colony he founded did not last, the account of it is worth repeating here for the details it gives on the economy and mechanics of sponsorship of such early communities on the mountain:

> Later he founded on the same day [at Tsari] the Yab-chos-sdings and the sGo-mo-chos-sdings monasteries, in which countless male and female yogins gathered . . . At the foot of the mountain, the place was filled with small huts, which could accommodate one hermit only. . . . He did not discriminate between those who offered him a thousand *zho* and those who offered him a needle and thread, and received all of them with tea and entertainment. . . . They [i.e., the Tselpa Kagyü] did not keep any monastery lands for the upkeep of the above two monasteries (in Tsari) but gained their livelihood by begging for alms. However they were able to distribute food to not less than a hundred hermits observing the annual seclusion (*lo-mtshams-pa*).[9]

There was sufficient interest in the mountain by the fourteenth century for this type of support to come from nearby populations and visiting pilgrims, as well as for large religiopolitical institutions like the Drigungpa sect to provide long-term sponsorship of their community at Yümé in the western part of Tsari.[10] During the early years of their reign (c. 1360), the Pagmo Drupa hegemony under Changchub Gyeltsen (1302–1369) set up a system of pilgrims' resthouses and provision caches at both the *néri* of Tsari and Tise.[11] This is one of the earliest records of what might be called state patronage of Buddhist ritual activity at *néri* mountains such as Tsari. Both the Drigungpa colony at Yümé and the network of pilgrims' resthouses still existed as important institutions at Tsari during this century.

Although the Drukpa sect naturally credit their own lineage with having first opened the *néri*, the available accounts show they were just one among a number of Tibetan Buddhist schools who maintained communities around the mountain. Their meditators enjoyed early sponsorship from both the parent monastery of Ralungthel in Tsang province to the west, and the nearby kingdom of Kyemdong in Kongpo to the east. The relationship with the people of Kyemdong was to endure up to the present century. The Drukpa Tantric community became and remained the leading group at Tsari only after the Fourth Drukchen incarnation was found in a minor aristocratic house of Kongpo, in the person of Ngawang Norbu, alias the great savant Pema Karpo (1527–1592). He established a new Drukpa power base directly adjacent to Pure Crystal Mountain by building up his own important monastery of Sangnag Chöling in the area of Char directly adjacent to and west of Pure Crystal Mountain.[12] He made various extended visits for meditation and pilgrimage at Tsari, and during the middle of the sixteenth century he established the Chikchar *drupde*, beginning the tradition still current in 1959 of placing thirteen yogins in a retreat hermitage there for their three-year training. He also founded the mountain's most patronized shrine, the Chikchar Dorje Pagmo temple, there in about 1570. On the forested slopes of the upper Chikchar valley on the northeastern flanks of the mountain there were other smaller temples-cum-hermitages established at the sites of the very earliest meditation communities, including those of Densa, Göpa, Üri, Zimkhang, and Sinbumtang.[13]

The Chikchar Yogins, 1940–59

The most well-known Tantric community of Tsari was the Drukpa *drupde* at Chikchar. It was abandoned and destroyed after 1959–60 following the Chinese occupation, but its practice lineage still continues in Indian exile. For at least the last three to four hundred years Chikchar has been the main staging point for all major circumambulation routes around Pure Crystal mountain. It had a domestic lay population living in substantial houses, some very popular temples for pilgrims' offerings with a resident body of monks, attendants (*kunyer*), and various functionaries (*létsen*), and a constant, year-round flow of pilgrims of all descriptions from throughout the Tibetan world. It functioned as the de facto seat of local government, as representatives of the Drukpa aristocracy of Char were resident there.

So Chikchar was, by all accounts, the most frequented site in the Tsari district, yet it also housed the main community of Tantric yogins in retreat in the surrounding forests. Its thirteen resident yogins were very distinctive, with their long, dreadlock-style hair, their beards, and their special striped robes known as *relcha*, or "long-haired's costume" (*relpaé chalug*). In appearance they resembled the archetypal Tibetan yogin saint Mila Repa; however, they were not just trying to cultivate an image. They were heirs to the same lineage of practice as Mila Repa, performing the same yogas at the same great *néri* mountains as he had done in the eleventh century. Aspects of their meditation practice demanded total identification with a chosen meditational deity (*yidam*), and they did not shave or cut their hair because to do so would have been equivalent to performing the act on the deity itself, hence reducing the benefits of their practice. As the yogin's song tells us:

> When I meditated for three years
> My meditating-hair reached to my waist.
> When I went on for another three years,
> My meditating-hair was in coils on the ground.[14]

Theoretically, they were engaged on a level of concentration where actions such as body grooming became superfluous; being beyond discriminations of acceptance or rejection of appearance, they left things au naturel. This approach was the exact opposite to that of the non-Tantric clerical practitioner of the monastery, and their special striped yogin's robes symbolized their alternative training and path.

The practice lineage of these yogins was the Khorlo Dompa system of the "mother" class of highest yoga Tantras used by the Kagyü lineage. This is precisely why they were at Tsari, as the chosen meditational deities on whom they would focus—Khorlo Dompa and Dorje Pagmo, together with their large retinue of initiatory beings—had their *né* there in Pure Crystal Mountain maṇḍala palace. This yogin's song expresses this notion:

> By performing your three years' meditation
> In the great *né* of Tsāritra,
> You won't need many retreat assistants;
> There are enough mother-goddesses and sky-goers![15]

During their three-year retreat (*losum chogsum*) at Chikchar, they would specifically prepare for and cultivate higher concentration exercises of the "perfection-stage" (*dzogrim*) of this system as found in the original Indian manuals. These practices included the "Great Seal" (Mahāmudrā in Sanskrit, or *chagya chenpo* in Tibetan) and the so-called mystic heat (*tümoéme*) and dream (*milam*) yogas. The specialist practice of the Chikchar yogins I want to focus on was the performance of the yoga of mystic heat, which is sometimes called the internal fire, because it produces a raising of natural body temperature.[16] In essence, the technique is a specialized harnessing and refinement of the natural libido or sexual energy in the body. The specific purpose of such a practice is to purify psychic defilement and delusion and activate the subtle body network in particular ways, and the physical rise in body temperature is a purely secondary feature of it. This practice is classified as a yoga of the perfection stage "which has signs," because it depends on meditating on the form of the internal psychic or subtle body. This body is constituted by the network of major and minor psychic "channels" (*tsa*), the subtle "vital energy" (*lung*) that is circulated through them, and "essential drops" (*thigle*) of "awakening energy" or "life-force" (*changsem*) throughout, together with the hierarchy of energy "wheels" (*khorlo*) along the central axis of the body.[17] Tibetans thus refer to this complex as the *tsalung thigle* or *tsalung* system for short. I discuss its use at Chikchar in particular not only because it has a very long history of practice there, but because for certain reasons the Chikchar meditators were widely known for their abilities in forms of this yoga.

By the early part of this century the Drukpa practice lineage of *tsalung* yoga at Tsari had declined drastically, and my informant Shérab Gyatso was sent to the Chikchar *drupde* from Sangnag Chöling monastery in Char in order to revive it. Shérab Gyatso received his full initiation into the lineage from Apho Rinpoché during his three-year retreat in Tsari Kyiphuk in about 1940, when aged twenty-five. When he later lived in Chikchar he taught the meditators who filled the thirteen or so places in the *drupde*. The candidates came of their own choice; it was not a compulsory part of any larger religious training system, although there were certain prerequisites for entry. The meditators had to be members of the Drukpa school, and almost all came from the regions adjacent to Tsari or from Tsari itself. Most were quite young, well under forty years old. This was no coincidence, as the optimum age for efficient *tsalung* performance was considered to be between about sixteen and forty. Practitioners had to be male. They also had to have strong motivation to undertake all the preparations required to perform the retreat training. Not only did they have the four hundred thousand preliminary exercises, plus an additional hundred thousand ritual formulas dedicated to the chosen meditational deities to recite after initiation, but they also had to arrange their own sponsorship for the three-year period. As they gained no direct support from either the main monastery or the government, they had to locate individual sponsors from surrounding districts such as Kyemdong, Nyel, and Dakpo. All such sponsors hoped to generate their own merit from such an act of support.

The *tsalung* practice was taught to the meditators, and the "Oral Instruction Lineage of Rechungpa" (*Rechung Nyengyü*) was followed, as was common in Drukpa training.[18] When meditators were thought to have mastered the particular practice of mystic heat yoga, they had to undergo something like an exercise, or ritual test. These were of two types. The first to be performed was the Rephu (pron. *Rimbik* in Tsari dialect), which literally means "casting off [the yogin's] cotton cloth." The second test was called Chure or "wet cotton cloth." The Chure was an exclusive performance and could only be personally witnessed by other practitioners of the yoga system.[19] For this reason, and also precisely because it was by comparison an open performance, I will detail the Rephu ritual as it took place at Chikchar in the 1950s.

Upon a Winter's Night...

Essentially, the Rephu ritual consisted of spending all Midwinter Night sitting nearly naked in the snow, in the extreme cold of upper Chikchar (elevation 3870 meter). In one sense it was a test of the yogin's mastery over the technique of mystic heat yoga, as proficiency did have the side effect of raising physical body temperature, hence giving the meditators the ability to withstand the intense cold of the ritual setting. But it was not a test in the normal sense of the word, as Shérab Gyatso, a supervisor of Rephu, explains:

> There was no pass or fail in the Rephu and other such exercises; it remained the knowledge of the individual meditators whether they reached the goal of proficiency in *tsalung* or not. People gossiped about who was good or bad of course, but only the meditators themselves knew about it. There was no absolute standard imposed, and no punishment for not performing. But those who were not good in practice used to get ill during the Rephu; the color would drain out of them and they would really shiver, and that's a sure sign you hadn't mastered it. But the supervisor didn't ask afterwards if you did it well or not.

Although it lacked strict criteria, the ritual exercise did have a certain evidential value. And this quality of the performance became the most socially important aspect, regardless of whatever may have happened in the mind and body of any individual yogin.

In the depths of winter each year, those meditators who were ready to undergo the Rephu began a regime of preliminary preparations. From the first day of the twelfth Tibetan month (approximately January) they moved out of the Chikchar *drupde* and lived outside in thin cotton tents.[20] Here they remained engaged in various preparatory yogic exercises until Midwinter's Evening, on the fifteenth day of the month. This day was chosen because, according to Tibetan lineages of the Khorlo Dompa system, it was the most potent time of the year one could make offerings to the chosen meditational deities and hope to gain paranormal powers as a result. On that evening the "eight functionaries" (*létsengye*), who were lay workers and patrons representing the eight traditional meditation and temple communities of Chikchar area, came to greet them and conduct them by degrees to the site of the ritual.[21]

The ground for the Rephu was a flat clearing up in the forests above Chikchar called Sinbumtang, or "Plain of One Hundred Thousand Si" (the *si* being an important class of early Tibetan spirits). This alpine meadow, named Serpangma ("Golden Meadow") in the early sources, was reputedly the site of Tsari's first temple built by Tsangpa Gyare. It was also the place where this first Drukpa yogin performed *tsalung* yoga, thus setting the ritual precedent for Rephu there. Before arriving at this ground, the yogins were taken to visit two additional sites: Zimkhang, which was the offering temple of Dorje Yudrönma, the local field-protector sky-goer goddess; and Densa, the seat of the incarnate lama. At Zimkhang the eight functionaries would bring a young girl to welcome the yogins. This person took the role of Dorje Yudrönma and was said to actually be the local sky-goer goddess during the ritual. She had to be a premenstrual virgin of a better class of family who had never had any kind of relations with a man. In the temple was a large bowl for the goddess in which she received her customary offering of barley beer. On this evening it was filled with the potent "first brew" (*changphu*) of local beer, and offered to the yogins by the girl who played the part of the sky-goer.[22] The yogins were permitted to drink directly from "her" bowl. They could consume what quantity they liked, but even a taste was sufficient. This beer offering transmitted the goddess's empowerment (*chinlab*) to the yogins and was believed to give them heightened ability in the circulation of their *lung* or "vital energy." The girl was escorted back to the village immediately after her duties had been performed.

The group then went on to Densa and performed the regular "offerings to the lamas" ritual. Here they had to prepare their costume for the night's performance. They could only wear light underwear, with about twenty centimeters of tightly folded cotton shawl (*zen*) covering them at the groin and a meditation band (*gomtha*) around the waist. Before setting out to the Sinbumtang they would all take turns singing different songs about their lineage, Tantra practice, and yoga, for example:

> On the Sinbumtang at Chikchar
> There is an excellent lion's throne.
> Our glorious Drukpa lineage
> Sit upon that throne.[23]

It was ten or eleven o'clock at night by the time they reached the snow-covered Rephu ground. At the site there was a flagpole covered in prayer-flags and a natural stone throne. The supervisor would stop there, and having collected the prayer-bead necklace of each participant, would throw these out onto the snowy plain one by one. Wherever a yogin's beads landed marked the spot where he would have to meditate until the next morning without moving. Each was given a very small pad or mattress to sit on. The meditation had to be performed regardless of the weather conditions during the period. If snow fell, meditators would have to unfold their thin shawls, drape them over themselves, and flick off the excess snow. At sunrise the following morning, around eight or nine o'clock, the eight functionaries would return to the site to greet the yogins.

At this point in the ritual, the esoteric and highly advanced Tantric yoga practice became transformed into a public spectacle of sorts. When the eight functionaries arrived, they would have with them quite a crowd of both local people and visitors to the region, including men and women, some of whom were patrons, who wanted to witness the event. They believed that they could obtain empowerment by direct sight of the meditating yogins, as these persons had in a sense temporarily become deities. The meditator's motionless bodies were arrayed around the snow-covered plain when this crowd arrived, and the functionaries would formally greet each meditator in turn. The yogins were then allowed to rise, unfold the thin shawls from around their waists, and drape them over themselves. It was a socially poignant moment, as ordinary men and women came face to face with an exhibition of the potent human powers that their religion claimed one could cultivate: control of the internal world, hence mastery over the external brute force of nature. Such a display of the power of Tantra was conducted at the site for centuries. One Tibetan account from the nineteenth century represents such a moment from the past as an inspiring encounter with this power:

> In order to exhibit the superiority of mystic heat yoga, the thirteen great meditators of the Chikchar *drupde* spent a night on a snowy plain at the foot of the snow mountain, wearing only a single shawl in the cold of the depths of winter. Early next morning the *tsulpa* patrons of Tsāri went to meet them carrying ritual parasols and victory banners, and as they witnessed them all coming forward with steam rising off their bodies an overpowering faith in these lineage sons of Mila Repa was born.[24]

As the ritual was observed in the 1950s, when each yogin got up from his meditation position, he sang celebratory songs to the crowd—not only to rejoice but to proclaim the inner reality of what was being witnessed externally. For example:

> On this present occasion I'll sing a happy song.
> On this present occasion I'll perform a joyous dance.
> When the reality of all the excellent lamas and Buddhas
> Arises in the primal expanse of my own mind,
> The yogin whose mind is purified rejoices![25]

I have no doubt that the ritual generated faith in the public observers. By any standards it was a remarkable feat of human endurance. In addition, there were other more lighthearted performative dimensions at this point, as Shérab Gyatso, himself a yogin, recalls:

> It was hard for the yogins, they had to look good. If they got up and showed that they had cramp in their legs or something, then everyone in the crowd would make fun of them and say they didn't do it properly. There was some playacting about this. Sometimes yogins put the thin shawl over their heads and pretended to sleep when the eight functionaries came to greet them. The functionaries would say, "You are a well-developed meditator, please arise," but there would be no movement. The senior man would come over to look, and then indicate to the crowd that the meditator had died of cold. The people would gasp in shock, but then laugh when they realized the joke. It was not all serious at the end.

After the welcoming, the yogins went to Üri temple and were greeted by people who lined the route. Then at Zimkhang they ate a meal that was laid out for them. Here they dressed in their normal robes once more. They performed the "offering to the lamas" ritual again. To complete the Rephu they went to the golden throne in the Chikchar Dorje Pagmo temple and performed the Dorje Pagmo offering ritual. Later the same day there was a community festival in Chikchar (see chapter 10), during which the eight functionaries performed a particular "yak dance" (*yakdro*) relating events in the story of the founding of Chikchar as a retreat place; then songs were sung and much beer was drunk by the villagers.

Tantric Space and Gender

To close this short account of Rephu, I must mention one aspect of the whole ritual process and the site, as it highlights a particular feature of life around the mountain:

the organization of local space with regard to gender and domestic life. Women were systematically excluded from certain areas around the mountain, and this practice appears to have its origins in the early establishment of Tantric meditation retreat centers there by male yogins and lamas. As mentioned in chapter 5, Pema Karpo's historical account of Pure Crystal Mountain notes a certain yogin of the twelfth century, Gyergom Shigpo (1090–1171), living there in retreat with a real woman as his ritual consort for Tantric practice, and that he was expelled from the site for doing so by his conservative colleagues.[26] More solid evidence is found in the biography of the influential fourteenth-century Kagyüpa teacher Barawa Gyeltsen Palzangpo (1310–1391). After Barawa had practiced at Tsari for three years, he made a law (*chatrim*) that women (*kyemen*, literally "the low-born") could not reside at the mountain. This apparently created some upset in the community of practitioners at the time it was announced.[27] The sources are silent about the long-term development and maintenance of such regulations, although local historians from Tsari now state that they were enforced in various forms until 1959.

For the twentieth century there exists a well-documented ritual exclusion of women associated with the presence of the Chikchar *drupde* and yogins practicing Tantric meditation in the area. This exclusion was applied in two contexts: specifically to the Rephu ritual, and more generally to the entire Chikchar area throughout the winter. At Chikchar in 1913, F. M. Bailey noted: "On the 15th day of the 8th [Tibetan] month when the pilgrim road is closed all women are obliged to leave Chikchar where there are several holy temples; they live during the winter at Yarap on the opposite bank of the river."[28]

Women remained at the Yarab settlement, or were not permitted past it, until the following spring sometime before the upper mountain was ritually reopened during the middle of the third Tibetan month (approximately late April to early May). This represents a period of exclusion of over half the year. Although located only a few kilometers from Chikchar, Yarab lay just outside the natural boundary of the sanctuary of Tsari, which was formed in the east by the Tsari River. My informant Shérab Gyatso offered this explanation: "In the past they didn't want women there in the winter because the yogins had to spend the night in the snow seminaked during the Rephu exercise, and it might have caused them loss of concentration if women were there. That was the rule in times past."

This rule was later relaxed to allow temporary visits to the site, such as to obtain empowerment at the ritual's end. Similarly, Bailey's informants told him: "All the women from Chikchar are obliged to live here [at Yarab] in winter, so that the monks in the holy temples can meditate without being distracted."[29]

These Tibetan reasons for the exclusions are based on the ritual requirement for male yogins to observe strict celibacy during the practice of *tsalung* meditation. This was a pragmatic requirement, since the technique involved the transformation of the libido energy, and chastity is one of the precepts for this particular lineage of yoga practitioners, and it seems to have been rather rigorously observed by the Drukpa yogins.[30] The exclusion of women from male clerical or Tantric space was found elsewhere throughout Tibet.[31] There also existed exclusions from male civic space in Tibet, ostensibly on account of sexual distraction.[32] In a broader context, the theme of women as a sexual distraction is familiar from Indian classical traditions on the tension between celibate, male asceticism and the desire and attachment represented in men's views of women's sexuality. The image of sexually active women as a major threat to male Buddhist meditators is found in Buddhist canonical literature.[33] Thus, what happened at Chikchar was not just a feature of Tibetan notions of gender and the body, and the particular Tibetan expression of Vajrayāna Buddhism, but was a longstanding feature of the Buddhist tradition as a whole.

In traditional Tibet, these older, originally Indic cultural forces succeeded in most instances in neatly dividing a male religious world from a lay female and domestic one. But the particular history of the development of Tsari as a cult site effectively collapsed them together. Places like Chikchar and Yümé functioned on one hand as celibate meditation communities, and on the other as public staging and servicing points for popular pilgrimages with the necessity of domestic residence by the laity. Whereas the *drupde* in Yümé had more or less died out this century, with women consequently experiencing only minimal restrictions on the use of ritual space there (see chapter 10), the categorization and use of space around the active *drupde* of Chikchar remained ambivalent right up until 1959. For example, while lay families maintained sizable households there, childbirth was forbidden as it was considered polluting, and pregnant women anticipating labor had to leave the settlement and go elsewhere in order to give birth. While local people made part of their income in the village through trading and selling various handwork products, such as cane baskets, they were forbidden to actually weave them within the precincts of the valley and went elsewhere to do so; the sewing of clothes was also locally outlawed. Thus, the seasonal exclusion of women between the closing and reopening of the public pilgrimage route, and over the winter period of specialist yoga practice, appears to have been, as much as anything, a kind of compromise for coexistence within the same space of two communities with opposing cultural definitions. (The question of women's exclusion from part of the mountain is pursued in more depth in chapter 7.)

Tantric Magic, Status, and Place

The Rephu is an interesting ritual, not because it may seem fantastic or exotic to us outsiders; but precisely because it was fantastic or exotic for insiders, for the Tibetans themselves. Oral and written chronicles or biographies, local dance dramas and operas, songs, folk tales, paintings, and other expressions of Tibetan life are pervaded by a mass of stories and references to the incredible magical powers of Tantric yogins. As is well known in the West, these stories have spread beyond Tibet and become part of the postcolonial cultural construction of that society by peoples in other times and places.[34] The Rephu is significant because it was more than just a story for Tibetans, it was a public demonstration of what Tantric practice could actually achieve. It was not a spontaneous miracle that always happened somewhere else to be seen by somebody else, but rather one of those rare predictable, scheduled, and accessible displays. And even though it was a knowable aspect of Tantra, public access to demonstrations of the power of mystic heat yoga did not make it taken for granted. It probably led to the generation of further stories and references out in the public domain, and there does exist a large collection of popular narratives about this aspect of Tantric yoga. Even in Chikchar where the displays were held every year, there were all sorts of local accounts in circulation based on real-life characters and events.[35]

This ritual is but one example of the fact that Tantra was not just an esoteric and secret tradition but had a public face in Tibet, a fact that had certain consequences in the social world. The public advertisement of Tantric powers and abilities only served to increase the symbolic capital of those associated with its practice. This was a singularly important feature in a society ruled by high-ranking Vajrayāna lamas and clerics and their supporters. Definitions of place and space were intimately involved in this process in Tibet. The fact that the ritual took place at Pure Crystal Mountain, a *néri* with a very high status that attracted visitors from throughout the Tibetan world, is not to be overlooked. The location's importance lies not only in the ritual's effectiveness as a form of public power display, but also in that the ritual could only happen there because of Tsari's particular definition as a place, and the fact that it did happen there served to reinforce that definition. Certain persons associated themselves with power places because an exchange of status took place at them that was important in the social world. Space had to be managed in relation to certain times and sites so that other persons, in this case women, would not jeopardize the functioning of such exchanges.

Circumambulation and Alchemy

There are three major and several minor pilgrimage routes encircling Pure Crystal Mountain. Although Tantric yogins and meditators might use any of these routes and the numerous sites on their itineraries as places of individual meditation practice, there are two types of pilgrimage that they specifically undertook on the mountain: the Tsekor or "peak circuit," and what I call the maṇḍala pilgrimage. Both are forms of ritual circumambulation (*korwa*), made in the clockwise direction prescribed by Buddhism. Here I will detail the unique itinerary of the peak circuit, most of which was performed only by male meditators and yogins prior to 1959. (As of 1983–84, the upper mountain has once again been opened for pilgrimage by Chinese authorities, and the higher altitude circuits I will describe here can now be performed. Thus, although I have had to use the past tense herein for accounts of certain rituals at Tsari, I will use the present tense for the pilgrimages that are still functioning.)

The peak circuit is the shortest of the five different circumambulation routes around Pure Crystal Mountain. It is also the one highest in average altitude and closest to the actual summit peak of the mountain. In relation to the representations of the subtle architecture of landscape at the site, this route can be said to be closest to both the highest palace of the chosen meditational deities in the maṇḍala, as well as to the central vase and spire of the great crystal *chöten*. This pilgrimage, and the maṇḍala pilgrimage described in the next section, were both more or less exclusive to male yogins. In theory any male pilgrim could pass over all, and any female could traverse part, of the physical routes of these specialized pilgrimages. But women could not engage in the rituals that yogins might perform on these circuits because they lacked access to the esoteric knowledge, initiations, and training that were required beforehand.

The Peak Circuit Itinerary

The Tsari Tsekor, or peak circuit, is an annual circumambulation, which can be performed as many times as a practitioner either wishes or is able to. Prior to 1959 the route was officially opened around the beginning of the fifth Tibetan month. Due to the high average altitude, it can only be easily performed between the fifth and eighth Tibetan months (approximately late June to October). It is a summer activity, as much of the route is covered in snow and ice at other times during the year. The route forms a loop that begins and ends at Chikchar (see figure 6.1). It usually takes from two to four days to complete, although the duration is totally dependent on what specific sites are visited and stayed at along the route. The written guides only describe small portions of the peak circuit route. The fullest descriptions of the basic itinerary are found in oral guides or maps. In the following example of one such guide, I have added the known approximate altitudes for the main points of the route:

> From Chikchar (3870 m), you cross over the Drölma La (Goddess Drölma Pass, 4900 m), and take a midday meal break in Miparong (Human Skin Ravine). From there, through the Shakam La (Dried Meat Pass, 4900 m), Champarong (Kindness Ravine), and Kardogtang (Dairy Food Scraps Plateau), you climb up to Tama Lamgo (Tama Flower Pass Summit, 4420 m) and spend the night there. After leaving there ascend with swift-footedness (*kangyog*) through to Khandro Tsogshong (Sky-goer Assembly Offering Basin) and take a midday meal break in Tagtsangrong (Tiger's Den Ravine). Then you cross the Shangü La (Stag Tears Pass, 5060 m) and cross the Damchen La (Oath Bound Pass) and have a direct encounter (*jelwa*) with the Kalā Dungtso (Conch-shell Conduit Lake, 5100 m). After this you traverse the Kyobchen La (Great Assistance Pass, 4900 m), and, having had a direct encounter with the Trakshe Lamtso (Trakshe Vitality Lake), you return to Chikchar. That is how the peak circuit is done.[36]

From Chikchar to the summit of Tama Pass, the route is the same as the Shungkor, or popular middle circuit, described in chapter 7. But from the Tama pass it deviates and crosses a high ridge, formed in part by the peaks of the so-called Four Khachö Mountains, which runs southeast down from the summit of Pure Crystal Mountain. Sometimes this shorter route is not taken, and the route continues on the middle circuit a little longer to include other empowered lakes and caves in the region of the key ritual site of Phodrang Yumtso, or "Turquoise Lake Palace," to the south. But from the summit of the Shangü pass back to Chikchar, the high altitude route, averaging close to five thousand meters, is unique to the peak circuit and also restricted to initiated persons.

Landscape of Power

Simple circumambulation of the main peak of Pure Crystal Mountain by this route is an aim in itself. It generates merit and empowerment if performed with the correct attitude of devotion, observation of ritual constraints, and physical performance. In addition to this basic ritual, however, Tantric practitioners and other élite pilgrims,

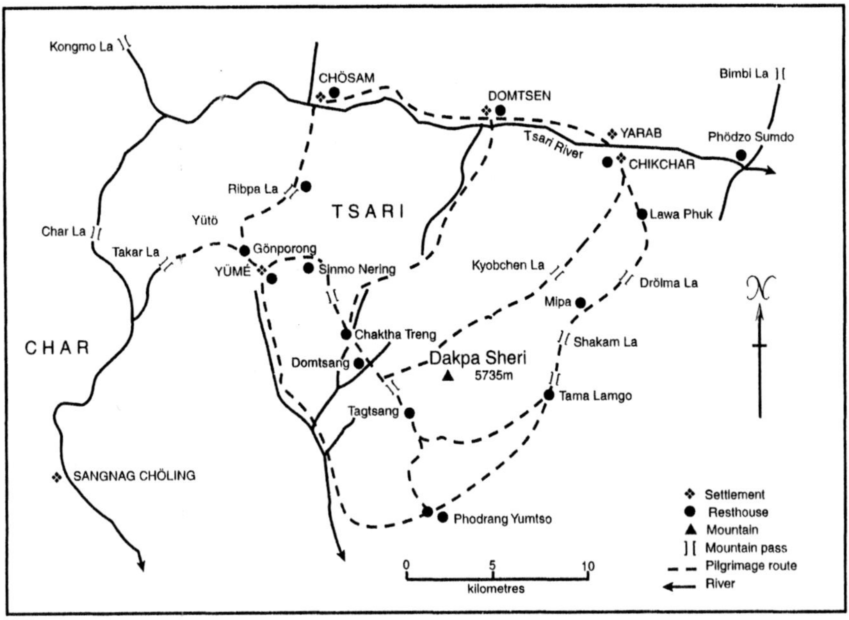

Figure 6.1. Pilgrimage routes of the upper mountain.

such as high-ranking clerics, use this strenuous high altitude circuit for other specific reasons. This high ground of the mountain is marked by many of Tsari's most potent empowered sites. This circuit circles closest to the central peak abode of the chosen meditational deities, allowing for the most intimate direct encounter (*jelwa*) with that edifice of natural architecture. On its alternate routes it visits the most important meditation caves in the area, where the Tantric yogins of the past gained their supreme paranormal powers in meditation, and it encompasses the primary lakes containing maṇḍala abodes and ritual substances of the highest ranking. Here one begins to enter the sphere of the celestial *khachö* purity zone, and the landscape and physical quality of the environment are charged in their very being by the immediacy of this interface. Oral and written narrative maps and guides reveal that in this region there are a myriad of sites and traditions connected with the ritual priorities of Tantra practitioners who perform peak circuits. I will give a few examples to illustrate these priorities.

On the peak circuit, the group of central mountains that constitute the main summit ridge running to the southeast—the Four Khachö Mountains—are places where advanced Tantric meditators can engage in Great Seal yoga in various caves. Here, in the high altitude cave of Dorje Phuk, for example, the Indian yogin Lawapa attained bliss in his Tantric practice. The area is described as a place of such attainment in a language heavy with references to the Tantric practices of deity visualization and *tsalung thigle* yoga:

> Thab Dorjeri (Ritual Scepter of Means Mountain) is the place for cultivating the perfection stage. . . . Shérab Drilburi (Bell of Wisdom Mountain) is the place for cultivating the generation stage. . . . At the center, the one called Thab Shérab Sungjuk Ümari (Central Convergence of Means and Wisdom Mountain), the yogic concentration of the convergence of the generation and perfection stages arises spontaneously, one's own body is purified in rainbow light, and so forth. It is extolled as the place for cultivating Great Seal yoga.[37]

At other spots one comes within very close proximity of the central maṇḍala palace, such as the lake of Kalā Dungtso, directly under the main north summit and the site of yet another important practice cave of an early yogin. In relation to the descriptions of these landscape features, the language of architecture gives way to the honorific language of anatomy and personal effects, as the chosen meditational deities themselves are right there in front of the practitioner. So it is said, "This Kalā Dungtso is like the upper torso (*kutö*) of Pure Crystal Mountain."[38] Here is a chance for direct physical encounter: "When Pure Crystal Mountain disrobes itself of its garment (*nabza masöl*) of mist and cloud, your meeting will be extremely close, and you must perform offerings and exert yourself in prayer."[39] What is more, the vital bodily substances of the chosen meditational deities can be found and extracted from the landscape itself, as their bodies *are* the body of the summit. In the waters of Kalā Dungtso there is a thick white suspension (perhaps an alpine algae or slim mould) that resembles semen. Yogins ladle and decant the waters in order to collect it. This "cream" is considered to be the generative fluid or semen of Khorlo Dompa, as well as, in an esoteric sense, the drops (*thigle*) of white awakening energy or life force (*changsem karpo*) that are circulated within the channel network of the subtle body during yoga. This highly empowered substance is used in Tantric alchemy and rituals.

Close by, on the opposite side of the main summit, is the Khachö peak Shérab Drilburi, or "Bell of Wisdom Mountain." Yogins understand that the elements of its name are a symbolic reference to the female chosen meditational deity and chief sky-goer goddess Dorje Pagmo, and that her body is this feminine half of the summit's landscape.[40] And it is here that "[f]rom the sky-goer [Dorje Pagmo]'s secret vagina a flood of white and red generative fluids flows down as *sindhura*."[41] Her menstrual blood, also conceived of as empowered subtle body-energy drops or red awakening energy fluid (*changsem marpo*), is available to the Tantric practitioner in the lake waters of Phodrang Kyomotso, or "Long-handled Ladle Lake Palace," so called because of its shape. This lake is also called Ocean of Sindhura, and the red *sindhura* powder suspended in its waters, which can be identified as a type of ochre resembling minium, is regarded as a most potent substance, being the chief sky-goer's menstrual blood. It can be consumed to gain direct empowerment. It is also prized for use in certain Tantric rituals, such as the construction of *sindhura* maṇḍala by drawing the design on a mirror's surface with the precious powder, or for certain steps in the initiation of practitioners into the meditation cycles of the Khorlo Dompa system. This *sindhura* powder is also used by lamas in divination rituals that invoke the important goddess Dorje Yudrönma who dwells at Pure Crystal Mountain, and who is counted as one of Tibet's chief protective deities.[42]

If substances around the peak circuit have a high ritual ranking, so, too, must the persons who go there and collect them. Those who wanted to make collections required advanced levels of initiation and spiritual cultivation, and the holding of this qualification by someone was public knowledge, that is, they were recognized as a lama or yogin by others. As I will show hereafter, the fact that certain qualifications were required also became public knowledge by virtue of the way Tibetans explained the supposed results of ritual breach in collection practices. Potential collectors of empowered substances required a sufficient resource of symbolic capital, which could be generated by means of Tantric ritual activity. To gather material such as *sindhura* at Tsari, male pilgrims (for no women are allowed near these locations; see chapter 7) must be Tantric initiates who have completed the Dorje Pagmo retreat practice or who have performed no less than thirteen middle circuits of the mountain already. Tibetans are always ready with narratives describing how terrible calamities struck pilgrims who visited the lakes and collected *sindhura* without these ritual qualifications.[43] The monk who went lame, the herder whose wife was drowned, and others in these stories are all the victims of the local protective gods of the mountain, whose wrath, once aroused, knows no bounds. Even those who are highly qualified are extremely cautious about their behavior when taking *sindhura*; it is not a practice to be taken lightly, because of the immense power of the place and its divine inhabitants. For example, Shérab Gyatso is a highly experienced Tantric yogin who knows the mountain intimately. In the 1950s he was one of only two persons officially authorized to collect *sindhura* on the mountain, as there had been some bad omens and "mishaps." Even Tibetan government representatives were not allowed to gather it; they had to get it from the yogins of Tsari. He once collected a sizable quantity, too much in his opinion, of the substance while performing a peak circuit. On his descent he became hopelessly lost in wet weather for several days before being found in a very rough state by some yak-herders. He sees a direct connection between these two events. An interesting footnote to this story is that the villagers of Tsari were very surprised when they saw this yogin looking stressed and in a disheveled state due to his ordeal. They could not understand how a yogin possessing Tantric powers could get this way, not realizing that one cannot effectively go without food and warmth unless seated in quiet meditation.

The abundant glacial water in streams and lakes on the mountain is also considered potent. In various oral and written traditions its sources and properties are cataloged and ranked, and like the other physical stuff of the upper mountain it can be ritually collected and consumed. Up here at certain spots one may be drinking the "urine" (*sangchab*) of the chosen meditational deity Dorje Pagmo, or the ritual water used in the Tantric consecrations of maṇḍala initiation, and thus gain empowerment, purification of defilements, or even various levels of paranormal powers.[44]

Yogins know that everything about the upper landscape of the mountain is charged with power and thus ritually significant as means toward their goal of physical and psychic refinement. Much of this is also general knowledge—for instance, any lay pilgrim on the mountain will continually "taste" the waters from streams and lakes to gain empowerment and purification. But Tantric practitioners are employing these substances in very different ways from the ordinary person, in terms of both the symbolic significance and the material efficacy that are attributed to them. So, for example, they may use materials from Tsari in constructing specialized ritual cakes (*torma*), circular feast offerings (*tsogi khorlo*), or maṇḍala rituals, although even here much of the significance of such uses is known to non-Tantric clerical and lay practitioners. The biggest difference in Tantric and non-Tantric ways of understanding and using the mountain's substances is in the yogin's practice of "essence extraction" (*chulen*) and the use of special preparations drawing on alchemical theories.

Tantric Botanists and Herbs of Liberation

The ritual collection of herbs and minerals by lay pilgrims at certain mountains such as Tsari is common practice in Tibet. Some of the main reasons for it I have already outlined. For more specialist purposes, traditional Tibetan doctors and pharmacologists also visit these sites to gather materials for use in medicinal preparations. At Tsari in the past, the collection of medicinal and ritual herbs also had a minor economic importance, as they could be traded and sold and were even expected as part of the annual tax payment from certain villages to the government. Some traditional Tibetan doctors combined the practice of pilgrimage with the collection of medicinal plants on Pure Crystal Mountain. The harvest of valued natural products such as *chartsa gunbu* ("summer grass, winter worm") from the meadows of Tsari continues today for a new Chinese market.[45] Tantra practitioners collect herbs and minerals there also. But the way in which they use them not only combines the layperson's view that they are empowered by contact with the place and the pharmacist's view that they have certain physical, chemical properties, but also recognizes that they either possess or are identified with the paranormal powers of the divine residents of the mountain, or can produce these and other powers and results when prepared and consumed in a ritually correct manner.

By far the most famous of these Tantric substances used at Tsari is the rare herb known as *tsa ludud dorje* ("adamantine serpent deity–demon herb").[46] Many now know of this so-called supreme herb as it is mentioned in a famous song, attributed to the Sixth Dalai Lama, about Pure Crystal Mountain and its empowered substances:

> Water from the glacier of Pure Crystal Mountain,
> Dewdrops of the *ludud dorje* herb,
> Balm of medicinal elixir;
> The beer-serving maid is the perfect cognition sky-goer [i.e., Dorje Pagmo].
> If one drinks it with pure Tantric commitments,
> There is no need to undergo bad rebirth.[47]

Recent analysis of the song shows how *ludud dorje* relates to the mountain and its divine inhabitants, what paranormal powers it is identified with, and how it was used by Drukpa yogins there in certain Tantric preparations, most importantly in the so-called rainbow-light pellet, a highly empowered relic pill for which the Drukpa are famous.[48] Most such details are known by any knowledgeable Tsariwa.

Here I will add some further materials on this and other such herbs and minerals from oral traditions about the mountain. Tsariwa all know of and also sing about the herb *ludud dorje*. For example, one such song goes:

> Pour some dewdrops
> Of *ludud dorje* into a teapot,
> Then please drink your fill,
> And you will not need to undergo bad rebirths.[49]

This is a simpler song than the more famous one just quoted, although it is very closely related to the same main theme. Comparing the two texts, one of course is lead to ask whether this is a local version of the one attributed to the Sixth Dalai Lama or his was a fancy literary version of this local oral one? Yogins who perform the peak circuit remain vigilant at certain points on the itinerary, particularly in descending from the Kyobchen pass toward Chikchar, for the occurrence of plants of *ludud dorje*. One needs a careful eye to identify this species from others of similar appearance that also grow on the mountain slopes. Serious Tantric practitioners will consult ritual manuals and guides and be tutored in taxonomic skills by their lamas in order to botanize efficiently. The sites of discovery of patches of the herb are usually kept secret or shared only with other initiated practitioners. The consumption of the herb is not only linked with obtaining Tantric paranormal powers and better rebirths, but also with cures for serious diseases such as leprosy (believed to be caused by the serpent deities, hence the plant's name) and the inducement of powerful hallucinatory and bodily effects. Most Tsariwa and pilgrims to the area have stories about it being encountered inadvertently by humans or animals.[50] Many unusual occurrences are attributed to the accidental ingestion of *ludud dorje* in the area. The most common of these narratives tell of lay pilgrims whose idle chewing on a plant stalk (actually *ludud dorje*) while circumambulating causes them to fly up in the air or have intense and lucid visionary experiences. The incidental grazing on it by wild and domestic animals is said to lead to miraculous self-produced markings and images of Buddhas and ritual formulas on their bones and horns, as well as bodily deformities. Some pilgrims collected the droppings of deer and other wild animals up on the mountain, as they maintained they must contain accumulated empowerment, and perhaps even *ludud dorje*, because the animals grazed everywhere and probably ate it at some stage.

Yogins and Tantric practitioners also seek out other species of alpine herbs for which the mountain is famous. These plants, like *ludud dorje*, are credited with possessing the paranormal powers of the sky-goers of Pure Crystal Mountain and being able to bring forth those powers in the yogin if consumed. Their use is also said to produce general physical vitality and to aid the *tsalung thigle* yoga practice. On the routes of the peak and middle circuits, those who know can collect and eat, either raw or cooked, a plant known as *khandro lapuk* (pron. *khandro limbik* in local dialect), or "sky-goer radish," which is said to help produce paranormal powers.[51] *Khandro lapuk* is believed to be the same as the sky-goer radish that was cooked and eaten by the Indian Yogin Lawapa while high on the mountain here, resulting in his departure to the *Khachö* pure abode. The precautions Tsariwa take when harvesting this plant are of interest: when they are uprooted, the excess soil must be immediately removed from the roots and placed back in the ground. If this is not done, it is believed that the divine residents of the mountain will cause rain to fall due to the disturbance of the substance of their telluric abode. Another prized plant is *lingchen*, or "giant ling," a species of a tall herb resembling a wild onion, found growing in high alpine pastures upon Pure Crystal Mountain.[52] It is collected, cooked, and consumed for the same purposes, just as the great yogins of the past did here. At still other points on the itinerary, a white alchemical stone known as *chongshi* is sought out and collected for use by yogins.[53]

All such collections and uses of substances around the peak circuit and elsewhere on the mountain by Tantra practitioners are ritually important within the general framework of a type of Tantric alchemy originally derived from Indian traditions, which Tibetans call "essence extraction" (*chulen*). One consumes these substances in small quantities, usually prepared as pellets, as a substitute for bulk food during periods of meditation and yoga. The "essence" (*chu*) of the materials that has been extracted sustains and revitalizes both the physical and the subtle bodies of the yogin. This is one way that consuming these substances is believed to produce paranormal powers, as it generally renders the circulation and control of vital energy (*lung*) more efficient. In addition, as I have already shown, Tibetans subscribe to notions of the substantial or physical presence or embodiment of either the paranormal powers of the sky-goers or even the sky-goers themselves in these substances. This belief is the basis for a widespread cult of sacred bamboo associated with the mountain and popular lay pilgrimage there (see chapter 7).

Maṇḍala Pilgrimage

Perhaps the most unique aspect of Tantric practice on the mountain is its use as a gigantic initiatory structure, a natural landscape maṇḍala, by way of a systematic ritual journey or circumambulation.[54] Such a treatment of the natural environment is truly an example of what Buddhists would call skill in means. To fully realize the mountain as maṇḍala, hence ultimately experience enlightenment, the practitioner must be a highly advanced Tantric adept with all the preliminary practices completed, and a holder of transmissions, instructions, and binding pledges in the Khorlo Dompa Tantra system. Then one is able to enter into the Pure Crystal Mountain maṇḍala and attain to the four levels of consecration or initiation (*wang*). This procedure involves a sophisticated ritual process with both physical external and psychic internal dimensions. During the ritual the yogin identifies with and becomes the chosen meditational deity Khorlo Dompa, and thus subdues the inner propensities toward defilement and ignorance in a reenactment of the original subjugation of Jigjay related in the origin narratives of the mountain maṇḍala.

The great Tantric expositor of the mountain Pema Karpo wrote a chapter in his guidebook which he entitled "Circumambulation There Interpreted as Walking the Graded Path of the Great Secret," the great secret here being the Tantric method of attaining enlightenment. This chapter delineates the process of maṇḍala circumambulation in outline, and although to the uninitiated it appears packed with esoteric detail, an extensive oral commentary is implicit. The following excerpt relates the first three stages of this process, which show the relationship between outer and inner landscape and ritual. The first section describes maṇḍala entry at Sexed Rocks, where one encounters and appeals to the door guardian in the same way, discussed earlier, the pioneer Tibetan yogin Yeshé Dorje encountered the field-protector sky-goer there when he first opened the *néri*. Then, at Chikchar, where one ascends the mountain onto the upper level, or "enters the palace," the Tantric commitment to total union with one's lama and the divine inhabitants of the maṇḍala is invoked before full ritual entry can be achieved. The second section describes how the mountain's weather, which is renowned for being extraordinarily wet, provides the initial vase consecration. The image here is of the sky-goers in the space of the *khachö* zone above sprinkling the purificatory waters of initiation down as rain and mist. Third, the traverse of the mountain's four "great" passes and ravines parallels the practice of the initial purification and activation stages of internal yoga using the flow of vital energy through the psychic channels and wheels or "centers." Note that the process of transformation is marked by the shift from ordinary to honorific terms for the body, speech, and mind of the practitioner here:

> Pray, and enter the door from the Sexed Rocks of Tibet. Because there exist the likes of fierce local guardians, they call out such things as, "You need to be careful!" As for the vision in Chikchar of all the lakes that liberate one from obstructions and enemies, that generate action, and that produce paranormal powers in the palace of divine heroes and sky-goers: first make the inner entry into the great Vajrayāna maṇḍala, then those who hold binding pledges and vows make the secret entry into it. After empowerment is bestowed, the great maṇḍala is revealed. . . .
>
> As for the azure clouds totally enveloping every direction, and the rising mists and the continuous downpour of rain, this is water with the inherent nature of the five nectars, coming out of a perfect vase possessing a topknot of white cotton, for washing living beings who are greatly afflicted in their sins. This opens the way for the essential drops of the body (*lu*) to awaken, gross defilements to be cleansed, and the adamantine body (*ku*) to be put in order. This is the vase consecration or nonregressing consecration, and as for the initiators, they are the chieftainesses of *khachö*. . . .
>
> Having descended the four great ravines [Parparong, Gönporong, Lhamorong, Tagtsangrong], and ascended the four great passes [Kyobchen-La, Shakam-La, Gayo La, Shangü La], offer many circular feast offerings in them. Also there, the generative fluid of the divine Lord and the generative particles of the divine Lady, both of whom are indistinguishable from one's lama, descend in the ravines of the four energy wheels through the seventy-two thousand psychic energy channels. And that itself then ascends the passes that are the disciple's own four energy centers. Orally tasting the five nectars that are the secret substances produces the conditions for the essential drop of speech (*nak*) to be dreamed, subtle defilements to be cleansed, and the adamantine speech (*sung*) to be put in order, which is the second consecration, called the "secret one."[55]

The text continues by relating the process of the third consecration, the "wisdom consecration," to drinking from the water of the twelve lakes on Pure Crystal Mountain that are maṇḍala palaces and ascending to the summits of the four summit peaks (Dakpa Khachöri, Shérab Drilburi, Thab Dorjeri, Thab Shérab Sungjuk Ümari). By doing so one activates the essential drop of the mind (*yid*), cleanses extremely subtle defilements and prepares the seed of adamantine mind (*thug*). For the so-called fourth consecration one "rests" (in meditative concentration) in the four caves (Kyobchen Phuk, Ömbar Phuk, Khachöri Dorje Phuk, Mikra Phuk), sitting on the four natural stone thrones, and then, moving to the pass of Gayo La, one sings an inducement to the female chosen meditational deity Dorje Pagmo abiding in the Turquoise Lake Palace. This action prepares the inner psychic faculty of adamantine-cognition. Finally the yogin must stride with intense energy to the place of Khandro Bumde and climb onward to the site of Machen, which completes the full maṇḍala consecration process.

Anyone familiar with the details of maṇḍala entry and consecration, the process of *tsalung thigle* yoga, and the mountain's basic topography will see at once what a sophisticated interpretation of the ritual relationship between outer and inner space this process represents. It is not just two different rituals happening at the same time, one outward and the other inward; it is the same ritual happening in two different modes simultaneously, as physical transit of the Khorlo Dompa maṇḍala constituted in landscape and psychical transit of the same maṇḍala constituted in the channels and other media of the meditator's body. As a result of successful maṇḍala circumambulation, the yogin experiences a state of bliss, which is indescribable, but understood as equivalent to a Buddha's experience of enlightenment. Because the outward journey is also simultaneously the internal purification and culminates in the realization of the symbolic union of the chosen meditational deities by way of yoga in the subtle body, the state achieved is specifically termed "Buddhahood possessing the seven features of father and mother face to face."[56] This state is, of course, what all the writings on Tsari variously refer to when they talk of yogins attaining the "supreme paranormal power" on the mountain; it is Buddhahood itself.[57]

Such a presentation admittedly reduces a highly complex ritual process to a glib routine. However, to go into further depth here would not only involve a breach of contract with my informants, but go well beyond the scope of this work.

The account just given may well have been inspirational centuries ago, but has anybody performed such rituals in more recent times? Yes. I have had accounts from two yogins describing abbreviated variations of this ritual scenario performed within the last forty years. But regardless of whether anyone actually still does this nowadays, what is important to recognize is that the major portion of this Tantric ritual takes place around the high ground of the mountain. That is, yogins use the immediate environs and central zone of the maṇḍala palace as it is represented in the mountain's landscape. They quite literally go high to get high! And, according to the theoretical prescriptions of the mountain as maṇḍala, that is exactly what they should do to achieve the results they aim for.

Historically, the landscape space of Pure Crystal Mountain *néri* was defined by Tantrists to serve the particular needs of their own ritual and social practice. The external places they designated as most highly ranked or ritually important have been marked off by both their practices and restrictions, so that the yogins' own inner spaces may be ritually utilized to maximum advantage. There are major social ramifications inherent in this process. In the following chapters I will show how the earlier prescriptions and proscriptions of this élite have set a pattern to which all other users and inhabitants of the mountain have had to adapt and conform. In chapter 7 I begin by describing and analyzing the three popular annual pilgrimage circuits of the mountain performed by all laypeople as well as non-Tantric clerical practitioners, that is, monks and nuns.

7

✦ ✦ ✦ ✦

Popular Short Pilgrimages

> [At Tsari] paranormal powers are bestowed in various ways:
> Directly in person to those who are advanced and superior,
> As visions of bodies and images to those who are middling,
> And also as lakes, rock mountains, and trees to those who are lowest.
> As the likes of this do not exist anywhere else,
> This is a magical place for sure!

This verse, whose composition preceded the rise of popular pilgrimage to the mountain, permits something for everyone at Tsari.[1] An élite of Tantric adepts converted the site for the practice of their esoteric style of ritual. But they, as Buddhists, also maintained a theory of the graded faculties and ritual status of personhood that took account of karmic condition and degrees of mental and physical cultivation and relative purity. Thus, they considered that all devout persons could benefit from visiting the mountain in their own ways. Advanced Tantric meditators might have been able to totally identify with the reality of the mountain as maṇḍala and the archetype deities in it, or at least enjoy the vision of its subtle and underlying representations as grand, divine palace, enormous crystal shrine, and so on. But the vast majority of "ordinary" (*sokyewo*) and "impure" (*madakdro*) persons whose faculties and status were held to be "lowest" (*thama*) experienced its manifest embodiment in the form of gross physical landscape features and substances, organic life forms and climatic systems. Not only were such persons believed to have lower grades of perceptual appreciation, ritual status, and purity, they also had to use correspondingly lower zones of space on the mountain's slopes, as I will show. Ordinary persons all knew some details of the alternative realities of the place and of its various representations. So, prepared with their narrative maps, they visited the site, constituting by far the largest proportion of practitioners in a ritual relationship with the mountain: peasant farmers and nomads, traders and criminals, nuns and monks, government officials, aristocrats, hunters, and so on.

The extent and development of later Buddhist lay and non-Tantric clerical visits to the site is difficult to determine before the seventeenth century, due to lack of sources. The available historical sources do reveal a continuing and increasing trend toward popular pilgrimage, which appears to have greatly overshadowed the use of the site by Tantric yogins in recent centuries. During the twentieth century, up to 1959, the primary ritual activity of ordinary pilgrims was a physically challenging circumambulation itinerary traversing the numerous radial ridges and valleys of the mountain in a clockwise direction. This route was known locally as the Shungkor (also Barkor), or "middle circuit." It had two important variant itineraries, the Ngakor, or "advance circuit," and the Kyemengi Korwa, or "women's circuit." In this chapter I will briefly describe each of these itineraries in turn and elaborate certain aspects of their performance.[2] Today only a modified form of the basic middle circuit, and the women's circuit itineraries are being performed again since pilgrimages on the mountain were officially permitted in the early 1980s by Chinese officials.

All three variants of the Shungkor were lower in average altitude, further from the main summit, and consequently longer than the peak circuit described in chapter 6. However, these circuits were still very physically demanding. For instance, to perform the full middle circuit over the course of about a week, one had to cross no less than seven steep mountain passes between four thousand five hundred and five thousand meters, make multiple ascents and descents of at least a thousand meters on consecutive days, in what were frequently miserable weather conditions, and all the while observe various codes of behavior and ritual performances with an attitude of single-minded devotion. Like all pilgrimages around the mountain, it was not an exercise to be entered into lightly.

Pilgrimage of Snows

The main middle circuit is an annual event that can be undertaken at any time throughout the Tibetan summer and autumn. Prior to 1959, a special ritual for "opening the doors of the *né*" (*négo chewa*) was performed on a variant of this route on the upper mountain. Its basic form was a single clockwise circumambulation by a procession of pilgrims. This opening route, known as the advance circuit (Ngakor), followed the initial portions of the middle circuit but then dropped to a lower altitude to complete it, thus avoiding the steep snow passes on the mountain's western slopes. This was done about the middle of the third Tibetan month (approximately late April), when the entire mountain was still snowbound, and the majority of the circuit involved walking over ice and deep snow. The middle circuit route was serviced during the summer and autumn by a series of small and basic pilgrims' resthouses, locally known as *tsulkang*. During the previous autumn, in preparation for the extreme cold of the advance circuit, the *tsulpa*, or resthouse-keepers, laid large amounts of firewood in store before closing their huts up for the winter. This wood was vital for the pilgrims in the advance circuit procession, who needed it for cooking and keeping warm during their icy journey.

During the second week of the third Tibetan month, the initial rituals for mountain opening began in the village of Yümé in the western part of Tsari (Tsari Nub). At that time the protective deities of the mountain were worshiped. This annual, week-long period of ceremony and festival was called Chölé Chenmo, or "The Great Religious Work," and as it was primarily a ritual performed by local villagers, I will defer full discussion of it until chapter 10. During the Chölé Chenmo in the 1950s a local ritual specialist from the Yümé area, the Chagchen Lama, began chanting the ritual formulae (*mani*) and prayers that accompanied the spring opening circumambulation of the upper mountain. The assembled villagers were all supposed to join him in this chanting exercise, which signified that the Chagchen Lama and his company of local pilgrim-assistants would soon go to start opening the snowbound pilgrimage trail by performing the advance circuit together. His helpers, six to ten young men, where termed "sons" (*butsa*), and the opening team collectively called the "Chagchen and sons" (*chagchen butsa*). During the course of the advance circuit, the Chagchen Lama called on all the deities of the mountain by chanting *The Great Oath Prayer to Tsari* (see chapter 5) along with other ritual formulae, while his young assistants broke a path through the snows, leading the way for a larger party of accompanying pilgrims.

Just prior to the 1950s, a more specialized tradition of annual mountain opening existed, as follows. The Yümé Chagchen of the 1950s was a knowledgeable local man who had taken over the role of annually opening the mountain from two hereditary lamas who came from the family house of Kyogo, not far from Yümé village, after that household and its ritual lineage declined and died out completely by the late 1940s. These two former hereditary lamas, associated with the Drigungpa community of Yümé, were known as the "Snow-cutter" (*Gangshak*) and "Snow-firmer" (*Gangten*). As their names suggest, they used certain magical powers generated by way of ritual formulae to facilitate the clearing of a path through the often deep spring snows encountered on the mountain, and to avert avalanches that might sweep down on the pilgrims. After the Yümé Chölé Chenmo festival had finished, the Snow-cutter and Snow-firmer lamas, together with villagers from western Tsari, went to Chikchar. At Chikchar, on the fifteenth day of the month, a community ritual in honour of the mountain's protective deities had also taken place to mark the advance circuit and mountain opening (discussed in chapter 10). The party arriving in Chikchar from western Tsari were joined by other hardy Tsariwa who were experienced on the mountain, along with hundreds of lay pilgrims, who came from surrounding districts such as Char, Dakpo, and Kyemdong.[3] The event tended to attract many Drokpa, or pastoralists, who did not always have the chance to attend during the summer season. On the nineteenth day of the third month the procession was formed, and it ascended the mountain and began the advance circuit. No women took part in this procession. Only oral narrative maps of the advanced circuit route exist (see figure 6.1); for example, here is one version remembered from the performance of the ritual in the 1940s:

> On the fifteenth day, able-bodied men only were assembled in order at Chikchar. After two lamas, the Snow-cutter and Snow-firmer, arrived from western Tsari, they chanted ritual formulae aloud and led the way in front, and it took a day to go to Lawa Phuk (Lawapa's Cave), then across the Drölma La (Goddess Drölma Pass), and into Miparong (Human Skin Ravine). From there, on the following morning, it took a day to go across the Shakam La (Dried Meat Pass) and then descend down through Champarong (Kindness Ravine) and Kardogtang (Dairy Food Scraps Plateau) to the Ömbar (Blazing Light) Ravine and Plateau. From there, they climbed up toward Khachö (Celestial Action), and having circumambulated the Phodrang Yümtso (Turquoise Lake Palace) they descended through the Dongmo Chuluk (Tea Churn Water Container) [a steep gorge or chute formed by the action of water]. Then in the morning they went up through Lokag (Lopa Obstruction) [a tribal toll station for pilgrims] to Shingkyong Torma (Local Field-protector's Ritual Cake), in the direction of Yümé. From there it was one day up to Dongrag Gong Og (Upper and Lower Stacked Tree Trunks). After that they made a direct encounter (*jel*) with the temple in Yümé and the Khandro Bumde (Community of One Hundred Thousand Sky-goers). Then those pilgrims from Dakpo, Kongpo, and Kyemdong crossed the Ribpa La (Hermit Pass), and those from Dakpo gathered in

> Chösam and returned home by crossing the Kongmo La (White Grouse Pass). Then the people from Kyemdong returned home by crossing the Bimbi La (Clay Nodules Pass). From Yümé, those people from Chayül, Nyel, and Char went on through Yütö, and after crossing the Pagsha La (Swine Flesh Pass) they returned variously through Kyünang and Sangnag Chöling.[4]

This particular route avoided many of the high altitude sections of the standard middle circuit because of the snows. It achieved this by dropping down into the valley of the Yümé river to the southwest of the mountain, the same valley up which the twelve-yearly "great ravine circuit" (Rongkor Chenmo) procession came before it arrived at Yümé settlement (see chapter 8). The advance procession also took the precaution of traveling by night or in the early morning before the thaw, often using flaming torches, as this avoided both the soft snows that made walking slow as well as the danger of avalanches. Clerics who recall this advance circuit in the 1940s mention the special lamas' work of chanting ritual formulae and offering ritual cakes (*torma*) and their magical powers as essential for clearing a safe path in the snow. However, it is revealing to hear the same event described by one of the *tsulpa*, the local people who assisted the lamas in the procession:

> The lamas know it (i.e., My God)! We had to dig out the snow. The lamas know it! There were two men who were the snow diggers [in front]. The lamas know it! There were the two lamas, and they used to order, "Each of you dig, each of you dig!" The lamas had young men with them who cut through the snow. There were about twenty men like that. Although they were told, "Cut through the snow" they couldn't cut through it very well. Those young men had to break through the snow [crust] bit by bit.[5]

It seems that the lamas chanted more than just magical formulae on the advance circuit! In addition to the snows, there were other obstacles to deal with. As the route dropped down at its southern point into the lower valley of the Yümé river, it crossed a piece of territory that the Lopa, the Arunachal tribal people living to the south of the mountain (chapter 8), considered to be their land. At a point on the route, a place the Tibetans called "Lopa Obstruction" (Lokag), the path was blocked by a wooden barrier. Here the tribal people waited and only let pilgrims pass through one by one on payment of a small toll or passage fee. The amount was not fixed, and payment could be offered in coin or parched barley flour, or any other bits and pieces the pilgrims happened to be carrying. These particular tribesmen came from the nearby borderland area of Lüng to the southwest in Charmé, or "Lower Char," right where the Subansiri River cut through the main Himalayan divide. The Tibetans accordingly referred to them as the Lungdu Lopa ("Lopas at Lung"), and, at least in the middle part of this century, these particular people had reasonable relations with their Tibetan neighbors, unlike many of the other adjacent tribal groups. Because of this, any local pilgrims—that is, from Sangnag Chöling, Charmé, and Tsari—were exempted from the toll.

When the procession was completed, and the pilgrims had left the area, the mountain remained closed until the summer pilgrimage season. Usually at the beginning of the fifth Tibetan month (approximately late June), when most of the snows had melted, the *tsulpa* resthouse-keepers went up and opened their huts once again. From then on pilgrims could perform the middle circuit. The great *néri* had its "doors closed up" (*négo dam*) once again with a ritual to mark the end of the pilgrimage season on the fifteenth day of the eighth Tibetan month (approximately mid-October). Many say this event roughly coincided with a certain annual natural phenomena—the appearance of many insect larvae all over the ground—so that pilgrimage became impossible anyway because of the high risk of crushing many insects, a sinful act for Buddhists in the progress of a ritual. The *négo dam* was celebrated with a three-day ritual held in the village of Chikchar (see chapter 10).

The Popular Middle Circuit

The Shungkor, or "middle circuit," around Pure Crystal Mountain was the most popular annual ritual at Tsari. From the beginning of the summer until the pilgrimage route was officially closed again, a constant flow of pilgrims performed this circuit. They came from all over Tibet and from Tibetan-speaking parts of Bhutan, Ladakh, and areas of northern Nepal. They were people from all walks of life and ranks of society, yet they all shared certain things in common. In terms of the Tibetan theories of personhood on which they drew to define and represent themselves, they all had degrees of impurity (*drib*) and gross and subtle moral and cognitive defilements (*dik drib*) obscuring their being in some way. They also all understood that Pure Crystal Mountain as a natural shrine or Buddhafield could be used as a zone of purification if approached in the correct manner. Its reputation as a place with the power to wipe away the "shadows" that clouded body and soul was well known in Tibet. This type of pilgrim describes his or her ideal ritual relationship with the mountain as being a rich regime of contacts utilizing body, speech, and mind, directed by the goals of physical and karmic purification and merit accumulation and performed with an attitude of faith and devotion. Their pilgrimage was also an opportunity to come face to face with the mountain's powerful protective deities and ask for favors, request forgiveness, and seek increases of fortune. How this ideal was acted out at the site and a few general social outcomes of the process as it occurred at Tsari in the 1950s are the focus of the next section.

Entering the Sphere of the Mountain Maṇḍala

All pilgrims begin the middle circuit on entering the valley of the Tsari River, northwest of the mountain (see figure 6.1). They descend from the various high passes that connect Tsari with adjacent districts to the west, north, and east. No matter which of these high passes they cross, as most return home by way of the same route after their circuit, they in effect close a ritual circle around the mountain. For nearly everyone this process entails passing through the places of Phökhasum and Chösam to the north in the first stages of the journey, reenacting the initial entry during the opening of the place by the heroic Tantric lama figures. At many stages throughout the journey the narrative maps of the route signify the local terrain with references to these past dramas. Continuing down the valley through the site of Sexed Rocks, they arrived right at the foot of the mountain in Chikchar.

Many pilgrims made various renunciations and vows as they entered the course of the Tsari valley and Chikchar, for they had now come within the sphere of the great natural maṇḍala or shrine that appeared in the form of the mountain. Men and women abstained from sexual relations, most gave up drinking alcohol and even tea, and if they carried weapons, such as firearms or the common short sword, they left off using them in any way until they were clear of the mountain once again. These were the general behavioral restraints common on most Tibetan pilgrimages. Some pilgrims silently or audibly recited ritual formulae for the duration of their circuit, often having vowed to perform a certain number while in the vicinity of the mountain. Pilgrims recited and committed to memory a standard and well-known prayer to the mountain before proceeding onto its upper slopes:

> Lamas of the Kagyü lineages, chosen meditational deities, gods,
> Sky-goers, and defenders of religion at glorious Tsāritra,
> Pure *né* of Khachö, I entreat you!
> Grant me the empowerment to purify bad deeds and obscurations,
> To dispel adversities and dangers,
> And bestow both the supreme and mundane paranormal powers.[6]

The purpose of this prayer was to generate faith in the mountain based on a correct knowledge of what or who was there and what exactly the performance of ritual motivated by faith might gain for one. Thus, one addressed the three types of powers that prevailed at the site—beings that liberate, beings that protect, and a place (*né*) that purifies—and requested the three possible results of ritual: purification, protection, and enlightenment. Through committing this prayer to memory, right from the outset pilgrims were aware of the great powers of the mountain and the purpose they themselves were there for.

There was no mistaking that this mountain was a serious place, and one had to act in accordance with that. The place is often described as being "fierce" (*nyenpa*) and "dangerous" (*drakchen*), even for those who are spiritually refined. Visitors were reminded of this from the very context that produced their entrance prayer. It was sung by one of Tibet's greatest practitioners, the Gelukpa reformer Tsongkhapa (1357–1419), after he got a crippling pain like bamboo splinters in his feet as punishment for his doubt and subsequent ritual breach when on pilgrimage there. A simple song, sung by pilgrims and local people, makes this point eloquently in the form of a pun on Tsongkhapa's misfortune:

> One ought not to say "Don't go
> To the place of fierce Tsari!"
> By all means go, but make sure
> That you don't get bamboo splinters in your feet.[7]

The whole attitude that the mountain, and by extension its resident deities, are fierce and dangerous is in keeping with the widespread Tibetan representations of the potentially martial or violent character of the indigenous mountain gods, and the consequent need to treat them and their territories with great respect. This shared feature is yet another reminder that the *néri* cult is a syncretistic one.

Horses and yaks could be ridden down the broad and open valley to Chikchar, although many walked, as it was more meritorious to do so, and the animals were used for baggage by those who traveled heavily laden. Coming close to Chikchar, an area credited with special properties that promote the acquisition of Tantric powers, pilgrims have to pass by a hillock with an irregular shape that is festooned with numerous prayer flags and marked by a small red shrine on which a fierce face is painted. This place is the abode of Chikchar Marpo, the "Red One of Chikchar," the powerful local protector of this forested alpine valley. He is a manifestation of none other than the Lord of Death himself, Shinje Gyelpo, who, as directional guardian stationed at the south of the Khorlo Dompa maṇḍala, has his own divine palace as a subterranean construction here. There are various local ritual observations in view of his presence. This site marks a boundary point where one must pay respects to the deity on entering his territory. Before 1959 any pilgrims mounted on an animal, even Dalai Lamas or other high incarnate lamas, had to dismount here and from then on only lead their animals in the area, or the auspices for a visit to the mountain would not be good.[8] If one failed to do this, the offering of one hundred butter lamps in the nearby Dorje Pagmo temple was a standard way to rectify the ritual error.

Leaving the Chikchar area and beginning the ascent onto the mountain, pilgrims were expected to adhere to a specific code of mental and physical behavior for the course of their ritual journey on the middle circuit. They learned of this unwritten code from the resthouse keepers, from monks and lamas, and from other pilgrims before their ascent. The code applied specifically between two points on the journey, from a small water source called Chumik Nagmo, or "Black Spring," at the base of the mountain above Chikchar settlement, through to a rock formation resembling a bird's head named Yümé Charok ("Yümé Crow"), above the western village of Yümé. The area defined by these two points was exactly that within which there was no permanent human habitation on the mountain in either villages or meditation retreat centers. The five main aspects of this code are as follows:

1. At the Black Spring pilgrims perform ritual ablutions, washing hands and faces and sipping the water, and try to imagine that their various impurities are thereby being cleansed. The body should be thought of as a pure vehicle for undertaking the journey.
2. It is also said that from here on, following the advice the sky-goers gave the pioneer lama Kyewo Yeshé Dorje when he made the very first circumambulation of the mountain, one should always keep a walking stick in hand, a hat for rain on the head, and heavy boots against the wet on the feet, and continue praying and making offerings (see the original narrative in chapter 5). There is more than just ritual precedent invoked here, for the recommended pilgrim's accoutrements constitute good practical advice, given the local conditions about to be encountered. The pilgrim's walking stick was in fact a local institution and one with some economic importance, as a particular type of stick was made by the residents of Chikchar and sold to pilgrims before they ascended the slopes.[9] The fancier types of these sticks, especially those few made of bamboo, were taken home as both a marker and a sort of souvenir of the visit to Pure Crystal Mountain. Most pilgrims used some sort of walking stick on the mountain's steep and slippery trails, and they often deposited these on the summit of one of the final mountain passes near the end of the pilgrimage, after which the terrain becomes easier. This summit is called Khargyug La, or Limit for Sticks Pass, and always has a pile of walking sticks adorning it.

3. The pilgrims should think of their fellow travelers on the mountain as inseparable "religious friends" (*chödrog*) or "*né* companions" (*nédrog*)—those who have committed themselves to the same ritual path and its conduct, an encounter with divine power, and common hardships. These types of associations forged through mutual ritual participation are a form of horizontal relationship that is fairly common in Tibetan society. Due to the duration of the Shungkor, which often required a good week to complete, the regular use of the system of pilgrims' resthouses, and the practice of traveling in small groups for reasons of safety, pilgrims often did get to know one another on the mountain.
4. As for mental conduct, the pilgrims should dwell firmly on their faith and any vows they may have made, and not become distracted and neglect these. In general, thoughts should be turned toward wholesome things.
5. The final point concerns "general deportment and conduct with bodily wastes" (*chölam chablam*). This code ruled out fighting, unnecessary shouting (a disturbance to the deities which could result in rain or snow), or doing anything unseemly with the body. One must refrain from spitting saliva anywhere and must only urinate and pass one's stool at ritually designated spots along the route, about which I shall have more to say later.

The Upper Mountain

Climbing the mountain from Chikchar, the pilgrims could spend from four to eight days to complete the high sections of the middle circuit. Here is an example of a brief Tibetan oral map of the route:

> First, from Chikchar men and women are permitted to go together as far as the summit of the Drölma La (Goddess Drölma Pass), and from there the women go back down to Chikchar. Then if [the women] go to Tsokar (White Lake) they have to pass through Lo Mikyimdün (Seven Households of Lo). If they don't want to go there, they pass through to Sexed Rocks from Chikchar, and those who go on from Dorje Drak (Adamantine Rock) as far as Chaktha Trengo (Iron Chain Narrow Entry Path) get there by evening. Across the Drölma La, [the men] take a midday meal break in Miparong (Human Skin Ravine), and then cross over the Shakam La (Dried Meat Pass). Up from Champarong (Kindness Ravine) and Kardogtang (Dairy Food Scraps Plateau) they go on and spend the night at Tama Lamgo (Tama Flower Pass Summit). They travel successively across the Pawo La (Hero Pass), Pamo La (Amazon Pass), and other passes, and then directly encounter Ömbar Lamtso (Blazing Light Vitality Lake). Whichever of the three routes to Phodrang Yümtso (Turquoise Lake Palace) one takes, the Go La (Doorway Pass), the Gyabkor (Back Circuit), or the Khandro Sanglam (Sky-goer's Secret Path), you arrive at Turquoise Lake Palace. After having a midday meal break there, they directly encounter Phodrang Kyomotso (Ladle Lake Palace). Descending from the Tagyugtang (Horse Race Plateau), they arrive at Khandro Tsogshong (Sky-goer Assembly Offering Basin), after which they make an assembly offering (*tsog*) there. Descending from there, they spend the night in the Tagtsangrong (Tiger's Den Ravine). Then they depart in the morning and arrive at Iron Chain Narrow Entry Path for the midday meal break. From there, having crossed over the Khargyug La (Limit for Sticks Pass) they arrive in Sinmo Nering (Ogress Long Meadow). Then they pass through Tamdrinrong (Tandrim Ravine) and reach Yümé. They go off to their various lands in the same way as they do at the time of the advance circuit.[10]

It is immediately clear from this account that women and men undertake almost completely different pilgrimages on the mountain. (I will discuss the alternative women's itineraries later), but that a great deal of minor ritual variety is possible along the fixed routes of both. Just what any individual pilgrim might do at the numerous sites of significance, such as caves, rock formations, springs, passes, view points, and lakes along the way was dependent to a large extent on what detailed knowledge of the site they were prepared with beforehand. One important aspect of this preparation for ordinary pilgrims was contact with the keepers of the pilgrims' resthouses, which were stationed on both women's and men's circuits. These people, the *tsulpa*, had much knowledge about the mountain and could transmit detailed oral narrative guides and maps to pilgrims concerning what they might encounter (*jelwa*) in the immediate area and how to get there.

While the basic ritual was Tibetan Buddhist circumambulation, on the upper mountain circuit men engaged in other rituals that one might find performed on any circumambulation itinerary or mountain cult in Tibet. These encompassed many classes of practice, ranging from those prescribed by canonical Buddhism to those associated with pre-Buddhist local deity cults and based on ritual logics attested in the earliest known Tibetan texts. Lay men also tended to focus on the powerful protective deities dwelling at the mountain rather than the meditation deities, although to many the exact distinction was not always clear, as the protectors could be regarded as manifestations of the meditation deities or members of their retinue, and so on.

At points where pilgrims enjoyed clear views of Pure Crystal Mountain's peak (see figure 7.1), they said prayers for protection, long life, or purification of defilements; confessed their sins; and so on, and made small offerings of butter and barley flour or set up prayer flags on the mountain passes. Some pilgrims deployed "windhorse" (*lungta*) images to the gods of the mountain to get good luck or fortune and success in worldly affairs. At one site, near the Tama Flower Pass, they prayed fervently for actual material wealth (money, gold, silver, precious stones, guns, etc.), and at another, Oath Bound Pass (Damchen La), they piled all kinds of imitation and real weapons (swords, axes, daggers, spears, even needles) on the pass shrine of the powerful protector Damchen Dorje Legpa. Because of the steepness and ruggedness of the alpine terrain they did not perform full-length body prostrations around the circuit, as was done at other major *néri* sites in Tibet. At many points along the route, but particularly at spots very close to the main summit and on passes, pilgrims pile up small cairns using stones carried from the mountain's base or set up simple altars in very large numbers. These are common Tibetan practices in relation to the worship of local deities, and I have seen it done often on mountain passes and close to the *né* of *yüllha* and local gods throughout Central and western Tibet. Rather than repeat here what is already familiar from other ethnographies of Tibetan ritual behavior, I will give examples of several practices that are more specific to the site of Tsari itself, and which express a certain belief about the place and the relationship with it that lay and non-Tantric clerical pilgrims maintained.

Most ordinary pilgrims did have a level of mental relationship with the mountain through prayer, the chanting of certain ritual formulae, and having a constant aware-

Figure 7.1. Pure Crystal Mountain viewed from the *Shungkor* pilgrimage route. (Courtesy Thupten Nyamtsur.)

ness of their actions in relation to ritual protocols. But it was nothing like the meditative identifications, visionary experiences, and collapsing together of inner and outer spaces that the serious yogin cultivated. Ordinary pilgrims brought themselves and the mountain together in other ways, by cultivating a direct physical relationship with it. This interaction involved various forms of consumption of substances, contacts by touch, collections of material, offerings made in exchange, and so on. The sheer physicality of these dimensions of ritual are very important to ordinary Tibetans as pilgrims and, as I have shown, can be to yogins as well. Such physical acts of contact are also found at other important places that Tibetans visit as pilgrims, so I will present a few examples that are specific to beliefs about Pure Crystal Mountain.

The Cult of Bamboo

My first example is not limited to the activities of male pilgrims on the upper mountain but covers all pilgrims on the middle circuit and its variations. It concerns the ritual collection and usage of bamboo canes growing on the mountain's lower slopes. At least in more recent centuries, the bamboo from Tsari has become a sort of identity-marker for the place in Tibetan thinking. This might be explained due to the relative exoticism of a very useful subtropical plant among dwellers on the cool and arid high altitude Tibetan plateau to the north. Bamboo is a rare material associated with the warm, damp *rong* or "ravine" country to the south and remote southeast. But even in Bhutan, a Tibetan Buddhist country to the south whose ravines and mountainsides abound with bamboo cane, Tsari bamboo has a particular ritual value.[11] There is far more to this bamboo than meets the eye.

The bamboo plants grow only on the lower slopes of the mountain, where either pilgrims collected it themselves or local people collected precut, and occasionally sold it to pilgrims at places like Chikchar or Yümé. The main area for collection is near Yümé, at the completion of the pilgrimage. Pilgrims used bamboo from Tsari in various ways. Sometimes, bamboo lengths were fashioned into pilgrim's walking sticks. These were an essential pilgrimage accessory on the mountain; they were constantly put to use crossing the rough and often steep alpine landscape or the many small streams throughout the area. But here again, as in the case of exoticism, one cannot reduce the importance of bamboo at Tsari to functional necessities. Tsari bamboo was used mainly in relation to the body, the household, and sacred representation (*ten*). Many local people and pilgrims cut out the nodes from the canes (*nyugtsig*) and strung these small sections around their necks on strings, a practice not unlike the other common Tibetan one of wearing strings with "protective knots" (*süngdüd*) that are distributed by lamas.[12] Sections of young tender cane with exactly three nodes on them were cut and shaped into bracelets to be worn around the wrist as a medicinal aid. Pilgrims often harvested large bundles of canes of various sizes and carried them away after their middle circuits were completed.[13] These canes were placed on the roof of the house as a sort of apotropaic device and were sometimes used on household shrines and distributed to friends and relatives for the same purposes. As well as other materials, monks collected bamboo from the site and used it to empower *ten*, such as *chöten* and bronze statues, by inserting the bamboo inside them during the special consecration ceremony that brought such objects and constructions "to life."[14]

Tsari bamboo was so popular with pilgrims because it was believed to physically contain the empowerment (*chinlab*) of the local sky-goer goddesses and of empowered substances in the local soil.[15] The nodes of the cane in particular were believed to have empowerment concentrated within them. Thus, bamboo was a portable source of the mountain's great powers, which pilgrims could keep close to their bodies and domestic environments for further contact. This belief in the power of bamboo is expressed in a common song:

> I made a pilgrimage around the peak of Tsari.
> There was bamboo at the rocks throughout the ravines.

The empowerment of the mother-goddesses and sky-goers
Is infused into the nodes of the bamboo.[16]

But pilgrims did not simply come and take bamboo from Tsari; I have called it a ritual collection precisely because it is closely related to the performance of pilgrimage there and a particular relationship with the mountain itself. Bamboo was collected *on condition* of pilgrimage there, and the main point of collection was significantly located at the finish of the pilgrimage. One had first to make a ritually correct middle circuit and so honor the sky-goers whose substance, in part, one was removing from the site. Failure to operate such an exchange was a breach of ritual protocol. It is not unlike the cautions that had to be observed when Tantra practitioners collected the empowered substances, such as *sindhura* powder, that they prized on the mountain. As pilgrims would sing, the sky-goer to be most respected was of course the Chieftainess of Khachö, the meditation deity Dorje Pagmo herself:

I made a pilgrimage around the peak of Tsari.
I cut bamboo from the ravines.
There is no reason for Dorje Pagmo
To impose a punishment on me.[17]

One can see that the ritual collection and later distribution of bamboo from Tsari by laypeople was one of the many processes by which the mountain's fame and identity spread in Tibetan popular culture. A gift of the sought-after empowered bamboo to friends and relatives at home was also a way for pilgrims to reinforce friendships and gain recognition for having visited the famous mountain.[18] These notions are found in another popular song:

I made a pilgrimage around the peak of Tsari,
I collected bamboo from its ravines.
Because of my Tsari pilgrimage, I have a gift,
I am able to present you bamboo with three nodes.[19]

One finds references to Tsari and its famous bamboo in a wide variety of songs that were sung in places throughout the Tibetan world. For example, a verse from a western nomad's marriage song compares the female partner's body to the bamboo:

Her figure doesn't resemble the bamboo of Tsari,
Her physique is like a lama's small box.
Its exterior appearance is nothing special,
Inside there are plenty of desirable things.[20]

In another northern plateau nomad's song, classified as a dancing song, we find:

Having erected bamboo from Tsari,
Take hold of the middle of the bamboo cane.
Having grasped the middle of the bamboo cane,
Twist the bamboo leaves down to the ground.
Having twisted the bamboo leaves down to the ground,
You will spread the Doctrine in Tsari.[21]

A third example is an interesting Tibetan or Bhutanese song whose subject, according to its recorder Sarat Chandra Das, is a slender bamboo cane (like much of the cane from Tsari) about one foot long, which is used as a straw to drink homemade millet beer in Bhutan and Sikkim. His explanatory notes appear to suggest it is a type of drinking song:

Explaining the cane of bamboo,
Best is the bamboo of middle Tsari:

Its base has the suppleness of
The mother beer-serving maid's tavern jewelry. But
If you say her tavern jewelry isn't supple,
Then go back to middle Tsari.

Its center has the suppleness of
The lord patron's arrow. But
If you say his arrow isn't supple,
Then go back to middle Tsari.

Its top has the suppleness of
The superior lama's staff. But
If you say his staff isn't supple,
Then go back to middle Tsari.[22]

This may well be a drinking song in some contexts, but it also makes various allusions to more esoteric activities. My yogin informant Shérab Gyatso suggests that "middle Tsari," written with the spelling *rtsa-ri gzhung* (pronounced *tsari shung*) here, can refer to a pilgrim performing the Tsari Shungkor, but that a Tantra practitioner familiar with Tsari might read this song differently. The expression *rtsa-ri gzhung* could also refer to the middle and principal vein or vital energy channel (spelled *rtsa*) of the psychic body of the meditator at rTsa-ri, the meaning of that spelling being "Vital Energy Channel Mountain," as discussed in chapter 6.

R. A. Stein, who has already alluded to this connection in another context, tells us that the central (*üma*) channel in the meditational body is represented by Tibetans as a thin, hollow bamboo reed with three nodes.[23] This analogy provides an alternative to the layperson's beer rising up the three levels of the bamboo drinking straw. Stein has also noted that "*bodhicitta* is made to rise through the central artery, starting from the sexual organ and ending at the crown of the head, by way of the three 'bamboo joints' of the psychic centres."[24] He has further attempted to show that the yogin's psychic transit up the central bamboo cane/channel can be symbolized by a journey up the center of the hypostatic body of the meditation deity Dorje Pagmo within the landscape of the mountain of Tsari.

The "mother beer-serving maid" (*ama changma*) of this song can refer to the chief female meditation deity of Tsari, Dorje Pagmo, mother of all the sky-goers around Tsari, who is termed the "perfect cognition sky-goer beer-serving maid" in another song about the mountain with strong Tantric connotations, that of the Sixth Dalai Lama discussed briefly in chapter 6. She is also the "owner" of the external bamboo, which pilgrims collect for their necklaces and beer-drinking straws. The three personal subjects of the song are the three that are most important to the Tantric yogin:

his meditation deity as symbolic female consort, his lama, and his worldly patron. To return to pilgrimage briefly, a cane stick with three nodes is listed as standard pilgrim's equipment in a Tibetan song recorded by Tucci, who comments that the pilgrim stick with three nodes alludes to the three means of liberation.[25]

Besides what they show us about the way Tsari and its bamboo are understood by Tibetans, I have elaborated these details here for several other reasons. This is a good example of how a song circulated in a popular lay context can also be redolent with Tantric references. I suggest the song may be meaningful to beer drinkers, pilgrims, and Tantric meditators alike. Although I am not in a position to answer such a question, it would be very interesting to find out just how much of what the yogin reads in the song is also seen by laypersons, especially those who sing it while sucking contentedly on their beer-straws. It is also a good example of how seemingly straightforward material can be potentially difficult to interpret and classify for non-Tibetans.[26]

Jewelry, Guns, and Excrement

While performing the upper circuits, all pilgrims, as I have shown, had to pay close attention to the ritual collection or removal of the mountain's valued materials and substances. This need for caution and ritual propriety can be understood in two ways: first, the mountain is an abode (né), and one has to deal correctly with its powerful inhabitants when taking their property; second, the mountain and everything on it are ontologically continuous with these divine inhabitants by way of their embodiment. These two Tibetan explanations are entirely compatible. Furthermore, all persons had a general ritual ranking in relation to the mountain: Tantric practitioners were higher than ordinary laypersons; those who had circumambulated it were higher than those who had not (the number of circuits performed was significant); and, as I shall shortly discuss, men were higher than women.[27]

Pilgrims of various ranking did not just take materials and substances on the upper mountain, they also left them behind. They were involved in certain physical exchanges with the mountain, in some instances involuntary and in others highly intentional. Due to the attitudes just mentioned about the mountain, anything exchanged with it or left behind there was also subject to particular attention. There was what some cultural theorists of Indic South Asia would call a certain transactional logic involved.[28]

The Turquoise Lake Palace (Phodrang Yümtso) ranked, along with Chikchar and Pure Crystal Mountain's summit area, as one of the most potent locations in the area. This alpine lake lay at the southernmost point on the middle circuit and was thus accessible to all rankings of male pilgrims. It was the site of an aquatic maṇḍala palace of the meditation deities and could also be thought of as a kind of portal into the heart of the great mountain maṇḍala itself. It was well used as a meditation site by Tantric practitioners, who entered it in a visionary manner, and for laymen it was an important place to make offerings and prayers to the mountain's chief protective deities, to drink of its waters to obtain chinlab, and to perform ritual ablutions. In this sense it was an exchange point between man and mountain. As with every major ritual on the mountain, there were alternative levels of approach.

For instance, for yogins and monks the different offerings, classed as *choga* or rituals of the initiated, that they could make at Turquoise Lake Palace were the three grades of maṇḍala offering, outer (*chi*), inner (*nang*), and esoteric (*sang*), using various types of symbolically designated substances (*chödzé*). Here I will limit my brief discussion to the gross material offerings and exchanges made there by lay pilgrims.

In recognition of the intensely powerful divine inhabitants that they were confronting here through the surface of the lake's waters, lay pilgrims made proportionally intensive material offerings to them. Together with a regular *sang* or fumigation offering and placement of prayer flags here, this offering consisted of throwing items of great value, such as jewelry, gold and silver, coins, and ritual objects made of metal into the lake, with an accompanying prayer. The practice is not a recent one; it existed long before the 1950s. An aristocratic pilgrim's account from the late eighteenth century notes that the party threw in as offerings items that included a set of metal ritual implements, a scepter (*dorje*) and bell (*drilbu*), ten *ngülsang* (approximately 370 g) of Chinese silver, and three *zho* (approximately 37 g) of gold.[29] In the late 1950s an informant from the Kham region of east Tibet visited the lake; he reports that he threw in his sister's turquoise and silver earrings, a gold ring, and a handful of small-denomination silver and copper coins as offerings.

The offering of jewelry, and especially turquoises, in this manner seems to have been quite common. Sometimes valuable objects or coins would be seen at the shore or near the outlet, but pilgrims did not dare to steal them and threw them back into deep water for fear of provoking the mountain deities, which, it was believed, could result in complete loss of merit, reversal of fortunes, and premature death.[30] There were two pilgrim's resthouses at the site, and it was said locally that sometimes the *tsulpa* who lived there in the summer used to take a few valuable items with them at the finish of the pilgrimage season. While the rituals of lamas and yogins mainly addressed the meditation deities at the lake, the lay pilgrims were also concerned to direct their offerings to the powerful and potentially wrathful protective deities dwelling on the mountain, the Lion-faced Tsari Shingkyong, Dorje Yüdrönma, Damchen Dorje Legpa, and others. Thus, these were not unlike many other lay offerings to the various classes of autochthonous protective deities or mountain gods that inhabited the natural and domestic environments. The practice of *soglü*, or "ransoming life" on the upper mountain has already been mentioned in chapter 5 (see n. 39). All such practices follow an ancient Tibetan ritual logic of using a gift or exchange for attracting, persuading, and rewarding the deities in various ways to gain some desired change of circumstance or some end over which the deities are believed to hold power. The *ngenchö*, or "reward-offerings," for example, require the offering of expensive material goods and wealth, but reproductions are usually substituted for the real thing.[31] At Tsari the real thing was used, and it had to be used to give the appropriate exchange value in terms of the way Tibetans considered the mountain and what they might be, or were, getting back from it.

In a related ritual action here, numbers of firearms, mainly Tibetan matchlocks, were thrown into Turquoise Lake Palace by pilgrims during the middle part of this century. Many of these guns, lying submerged on the lake bed, are still visible through the clear waters to pilgrims circumambulating the shores in recent years. These guns were thrown in by hunters and by pilgrims from eastern Tibet who had been involved in skirmishes with invading Chinese military forces or in intertribal feuds and raids. The owners of these guns had taken many lives and were extremely defiled, as they had upset local gods who are believed to own game animals, and committed murder, one of the cardinal sins of both Buddhist and Bönpo ethical systems. The guns themselves, however, were in general considered items of great value, sometimes even treated like companions, and often represented the most treasured possession a Tibetan man might own during his life. Firearms that had killed many animals and men were also commonly believed to possess a magical power of their own by virtue of the carnage they had wrought. To be rid of the bad luck and illness the gun owners believed the local gods had brought down on them and their houses, and to attempt to clear the heinous sins of intentional killing and murder, men made the dramatic gesture of hurling their prized weapons into the sacred waters while swearing off killing and praying for relief and purification in this life and the next. In this lay ritual, a clear distinction between the *néri* cult with its Buddhist nature at Tsari and the local mountain cult can be seen. At local mountains Tibetans deposited weapons of all types in *tenkhar* shrines or used them in their rituals, and hunters, warriors, and soldiers worshiped the local mountain gods for victory in war and success in hunting. At the *néri* they deposited their weapons for the opposite reasons: to reverse the negative effects of all kinds of killing.

These offerings were an intentional form of human exchange with the mountain. The need to defecate, urinate, and expectorate while on the middle circuit were involuntary forms of personal substance-exchange with the mountain. The excretion of body waste of any form was considered extremely polluting on the upper mountain. Spitting or even clearing the nose is not allowed after the Drölma Pass summit. From there on also to the Domtsang pilgrim's resthouse defecating and urinating, which take place of necessity, are restricted to special sites along the route. Before 1959 these were ritually designated and marked by the ritual formula *Oṃ Ah Hūṃ* written on certain rocks, and pollution could be minimized by stopping at such spots. The restrictions on excreting bodily substances applied to all the high altitude areas of the mountain, those closest to the main summit. In fact, all human domestic operations on the high zone of the middle circuit were managed in order to avoid pollution.[32] At other landscapes, bodily discharges would not be an issue for concern, but here the pilgrim was walking within proximity of the Khachö Pure Abode around the upper mountain, and on a maṇḍala palace itself there was every cause for concern about ritual observances that avoided pollution.

While male pilgrims were being careful to answer the call of nature correctly on their clockwise circumambulation of the high slopes of Pure Crystal Mountain, elsewhere in the area their female counterparts and companions were walking off in the opposite direction, and not necessarily because they wanted to.

Born Low, Stay Low: The Women's Circuit

It is already obvious that a person's ritual rank or status correlated with the definition and use of the space around the mountain. But this correlation was not based purely on what type of practitioner a person might be and what level of cognitive abilities they were held to possess; it also related to Tibetan notions of essential gender differences and the body. Just by being born in a female body, all women automatically ranked lower than all men in relation to the mountain. Therefore, all of them—whether laywomen, nuns, or yoginīs, local residents or pilgrims—were banned from performing the peak circuit and much of the middle circuit, excluding them from a large area of the mountain coinciding with its main places of power.[33] This control of access to ritual space operated, according to Tibetan explanations, on a somewhat different logic from that (i.e., sexual distraction) which justified seasonally banning women's presence around the mountain's meditation communities. The ritual exclusion of women on such a large scale has not so far been reported for other Tibetan *néri* sites, although accurate ethnographic and ethnohistorical knowledge of most *néri* cults remains quite limited at the present time. It is safe to say, however, that the *néri* mountains in general offered much greater ritual access to women than did the almost exclusively male local Tibetan mountain cults.

Although there exists an extensive body of Tibetan writings about Tsari and Pure Crystal Mountain, apart from a few most brief references, all the texts are completely silent on the longstanding fact of women's exclusion from complete pilgrimages around the mountain. I think it is significant that the various formal references that exist to the ranking of persons and their relationship to the site do not mention gender as a factor, yet it is implicit. It is a commonplace of Tibetan Buddhist definitions of personhood that women are generally at the lowest ritual rank. There are only scraps of historical information concerning the exact origins of women's exclusion from the upper mountain and the development of the practice over time. Those data relating to women's exclusion from the Tantric meditation communities of Pure Crystal Mountain have been discussed in chapter 6; they date back to the twelfth century. However, our earliest actual record of women's exclusion from the upper mountain pilgrimage routes is not Tibetan but was made by the Jesuit missionary-traveler Ippolito Desideri while visiting the nearby Dakpo region in about 1720:

> The other place the Thibettans venerate exceedingly is called çe-ri (Tseri or Tsari). . . . Troops of pilgrims, men and women, go thither to walk in procession round the foot of the mountain . . . It is considered a sacrilege for any woman, even for nuns, to go to the upper mountains; and there is a point beyond which they are forbidden to pass.[34]

Like male pilgrims, women could begin a middle circuit from Chikchar, but upon reaching the exact summit of the Drölma Pass women pilgrims were permitted to walk exactly seven steps further down the other side toward Pure Crystal Mountain before returning back the way they came.[35] Women were thus banned from a twenty-five to thirty–kilometer stage of the middle circuit between the summit of the first major pass, the Drölma La to the east, and the Domtsang pilgrim's resthouse to the west of Pure Crystal Mountain peak (see figure 6.1). This ban included by necessity the entire peak circuit, as it too was reached by way of the Drölma pass. According to the Tsariwa and pilgrims, this was the extent of the exclusion up to 1959. The exclusion of all women from the upper mountain is still being strictly enforced by Tibetans since Chinese authorities allowed pilgrimages on the mountain again in the early 1980s.[36]

The Women's Circuit Itinerary in the 1950s

Although women pilgrims were prevented from accomplishing clockwise circumambulation of the upper mountain in conformity with orthodox Buddhist ritual performance, they did have an alternative route for completing what they could of the pilgrimage. But they had to do so by making a partial counterclockwise circuit, in reverse of the prescribed ritual order. The Kyemengi Korwa, or "women's circuit" (more literally, "the low-born's circuit") retraced a route from the Drölma Pass summit down to Chikchar and back up the Tsari River again to the important site of Sexed Rocks.[37] It then took a unique route up the northern flanks of the mountain and rejoined the main route of the middle circuit, which could then be followed to its normal conclusion at Yümé. This route has been used by women since at least the late eighteenth century.[38] There were also several short extensions to the women's itinerary that the pious could perform if they wished. A Tibetan oral narrative of the full possible itinerary is as follows:

> When women started from the base of the mountain they reached Lawa Phuk (Lawapa's Cave), and just below there the Khandro Trütso (Sky-goer's Bathing Lake), then they ascended to the Khandro Doénying Phuk (Sky-goer's Stone Heart Cave), the *né* of Dorje Yüdrönma. Then they went to the Drölma La (Goddess Drölma Pass) and did their seven steps down and returned to the Doénying Phuk. Then they traversed the face of the mountain north across to a lake called Bongbu Lamtso (Ass Vitality Lake), the *né* of the ass that is the mount of Pelden Lhamo. Some women, not many, went across further to visit the Trakshe Lamtso (Trakshe Vitality Lake), the *né* of Gönpo Trakshe, but this was a very rare occurrence. Most women descended from Bongbu Lamtso and continued on to Domtsen (Sexed Rocks), then continued on to Dorje Drak (Adamantine Rock) near Domtsen, then on to Chaktha Treng (Iron Chain Narrow Path) directly up the mountain. They were allowed a little further to Domtsang (Bear's Den) resthouse, but then they had to return to Chaktha Treng. They crossed the Khargyug La (Limit for Sticks Pass) to Sinmo Nering (Ogress Long Meadow) and on to Yümé to finish.[39]

Some women pilgrims visited Tsari without ever ascending the mountain on these special women's routes. They chose instead to remain around its base, or to perform another short, demanding, and unrestricted pilgrimage to the closely related site of Tsari Tsokar, or "White Lake," a glacially fed alpine lake some forty kilometers east of Pure Crystal Mountain's summit.[40]

Tibetan Explanations of Women's Exclusion

The preceding summary shows the limits placed on women's ritual movement on the upper mountain. It is worth discussing the various Tibetan explanations for these controls here, as they further reveal commonly held attitudes about the ritual relationship between persons and the *néri*. Among the Tibetan oral accounts about women's exclusion, some are in the form of direct explanations, and others deal with the consequences of women defying the restrictions placed on them at Tsari. Together both types use discursive constructions of gender, body, and powerful landscape. I will present several here to show the variety in the accounts, as well as that there is a contest of meaning over the reasons for exclusion between accounts given by laypersons and those of clerics and lamas.

During his visit to Tsari in about 1883–84, the 'Pandit' explorer named Kinthup was given the following narrative by Tsariwa:

> [F]ormerly a goddess, named Drolma, who wished to judge the moral behavior of men and women, laid herself across the pathway at the summit of the [Drölma] pass. A man came by and found the road blocked by the goddess, who was disguised. So he asked her with kind words to get out of his way. In reply the goddess said, "My brother, I am so weak that I cannot stir; if you pity me, please find another road, if not, cross over me." On hearing this the man took a different road. After a short time a woman passed that way, and she also saw the goddess and told her to give way; the same reply was made by the goddess, but the woman crossed over her and went on. Therefore, from that day, women have been forbidden to pass over, and from that day the pass has been known as the Drolma La.[41]

Very similar versions of this narrative still circulate today. Another narrative I heard is more widely known, and has several variants:

> There was a government minister from the aristocratic family of Doring.[42] His daughter was very arrogant, and when she learned that women could not perform the middle circuit and the peak circuit at Tsari she disguised herself as a man. Defying the restrictions, she crossed the Drölma La, and circumambulated Pure Crystal Mountain and the zone of exclusion. Finally she reached the resthouse at Domtsang, the official limit for women at the other end. When there she boasted that it was all nonsense that women couldn't do the pilgrimage, saying, "So what, I did it!" And then in the night she disappeared from the resthouse. A *migöd*, a huge hairy beast, came and quietly stole her away out of the resthouse. Nobody noticed. The *migöd* pulled down a large tree and put her body in it and then threw it up like an arrow. The people there went in search of her, and finally after many days of searching they found her in a large tree. The tree trunk had been split down the middle, her body laid into this split, and then the tree sealed back up again. She was dead, and parts of her body were sticking out either side. This was done to her as punishment by the Tsari Shingkyong, the local protective deity who had manifested as the wildman.[43]

In some variants it is the minister's wife who breaks the restriction due to her envy of the male pilgrims, or in defiance of her pious husband's plea not to proceed. In others the daughter is killed by a snow avalanche that is caused by the protective deity. Desideri was also told about such consequences for women crossing the forbidden threshold: "This they never attempt as they believe that any woman who dares to pass this point will be put to a fearful death by the Kha-ndro-mà [i.e., sky-goers], the tutelary goddesses of the place.[44]

But her death is not enough. The story is always recounted with the ending that from then on the Doring family are obliged to pay a regular tax to the pilgrims at

Tsari, both as a fine and a form of expiation of the sins brought on the family by this unruly woman. This taxation did in fact occur in the late eighteenth or early nineteenth century.[45] The tax was imposed by the Tibetan government in order to appease the Tsari Shingkyong, the powerful lion-faced protective deity who presided over the site. It is an example of the direct and ongoing interests the Lhasa government had in the mountain as an important site for maintaining the countrywide cult of major protective deities (see chapter 10).

These accounts were told to me by laypeople to explain the exclusion of women, although the story of the Doring family is also sometimes told by monks. These accounts offer a discourse on feminine character and its relation to the mountain's divine inhabitants, along with a less well-developed masculine character discourse. Feminine character is presented as disrespectful, irreverent and arrogant, impetuous, and envious.[46] And as if to emphasize by contrast, the male figures are reverent, considerate, and cautious. The divine residents of the mountain are disturbed as a result of these feminine character traits and respond with prohibitions or certain death. The burden of their response falls not only on the unruly women but extends through them to the male world of taxation and state administration; at Tsari women must be controlled by men's rules so that the goddesses and gods are not upset.[47]

It is interesting that on hearing these accounts monks often disregard them, or disparage them as "ordinary people's stories." Their alternative accounts contain a completely different set of discourses to give meaning to the exclusions. Several monks gave me a type of account that centers on the relationship between the psychophysical and soteriological status of the female body and the powerful nature of the mountain's landscape, as follows:

> Because it is such a pure abode (*nédakpa*), inside the maṇḍala palace [of the mountain], that is why women are not allowed. There are maṇḍala in many of the powerful sites on the mountain, such as the three vitality lakes (*lamtso*) of the [Tantric] deities; lakes such as the Phodrang Kyomotso, Phodrang Yümtso, and the "Ocean of Sindhura." They have maṇḍala of the gods and goddesses within them and are supposed to be too pure for women to visit. Wherever there are maṇḍala [on the mountain], women can't go. The main reason is that it is a palace of the deities, and a maṇḍala.[48]

These conceptions of mountain as maṇḍala palace, containing other maṇḍala within it, and other conceptions defining powerful landscape are related to further discursive themes of soteriological (i.e., karmic) status, bodily purity/impurity, and self-control, which also serve to construct femininity and masculinity through difference. These themes are exhibited in the following accounts:

> The only reason is that women are of inferior birth, and impure. There are many powerful maṇḍala on the mountain that are divine and pure, and women are polluting. Women can go on the ravine circuit because you don't have to pass over any power places [as it goes outside the boundary of Tsari's natural maṇḍala]. And if women went on the peak circuit and middle circuit they would be stepping on the power spots, and we believe that women are lower than men, and more impure, that's why. But when they go to Drölma La summit they walk just seven steps down the other side. On these seven steps they pray that in their next life they will be reborn as a man so they can complete the pilgrimage.[49] The *né* is so powerful this is possible.[50]

And further:

> There are places where you can't go because its so pure, and you could make them impure. You can't just go to the toilet anywhere at Tsari, that is why women can't go but men can. You need to have self-control over your personal desires and needs and wait until the allocated spot is reached. At certain spots on the mountain where the ritual formula Oṃ Ah Hūṃ appears on the rocks, these are the spots where one can do one's toilet so that pollution is avoided. This applies to areas on the peak circuit and the middle circuit in the central part. After the Drölma La is crossed and then all the way through to Domtsang there is a restricted area for ablutions. There used to be a text listing them all, but I can't remember it now. This tradition comes from the need for being extremely prudent and careful when in such a great power place as this.[51]

Other accounts give us further concepts of women's bodies being problematic because they are linked to sexuality in various ways at the site:

> The reason why women can't go up there is that at Tsari there are lots of small, self-produced manifestations of the Buddha's genitals made of stone. If you look at them they just appear ordinary, but they are actually miraculous phalluses of the Buddha, so if women go there these miracles would become spoiled by their presence, and the women would get many problems also. They would get sick and perhaps die prematurely. It is generally harmful for their health, so that is why they stopped women going to the holy place in the past, for their own benefit. The problem is that women are low and dirty, thus they are too impure to go there.[52]

Here the same themes of women's low and impure bodies is negatively and dangerously related to a "sexed" (*tsenchen*) landscape, from which they are excluded. This view contrasts with the lay traditions about the important site of Domtsen, or "Sexed Rocks," discussed in chapter 5. I note here in passing that Tibetan landscapes and power places can be not only sexed but also gendered.[53]

Earlier I noted that there is a discourse on women as a sexual distraction given to account for the periodic exclusion of women from the retreat centers of Chikchar, and I showed that this theme used in clerical accounts of exclusion is also typical of a wider Buddhist context. Similarly, the inferior karmic status applied to women here is at least implicit in Indian Buddhism and is explicit in Tibetan Buddhist sources.[54] Likewise, notions of the bodily impurity of women are also implicit in Indian Buddhism,[55] and they have long been explicit in Tibetan Buddhism, although in Vajrayāna tradition at highly developed levels rejection becomes acceptance as the inversion logic of Tantra transforms substances like menstrual blood from dangerous and polluting into bliss-giving and liberating in quality.[56]

Social Realities and Soteriological Promises

Thus far, I have not searched for some elusive historical origin of the tradition of women's exclusion from the upper mountain pilgrimage routes, nor any single, more convincing reason for its existence.[57] Such analytical strategies divert one from the point that the exclusions are about the complex operations of social power in certain relations and practices. The foregoing accounts show how Tibetans explain these circumstances in terms of their own worldview, and it should be clear that this process is far from being socially uniform or static. The story of the woman of the Doring family, and the penalties that aristocratic house incurred from the state, show that gender definition in ritual at the mountain was also far from being unproblematic. It was at times actively resisted and contested by women, a circumstance that continues right up to the present day.[58] In general the ritual restrictions did not exist to protect women from the effects of the mountain but to protect the mountain from the effects of women. The maintenance of its purity would thereby be better ensured. If it remains pure, it is believed that it will continue to be an especially powerful zone of potential transformation for its ritual users. In this way the exclusions work to increase the status of the place with pilgrims and meditators, and it is men, particularly élite male clerics, as pilgrims and meditators who stand to gain the overwhelming share of the benefits of this arrangement. They continue the accumulation and maintenance of social status or prestige in two related modes: through the claimed results of effective ritual performance and its public recognition in ranking; and by way of monopolizing the actual definition and control of space.

Overall, the sophisticated representations of the mountain detailed in earlier chapters give a full ordering of the landscape as a context in which women's exclusion may be understood in relation to certain Tibetan social constructions of the female person. The restrictions provide a hierarchy of vertical and horizontal space within which women may only use the lower-outer zone, all men use the middle-inner zone, and only spiritually advanced or purified men use the higher-central-inner zone. Purity, gender, and altitude are linked in similar ways in other Asian mountain contexts, and such a Tibetan construction of space is not unique to the landscape of mountains that are represented as Tsari is.[59] In Tibetan thinking in general, a hierarchical ordering of space that places maximum status on centrality and vertical height is pervasive; it is applied to the body, dwelling house, temple, world-system, and cosmos. In all these schemes, beings—both human and divine—are systematically arrayed on the basis of ranked qualities and properties. What is significant about the case of Tsari is that it gives a clear example of a Tibetan social context, that is, complex rituals relating persons and places, where both sex and gender are explicitly invoked as being important factors of this ranking. While élite, clerical explanations may provide explicit and often elaborate theories for the powerful definition of gender at Pure Crystal Mountain, in many respects such theories could also be viewed as a sophisticated reframing of popular beliefs and practices that have perhaps been of long standing in the small-scale, preliterate world of local Tibetan community life and traditions. How might this be so?

In other contexts, as I have just observed, Tsari is primarily a self-created category of power place, and its power predominantly flows from itself to the persons who encounter it, rather than the other way around. Having this type of power it is considered to be "fierce" and "dangerous," even for those who are spiritually refined. This danger is partly why the site is said to be hazardous to women's health, why special caution is required to control one's desires and needs there, like potentially polluting bodily functions, as well as why violations of the exclusion traditions through disrespect and arrogance produce such terrible punishments as suggested in the foregoing narratives. For Tibetans this terrific power is personified by the protective deities, such as the lion-faced Tsari Shingkyong. The lay explanations of female exclusion invoking feminine character traits are based on common notions of mutually binding relationships between such local gods and humans. On this point Tsari, perhaps more than any other *néri*, reminds one once again of the strong similarities and links between the *néri* cult and that of local mountain worship all over Tibet. In local mountain cults, women are excluded from the major ritual events and from access to the high space closer to or on the mountain summits where these often take place.[60] The high slopes of the local cult mountain are male space, and the deities dwelling in such places are also believed to be displeased by women or hostile towards them.[61] The local mountain cult has remained an important ritual site of gender definition in the local Tibetan social world, but it lacks something its more sophisticated cousin at the *néri* such as Tsari has to offer: the promise of female mobility.

Many Tibetans say that it is, at least theoretically, easier to transform a negative character trait than to transform a negative bodily attribute in any one lifetime.[62] Although this is a very general statement, it is perhaps part of the position from which Tibetans read the accounts of women's exclusion; gender-related attributes are more malleable than sex-related attributes. From this position the clerical accounts together provide a much more total discourse for exclusion. While it may be possible to change one's character, particularly through Buddhist education and practice, changing bodies is quite another matter, which requires a change in karmic status and at least another rebirth to accomplish. Since all women, even yoginīs, are banned because of their bodies, all will have to wait until their next birth to see if those seven steps across the Drölma La worked to give them a male body and qualify them for the whole pilgrimage. It should not surprise us that a Tibetan Buddhist ritual at Tsari invokes karma and rebirth both to exclude women and to offer the promise of a liberation from the restraints of women's lives if the prescribed ritual is observed. Tibetans will cite karma as an important element in attributing female gender and also to account for the difficulties of women's lives. There also exist sentiments and practices focused on the spiritual and mundane desirability for women to be reborn as men.[63]

In addition to the manifold pragmatic concerns (health, long life, fertility, wealth, power, etc.) that all ordinary pilgrims brought with them to the *néri*, they were also strongly motivated by the promise of a soteriological mobility that the local mountain cult did not offer. This promise offered a future status that held a particular appeal for women, as they were graphically reminded of the reality of being "low-born" (*kyemen*) during their ritual encounters with Pure Crystal Mountain. Finally, in a comparative context, one should note that both the exclusion applied and the promise offered to women at Tsari are not unique to Tibet. They are fundamentally the same as those found in other Asian Buddhist mountain cults where traditions of local mountain worship have been converted in terms of the universal representations and rituals of introduced Tantric Buddhism, as happened, for example, in Japan.[64]

Although all women were denied annual ritual access to the upper mountain, they were free to participate in what was certainly the best known and perhaps the most prestigious ritual event to be staged around Pure Crystal Mountain, though their chance to do so only came once every twelve years: the long Tsari Rongkor Chenmo, or "great ravine circuit" procession. This ritual was famous throughout Tibet as a special opportunity to satisfy the common goals of most pilgrims—purification of defilement, harvest of empowerment, accumulation of merit, and attainment of mundane potential—but its high status was directly related to very much higher stakes, perhaps even the loss of life itself. I will now give a detailed narrative account and analysis of this major Tibetan ritual, which was the only pilgrimage at Tsari that any "body" without exception could perform if he or she so wished, or dared.

8

✦ ✦ ✦ ✦

Barbarian Tributes and Great Processions

> Every hardship and every pain increases the blessing of pilgrimage, and even death on pilgrimage is the best of all deaths.
>
> R. B. Ekvall and J. F. Downs, *Tibetan Pilgrimage*

Once every twelve years, at the beginning of each monkey year in the Tibetan calendar, large crowds of pilgrims assembled and camped at the base of Pure Crystal Mountain.[1] They gathered there in preparation for the long pilgrimage procession known as the Tsari Rongkor Chenmo, or "great ravine circuit of Tsari." When performed in full, this clockwise journey circumscribed the outer perimeter of the great, sublime landscape maṇḍala that radiated outward around Pure Crystal Mountain (see figure 8.1). The prominent reputation this event enjoyed throughout Tibet was based on the fact that it involved intense physical hardships, even at times actual mortal danger, due to the prevailing conditions along the route. The procession's great attraction came from beliefs that the place itself and the journey were powerful enough to effect strong personal transformations in the participants. It was believed to be a particularly efficacious means of cleansing the great defilement resulting from the killing of animals, acts of homicide, and even parricide. For some, the deaths they had caused could be dealt with here ritually by facing the prospect of death itself, while for most the possibility of death during the procession held the promise of rebirth in a Buddhist paradise. Yet, ironically, as I shall show, participation in the great ravine circuit could also entail the necessity of taking human life.

Unlike the four other pilgrimage circuits performed around the mountain, which had certain restrictions of access placed on them, the great ravine circuit was open to men and women from any social or religious ranking, to both Buddhists and Bönpo, and to members of other ethnic groups. They came from the high Himalayas and all parts of Tibet to participate in the procession: from Tsang and Ladakh far to the west, from Ü and Lhasa in the center, from Lhokha, Bhutan, and Monyül to the southwest, from Kham as far as Dartsemdo to the east, from Amdo and the high Changtang plateau to the north, and from the districts in the immediate vicinity of Tsari itself, such as Dakpo, Kongpo, and Powo. Their total number usually reached or exceeded twenty thousand persons.[2] The composition of the procession itself reflected much of the complex cultural, ethnic and political map of the Tibetan-speaking world.

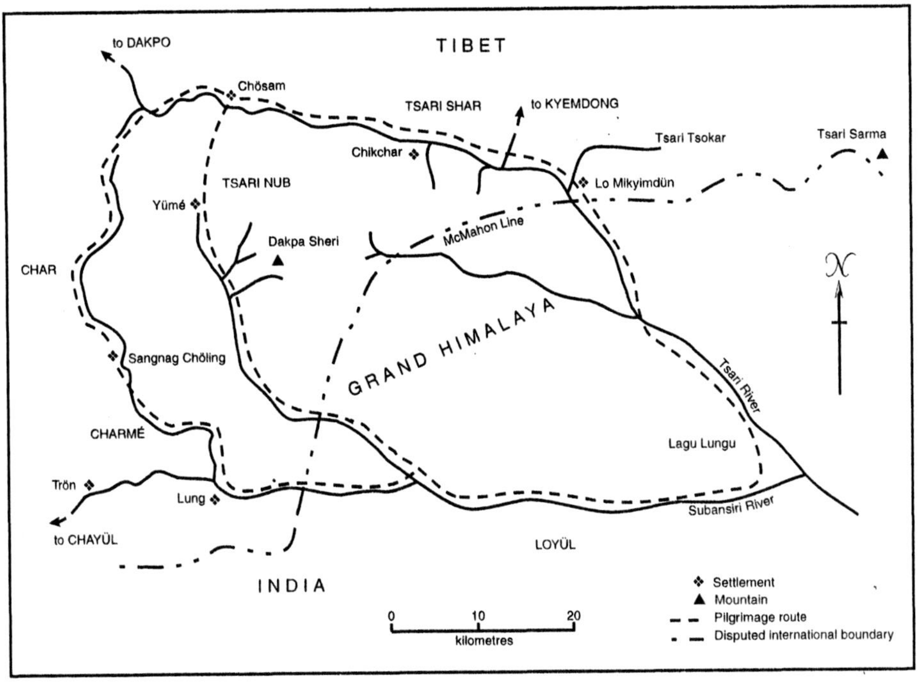

Figure 8.1. Rongkor Chenmo procession route.

Ever since its beginnings in the early eighteenth century, the Tsari Rongkor Chenmo procession and its associated rites enjoyed the direct patronage and logistical support of the Central Tibetan government and aristocracy. It was clearly always a ritual of regional religiopolitical import, and thus suffered its demise along with the collapse of the Lhasa regime in the late 1950s. Therefore, unlike other Tibetan pilgrimages that have recently enjoyed a popular revival at Tsari and elsewhere throughout Tibet, Rongkor Chenmo will most probably never take place again, especially given the context of the ongoing Sino-Indian disputes over the de facto international border in the area.

Because the Rongkor Chenmo procession and its associated ceremonies was one of the largest traditional Tibetan pilgrimages, and one directly orchestrated by the Lhasa state, it warrants comprehensive treatment. In this chapter I give a description of the ritual based on Tibetan eye-witness accounts of the events at Tsari in the monkey years 1944 and 1956, with reference to the small body of written records concerning the tradition. I will also consider the soteriological and social dimensions of participation in the procession from the pilgrims' point of view. In chapter 9, I provide a detailed analysis of the cultural and political significance of these rituals for Tibetan society in the middle of this century.

Preliminary Preparations

Considerable resources and organization were required to stage such a large-scale event as the great ravine circuit in so remote a location as southern Tsari. With the coming of the sheep year preceding the monkey year, certain preparations were begun well in advance. First, two government officials had to be appointed in Lhasa to organize the proceedings. Their most important task was the negotiation and payment of the Lodzong, or "barbarian tribute," that immediately preceded the actual procession, and the collection and transportation to Tsari of the materials and personnel required for this procedure. The barbarian tribute was a kind of safe passage fee that had to be given to the neighboring Tibeto-Burman-speaking Himalayan populations whom the Tibetans referred to as the Lopa, a name with strongly pejorative overtones meaning "barbarian" or "savage" (from *lalo*). In general the term *lopa* is also a blanket Tibetan designation for many different groups of far eastern Himalayan peoples. They are usually described as "tribes" in the anthropological literature, with the main populations who inhabit the upper Subansiri River basin immediately south of Tsari being identified as groups of "Dafla" and "Hill Miri," such as the Nishi (or Nisü), Sulung, Boru (or Bori), Nga (or Na), Tagin, and Gallong, among others.[3] Local Tibetans had their own specific classification of these tribes (which I will introduce hereafter). Since much of the procession's route passed through territory that was either used or occupied by various of these hill peoples, the Tibetan organizers of the procession were obliged to pay them tribute before the pilgrimage could take place. In return, tribespeople swore an oath of nonmolestation of the pilgrims.[4] The ceremonial transaction of these affairs constituted the Lodzong. The officials also had to arrange for armed troops from surrounding districts to be dispatched to Tsari. These soldiers, together with some local militiamen, were used to guard against attacks on pilgrims by hostile tribals that could take place along the route. The importation of extra food supplies into the Tsari district also had to be coordinated. Finally, the government officials had to travel to Tsari and accompany the pilgrimage for its entire duration.

Of the two government officers regularly selected in Lhasa, one was classified as a "monk official" (*tsedrung*) and the other as a "lay official" (*drungkor*). Like most such officials in the Tibetan government, those appointed to supervise the Tsari Rongkor Chenmo were from aristocratic backgrounds and generally held middle to higher rankings in the state bureaucracy.[5] Prior to the pilgrimage, certain goods and produce were collected from throughout administrative districts of Central Tibet as a form of tax to support the event. This collection was done mainly by the government officials and partly by Tsariwa who made wide-ranging, government-sanctioned begging tours and trading trips during the winter off season when they were released from pastoralism and work on the annual pilgrimages around the mountain. The senior male taxpayers (*trelpé apha*) from communities living around the mountain also held some responsibility for the gathering of this tax in the districts surrounding Tsari. The collections had to be completed about half a year before the rituals commenced. Many of these materials were accumulated prior to each monkey year at local monasteries and the nearby government administrative centers (Dzong), such as Kurab Namgyel Dzong to the north in Dakpo, which was partially responsible for Tsari district.

From about the tenth Tibetan month (approximately November–December) of the sheep year onward, over one hundred yakloads of materials for the barbarian tribute were transported far to the south to a place called Tsari Maṇḍala Plain (Tsari

Kyingkortang), the major staging point for the procession. Maṇḍala Plain was located in a ravine almost at the mutually acknowledged border between the Tibetan administered (i.e., tax-paying) area and the tribal lands to the south of Tsari. To reach this place, pilgrims and administrators had first to cross one of the high passes that connected Tsari with surrounding districts and descend into the Tsari River valley. By traveling down the valley past Chikchar village, the main staging point for all the higher altitude pilgrimage circuits, they effectively began their long circumambulation around the base of Pure Crystal Mountain. This passage was the beginning of a huge circle formed by their ritual journey, which would be closed on the successful completion of their great ravine circuit.

Following the valley below Chikchar, the pilgrims came to a river confluence marked by a single household and a pilgrims' resthouse. The place was fittingly named Phödzo Sumdo, or "Triple Confluence [Where] Tibet Ends," as it was here that another world indeed began for the travelers. At this point the Tsari River drops suddenly in a tumult of rapids for a thousand meters through a steep, narrow gorge. Leaving behind the flat alpine meadows and the coniferous forests of Chikchar, more broadleaved trees and an ever-increasing variety of plants cover the steep valley walls in a dense scrub. Descending the narrow paths to Maṇḍala Plain and further to the great ravine circuit below, another ecological zone was entered, for most pilgrims the beginning of a terra incognita. Here was the threshold of the *rong*, or "ravine," country, those lands below the high plateau that lay at the southern extremity of the Tibetan world-space. Although few ventured there, up on the arid, cool, and treeless highlands one heard or read about this other world; of its wet, warm and verdant jungles with exotic species such as monkeys, tigers, and bamboo; and of its human inhabitants, a barbarian race naked, lacking the civilization of Buddhist culture, and dangerous with their poison-tipped arrows.

Maṇḍala Plain lay adjacent to the tribal territory the Tibetans referred to as Loyül, or "Lopa country." The plain itself was located not far below the frontier village of Lo Mikyimdün, or "Seven Households of Lo," a name explained by local Tibetans as referring to a story about the original seven ethnic Tibetan families who founded this village in tribal territory long ago. The settlement contained some eighty households scattered on both sides of the river, interspersed by patches of cultivation and vegetation. Since this village was at a lower altitude, (3,000 m) it rarely snowed and was much warmer there than in the upper Tsari valley. The villagers could grow tobacco, potatoes, and wheat here, crops not seen up on the plateau. Due to the high rainfall they could not employ traditional architecture, and they had to build their houses with pitched, wooden-shingled roofs. Even the local Tibetans were different, as a result of their environment and their occasional intermarriage with their tribal neighbors, some of whom also lived in the village. Unlike most pilgrim visitors, the local people wore lighter and shorter tunics and habitually carried swords; some went barefoot or smoked pipes; and many had a knowledge of the tribal languages used by their southern neighbors.

The great ravine circuit was usually scheduled to commence around the time of the full moon in the first Tibetan month (approximately February–March) on a date considered astrologically auspicious. However, all those participating in it, pilgrims, officials, and troops alike, had to begin their journeys to Maṇḍala Plain many weeks or even months in advance of this date. Long travel times were not unusual in Tibet, but it was winter, and the Tsari valley could only be entered by a number of high passes that when snow-bound or beset by bad weather could cause delays. From the time the first pilgrims arrived, it took up to four or five weeks for them all to assemble at Maṇḍala Plain.

To assist in the staging of such a large ritual, various other civil and religious personnel began to converge on this remote spot: a high Drukpa lama and some monks from Sangnag Chöling monastery in Char; monks from the Drigungpa retreat center at Yümé; the Drukpa religious administrator (*Dordzin*) from Chikchar; officials from the local Dzong; and the senior taxpayers or headmen from the villages of Tsari. Local people from the upper and lower Tsari valley had to contribute their labor at different times during the proceedings. This work was counted as a tax obligation, which most villagers usually had to provide annually to the government in the form of corvée labor (*ula*). In addition, up to two hundred armed troops were assembled.[6] About twenty regular soldiers accompanied the government officials from Lhasa, and between fifty and one hundred troops were sent by the Dzong from local militia in surrounding districts, particularly from Chayül, Dakpo, Kongpo, and Powo. Some Tsariwa were also temporarily drafted to make up the troop complement. In payment they received food rations and a blanket but no wages in cash. They were required to use their own Tibetan-style matchlock firearms, if they possessed any. Tibetanized tribal men where recruited for specialist duties during each great ravine circuit. The Tibetans classified them as "forest Lopas" (Lonag) whom they called the Charlo, as they lived in forest on Tibetan territory in parts of Charmé south of Sangnag Chöling. They could speak Tibetan and wore Tibetan-style woolen robes but retained many of their tribal accoutrements and hunting equipment. Other similar men were recruited from the Trön and Lung areas along the Loro River close to the frontier. The forest Lopa recruits were known to the local Tibetan communities where they lived, thus trusted. These tribal men were used as guides and trailblazers in the dense jungle through which much of the great ravine circuit passed; they also served as translators if other tribals were encountered along the route. The government officials gave them hatchets and thick yak-hair ropes for clearing trails and preparing river crossings, and they kept these as payment at the finish of the pilgrimage.

The Tsariwa say that long ago, Gesar, Lord of Ling, the heroic king of the great Tibetan epic, pitched his camp here on Maṇḍala Plain when he visited Tsari in order to suppress the "Evil One of the South," Shingtri Gyelpo, and the wicked "Minister of Mon," Kulha Thogyel.[7] This local story prefigures well the pitching of the government camp and the enactment of the barbarian tribute that had to take place here before each great ravine circuit could start. As groups of organizers and pilgrims began to arrive, grand white tents adorned with Buddhist symbolic designs belonging to the government and local monasteries were erected on the Maṇḍala Plain to accommodate the officials, lamas, and monks, and for the performance of Buddhist rituals. Other well-appointed, private cloth tents were erected by the servants of those aristocrats who had come to perform the great ravine circuit. Then there were many more humble tents and small makeshift shelters and encampments established by pilgrims of every description. The range of these different assembled camp dwellings itself formed a visible index of the relative social rank and power of the would-be participants.

Both the lay and monk officials arrived from Lhasa, the latter carrying a set of the incumbent Dalai Lama's ceremonial robes on his back. These had to be carried, as no one except a Dalai Lama could wear them, and they were destined to journey around the entire great ravine circuit in this manner. The presence of the robes on the pilgrimage was a form of substitution for the Dalai Lama's personal presence during the ritual. Because of their symbolic value, much of the welcoming etiquette and ceremonial ritual used for the personal arrival of a Dalai Lama was prepared and then accorded to the robes that the monk official brought. After the government party from Lhasa had arrived and established itself, various preparations began around the camp for the transaction of the barbarian tribute and the several religious protective rituals that attended it.

The Barbarian Tribute

The exact timing of the Lodzong, or barbarian tribute, was difficult to figure, as it depended on when the tribes who were to participate would come up the ravines and out of the forests to the south. Village workers from the main government tax households (*trekang*) of Lo Mikyimdün village attended to preparations. They erected the large government tents on the center of the plain. The many loads of goods that were to be used in the negotiations had to be unpacked and sorted. Some workers cut lengths of timber for use in the tribute ceremony, and members of each *trekang* had to build bamboo shelters for the leading members of the various tribes to use during their stay. Meanwhile, the translators, several Tibetans from Lo Mikyimdün village who spoke tribal dialects, were dispatched down the ravine into the thick forest. Here, they hoped, they would find the tribal parties gathering in anticipation of the tribute ceremony, and would invite them to leave the cover of the forest for a few days and negotiate a settlement out in the open on the Maṇḍala Plain. From a Tibetan point of view this emergence was essential, as the favored method of tribal attack was hidden ambush in dense forest, where pursuit and retaliation even with firearms was ineffective.

To the Tibetans the area to the south called Loyül was a vast tract of rugged, virtually unknown country. It was also an ethnic jigsaw puzzle of peoples who spoke different languages and had different customs and appearances. The Tibetans fought at times with some groups of these peoples and traded with others. When it came down to the question of which tribe would attack pilgrims, and which tribe would accept the tribute and take an oath of nonmolestation, it was often hard for the Tibetans to know exactly who they were dealing with for any one Lodzong. They identified several different tribes who came to participate in the negotiations on the basis of the altitude at which they were known or thought to live, and by their other attributes. Although they did not always know exactly how many regional or subregional groupings were involved, the two main and two subsidiary groups who were entitled to receive the barbarian tribute in the 1940s and 1950s were classified as follows:

1. Chebu Lopa, or "naked Lopa" tribes, who were specifically called Tinglo, or "Lopas [from the Valley] Floors;" and sometimes Mérongwa or "Ones from the Lower Ravines" (see figure 8.2).[8]
2. Lonag, or "forest Lopa" groups, who were called Khalo, or "Lopa facing [Tibet]," living higher up in the forests closer to the Tibetan border villages (see figure 8.3).[9]
3. Lungdu Lopa and Trön Lopa, who were Tibetanized groups living in Charmé near the border, a few of whom the Tibetans employed as translators with the Tinglo (see figures 8.3 and 8.4).
4. Mikyimdün Lopa, who were also Tibetanized, living south of, and occasionally in, Lo Mikyimdün village (see figure 8.5).

As the latter two Tibetanized groups had come under much stronger Tibetan influence by the mid–twentieth century, their part in the tribute was not so problematic. If satisfied with the payment, they generally helped the procession by preparing bridges, wooden ladders, and fords at difficult parts of the route. The other two groups, in particular the Tinglo, were regarded as more hostile and unpredictable and as perpetrators of violence against pilgrims, so their role in the whole

Figure 8.2. Subansiri tribal peoples at Charmé identified as Tinglo or Mérongwa Lopa.

Figure 8.3. Tibetanized tribesman at Charmé identified as Khalo.

process was more critical. Since these peoples generally lived lower in the valleys, hence further away from Tsari, the Tibetans regarded their claims to Lodzong entitlement as less legitimate.

With representatives of the Tibetanized groups already present, the government translators had to find, make contact with, and lead the Tinglo and Lonag groups up and out of the forested ravines onto the negotiating area. Three or four different chiefs came with large parties of hundreds of warriors. Whole families also accompanied these armed men. When the tribal groups finally left the forest and entered the plain, the Tibetans were confronted by the warriors they considered to be their enemies. For the Tibetans, especially the unseasoned pilgrims and officials, these people presented a striking contrast to themselves. Many men and women were almost naked, with only small coverings over their genitals. Their bodies looked strong and muscular and were adorned with finely crafted cane accoutrements and heavy metal jewelry. In their hands they carried iron-tipped spears, bamboo bows, and iron-tipped arrows dipped in lethal poisons made from herbs such as aconite

Figure 8.4. Tribal priest at Charmé identified as Charlo.

(*tsendug*).[10] Others of rank and wealth were draped with wool blankets and carried Tibetan-style metal swords and knives. Some wore Tibetan-style tunics. Those not wearing woven cane helmets or feather headdresses had their long hair fastened into a ball at the front of their heads with large bamboo pins.[11] Many were smoking continuously from pipes. At some points in the proceedings they made a mock show of force, brandishing their weapons, dancing together, and screaming out battle cries. The onlookers knew that these people would be the ones who might murder them; steal and extort from them, or capture and enslave them down in the ravines if the tribute and oath-swearing were not completed to their satisfaction.

The government officials ordered that each be given a *dre* measure (about 1.5 kg) of parched barley flour, which took the workers many hours to distribute. At night, the Tibetans could see the warriors dancing around their campfires to the music of simple instruments. In the morning the tribute was transacted. The two government officials were seated on wooden chairs in the center of the plain. The senior representatives of the government tax households were arranged behind them, standing. The tribal chiefs and groups of their warriors were scattered over the plain directly in front of them. For the purposes of the Lodzong, the taxpayers were termed *lodag*, or "Lopa owners," in the proceedings. This meant that the corporate tax households

Figure 8.5. Tibetanized tribesman at Tsari identified as Mikyimdün Lopa.

(*trekang*) or community groups they represented each constituted separate tax sources for the various tribal leaders and groups. Thus, one *trekang* might be charged with paying the tribute tax for a particular group of tribal people whom they "owned" as a tax responsibility, although only a small portion of the goods they offered came from the collections by the Tsariwa. Most of the goods used came from the collections by the Lhasa administration, some were individual donations by wealthy nobles, and on occasion the officials who negotiated had to give some items of their own property that they held in reserve, if the bargaining appeared to be on the point of collapsing. During 1956, to ensure a good settlement, extra donations were solicited from the waiting pilgrims as well.

With the help of the interpreters the first payment of the tribute was made to the tribal headmen or chiefs. Although the tribal peoples had no written languages, through the use of notched tally-sticks recording past tributes they knew almost exactly what had been given them previously, both in quantity and quality, and they insisted that this amount was therefore the minimum they should receive in payment.[12] Older men who had been at previous Lodzong also came to give oral advice on what to accept. The Tibetan officials for their part had lists of previous tribute payments, and the matching of tribal and Tibetan expectations and records formed the bulk of the negotiations. These often became tense, with the translators moving between the two parties having to convey messages of dissatisfaction in both directions as diplomatically as possible. To avoid trouble on the coming great ravine circuit, the Tibetans ultimately had little choice but to pay what was demanded. Each chief was given a Tibetan woolen blanket, a knife or sword, a hatchet, and a yak. Then, general payment of a wide range of articles was distributed among all those attending. This payment mainly consisted of many small bags of salt, sugar, and parched barley flour;[13] large quantities of coloured beads and shells for women's jewelry;[14] cotton and woolen cloth; yak tails (only white ones); long and short Tibetan swords; hatchets, metal bowls, and the bells used on pack animals; Tibetan Buddhist ritual instruments, including bronze bells, large and small bronze or bell-metal cymbals,[15] and perhaps a few domestic animals.

After the formal payment of goods was completed, preparations for the oath-swearing ceremony began. The Tibetan government workers cooked large copper pots full of a meat and barley dumpling stew, which they offered to the gathered tribesmen. A ritual gate was built, with elements of both Tibetan and tribal design included, which the warriors had to pass through as they took the oath. Tibetan workers cut a large tree into three sections; two of these were erected in the ground, and the third was lashed across the top. On top of the crossbar the Tibetan officials and monks fixed a statue of Chana Dorje, a Tantric deity whose appearance is wrathful and who defends the Buddhist doctrine. They also placed a Buddhist religious text next to it.[16] The Tibetans considered that the tribesmen would not understand the religious meaning of these items, and they placed them there mainly in order to frighten them into obeying the oath. Through the translators the warriors were told that once they had passed under the deity on the gate they would have extremely bad fortune in the future if they broke their oath, due to the wrath of the god.

In turn, the tribesmen consulted with their priest (see figure 8.4) and arranged various items on the gate that were of ritual significance to them. The Tibetan government had provided several yaks, which the tribesmen were to sacrifice during the oath-swearing ceremony. These were firmly tied to the sideposts of the gate. It was actually these animals that the tribesmen referred to as the tribute in their own languages. The yaks were swiftly sacrificed with the stroke of a long sword and the invocation of the tribal priest. As soon as this was done, many warriors moved onto the scene, and events began to unfold rapidly. Chunks of meat from the freshly slaughtered animals were attached to one sidepost, and a piece of Tibetan wool, a ball of barley-flour dough, and a length of white cloth were attached to the other sidepost. To the horrified Tibetan onlookers, it seemed that the sacrificial animals were still alive as the crowd of sword-wielding tribesmen quickly drained their blood and stripped the flesh and entrails from their carcasses.[17] The senior taxpayers attended the event and organized for blood from the severed throat of one of the sacrificed yaks to be collected in a large copper pot they supplied. A skein of wool was dipped into it and soaked. Then the chiefs and all their warriors had to pass through the gate, cut off a piece of the raw yak flesh, and eat it. As they passed through, the Lhasa officials instructed them not to kill or rob pilgrims during the coming great ravine circuit, and each had to swear to it in turn. On the far side of the gate the senior taxpayers took pieces of the bloodsoaked wool, which they called nose-wool, and smeared blood onto the noses of the warriors with it. This marked them as being oathbound.[18] Some of the warriors were reluctant to participate in this ritual, and the Tibetanized tribesmen from Lo Mikyimdün and Trön village had to help ensure that they passed under the gate. The Tibetans considered this passage the most important component of the ritual for ensuring nonmolestation of pilgrims by the tribesmen during the pilgrimage procession. They held that the giving of goods in tribute was no guarantee of their cooperation, and the sacrificial gate and its attendant oath-swearing ceremonies had the most influence over them, because these rituals were partly derived from tribal customs.

In addition to the oath-swearing, several Tibetan Buddhist rituals intended to effect a safe passage of the great ravine circuit were performed by Drukpa and Drigungpa monks from Tsari. The monks had their own tent in which they chanted numerous prayers for protection. A ritual dance (*cham*) to propitiate and honor the dark, lion-headed god Kunga Shonu, who was the Tsari "field-protector" (*shing-kyong*), or main protective deity who presided over the region, was performed by the monks from Sangnag Chöling.[19] Part of the significance of this ritual was that the southern tribal peoples were popularly believed to be wrathful human embodiments of the protective deity's retinue and thus susceptible to his will. As these Tibetan Buddhist rites progressed, the tribesmen finished eating and drinking the last flesh and blood of their sacrificial yaks and began to carry off their latest tribute goods back down into the ravines. Now that the Lodzong and the protective rites were drawing to a close, the organization of the enormous procession could be accomplished, and the pilgrims would finally depart.

The Great Procession

Over about a six-week period before the commencement of the great ravine circuit, pilgrims continued to arrive at Tsari in large numbers. Those with time to spare before the procession departed would visit and worship at local power places along the course of the Tsari valley on their way down to Maṇḍala Plain, such as the Sexed Rocks, known for their bestowal of powers and fertility, and Lugyel Wangdrak ("Mighty Serpent-deity King Rock"), believed to cure diseases of the skin, even leprosy. At Chösam, the first village of Tsari district the pilgrims arrived at, the local shrine-keepers would bring out various sacred objects stored there in the monkey year. These relics included such items as the walking sticks of heroic lamas said to have opened the mountain, which bore their handprints; stones with their footprints on them; and a miraculous female deer's antler (see hereafter). To begin their great ravine circuit here, pilgrims made offerings of cash and kind in return for being empowered through having such relics contact their bodies. This procedure was regarded as a preliminary bodily purification for the pilgrimage, and it was accompanied by the confession of one's bad deeds. Further downstream, at the Dorje Pagmo temple in Chikchar, the wealthier pilgrims sponsored special offering rituals dedicated to the meditation deities, sky-goers, and protective gods, and also made donations to the community of meditators in that place. Some early arrivals were able to observe the completion of the Rephu yoga examinations. When they arrived at Maṇḍala Plain, they found a crowded and ever-growing encampment, packed with waiting pilgrims.

The newness of the surroundings, the large number of different peoples, and the mounting expectations about the coming procession gave the place a charged atmosphere. Groups of friends, relatives, and "fellow countrymen" (*phayül chikpa*) were meeting up in the crowded camp and organizing their march in the procession together. Some spent their waiting days engaged in religious practices—dedicating themselves to the performance of prostrations, the recitation of prayers, and the making of offerings—to capitalize on the powerful environment of Pure Crystal Mountain and spiritually prepare themselves for the coming pilgrimage. Others passed their time in more worldly activities such as dice games and gossip, cleaning their rifles, and preparing their equipment and provisions. As the days passed the campsite became overcrowded and befouled, and in the cool of the mornings one could not even see the sky due to the thick blanket of campfire smoke that hung over the area.

As the starting date for the pilgrimage drew near, two logistical problems increasingly occupied both officials and pilgrims: food supplies and the formation of a ranked and orderly procession. These were vitally important matters because of the duration and nature of the journey. Traveling fast under ideal conditions, the whole route of the great ravine circuit could be covered in about ten days. Each monkey year the bulk of the pilgrims took a minimum of fifteen days to cover the entire distance. The slowest among them required three or four weeks to complete it. Since most of the route passed through areas that were unpopulated or only sparsely inhabited by tribal peoples who remained for the most part unseen and uncooperative, pilgrims had to carry all their own food, as there was no chance of being resupplied en route.

During the wait at Maṇḍala Plain, even the best-organized pilgrims continued to use up the rations of food they had purchased on the trip south. Due to the local ban on cultivation, butchering, and hunting around Pure Crystal Mountain, the district was already food-deficient, and local supplies from the upper valley and Lo Mikyimdün village could not be relied on. With such large numbers of pilgrims, extra provision had to be made for food supplies. Government officials organized the transport of several thousand loads of parched barley flour to Maṇḍala Plain from the estates in neighboring districts, especially from Dakpo to the north, and arranged for its distribution in rations of several *dre* per pilgrim.

Food could also be purchased, but because of its scarcity and its necessity in the weeks to come, it became the object of speculation. Families of Tibetanized Charlo people from the southwest came to Maṇḍala Plain each monkey year specifically to trade and sell both food and their local wares, such as bamboo items, to pilgrims. The Mikyimdün Lopa also made a business out of food sales, as did a few Tibetan traders who carted supplies there from the highlands. The prices were inflated many times above the normal rates.[20] The tribal traders would wait until the first batches of pilgrims began to depart before they sold their food supplies. As the ordered departure was spread over five or six days, those pilgrims leaving last would continue to use up precious supplies at camp and then be forced to pay the trader's extortionate prices.

The Lhasa government and local officials had the task of forming the thousands of pilgrims into a series of large, single-file lines called *sho*, or "columns." One *sho* was dispatched into the ravine at the beginning of each day, so as to leave a sufficient gap between them. This wait was necessary because most of the trails, bridges, and galleries forming the route were narrow and, in many places, precipitous, allowing only one pilgrim to proceed at a time. When the way became blocked, as it invariably did, by one type of mishap or other, a great ravine circuit traffic jam, referred to as *shokag*, a "jammed column," would result due to the difficulty of passing in many places. The initial spacing between the *sho* was supposed to allow time for such holdups to be cleared so that the total number of pilgrims following would not also be seriously delayed, although the columns often connected after a time. Such arrangements were justified in purely practical terms.

Each *sho* had a leader, an identity, an internal structure, and a ranking in the order of the whole procession. The leaders were called *tongpön*, or "master of a thousand," although the *sho* often contained many more than that number of pilgrims. For instance, the *sho* of pilgrims from Central Tibet in 1956 had about four thousand in it. The four main *tongpön* were identified as Depa Shung, Drukpa Sang, Drigungpa, and Lonag. The first was a Tibetan government (Depa Shung) official who, in effect, represented Central Tibetan state interests. The second two represented the two Kagyüpa subsects and their aristocratic patrons, who together controlled and maintained the estate lands, monasteries, shrines, and sites of Tsari and some of its neighboring districts. The Lonag, or "forest Lopa," representative was a member of that Tibetanized tribal community in Charmé. In 1956 there was also the so-called Yabshi *sho*, formed by and named after the Yabshi Shika in Chayül well to the west of Tsari, being the estate (*shika*) held by the Fourteenth Dalai Lama's natal family after they were ennobled following his recognition. In addition, the large parties of Khampa pilgrims from eastern Tibet grouped together and selected independent leaders of their own, so there were a Trehor Khampa *sho*, a Nyarong Khampa *sho*, and so on, reflecting the different districts the pilgrims originated from.

The largest *sho* were named after their regions and leader so that, for example, the column formed behind the Lhasa official was called the Depa Shung *sho*. Pilgrims joined the *sho* that they felt best represented them and their interests and in which they might best find support on the very difficult pilgrimage ahead. They chose on the basis of natal and residence place, the Tibetan sect (or monastery and lama) with which they had a connection, and the presence in the *sho* of other members of their clan, family, and friendship groups. Language was also an important factor, as many of the pilgrims from far-flung locations could barely understand the very different Tibetan dialects spoken by their fellow-travelers. For most pilgrims all these categories were, in any case, compounded on the basis of their home place, and the general composition of the *sho* reflected regional or provincial zones of Tibet. Within each *sho* the same pattern applied, and many pilgrims organized themselves into ever smaller subunits based mainly on their country, province, locale, village, and household. Based on the stories of past tribal attacks, some pilgrims also chose purely on the basis of "firepower," the total number of guns carried by others in *sho*, so as to be well defended. This firepower was also a factor in the internal arrangement of the various *sho*, as leaders identified those with firearms and asked them to travel spaced out at regular intervals along their columns.

The ranking of *sho* in the processional order was determined in several ways. The first *sho* was headed by local peoples from around the mountain, since they knew the route, as well as those from Char, Monyül, and Bhutan. These peoples were held to be most familiar with and best adapted to the conditions of great ravine circuit travel, as these were most like the places where they lived along the southern Himalayan borderlands. They would forge and clear a trail for the other highland pilgrims to follow. The ranking of the other *sho* was determined by the leaders rolling dice; highest scoring went first, and so on.[21] To be near the front of the procession meant finishing fast, thus avoiding the risk of being delayed and running out of food and having to carry extra supplies to cover this possibility. It also meant that if pilgrims were stranded by problems, they had more chance of getting assistance from the other *sho* and not being abandoned in their wake. In the past, the monk official bearing the Dalai Lama's robes went up the front of the procession, but due to the threat of tribal attacks the procession was led by the lay official in 1944, and the local governor (*dzongpön*) of Chayül in 1956. A large party of armed troops also went in the forward *sho* to guard against tribal attacks, while the remainder accompanied the subsequent *sho* spaced out at intervals between groups of unarmed pilgrims.

With the ranking of the *sho* completed, all the preparations culminated in the daily dispatch of the great columns in procession down into the ravines of Tsari. For most of the next two weeks the pilgrims would walk narrow trails under cover of dense subtropical forest and through undergrowth, climb the cliff-sides of ravines, cross slippery tree trunk bridges over rushing torrents, and continue to ascend and descend the steep ridges that came in punishing succession. The hot, humid, still air and the frequent rains down in the *rong* were a very oppressive traveling climate for the highlanders, who had just descended from midwinter at home. For the most part, personal comfort and hygiene were at a minimum during the journey. The thick woolen Tibetan clothing the pilgrims wore not only was too hot but also became waterlogged and began to rot in the warm weather. Some pilgrims suffered cuts, sprains, and even broken bones in mishaps on the most difficult and dangerous sections of the route. Wounds and sores quickly became infected in such conditions, and many suffered gastrointestinal problems, as in most places where they spent the night it was not possible to make fires for boiling water or cooking food. Everyone got uncomfortable bites from insects and leeches. Some pilgrims carried supplies of traditional medicines to help treat all these problems en route.

Many of the pilgrims were used to traveling long distances and camping out as a fact of life up on the high plateau, but these conditions were different and much harder. None of the familiar beasts of burden could be used. There were no open campsites and no place or means to make fires easily or restock any sort of supplies. Almost everybody had to carry all the requisites for life on their own backs. Those who had raincoats and blankets slept under them; others erected makeshift shelters if they could; and many just slept on the trail where their column halted for the night. Many pilgrims remember having to tie themselves with ropes and sashes to trees and bamboos on steep sections at night, so as not to roll off the path during their sleep. Their supplies consisted of the dried, portable foods used by most Tibetan travelers: parched barley flour and popped whole roasted barley grain, strips of dried meat, butter and dried cheese, salt, brick tea, and perhaps a little dried fruit. Not only were these light but they required little or no cooking before consumption. Although they were heavily loaded, to carry enough to eat well for two weeks was virtually impossible, and food had to be strictly rationed. A few, mainly wealthy aristocrats, did not have to travel this way. They either hired porters before setting out or brought their retinue of personal servants along. A few invoked their entitlement as government representatives to exact corvée labor in the form of personal transport from the local people of Tsari, whom they recruited as porters for the procession.[22] Thus they had small tents and bedding to set up where possible, could eat and drink well, and could carry other items for personal use and comfort. The egalitarian social ethic that pilgrimages, in theory, according to many Tibetans, were supposed to foster was certainly not evident in practice to those of humble means who observed the relative comfort of aristocratic travel on the procession.

While the entire circumambulation of the mountain via the ravines covered over 150 kilometers, the distance from Maṇḍala Plain to sites such as Yümé and Chösam, where the event ended and the pilgrims separated, was about a hundred kilometres. The actual route between these points was not marked by inhabited sites that appear on any Tibetan or Western maps (see figure 8.1). All the pilgrims knew was that they were to the south of Pure Crystal Mountain most of the time. Otherwise the geography had no points of reference for them except the unseen presence of the mountain itself always to their right and the site that marked the end point of the procession. Only the Tsariwa who regularly performed the great ravine circuit and the local tribal people had names for certain landscape features and campsites along the route. Only two sites stand out in the memories of pilgrims. The first, encountered some days into the procession, was the demanding "Nine Hills and Nine Valleys" (Lagu Lungu) section, which crossed over a series of ridges (see figure 8.6). It was here that hostile tribesmen commonly attacked the procession. Descending from this area, pilgrims eventually passed the place known locally as Takshing, which was the only sacred site of any note. It was regarded by the Tsariwa as the Tantric charnel ground named Ngampa Tratrok ("Awe-inspiring Screams"), where certain Tibetan Drukpa lamas had meditated in the past. Various charnel grounds are represented as surrounding the perimeter of the Khorlo Dompa maṇḍala, and the position of this site on the great ravine circuit accorded with Tibetan perceptions of Pure Crystal Mountain's sublime maṇḍala geography. Like many of the charnel grounds described in the Tantric Buddhist ritual texts, Takshing was marked by a huge tree in which the chief Tsari field-protector was said to dwell. In addition, the self-manifested forms of animals that frequent the charnel grounds, such as jackals and vultures, could be seen on the rocks there.

Violence and Death in the Ravines

As pilgrims walked this long route, they often held onto the backpacks or robes of their friends or kinsmen in front of them so as not to lose their position in the *sho* and thus become separated from their traveling companions. If one got left behind, it might take days to find and regain one's position in the column because of the

Figure 8.6. Detail from Tibetan painted map showing Rongkor Chenmo procession route with pilgrim's supply tent and tribal dwellings. (Copyright British Museum.)

difficulty of passing in many places. When the trail became seriously blocked in critical spots, forward progress was only in the order of a few hundred meters per day. In these conditions tempers naturally became frayed, and when there were bad blockages of the route, minor arguments and fights could break out. On the precipitous stages the advance guides had fixed ropes and made ladders of notched tree trunks to help climb cliffs and negotiate narrow trails. Some tribal people built log and cane bridges over the many rushing torrents that needed to be crossed. At certain of these the builders, who were armed, would wait and demand a toll from all pilgrims who passed the conduit, with the exception of the *tongpön*, who were accompanied by parties of armed troops. At these spots there was no alternative route possible, and with hundreds of pilgrims building up in the moving *sho* behind, there was no choice but to pay what the tribespeople asked. But not everyone yielded meekly in accord with the nonviolent spirit of Buddhism. In 1944 disputes had already erupted prior to the procession's departure between heavily armed Khampa pilgrims and some tribal warriors at Maṇḍala Plain. These men challenged the warriors at one of their toll stations in the ravines by refusing to pay, and a bloody fight broke out with swords, matchlocks, and bows, resulting in numerous deaths on both sides.

The worst type of encounter with the tribespeople was a full-scale attack in which pilgrims and officials alike might be murdered by poison-tipped arrows or knocked off the steep trails by boulders and stone that were rolled down via shots from above. The tribals preferred a remote ambush-style of attack to direct encounters, using the dense forest cover for protection from Tibetan gunfire and pursuit. The pilgrims and even the armed militiamen themselves greatly feared such attacks, as they knew they were powerless against the hidden bowmen with their lethal arrows, and there was literally nowhere to run to on the narrow trails. In 1944 the worst tribal attack ever remembered took place, an unprecedented massacre with scores of Tibetan deaths and casualties. According to the Tibetans, the tribal chiefs were highly dissatisfied with the tribute payment they received, and vowed to murder the Lhasa officials who had conducted the ceremony. But when this plot failed they turned on the procession at large, butchering whomever they could.

In some areas, such as the rugged Lagu Lungu, tribals intent on robbery would target pilgrims when the *sho* became spread out in the difficult terrain.[23] They stole jewelry, ritual objects, supplies, and even clothing; the Bhutanese raw silk shawls were a highly coveted item. During such thefts pilgrims often did not resist, for fear of being hacked to death with swords and hatchets or thrown off cliffs and into rivers. In addition to death and injury, pilgrims also faced the prospect of being captured as slaves or hostages for ransom, especially if they were young or female, as these were standard practices of tribal warfare to the south. (There were past cases reported when ransoms later secured the release of Tibetans captured on the procession.) To protect themselves, many pilgrims carried guns and swords. Since the turn of the century, automatic pistols had been a favored "companion" of some of the wealthy pilgrims and the administrators, as they were light and could be fired repeatedly, unlike the more cumbersome and slow Tibetan muzzle-loaders.[24] One informant made the great ravine circuit in 1956 as a young man with a group of his peers. None owned a firearm nor had much money, so the six pilgrims purchased a rifle jointly and carried it on their procession to shoot tribal warriors if need be. Pilgrim groups from Kham always attended the processions heavily armed.

Tribal attacks did pose mortal dangers. But for everybody, even the privileged, just walking in the procession involved general hardships of all types, which were unavoidable. In extreme cases, pilgrims who became seriously ill and injured would have to be left on the side of the trail and would die there, succumbing to infections or eventually starvation. A Tibetan lama described such conditions en route in 1812:

> On the journey I saw some people close to death due to illness, and also the corpses of some that had died. For them I provided assistance by way of blessings for a safe after-death journey and the transference of consciousness. I saw some who went on their way after abandoning their own sick friends, and the latter then wept since they were stuck and unable to carry on. I approached and consoled them saying, "The pilgrimage is not yet over. Rest for a few days and then continue when your strength

> is sufficient," and went on after leaving them medicine and provisions. . . . When I saw that everyone suffered hardships compassion arose in me.[25]

His account remains a valid description of the experiences of pilgrims a hundred and fifty years later, although by 1956, and in the wake of heavy pilgrim death tolls, better government logistics and support had lowered fatalities and casualties dramatically. Death by starvation did occur in the final stages of the pilgrimage. Food became critically short or even completely exhausted for many. It is commonly said that pilgrims with no food chewed the spent yak leather soles (*atre*) of their Tibetan-style boots in desperation. In fact, this practice served as the basis for an insult the local people used towards troublesome (and probably hungry) Khampa pilgrims from East Tibet, who often stole food when passing through the villages after the procession: *Khampa rongkor atre zakhen*, or "Khampa, eater of old boot soles on the Rongkor!"[26] The terrible starvation on past Rongkor processions even fueled rumors of pilgrims cannibalizing their dead companions en route.[27] Running out of food was worst for those who took the higher and harder route up to Yümé and north over the Ribpa La pass to Chösam to finish. Exhausted pilgrims, particularly the elderly, would arrive at the resthouses in these places, highly dehydrated and starved from pushing themselves to reach the end, and although they were given food, some were past the point of being able to ingest anything and died a day or two later. In 1956 the government and some wealthy families organized about thirty–forty horse and mule loads of food rations to be taken to Yümé to feed hungry pilgrims who finished there. Parched barley flour was distributed in measures of one–two *dre* at the Yümé bridge as pilgrims crossed it to enter the valley.

Harvesting Power and Merit

Unlike the upper circuits of the mountain, the great ravine circuit had no specific itinerary of power places and worship sites to visit or rituals and offerings to be performed. Tibetans commonly represent the mountain in one architectonic form as a great *chöten* or reliquary shrine, and like the *chöten* in any village, they simply circumambulated it on the great ravine circuit, nothing more, nothing less. The ritual requirement of the procession was that simple: a long and difficult walk in mountainous country. Of course, as with any circumambulation or similar ritual, it was believed that defilements would not be washed off nor merit effectively accumulated if pure motivation and behavior were not maintained during the practice. These must be based on faith in the Buddha's teachings and a vigilance of, and control over, negative propensities of body, speech, and mind. A Tibetan proverb neatly expresses this notion, but with a particular irony in the case of the conditions often prevailing on the great ravine circuit:

> Whenever you visit a power place
> Don't let your body and mouth
> Part company with your mind.
>
> And whenever you fight on the battlefield
> Don't let your sword and shield
> Part company with your hands.[28]

As with any circumambulation ritual, pilgrims could increase the merit generated by chanting prayers or ritual formulae to themselves as they moved along, which many did. But because of the conditions that prevailed, pilgrims could not perform a prostration circuit by measuring their body lengths along the path, as was often done on other popular mountain pilgrimages such as the well-known circuit of Tise or Mount Kailas in far western Tibet.

Besides the basic act of circumambulation and its possible amplifications, the other important ritual dimension of the procession for many pilgrims was the collection and consumption of empowered natural substances, a fundamental activity in Tibetan pilgrimage and ritual relationships with place. Because Tsari was considered such a tremendously powerful environment, all its natural substances were sources of empowerment. Although the purity and potency of substances at the site was generally ranked in relation to height and their proximity to Pure Crystal Mountain's peak, materials collected low down on the great ravine circuit were still highly prized by pilgrims. Their value was high because of the rarity and difficulty of their collection—only once every twelve years under very difficult conditions; and also by association with the ideology of the procession itself—that it was considered extremely efficacious for the cleansing of pollution (*drib*), for the karmic purification of bad deeds (*dik*), and for increasing the chances of higher rebirths. In fact, it was considered that even "[t]he animals who eat the herbs and drink the water [here] have their defilements cleansed and will obtain a human body in the future."[29] Such was the power of the environment through which one proceeded.

Materials collected included bamboo, soil (sometimes called *nésa*, "*né* earth"), stones (*nédo*, "*né* stones"), and water. Pilgrims would store small quantities of these substances in their garment pockets or fill containers with them as they traveled—or they might be consumed on the spot. Such was often the case with water, and pilgrims would drink small amounts from the many streams that flowed down from Pure Crystal Mountain's peak high above, washing down the empowerment of the sublime abode of the deities. Some referred to this stream water as "the water that liberates living beings [from cyclic existence]" (*chu drowa drölwa*). Bhutanese pilgrims found and collected certain leaves and nuts from various trees they knew of for making wads of pān or *doma*, a mild narcotic. For them this was an enjoyable way of being empowered by consuming the place. Many of the items and substances collected, like those obtained on the upper mountain routes, were carried back to pilgrims' home regions to be distributed to grateful friends and kinfolk and used as highly valued, portable sources of the mountain's power.

After passing Takshing charnel ground, the procession reached the site of the Doring resthouse, built on a spur above the Char River. This supply tent or hut (see fig. 8.6) was sponsored by the Doring estate and was the first contact the pilgrims had with their own civilization since departing on the procession. Here in 1956 the pilgrims were met by people of the Tibetanized Charlo tribe whom the Tibetan authorities had dispatched with many sacks of popped corn, which they distributed in one-*dre* rations to famished pilgrims. In this area the procession divided into two groups, in accord with onward travel plans after completion of the circuit. One group continued west, negotiating the lower gorges of the Chayül River (i.e., the upper Subansiri River), and then followed its northern tributary, the Char River up to Sangnag Chöling monastery to finish. As these peoples from western and southern parts of Tibet and from Bhutan had all initially transited here en route to Maṇḍala Plain, they effectively closed their great ritual circle around Pure Crystal Mountain. The second group headed due north, ascended the valley of the Yümé river immediately west of the mountain, and crossed the Ribpa La pass to complete their great circle at Chösam. From here they would cross the passes north and east heading for their home places in central, northern, and eastern Tibet. With the procession completed, no Tibetan would venture back down into the ravines of Tsari for another twelve years.

Endings and New Beginnings

As all the thousands of pilgrims departed from Chösam early in the monkey year, few were aware of a miraculous event that was taking place in the area, although quite a number had seen a sign of it in the form of a miraculous relic—a female deer's antler—when passing here a month or so ago. An auspicious sign had attended every great ravine circuit procession for as long as local people could remember. At the beginning of every monkey year, a female deer (*shamo*) miraculously grew a single, central antler (*üra*) on its head, called *shamo üra*. Examples of *shamo üra* were, and still are, preserved in some of the local resthouses and shrines around Tsari. This deer always lived alone, quite apart from all other animals. It was believed to be an incarnation of the Buddha. Toward the end of the monkey year it would die of natural causes. A Tsariwa's tale relates the death of this deer both as a moral against taking life in the precincts of this great power place and as a metaphor of the pilgrim's possible karmic transformation in the ritual:

> One day, toward the end of the monkey year, around the Jewel Hill (Norburi) behind the pilgrim's resthouse at Ribpa La pass, rainbows appeared all day, and a light like a burning fire appeared throughout the night. A local herdsman, Yakdzi Dawa Trakpa, saw this and thought to himself, "These are very auspicious signs, like those which appear when a special lama is born." He went over to the hill and saw a female deer, which had a miraculous antler, lying on the ground slowly dying. He was about to kill it and cut off the antler to keep. Just then the lion-faced sky-goer goddess appeared and told him, "Do not kill this female deer, or cut off her antler. If you do, you will have great misfortune, you won't take a good rebirth for another five thousand years!" So Dawa Trakpa didn't cut off the antler in heed of the warning. The deer died and its body went to the northern kingdom of Shambhala.[30]

As the monkey year drew to a close and the bird year arrived, a new female deer was born there. It too would wander the powerful mountain in solitude for another twelve years until its own miraculous transformation, death, and passage to a Buddhist paradise marked another great procession of the ravines of Tsari.

Transformations and Rewards

As was the case for the other Pure Crystal Mountain pilgrimage circuits described in previous chapters, purification and personal transformation were fundamental themes in the motivations and practices of Rongkor Chenmo pilgrims. And as with the other pilgrimages, these themes have their own particular dynamics in the context of the procession.

Any Tibetan who knows about the great Tsari procession can tell you two things. First, it was dangerous and difficult; thus, before leaving home to perform it, you took care to say goodbye to all loved ones, as it might be the last time you see them in this particular rebirth. Second, whether you lived or died during it, just by your undertaking the procession with a strong commitment and clear attitude of faith your bad karma would be cleansed and you would attain a better rebirth, perhaps even directly into a Buddhafield. Indicating the strength of these sentiments, both the themes of leaving loved ones to face the dangers of Tsari and the strong commitment its pilgrimage required were frequently employed as metaphors or referred to in Tibetan songs about intimate relationships.[31] Such commonly heard statements about the event contain the basis for two notions of personal transformation for pilgrims. The first is that by facing dangers with faith the ordinary person is transformed into a type of hero or heroine, and the second is that the sinner is transformed into a purified being.

The Heroes and Heroines Return

Barbara Aziz recently suggested that "pilgrimage is a cultural idiom for 'becoming the hero/heroine'—a means for negotiating a divine connection with the legends of a people and place providing specific heroic or valorous ideals."[32] Here her comments relate to measuring up to ideals of human perfection, following the footsteps of saints, and so on. But it seems that Tibetan views of the heroism of the great ravine circuit practitioner are not about these things at all. They are instead about being a tough and able (and lucky!) traveler in the face of all the legendary hardships of the route: poison arrows, cliff climbing, hostile jungle, lack of food, illness, injury, and so forth. The value placed on toughness and physical ability (on which I will comment further in chapter 9) figured in the ordering of the procession as well. This ability and endurance in the face of a challenge is perhaps closer to the heroism of our famous mountaineers or explorers, than to a religious heroism. Many Tibetans contend that the Rongkor Chenmo was the most difficult pilgrimage in Tibet, and that if one completed it then this showed one could travel anywhere in the country, regardless of the conditions. Interestingly enough, the completion of intensely demanding mountain pilgrimages in other Buddhist cultures are seen in exactly the same way.[33] A pilgrim remembers returning home from the great ravine circuit:

> When I came home after the Rongkor, I was treated a little specially by people when they found out that I had finished it. They treated me well when they found out—they put me up in their houses and fed me. They asked for stories about the journey and its dangers, so I told them all.[34]

To some extent, this heroism was not experienced by the pilgrims until it was socially ratified for them by their friends and acquaintances.[35] The modern Tibetan iconoclast Gendün Chöphel (1903–1951) even directed his sharp satire at such heroic storytelling in one of his poems of the 1930s, a piece obviously aimed at the pious bragging of the Lhasa aristocrats he so despised: "They go on pilgrimage to Tsari for their renown. . . . They recite the speech of the conqueror to get some recompense."[36] Talking to Tibetans about the ravine circuit, one finds many who are ready with a gripping account of the dangerous pilgrimage but have never been near Tsari—they relate the heroic journey of their uncle or cousin or a woman from their village.

Between pilgrims who have been on the Rongkor there is a degree of mutual recognition of each other as "Tsari-goers," as only they can really understand what one had to go through to perform the ritual. This was not a shared identity as hero, but rather of sharing hardships together, of having been through thick and thin with someone, as we might say. This bond is another dimension of the concept of "religious friend" (*chödrog*) or "*né* companion" (*nédrog*) as a form of horizontal relationship that could occur on pilgrimages. A song that was sung after the pilgrimage captures this feeling of solidarity through a juxtaposition of the ritual activity itself and the major concern one performed it for, that is, to deal with the problem of accumulated sin:

> We are religious friends who have circumambulated the *né* of Tsari.
> We are friends in sin who have killed the white grouse.[37]

Killing, Purification, and Death

Transformation through the purification of one's sins and embodied defilement is the central theme of the Rongkor pilgrims' experience in terms of the ritual redefinition of identity. This theme is, of course, pervasive in Tibetan pilgrimage traditions and other forms of lay belief and worship rituals in general. What is different in the context of the Rongkor and at other *néri* mountains are the extremes to which the purification theme is taken and also its links to death in various ways. The oral and written tradition of pilgrimage guidebooks for *néri* are full of references to their great moral cleansing power, such that even the most defiled individuals and monstrous sinners will be purified, avoid rebirth in hell, and the like. Such claims can rightly be regarded as a traditional Buddhist promotional device used by a religious élite to manipulate participation in their cult. And the evidence is unequivocal that traditional Tibetans as pilgrims took these claims at face value in the context of their general world view.

Contrary to recent attempts at portraying prediaspora Tibetan social history as nonviolent and ecologically correct, the bulk of evidence reveals that social violence, warfare, murder, hunting, and butchery were not at all uncommon outside of the relatively small Central Tibetan settled agrarian zone.[38] But as Buddhists, even the most ruthless Tibetan warriors and successful hunters were concerned about the burden of sins that would cause them to take rebirth in one of the hell realms. Like other religious systems, Tibetan Buddhism offered various ritual means for dealing with this problem, not least that of pilgrimage. The heaviest karmic burden is generated by killing, especially if it is intentional. It was commonly believed that the Rongkor could purify the bad karma of the most heinous crimes, including all types of killing, from hunting to murder and parricide. The popularity of the procession stemmed from the belief that it was a sort of once-only and total ritual treatment for great burdens of sin and defilement. While one Tsari Rongkor was considered sufficient to achieve this transformation, at other *néri*, multiple circuits might be required. For example, at least two circuits, each requiring a month, around Mount Targo and Lake Dangra on the bleak Changthang plateau are recommended for straight forward murder and thirteen circuits of distant Mount Tise for an accidental death.[39] Central Tibetans joke that the Rongkor procession was so popular with groups of well-armed, rough-and-ready Khampas from the east because they all had murders or battle deaths on their consciences for which they sought purification.[40]

There is a sense of bodily transformation involved in the purification of such sins that is related to the physical hardships the procession itself requires. One informant simply put it this way: "The ravine circuit is very rugged, and you have to suffer a lot physically, and the more you suffer, the more you wash off your sins and purify yourself. That is why people don't mind if it's very hard."[41] The results of the individual hardships of each pilgrim were attested in a wider context. The once defiled, then suffering, and now morally pure pilgrim's ritual body was socially and publicly recognized in the welcoming ritual for the branch of the procession that finished at Sangnag Chöling monastery in Char. Its form represented a dramatic reversal of the social and moral ranking normally accorded to monks and laypersons:

> The monks used to lay their large shawls along the ground on the path, like a carpet for the pilgrims to walk on, because they were now purified by the circumambulation. They, and others who could not make the journey, made offering there to the pilgrims, as they wanted to get the empowerment of these purified persons.[42]

The other related dimension of performance was personal transformation through risk-taking and the proximity of death. "All were expected to be ready to sacrifice everything, even their lives if necessary, when they chose to follow the large circle going to Rongkor."[43] The notion was that pilgrims had to overcome every doubt, even fear of death itself, through the sheer power of their faith. This is a case of fighting fire with fire; one needed to personally face death to have the power to deal with the consequences of death, that is, death caused both by killing and one's inevitable cyclic death and subsequent rebirth.

The question arises of ritual death and suicide on pilgrimage, which were not unknown on other popular Tibetan *néri* mountains.[44] There are many links between pilgrimage, death, and suicide in the Indian-influenced Asian context, both Buddhist and Hindu.[45] In a sense placing one's life at risk on the ravine circuit was tantamount to suicide, and in some cases participation could only be described thus. Especially for old people, dying on the ravine circuit was their last chance to become purified before another rebirth. Some old people regretted not dying at the mountain when they performed the Rongkor Chenmo because of the popular belief that death at this great power place on earth meant direct progress to a Buddhafield or heaven. Gregory Schopen has recently demonstrated that early Indian Buddhists believed death and ritual burial in close proximity of a reliquary shrine, equated with the Buddha's living presence in the form of his relics, resulted in rebirth in Buddhist heavens.[46] The same ideas are associated with death and burial in the presence of the Tantric saint Kōbō Dashi at the huge cemetery on the Japanese Buddhist pilgrimage mountain of Kōya-san. Tibetan beliefs about dying on the Tsari Rongkor Chenmo, at the base of a mountain commonly represented as a gigantic reliquary shrine housing the Buddha in his Tantric emanations, are completely in keeping with these other Buddhist ritual contexts. In fact, one hardly needs to inquire far into other traditions of pilgrimage to find parallel ideas. The obvious South Asian comparison here is the wish of elderly or sick Hindu pilgrims to reach the holy city of Kashi or Benares so as to be able to die there. Tibetan *néri* pilgrimages such as the Rongkor Chenmo should be seen within the whole history of Buddhism as a popular religion in Asian societies. They conform to the general pattern found throughout Asia of a Buddhist monopoly over rituals and beliefs concerned with death and dying (as opposed, for instance, to birth and fertility).

9

✦ ✦ ✦ ✦

Statecraft and Status in Contested Territory

The Tsari Rongkor Chenmo procession and Lodzong tribute were clearly at times a game with high stakes involved for all players. As I have shown, the attendant risks and dangers were perceived as having soteriological and social advantages according to the beliefs and experiences of the pilgrims. How, then, is one to characterize the participation of the other two parties attending and the relationship between them: the Tibetan state and its supporters, who regularly invested so many resources in staging this ritual in a remote, rugged border region, and the Himalayan tribal groups, who faced the possibility of armed resistance or arrest from Tibetan forces both during the Lodzong and the procession? Here I want to demonstrate that for both the Tibetan state and the tribes, the events were in part about generating and maintaining prestige or status in terms of their respective worldviews, values, and practices. Here I analyze how the Tibetan state and its élite supporters did so by examining the origins and development of the Rongkor and Lodzong and the role such rituals played in the operation and constitution of the traditional polity. The tribal participation can only be appreciated in terms of the complex history of Pure Crystal Mountain as an increasingly contested territory during the twentieth century, and the types of cultural models and social systems through which they responded to these changing local conditions.

Ritual and the Polity

The Lhasa-based Central Tibetan polity was systematized in the seventeenth century under the rule of the Great Fifth Dalai Lama (1617–1682) and his powerful regent, Sangye Gyatso (1653–1705). It continued, in various forms, under the joint hegemony of the Gelukpa sect and factions of the aristocracy until 1959. From Western points of view, this polity often described as a religiopolitical system of hierocracy or theocracy, and indeed its fundamental self-definition was that of "religion and political affairs joined together."[1] This polity has often falsely been assumed to have functioned as a highly centralized and integrated entity, operating over a very extensive territory. Recent commentators have better characterized the traditional Tibetan polity as a more complex and unstable ethnic and political assemblage, sharing and in part constituted by a number of cultural institutions.[2] This picture is closer to that of the "galactic polity" suggested for Thailand by Stanley Tambiah, and the "imperial-formation" model that Ronald Inden has proposed for precolonial India.[3] A feature of these alternative representations of historical Asian polities is the significant role they are willing to accord to ritual and ceremony in the operations of statecraft and in the definition of states as symbolic and ritual entities. This role is deemed important for various reasons: first, because ritual and ceremony themselves were the arena in which the dynamic constitution of complex political formations was worked out, in the form of "ongoing dialectical and eristical relations";[4] second, because on the ground there was often little actual political control or ability to enforce order in the local affairs of daily life; and third, because, as Geoffrey Samuel rightly points out in the case of Tibet, the interests of the polity lay ultimately in the control of persons rather than in the control of land.[5]

If rituals are considered important to the definition and operation of traditional Asian polities, how then do they allow for the hegemonic appropriation of power in specific cultural contexts? Many theorists since Emile Durkheim have viewed rituals and rites as being forms of social control in various ways. In general, they assume that rituals are instrumental, that is, intended to serve political interests or ends that are somehow beyond or outside the scope of the specific practice of a ritual. In viewing rituals as modes of social control, power is most often seen as being substantialized in the means of both persuasion or force, for instance as symbols or arms, which élites monopolize to manipulate others and maintain dominance. However, some, such as Michel Foucault, have argued against unidirectional and substantive notions of repressive power, stressing rather an analysis of the relational nature of power as being both constituted by and embedded in social practices and relations.[6] Here power works indirectly as strategic and dynamic negotiations rather than being wielded wholesale as violence or persuasive display. In terms of control, what distinguishes power from violence is its complex and subtle presence in the social fabric of everyday life. Power, as a relation, is predicated on the possibility of freedom to act within the context of actors' socialized bodies. Also, the practice theory of Pierre Bourdieu and others has attempted to show how the essentially arbitrary practices and relations within which social power operates become naturalized as legitimate.[7] These processes involve a certain view of reality that entails that specific social distinctions are produced and modified in such a way that conditions, such as asymmetries, are taken as being "natural" or "normal" by social actors.

In her overview of theories of ritual, Catherine Bell has used such conceptions of power and the habituation of its workings to reconceive ritual as being a strategic mode of action.[8] Thus, she advocates an analytical focus on the process of "ritualization" in terms of the core characteristics of practice (strategy, specificity, misrecognition, and redemptive hegemony) rather than just the fixed actions, symbols, and paraphernalia that go to make up a "ritual." Some of her critical observations and distinctions are pertinent, I think, to an understanding of ritual in relation to recent models of traditional Asian polities. For example, she argues that "ritual systems do not function to regulate or control the systems of social relations, they *are* the system, and an expedient rather than perfectly ordered one at that."[9]

> Closely involved with the objectification and legitimation of an ordering power as an assumption of the way things really are, ritualization is a strategic arena for the embodiment of power relations (p. 170) . . . [that] produces nuanced relationships of power, relationships characterized by acceptance and resistance, negotiated appropriation, and redemptive reinterpretation of the hegemonic order (p. 196).[10]

I would suggest that Bell's notion of ritualization, and the view of the premodern Tibetan polity as a complex and changing formation in which ritual and ceremonial performance were important, offer a promising analytical framework for understanding the Tibetan state's role in the Tsari Rongkor Chenmo and Lodzong described in chapter 8. I will begin by considering the origins and development of these events.

The Origins of the Rongkor Chenmo

Unlike other major Tibetan pilgrimages that have lengthy guidebooks containing narratives and other data purporting to explain their origins, the great ravine circuit and barbarian tribute appear to have no surviving written manuals. However, there are at least six brief, contradictory accounts, all of which follow a familiar Tibetan pattern of trying to fix, retrospectively, the precedent for such a ritual in the actions of some former saint or culture hero.[11] The very diversity of these accounts is itself further indication that a written guidebook never existed for the Rongkor Chenmo. Only one such narrative is of interest, the story of a lama on the run whose journey itself describes the route of the future procession:

> In later times, there was a lama named Lodrö Gyatso, the personal disciple of the lama Shakya Rinchen in Kongbu Shetö, who was the rebirth of Mîpham Lodrö. He was the son of a military officer from Trön Karutra [southwest of Tsari]. Because he murdered a man on account of a woman, he fled into the *rong*, and from the confluence of the Yümé River he went up. He arrived at Lo Mikyimdün. After that he went before his lama. He completed a great deal of penance [for the killing, and set off] according to the lama's prophecy, "Go to meditate in the Ngampa Tratrok charnel ground at Tsari. You will obtain the paranormal powers of Great Seal yoga." And although many of the Lopa's poison arrows pierced him, they were unable to harm him, as his faith had grown. A connection between the Lopa and the Tibetan people arose after this, and the practice of the Rongkor Chenmo was established [by] Lelung Shepé Dorje in accordance with a prophecy of Orgyen Rinpoché. With patronage by a Dalai Lama's mother, the government made the Lodzong.[12]

Several key issues are indicated here. First, it might be noted that this story is a good example of how the initially mundane and arbitrary, that is, escape from the scene of a crime of passion and an act of penance, can attain ritual signification through routinization and repetition.[13] The story of Lodrö Gyatso itself is a dramatic symbol of the Tibetan Buddhist ideology informing Rongkor performance: the accumulation of karmic defilements (especially through murder), a journey around, together with sincere Buddhist practice at Tsari for purification, and the attainment of advantages in this life and, by karmic extension, future lives as well. One is also led to believe that both Rongkor and Lodzong practice were always part of one whole process, and existed by virtue of each other. The Tibetan perspective does not separate the procession as a religious act from the tribute as a political one by applying abstract analytical categories.

The narrative indicates that those who initially established and patronized the rituals were leading incarnate lamas and members of the aristocracy and the Lhasa government itself, some of whom I shall discuss shortly. Although the exact date of the first Rongkor Chenmo remains unknown, its initiators appear to have set it up before the middle of the eighteenth century.[14] The Rongkor Chenmo and Lodzong continued to be the focus of Central Tibetan élite and government interest and sponsorship right up until they were last staged in 1956, and the names of highly ranked aristocratic families and influential clerics are traditionally associated with the events. The historical timing of this type of support being given to the establishment of a major ritual by the state and its allies is significant. The development of a new Central Tibetan Gelukpa state during the same general era saw the channeling of significant resources into symbolic and ritual institutions of religiopolitical importance.[15] Here one could mention the building of the great Potala palace overlooking Lhasa as an explicit reference to the mountain paradise of the deity Avalokiteśvara, of whom the Fifth Dalai Lama who headed the new state was recognized (and promoted himself) as being an emanation. Large public ceremonies in Lhasa such as the Tsogchö Chenmo and Tsogchö Sertreng and the addition of the Yasor or temporal dramatics to the Mönlam Chenmo festival calendar were all initiated at this time. The Lhasa Mönlam Chenmo ceremonies, for example, were a "public display of the state's monopoly of temporal power and of the Buddha's and the lama's monopoly of spiritual power; they restructure the Tibetan social and religious order."[16]

There is, of course, no single reason to postulate élite and state sponsorship and maintenance of the Tsari Rongkor procession at this time. But the general cultural context is clearly one in which the importance of the area of Tsari as a *néri* increased significantly for various reasons among the now dominant Gelukpa sect. One aspect of this attraction to the mountain is its association with major Gelukpa saintly figures, including the sect's founder, Tsongkhapa (1357–1419). His biography records that he performed pilgrimage on Pure Crystal Mountain in the summer of 1395 and had various powerful experiences.[17] The development of a cult of Tsongkhapa as the leading Gelukpa saint was already strong by the time the sect came to power in Tibet during the mid-seventeenth century. In the cult of Tibetan and other saints in general, the holy places at which they attained sublime meditative experiences, or even simply visited, ranked especially high as desirable places of pilgrimage and practice. The Lhasa élite actively sponsored the cult of Tsongkhapa on the mountain. For example, in 1794 an influential Lhasa aristocrat visited the saint's meditation cave there and had it restored using government corvée labor, and the setting up of a large image of the saint at the site is also noted.[18] As a legacy of this cult, and despite the virtual monopoly of textual traditions about Tsari by the Kagyüpa sect, one of the most popular short pilgrim's prayers to the mountain is attributed to the activities of Tsongkhapa himself.[19]

A second factor in the buildup of Gelukpa interest in the *néri* cult is their participation in the Tantric lineages of Great Seal yoga, in particular the system based upon the meditation deity Khorlo Dompa, the principal Tantric deity associated with the major *néri* since their beginnings.[20] The pilgrimage and retreat places in Tibet associated with Khorlo Dompa and the *néri* cult thus became increasingly important to more mystically inclined Gelukpa practitioners over the centuries.[21] An indicator of this rising interest is that by the seventeenth century they had developed their own new "branch" (*yanlag*) Khorlo Dompa cult site which was closely related to the *néri* tradition, in the neighborhood of Lhasa.[22] Other *néri* were steadily brought under Gelukpa influence as part of a state policy, initiated by the regent Sangye Gyatso, of converting, standardizing, and regulating many major and minor religious institutions throughout Tibet. When the Lhasa regime took control of Kagyüpa monasteries and shrines at the related western Tibetan *néri* mountains, it initially gave them support, but it soon ceased, and so various sites declined seriously during the eighteenth century.[23] However, during this same period of Lhasa's apparent neglect of distant western Tibetan *néri*, both the authorities and the Gelukpa sect became increasingly interested and involved in Tsari and its traditions. This manifested itself in the development of the Rongkor Chenmo and regular government sponsorship of local worship of the protective deities of the mountain. By the nineteenth century, the Gelukpa monastic cult had even taken an interest in Tsari as a ritual site, and large parties of Gelukpa monks regularly traveled from Dakpo Tratsang and other monasteries to Chikchar to perform the Drukchuma rites dedicated to Shinje Gyelpo on a large scale at the foot of the mountain. In addition to all this, there is another set of political and personal factors involved here, as well as the agency of some important individuals, to consider.

The foregoing short, surviving origin narrative attributes the great ravine procession and barbarian tribute at Tsari to the inspiration of the incarnate Gelukpa lama of Olkha, Lelung Shepé Dorje (b. 1697) and the sponsorship of a Dalai Lama's mother and the government.[24] Although there is no independent historical confirmation of these details, there is at least evidence to regard the agency of Lelung Shepé Dorje and his connections with various Dalai Lamas as being central here. Lelung was, like both the Fifth and Sixth Dalai Lamas, from a southern Tibetan family. He was ordained by the Sixth Dalai Lama in 1703–4 and met him again in 1706 shortly before the latter died. He then met the Seventh Dalai Lama in 1710, and he later maintained correspondence with him. In the early decades of the eighteenth century, Lelung, along with quite a number of other visionary lamas, mainly the Nyingmapa "treasure discoverers," was active in the southeastern borderlands of Tibet.[25] He made an extensive tour of Tsari and adjacent areas in 1719–20, and his oeuvre is full of guide books to nearby holy places and works on the cult of Tibetan protective deities.[26] Lelung based some of his longer ritual texts on the "secret visions" of the Fifth Dalai Lama, and it is in this esoteric corpus that the "Great Fifth" relates a vision he had of the dark, lion-headed protector Tsari Shingkyong, who also presided over his own natal place in southern Tibet.[27] Both the Fifth Dalai Lama and Lelung went on to compose various short ritual texts dedicated, among others, to the chief protective deities of Pure Crystal Mountain and Tsari district.[28] Their religious interest in and knowledge of the *néri* and its cult was shared by the Sixth Dalai Lama. His well-known esoteric song about Pure Crystal Mountain leaves no doubt that he must have possessed specialist knowledge of this *néri* in order to compose such a sophisticated verse, and a passage in his so-called secret biography (which claims that he lived long after his reported death) even has him go on pilgrimage to Tsari incognito during 1710.[29] To add weight to the complex of such spiritual connections with the famous *néri* of Tsari, which were shared by these most important Gelukpa figures of the late seventeenth and early eighteenth century, the Fifth Dalai Lama himself had several personal and political associations with the area. He was connected to the Drukpa Kagyü of Char, the custodians of Tsari, as the Fifth Drukchen incarnation, the head of the sect, was his cousin. The Fifth Dalai Lama also appears to have had respect for the scholarship of Pema Karpo, his cousin's previous incarnation, whose developments of the cult of Pure Crystal Mountain were so important. There was for a period preferential treatment of the Drukpa by the Gelukpa state at this time, especially in the light of the difficult relations Lhasa had with both the Karmapa sect and the Drukpa in Bhutan. And, partly in view of their strategic position on the southern border, the Dalai Lama accorded the Drukpa incarnations highest official ranking immediately after himself, even higher at the time than the Panchen Lama.[30]

At this point one could continue to catalog the interests and connections—and there are many—of the Central Tibetan élite with Tsari and surrounding regions. They are all clear evidence not only of why this *néri* mountain was chosen when it was but also of why it remained important to the Gelukpa polity and its powerful supporters. Not only is the origin of the Rongkor Chenmo and Lodzong to be found here, but also, it would seem, that of other ritual institutions of the cult of Pure Crystal Mountain, which remained vigorous until 1959. The annual worship of the important protective deities of the mountain also came to be sponsored directly by the state, a tradition I will discuss in chapter 10.

Élite "Benevolence" and Misrecognition

It is frequently noted that discursive themes of *dulwa*, or "subjugation," "taming," and "civilizing" are pervasive throughout Tibetan narrative and ritual complexes. The Rongkor origin narrative also draws on the theme of superior Buddhist magic and its implicit civilizing power triumphing over local evil and barbarity identified with the Lopa, the tribal peoples to the south. The narrative is the initial depiction of the relationship between the Tibetans and the Lopa at Tsari, and indeed represents a dominant Tibetan representation of such interethnic contacts throughout this part of the borderlands.[31] One might be tempted to interpret the entire scenario that took place at Tsari as a kind of exercise in Buddhist subjugation of barbarian borderland peoples and what they represented, or even as a form of Buddhaization or Tibetanization. In my thinking, and that of my informants, the relations between Tibetan and tribal populations defined by the staging and practice of Rongkor and Lodzong could not be regarded as exercises in subjugation or conversion. It is, rather, the existence, display, and deployment of the powers and values of Buddhism as they are embodied in the Tibetan polity, and the material efficacy associated with that, that are of central importance. The Tibetan state actually had little choice but to give in to the tribal demands in order to avoid massacres, but it was the way in which they went about doing so and how that was perceived by those present that was important.

Although my informants and I arrive at this same general conclusion, we do so from different points of view. All Tibetan informants saw their own and the Lhasa regime's role in terms of Tibetan Buddhist practice and its goals, and the support and enabling of these by a Buddhist state. A large part of the way in which they conceived of the polity was as a religiopolitical formation headed by a human incarnation of a Buddhist divine savior, Avalokiteśvara, partly ruled and administered by various other incarnate lamas and clerics, supported by Buddhist aristocrats, and itself defined as a system existing for the overall benefit of Tibetan Buddhism and its followers. This image is persistent in Tibetan accounts in general, despite the fact that many persons of lower rank also freely acknowledge the existence of gross asymmetries in the social system and the hardships of having to live within them.

The way informants characterized the logistical support that the government and its aristocratic allies provided for the procession—the officials and their escorts, the tribute goods, the donations of extra food rations, the armed troops, translators, guides and other workers, and so on—accords with this view of the polity as a whole. All pilgrims and local organizers who participated spoke specifically of the government and the aristocrats who were involved as "sponsors" or "donors" (*jindag*) and of all the resources that they marshalled as "gifts" (*jinpa*, or "alms" in a more technical Buddhist sense). Being employed in the services of staging a Buddhist ritual, they were conceived of as forms of meritorious or auspicious activity, resulting ultimately in a soteriological benefit (i.e., better rebirths) for the donor. And by way of these gifts, soteriological benefits were facilitated for the individual pilgrims as well, as they allowed for the chance to undergo the positive psychophysical transformations believed to result from completing the event. In this respect, all pilgrims expressed gratitude about the government's participation.[32] As for dealing with the tribal peoples and the conditions of Loyül, the procession and tribute were an example of the superior worldly resources and Buddhist powers (both material, political, and magical) embodied in the polity and its representatives and of their being redistributed in terms of the perceived function of the state. The deployment of these strategies and the successful completion of the pilgrimage were proof of these powers.

This Tibetan view of the events is of course made more explicit through inquiry, but in practice it was implicit and represents what was assumed by participants. They constructed their own and others' participation in the ritual as meaningful social action on the basis of this view. From an outsider's perspective, I present an alternative view that implies that the practice of the rituals entails a misrecognition of means and ends, producing what Bell calls a "redemptive reinterpretation of the hegemonic order."[33] By examining the ethnography of the procession's staging, I will suggest various ways in which this description is valid in terms of participation being a strategic mode of practice. Central to this exploration is an analysis of related systems of material and symbolic capital, the ordering of space and bodies, and the role of innovation.

Taking Center Stage

As noted, the government and the aristocrats were conceived of as sponsors or donors providing resources as gifts for the pilgrims. But what of the actual origins of these resources, and the impetus to provide them in the form of the staging? The majority of personnel under government service for the event, troops included, were involved on the basis of special corvée labor (*ula*) obligations, and others, such as the Tibetanized tribal guides, received their modest equipment as a one-off payment. Most of the tribute goods were collected from the populace in the form of a tax designated for the event, as was usual in the Tibetan fiscal system. Aristocratic houses, such as that of Doring, who "donated" food, did so by redirecting surplus production that they obtained through free peasant labor, under the obligations of the *trelten* contract system, or that they collected as a direct tax. It is very important that the orchestration and redirection constituting these Tibetan economic processes were perceived in terms of "donor" and "gift" in the context of this ritual sponsorship. Such identification serves to increase the symbolic value of all forms of patronage of such rituals. Those identified as the patrons can be seen to have potential benefits in terms of gaining prestige in the eyes of the population at large as well as of generating necessary status within their own ranks, as I will now discuss.

It is known that, in general, the Tibetan government allotted a portion of its annual income for grants to finance religious ceremonies.[34] There have been few in-depth studies of large rituals that involved the Central Tibetan state, but Joachim Karsten's work on the Yasor shows that the high-ranking aristocratic lay officials had to donate men and also finance the parades. He describes this activity as a "duty," as being "obligatory" and states that the organizing, arranging, and financing (which was a great expense) would show officials' capacity for government posts.[35] Melvyn Goldstein also notes the "frequent necessity of large gifts to secure the higher positions [of government]" and the great expenses of ceremonial responsibilities that characterized the political mobility of the upper aristocracy in Tibet.[36] These comments indicate that such activities requiring the investment of material capital could generate the necessary symbolic capital to make it into important government posts. The higher the ranking one attained, the closer one got to the center and its power, that is, access to the Dalai Lama and the regent, and the Kashag, or "cabinet," which was the highest lay political body in Tibet and a stronghold of the nobility. Luciano Petech's analysis of Tibetan aristocratic political life concludes that "the social and political status of the nobility as a whole could oscillate only between very narrow limits."[37] In addition, Goldstein notes, "One of the most salient features of traditional political life in Tibet was the intense and pervasive competition for power and prestige that took place within the ranks of the politically relevant, particularly within the aristocratic lay-official segment of the government."[38] It was a tight and competitive system, and the patronage of ritual and ceremonial was a possible, and at times necessary, avenue for status maintenance and mobility within it. I suggest that the involvements of highly ranked lay and ecclesiastic members of the Tibetan élite in the origins, maintenance, and orchestration of the Rongkor Chenmo and Lodzong were as much related to the need for generating social prestige within a small echelon of Tibetan society as they were about services to Buddhism and the generation of merit. But it seems that these were not the economics that were assumed by ordinary Tibetans as participants in the rituals.

It is clear that the logic of the whole procession necessitated élite support for its successful completion. The important point is that the deployment of resources and logistics were accomplished as a mode of strategic action, as ritualization. The requirement of conforming to various schemes of spacial organization was central to all aspects of the events. At points within these schemes, mythic/traditional and symbolic precedents were evoked. These arrangements can be seen to generate distinctions that reiterate a certain view of reality—although not a static one, as they also allow for that view to be contested, negotiated, and modified within the context of certain relations of power.

The initial positioning of the tents and personnel during the preliminaries leading up to the Lodzong established the most common Tibetan Buddhist hierarchial ordering of space, the maṇḍala. Not only was this positioning done on a site, Maṇḍala Plain, already popularly designated as such, but it evoked the popular tradition of Buddhist victory over the forces of evil there by another legendary Tibetan ruler, King Gesar. The large ceremonial tents, themselves no less markers of rank and power in Tibetan society than the castle, were pitched in the center of the designated maṇḍala, equivalent to the supreme abode of the highest deity.[39] It was here in this ideal center that representatives of religious and temporal authority resided, and presided in their turn over both the negotiations and the Buddhist protective rites for the success of the procession. And it was known to all those on the periphery that here, too, lay the source and control of the various material forms of the state's authority and efficacy attendant on the proceedings: the tribute goods, the armed troops, the local guides, translators and other workers, the supplementary food supplies, and so on. Many of these forms were featured again during the course of the procession.

Pilgrims were putting themselves in a situation where they were potentially physically dependent on the powers of the state in a number of respects for survival. The atmosphere in this setting was already charged with a certain degree of anticipation. All pilgrims knew in advance, by way of reputation, the personal challenges and dangers they and the others would have to face during the procession. This anticipation only served to lend importance to the élite persons and their supports (magicoreligious, logistical, material, and military), controlled from the center of this organizational maṇḍala. Similarly, the tribute arrangements centered on the seated and uniformed officials, while their tax-paying subjects had to stand behind them. This ordered scheme, with its trappings of high society (e.g., chairs and lavish costumes), contrasted with the relative chaos of the scattered tribal groups opposite it in the setting of a wild mountain valley. All pilgrims who witnessed the proceedings from the periphery could see that nonviolent Buddhist oath-swearing, religious dance, and protective prayer rites were taking place alongside spectacular animal sacrifice, the anointing of bodies with fresh blood, the consumption of still-warm flesh, and so on.

All these factors dramatically structured and reiterated a range of distinctions, such as powerful/subordinate, benefactor/recipient, Buddhist/non-Buddhist, civilized/barbarian, moral/amoral, and active male/docile female. By virtue of the relative positioning, required movement, and marking of persons in the context of the representational systems that were invoked, these distinctions were more than just external and objectified; they became encoded or impressed on the social bodies of the participants. And these included many thousands of women and men from every part of the Tibetan world, a more or less complete cross-section of the constituents of the complex Tibetan polity. After the tribespeople had departed, this whole process was rehearsed differently in another mode of ritual action—the ranking of the procession.

Processions and Power

Processions feature in the social life of many cultures as both large-and small-scale forms of public ritual. They are, in a Durkheimian sense, representations "in which some members of society represent their theories and systems of classifications and constructs to themselves and others."[40] Their characteristic form is of groups of people, ranked in order, connecting places together and defining areas of space by passing over territory along prescribed routes. William (Bo) Sax has observed that in this ritual form, as a collective representation, "[t]he linear order of procession is an icon of society, and that is why to lead the procession, or to define its form, is to claim authority over land and people. Disputes over such things as the order of procession . . . have therefore to do not with 'empty' forms or 'mere' symbols but rather with tremendously potent political actions."[41] The action of constructing this representation from human materials, that is, pilgrims' bodies, is the very ritualization process that "produces nuanced relationships of power, relationships characterized by acceptance and resistance, [and] negotiated appropriation."[42] The relational nature of power embodied in dynamic and strategic ritual processes accommodates innovation rather than reproducing static structures. This is certainly the case with the Tsari Rongkor procession.

Each major column or *sho* in the procession had a leader, an identity, an internal structure, and a ranking in the overall order. My informants attributed the logic of this ordering to utilitarian or functional concerns. In part, I would not want to disagree with such thinking, for instance, the fact that since local people and southerners probably were more familiar with the conditions, they want first. Joining a *sho* and ranking in a particular part of it because it represented one's interests through sectarian, regional, or kinship identities probably did ensure some better support in hard times. And the fact that the Dalai Lama's robes were carried by the Lhasa officials, who therefore went first, was because the Dalai Lama was not there in person. But beyond these purposes, the appropriation of leadership and the power of ranking the *sho* were as much a part of the construction of the social icon and a form of strategic action as these practical concerns might seem to have been.

From the beginning of the proceedings, the structuring was orchestrated by government officials and local lay and clerical authorities, and the chief representative (an official and his troops) of all these powers was placed in the premier position, at the head of the whole procession. Similarly, each *sho* was headed by the *tongpön*, who represented another level of these powers. The primary symbol used to define this overall hierarchy of spacial ordering is found in the main palladia or sacra that accompanied the entire proceedings: the ceremonial robes of the Dalai Lama himself, carried by the monk official from Lhasa.[43] It is well to remember here that such an item was more than merely symbolic to Tibetans. They believed the garment possessed empowerment (*chinlab*) through physical contact with the Dalai Lama's person. His power, and the combination of spiritual and temporal authority that he as head of state embodied, were in effect substantially present during the rituals. The innovation of new *sho* and *tongpön* as leaders is of particular interest. It shows on the one hand that control over the ranking of the procession concerned the highest members of Tibetan society and their agendas, and on the other that this control and ranking itself was actively contested.

A local official from Tsari attributes the appointment of the Lonag *tongpön* for various practical and political reasons to the progressive military chief Tsarong (1885–1959).[44] Tsarong was, in his day, one of the richest and most influential men in Tibet and a major favorite of the Thirteenth Dalai Lama (1876–1933), who had himself been to Tsari on pilgrimage in 1900 and whose natal place of Langdun in Dakpo was just to the north of Pure Crystal Mountain.[45] Tsarong's involvement in Rongkor organization is even less surprising when one learns that he was also a close relative of the Drigung Kyabgön lama, one of the leading incarnations of a Tibetan Buddhist school administering the Tsari area. Tsarong is said to have made the appointment when he performed the Rongkor.[46] The second appointment concerns that of the Khampa *tongpön* and the overall ranking of the various Khampa *sho* in 1944 and 1956. Pilgrims from far distant parts of the eastern Tibetan marches (i.e., Kham) were particularly high in number during these last two Rongkor years,[47] this fact was partly due to increasingly violent Chinese colonial practices in their home districts.[48] The groups of pilgrims from Kham appointed their own leaders, thereby asserting authority by defining their own part in the procession independently of the Central Tibetan officials. Moreover, the normal ranking by dice did not apply to the Khampa *sho*, who went up near the front of the procession in both years. Regardless of the outcome of the dice throws, the Khampas said they had won and went to the front anyway. They were undisputed, as nobody wished to challenge the large parties of heavily armed and easily provoked easterners.

Both these cases illustrate aspects of the process of polity formation by ritualization. The appointment of the Lonag *tongpön* appears to have been made partly to further integrate the already Tibetanized tribes of Charmé into the Lhasa-based state. There are two clear reasons for this action: to help defuse the recurring frictions and armed conflicts between tribals and Tibetans around Tsari (discussed hereafter) and thus stabilize this part of the borderlands; and to maintain the flow of trade in the area, especially the government's control over it and access to rare and specialized goods and produce in demand in the élite circles of Lhasa and the large Gelukpa monasteries of Central Tibet.[49] As for the new Khampa *sho*, they must be viewed in relation to the changing Tibetan polity. During the late nineteenth and the twentieth century, the eastern areas many of these pilgrims came from existed as either autonomous political entities or were actively involved in various contests for control with the Central Tibetan regime. From the 1920s up to 1950, the prestige and authority of the Lhasa state had also waned significantly in the east, such that many easterners felt little loyalty toward it even in the face of imminent Chinese occupation.[50] This is the dynamic context of polity in which the Lhasa administrators sought to rank the easterners according to their own scheme, and in which the Khampas contested and appropriated that right for themselves.

If processions are also a form of reflexive, metasocial representation, then what is the ordering of the Rongkor procession displaying to Tibetans themselves about the makeup of their society and the competing values that are called into play?[51] First, the ranking shows an assertion of overall authority by an élite of central government clerics and officials, and aristocrats, that was for the most part accepted. When it was challenged, by a belligerent faction from the periphery, it was toughness and force of arms that were able to assume organizational power. Toughness or hardiness and physical ability also defined those who were able to lead: soldiers (many of whom were local) and southern borderland peoples. Quite apart from any practical arguments for ranking, this is the way the Central and West Tibetans defined these people in relation to themselves. In contrast the groups from East Tibet obviously did not make this distinction in relation to themselves or consider it significant when it came to ranking.

Furthermore, the main internal organizing principle of the procession was localized identity, determined by residence or natal place; dialect; and community, clan, and affinal categories. This type of organization prevailed on other Tibetan pilgrimages I have attended in Tibet, India, and Nepal. Recent fieldwork on the long procession around the *néri* mountain of Amnye Machen in northeastern Tibet showed that pilgrims traveled in discrete homeland or family based units and hardly mixed with other groups at all, except at sites of particular interest or sanctity en route.[52] This type of ordering is one of the most pervasive ways in which Tibetans group themselves together socially. Its classic, pre-1959 institutional form would have to be the internal organization of Tibet's most powerful social body, the Gelukpa monastic populations in the county's major religious establishments.[53] Although there is no doubt that Tibetan pilgrimages did at times promote certain types of horizontal relationships, there is no evidence to suggest anything like Turnerian communitas or antistructural processes occurring during such large Tibetan ritual journeys to sacred mountains.[54] If any Tibetan pilgrimage is to be used to test Turner's theoretical perspectives, it should be the Dukhor Wangchen, those massive and presently most important of Tibetan diaspora rituals classifiable as pilgrimages, which are regularly staged in North India and elsewhere in the context of a new nationalism and the redefinition of a modern Tibetan Buddhism.

The Rongkor Chenmo procession, read as social icon, displayed a fundamental parochialism of identity that in large part defined, and still defines, Tibetan society. From another point of view, these distinctions marked the complex of units in the fluctuating ethnic and political formation that was "Tibet." At different points in the proceedings at Tsari, during each monkey year, the process of this polity's ongoing constitution took place in what were for Tibetans the pursuit of soteriological goals through Buddhist ritual.

Ritual across Ethnic, Political, and Cultural Divides

In general, and contrary to many popular depictions, the grand Himalayan chain never acted as an impenetrable geographical barrier that served to isolate Tibetans from their South Asian neighbors. Indeed, particularly from the Monyül corridor westward, the Himalayas are crossed by numerous passes and travel routes that Tibetans have long used to journey to the southern flank of the mountains and the plains of India beyond. However, Loyül, the area of the Subansiri basin to the south of Tsari, was not traversed by them at all for either trade, domestic, or religious purposes. This avoidance was not only due to the apparent martial nature of some of the numerous remote, small-scale, preliterate societies of the southeast borderlands; the Tibetans themselves believed strongly that they had less in common with these "uncivilized" peoples than with any of their other more Tibetanized and Indic, Chinese, or Central Asian influenced neighbors. Moreover, when crossing the mountain divide here, the ecology changed rapidly into a rugged and heavily forested subtropical hill country, which highlanders from the plateau found hostile and oppressive in general. Loyül thus formed a vast geographical and ethnic barrier to Tibetan penetration from the north, the only major (and then, only partial) exception being the twelve-yearly great ravine circuit processions around Pure Crystal Mountain.

Given the general lack of formal or sustained contacts between Tibetans and their tribal neighbors along this extensive borderland, the Rongkor, and the Lodzong in particular, constituted a unique local political institution, one in which the relationship was mediated through ritual. It is also known to have been an enduring one, and the few written records from the early nineteenth century show it had a general continuity of form lasting until 1956. Almost all our material on Rongkor and Lodzong comes from the Tibetan perspective. However, ethnographic data on Subansiri tribes recorded just before their forced administrative and military contacts with the Indian state in the 1950s offer some possibility of appreciating ways in which they constructed their relations with the Tibetans through these rituals and the events surrounding them. There are at least three aspects of the relationship that one can consider from the tribal perspective: the changing regional and historical context of their hostility toward Tibetan pilgrimage processions; the tribal values, practices, and cultural models that informed and defined the encounters between the two groups; and the role that status and identity definition played.

The Historical Context of Tribal Attacks

If Tibetans are asked about why the tribals regularly attacked, stole from, and killed pilgrims at Tsari, they reply that it is because they are "just Lopa," and Lopa are "savages" or "borderland barbarians" who indulge in meaningless killing and violence and do not follow the Buddha's doctrine, which teaches respect for the lives of all sentient beings. A classification of self and other is invoked to explain the longstanding hostility, both threatened and actual, that has accompanied ravine circuit processions. (I will return to the theme of essential Tibetan notions of ethnicity.) But the attacks on Tibetan Rongkor pilgrimage parties, as well as their cessation at times, did not occur because the tribal peoples were essentially hostile and violent or easily susceptible to being bribed. This particular interethnic violence and its pattern must be appreciated through a larger context of changing tribal-Tibetan relations, ecological and demographic factors, colonial and state policies, and the specific cultural patterns of the Subansiri peoples themselves.

Until the 1950s, the upper Subansiri basin remained one of the most inaccessible parts of the region, and its peoples along the southern flanks of Pure Crystal Mountain were one of the least-known populations of South Asia. Only a handful of outsiders penetrated the margins of the area from the south;[55] from the north it remained completely unknown below the last Tibetan settlements. Despite this apparent remoteness, the various small tribal societies in this area were far from being the static social product of a forgotten world frozen in primitive time. Rather, they appear to have been dynamic and unstable entities, partly due to certain local pressures and as a result of being caught between two larger and changing worlds—Tibet to the north and British colonial India to the south—that gradually made their presence felt.

The different populations of Nishi (or Nisü), Sulung, Boru, Nga (or Na), Tagin, and Gallong who inhabited the higher valleys of the Subansiri, Kamla, Sipi, and Khru catchment areas adjacent to Tsari before the 1950s shared an overall linguistic uniformity and general similarity of customs. However, they ranged from being stockless hunter-gatherer groups with only limited cropping to those with semipermanent settlements practicing shifting slash and burn agriculture (*jhuming*) and tending mithan oxen (*Bos frontalis*) at lower altitudes, or growing maize and wheat and keeping sheep and cattle in higher altitude settlements. The higher groups had become partly Tibetanized, in appearance at least, and acted as the conduit for Tibetan trade to the lower zone. Some of them freely intermarried and maintained shifting alliances with the lower Dafla groups also, such that in actions against the Tibetans a collection of different tribes from throughout the region might be aligned. At other times these same groups fought among themselves. The changing relationships between them as well as their reactions toward outsiders were determined by a number of factors.

The area in which these peoples lived was not an endless tract of empty jungle-covered hills. There where other tribes on all sides, and the availability of suitable sites for cultivation and settlement was limited. Quite apart from local social vicissitudes (feuds, etc.), the potential mobility of populations in the area faced increasing environmental constraints. The widespread shifting agriculture practice of clear-felling and burning forest on a ten-to-fifteen-year cycle left large areas throughout these catchments denuded, and with decreasing fertility due to periods of quick, successive cropping. This environmental factor appears to be part of the reason for patterns of migration in the Subansiri basin as a whole, and it meant that population pressures increased in certain areas.[56] Early in the twentieth century, hostile Tibetan actions added dramatically to these factors as they effected the peoples immediately adjacent to Tsari. In 1906 border groups of Nga and Boru (or Charlo, Khalo, and Dakshing Lopa to the Tibetans) were enticed by the Sangnag Chöling Drukpa to shift their trading activities to that place, thus abandoning their traditional trade with the

Tibetan government village of Trön to the southwest near Chayül Dzong. Upset by the sudden loss of trading opportunities and revenues, the Trön Tibetans killed well over a hundred of the tribals in what was tantamount to a series of cold-blooded revenge massacres.[57] After a tribal counterattack on the defenseless villages and shrines of neighboring western Tsari, which were not at all involved up to that point, the Tibetan government mustered five hundred troops from Dakpo and surrounding districts and pursued and punished the attackers.

The war ended quickly, but it shifted Tibetan-tribal relations and territorial claims in the area dramatically and permanently. Until then the Nga and Boru groups had claimed all the land at Tsari as their own, except along the main Tsari River valley to the northeast, including the Chikchar area and up to the summit of the Drölma La pass.[58] They regarded all southern flanks of the mountain right up to the high altitude pilgrimage routes as their traditional hunting grounds, and pursued game there every autumn, a well-documented practice that continued up to 1959 and later. The border villages of Yümé and Lo Mikyimdün at Tsari paid them annual taxes accordingly. The list of these annual taxes paid by Yümé to the tribes reads like a miniature Lodzong payment—barley flour, swords, spears, and salt.[59] In fact, the payment arrangements at the later Lodzong, which were based on the main government tax households (*trekang*) of Tsari as "Lopa owners" (*lodag*), are strongly suggestive of the incorporation of this earlier arrangement into the later tribute system.

After the 1906 war the situation was reversed, and those tribals who remained within a certain zone close to Tsari and Charmé had to pay taxes to the Tibetan government instead. Many of them had been forced to migrate south into the Subansiri basin, losing their trading advantage, having to live as nomadic hunters and leaving their high villages and fields abandoned in what was now technically (i.e., on the basis of taxation) Tibetan territory.[60] This situation was also to have lasting domestic consequences for the Tsariwa in terms of security. Troops were stationed over the winter in Yümé to protect the temple, and a local militia was formed in Lo Mikyimdün to defend against retaliatory attacks. The recorded hostility of the upper Subansiri peoples toward Tibetan pilgrims at Tsari, and the great importance these peoples placed on the Lodzong payments, were directly related to these developments early in the century. Individual tribesmen who had trading partnerships with some of my informants used to repeatedly remind the Tibetans of this incident, and that there was an outstanding score to be settled even after several generations. The large 1944 massacre of pilgrims by tribals can be partly attributed to revenge acts against the Tibetan government by displaced Nga and Boru in alliance with lower dwelling Dafla.[61] I will turn to tribal notions of dispute and fair settlement shortly, but first I will explore the other external pressure that increasingly influenced tribal behavior toward Tibetan pilgrims and moved Tsari and its pilgrimages onto the stage of regional geopolitics—the practices of British colonialism and the Indian state.

Lines upon the Map

Within the context of a long, slow process of attempting to exert administrative control in northeastern India from the nineteenth century onward, the British colonial government sent its first contact group to visit the upper Subansiri area during the winter of 1911–12. The so-called Miri Mission was a badly staged, semimilitary expedition that ended prematurely in a bloody confrontation with tribal peoples in the area. Following closely on Tibetan actions to the north in 1906, this first negative contact with their would-be administrators to the south only served to increase pressures on the local populations and harden their attitudes against any foreign claims over or passage through their territory. According to the tribal notions of honor and intergenerational responsibility for attending to unsettled scores, like those that plagued the Tsari Rongkor in the wake of 1906, the ancestors of victims of the Miri Mission were still intent on revenge when British India reestablished contact with the area in the mid-1940s.[62] By that time a number of invisible lines crisscrossed the tribal territory, drawn on remote maps according to the competing designs of distant powers the tribes had little or no knowledge of. The interest focused around these abstract lines eventually led to the radical upheaval of life in both upper Subansiri and Tsari itself, and the eventual demise of the Rongkor traditions.

The Subansiri basin continued to change its administrative identity following the Miri Mission; in 1912–13 it was included in the Western Section of the North-East Frontier Tract, although its northern border remained undefined; in 1914, following the Simla Convention, signed by both the British and Tibetan governments, the northern border was established along the so-called McMahon Line; in 1919 the area became the Balipara Frontier Tract of the new North-East Frontier Agency (NEFA); after years of neglect, interest in the area rekindled in the wake of World War II and, following renewed contacts with the region, in 1946 it became the separate administrative unit of Subansiri Area; after Indian independence, and due to Communist China's claims over Tibet, in the 1950s it became known as the Subansiri Frontier Division of the NEFA, within which a great deal of regulatory activity began to take place as the Indian government strove to rapidly assert its inherited and long-dormant claims over NEFA and the McMahon Line. The pace of new controls over tribal lives was such that by 1956, the year of the last Tsari Rongkor and Lodzong, the leading anthropologist-administrator of NEFA could plainly assert referring to the upper Subansiri and the ethnographic accounts of conditions there in the 1940s, that "the situation today is very different. Wars and kidnappings and cruel punishments, so fully described in these books, have come to an end and, even in the remotest valleys, officers of the Administration are braving loneliness and every kind of hardship to bring relief and a fuller life to the people."[63]

Occupied by the increasing presence of the Chinese in their own country, the Tibetans had little idea of what was taking place just across the mountains to the south. Tibetan accounts of the 1956 Rongkor and Lodzong are unanimous in stating that the Lopa caused no incidents at all that year because the Lhasa government had given a satisfactory tribute payment, made them all swear the oath successfully, and performed the appropriate rituals. However, it is almost certainly the fact that a vigorous decade of Indian administrative contacts had already either broken the spirit of the upper Subansiri tribes or made conditions too unconducive for them to attempt any aggravation of their northern neighbors and risk a political incident during this increasingly critical period of Tibetan, Indian, and Chinese relations. The reality was that by the late 1950s, armed Indian border patrols were already stationed just down the valley from Maṇḍala Plain, ready to deal with any sort of trouble on their side of the McMahon Line.

It is well known that the Tsari area figured as one of the special concessions granted the Tibetans during the formulation of the notorious McMahon Line as a formal Anglo-Tibetan border in 1914. The "exchange of notes" document to the Tibetan government from Sir Henry McMahon only mentions access to the peripheral sites of New Tsari and Tsari Tsokar, or "White Lake," to the east of Pure Crystal Mountain as special concessions by the British: "If the sacred places of Tso Karpo and Tsari Sarpa fall within a day's march of the British side of the frontier, they will be included in Tibetan territory and the frontier modified accordingly."[64] This arrangement represented a minor concession at best, as these *né* where in any case both at higher altitude, not over on the southern flank of the Himalaya proper, and thus logically more within Tibetan territory. The line on the map in this area that the Tibetans agreed to included all the upper parts of Pure Crystal Mountain, the entire Shungkor pilgrimage circuit, the Tsari border villages, and the associated *né* to the east within Tibetan territory (see fig. 8.1). At the time, the Tibetans appear not to have pressed for special concessions of access to the area of the Rongkor to the south nor claimed it as their territory. For their part, the British were well aware of all Tibetan activities around Tsari during the period, based on the intensive intelligence-gathering mission of the colonial spies F. M. Bailey and H. T. Morshead in the area during 1913, at which time Bailey became the first European, and one of the only ones, to perform the Tsari Shungkor pilgrimage.[65] Bailey's detailed advice to McMahon appears to have been critical to the latter's arguments for fixing the border around Pure Crystal Mountain. Thus McMahon "ignored, deliberately, the fact that the entire region was regarded by the Tibetans as being sacred, and that every twelve years a pilgrimage, the *Ringkor* or "Long Pilgrimage" [i.e., Rongkor], was made by hundreds of thousands [sic] of Tibetans down the Subansiri-Tsari . . . some twenty miles or so south of the McMahon Line"[66] while granting the more minor modifications to the east to "meet Tibetan religious susceptibilities."[67]

It is hard to imagine the Lhasa state abandoning one of its major rituals during the rule of the strong Thirteenth Dalai Lama. At the time the Tibetan government accepted this line on the map as a border in the area, it probably did not think the British in India to be even a remote future threat to the continued performance of the Rongkor, especially compared with the Lopa or the Chinese. There is also the question of whether the Tibetan government expected that this abstract border would ever be implemented within the foreseeable future, and it seems clear that it hoped it would not. The Tibetans were playing a game of higher stakes over the McMahon Line right from the outset, one that continued to catch them in a double bind over the agreement. While they initially hoped that acquiescing to McMahon's border might ensure positive British pressure on China to accept the Simla Convention as well, and later that not protesting its actual implementation might ensure British support in dealing with China, at the same time they remained unhappy about it, as the documents of 1945 Anglo-Tibetan negotiations show: "The Tibetan legal arguments, though far from cogent, reveal their strong commitment to maintaining control over NEFA and thus their unwillingness to accept the McMahon Line."[68]

This small chapter of a big game played from 1914 onward led to the permanent end of the Tsari Rongkor only forty-five years later and the definition of the area as a strategic zone subject to heavy Sino-Indian militarization. In 1956 there was for the first time a foreign presence at the Rongkor pilgrims' camp at Maṇḍala Plain, that of the Chinese. Some Chinese officials in Central Tibet dispatched several small medical teams to Tsari. One was temporarily stationed at Chikchar and the other visited Maṇḍala Plain. The medics treated and dispensed medicines to sick pilgrims who were traveling to or camped at Maṇḍala Plain. When the procession was due to depart, they withdrew and did not participate further. These apparently innocent medical teams are now seen by Tibetans as an important reconnaissance leading up to the Chinese occupation and border claims of 1959, a view not without substance. Chinese troops marched to Maṇḍala Plain only three years later. It was there on August 26, 1959, that the very first violent conflict in the Sino-Indian dispute over the McMahon line erupted, as a Chinese force of two to three hundred crossed the traditional border at Maṇḍala Plain and drove out Indian frontier troops stationed at the advance post of Longju in the lower Tsari valley.[69] At this time China accused India of collusion with local Tibetans at Tsari, calling them "traitorous rebel bandits," although there is no record of any Tibetan armed resistance in this area. Nehru immediately ordered the Indian army to assume direct defense responsibilities in the Subansiri-Tsari border zone. In the Colombo Conference proposals of 1963, the area below Lo Mikyimdün village where the Rongkor had run was designated as a disputed zone for special negotiations. The Chinese army maintains an advance military base in the area of Lo Mikyimdün village to the present day.

While the activities of agents remote from the actual pilgrimage itself combined at different times to encourage either an aggressive or a docile tribal disposition toward the Rongkor pilgrims and Lodzong administrators, the form and pattern of any particular tribal-Tibetan encounter was often heavily determined by the cultural models, systems of values, and practices prevailing among the upper Subansiri peoples. Some of these were used by the Tibetans as essential markers of difference in defining their own ethnic identity against that of the "Lopa" during the encounters facilitated by the tribute and procession. One might ask how the relations of competition focused on the mountain were seen in different terms by both parties involved.

Models, Values, Practices, and Identities

Clearly, the southern parts of Pure Crystal Mountain became an increasingly contested territory throughout this century. Yet Tibetan explanations of tribal violence against pilgrims are dominated by the idea of tribals' dissatisfaction with their tribute payments. Surprisingly, the notion that the Tibetan pilgrims were trespassers on tribal lands for which the correct "rents" (*satrel*) had to be paid—or retaliation followed—hardly figures, except in the minds of the few Tsariwa who lived at the border. The territory that pilgrims passed through was considered uninhabited by them, as it lacked permanent settlement or cultivation. And apart from a few ephemeral signs of the hunter-gatherer, woodsman, or traveler's presence, the tribals remained unseen by the pilgrims, except, of course, when confrontations occurred. In any case, their historical narratives described the visits and the religious and "civilizing" activities of a string of great Buddhist saints and yogins in the area, thus constituting it as an important part of "their" power place. The turn-of-the-century tribal claims of ownership and the actual Tibetan tax payments for use of the southern parts of Tsari had been forgotten by the 1940s and '50s, and replaced by the idea of tribute under threat of violence constructed in terms of essential Buddhist versus barbarian identities.

The Tibetan use of the term *dzong* to describe the government negotiations with the tribals at Tsari chiefly denotes the giving of goods in return for safe passage of pilgrimage processions. In the standard dictionaries the term is glossed "fee for safe-conduct," which agrees with this definition, but also "the act of accompanying, escorting."[70] Thus, the term could also have been used to refer to the government presence and support throughout the pilgrimage. I have translated *dzong* as "tribute," as this word captures well the meaning of the actual transaction from the Tibetan point of view, and because in standard English it defines both a political relation of submission between two parties and a payment as "a price of peace or protection."[71] However, the tribal interpretation of events described by and related to Tibetan *dzong* was somewhat different.

Tribute as a form of political relation has often been cited as practiced by Tibetan rulers in conjunction with neighboring states in high Asia. However, it has rarely been convincingly established exactly what tribute meant to both parties concerned as a type of relation in any particular instance or context. The use of *dzong* at Tsari is not necessarily a Tibetan innovation but is a tribal one, although the Tibetans were no strangers to such arrangements. Throughout the tribal hill districts of what is now Arunachal Pradesh, and in parts of Assam, the practice of so-called tributes was a common form of political relation both between tribes and between tribes and the British colonial rulers of India.[72] The tribes of the Subansiri area in particular, referred to generically as Dafla and Miri in British colonial sources, had a history of conflicts and tributes with colonial administrators dating back at least to the early nineteenth century.[73] The seminomadic Hill Miri, possibly one of the tribes historically involved at Tsari, were paid a form of tribute (originally in produce, later in cash), called *posa*, by the government. But each party had its own view of the practice. The Miri saw the tribute as a kind of rent for the use of their ancestral hunting lands by recent Assamese settlers; the government saw it as a fee or payment with which the hill tribe could be bought off from raiding the plains.[74] These alternative constructions of the meaning of tribute seem to parallel the situation at Tsari, where the Tibetans also regarded the Lodzong as a payoff to stop attacks. In contrast, the meaning of the payments (and the associated attacks) for the tribes can be seen to center around ideas of fair compensation and rent and intergenerational responsibility for maintaining honor, and aspects of the actual payment and actions often taken are closely linked to status in various ways. The ethnographic accounts of life in one tribal society in the upper Subansiri basin, the Nishi (Nisü), who were almost certainly attacking pilgrims, reveal several points of importance here.

First, if tribesmen believe they have been wronged in a dispute, for instance over property, unpaid debts, theft, or even violence, it is established practice to mount a retaliatory raid on the perceived perpetrators and their kinsmen. Such acts are supported by the community as a valid form of self-help in a social system with no centralized authority. The outcome of raids can range from theft and kidnapping of slaves or prisoners to violent injury and murder, much as was the result of raids on the pilgrimage processions. And, just as occurred on the ravine circuit, surprise ambush was the favored form of attack. Raiding and retaliation in disputes could become extremely protracted, spanning generations, with the responsibility to deal with them being inherited by a clan lineage. The long memories of the 1906 war and Miri Mission just mentioned are good examples of this principle in relation to outsiders. But within the tribal culture, such grievances very often ended with compensatory payment rather than killing or violence.[75] Such disputes could be settled in mediated debate, where the two sides lined up facing each other and compensation was negotiated, and the settlement might involve the transfer of goods of considerable value before satisfaction was reached. The lists of goods exchanged in such tribal compensation arrangements are in fact often remarkably similar to those for the Lodzong transactions.[76] Finally, relations could be normalized with a peace pact through the swearing of binding oaths witnessed by the gods and accompanied by the sacrifice of a mithan ox. Once again, the details of execution of such oath ceremonies are more or less identical to those found in the Lodzong.[77] In fact, the Lodzong appears to be mainly a tribal ritual form with certain Tibetan elaborations added. One can see that from the tribal point of view, the whole cycle of events that took place at Tsari during this century was for them a version of normal social relations concerning the fair settlement of dues, and that a part of that was the use of socially sanctioned violence.

Such violence was wholly unacceptable to the Indic Buddhist morality found in the orthodox Tibetan point of view. Unjustified social violence, in particular, led to the downgrading of moral status and had consequences after death by way of bad karmic fortunes. Quite the reverse was the tribal worldview; violent and aggressive acts that lead to successes and gains were valued by the Nishi. This point is nicely reflected in Nishi eschatology:

> On their way to the Land of the Dead, a land imagined similar to this earth, the departed have to pass a deity who acts as gate-keeper of the nether world and subjects the new arrivals to an interrogation regarding their doings in life. Those who can point to successful raids, the capture of prisoners, the acquisition of many wives and slaves, all symbols of worldly success, are received with honour, whereas little notice is taken of the meek and peaceful who have led an inconspicuous life.[78]

In Nishi life, martial and economic success were the kind of conduct that led to the acquisition of status or prestige.

While this worldview may count toward an explanation in theory for the motivation behind tribal violence against pilgrims, there is at least one other compelling social and material complex in Nishi society that reveals motivations for tribal involvements with Tibetans at Tsari. Descriptions of Nishi life all note the value placed on building not only large affinal networks but also networks of ceremonial friendship. Such ceremonial friendships were most often forged by the ritual exchange of valuable property. The most highly valued item in Nishi society was the Tibetan prayer bell, and it was the most prestigious item of exchange with which to cultivate solid alliances and friendships of this type; "among Daflas the purchase of a valuable prayer-bell (*maje*) creates between seller and buyer ceremonial ties comparable to those between families linked by marriage, and such ties add materially to a man's prestige and security."[79] Tibetan prayer bells, minus handle and clapper, were not regarded as musical instruments; rather, they were attributed divine origins, named, gendered, and passed on through descent lineages. The tribal warriors who attended the Lodzong were connoisseurs of these bells, accepting only the finest, oldest specimens, especially those with sacred syllables cast on them. Such items were intensely sought after, and their possession generated a great deal of status and was linked to economic and political power. As Christoph von Fürer-Haimendorf put it, "the owner of a famous bell, worth perhaps eight to ten mithan, gains as much prestige in Dafla society as the owner of a painting by Cézanne or Picasso acquires in European circles."[80] Outside of Nishi life, it is significant that Tibetan bell possession and exchange were also important to status acquisition and ranking and systems of value and currency in trade deals among the Apa Tani and Miri societies far to the south.

A few new bells did come into circulation through sporadic tribal trading contacts with Tibetans along the frontier to the north, but the Tsari tribute was a regular and reliable source of bells of the highest quality for the leaders of the groups who attended. What is more, some Tibetan pilgrims practiced devotions using these ritual objects during the long progress to the procession's departure at Maṇḍala Plain, and carried and used them during the course of the pilgrimage itself. Pilgrims might thus be the targets of attack, theft, or kidnapping down in the ravines in an effort to obtain the highly prized bells. The Tibetans have a range of popular narratives to account for why their ritual implements are so sought after by the tribals and their part in the Lodzong transactions as well. The usual plot is that earlier Tantric lama heroes, such as Padmasambhava or Thangthong Gyelpo, who originally opened the procession route or a "hidden land" (*beyül*) in Loyül in order to meditate there, encountered the Lopa and overcame them with magical powers. The tribes were very impressed, and the departing saints offered them as gifts the only possessions they carried, their standard Tantric ritual accoutrements—the bell (*drilbu*) and "thunderbolt" scepter (*dorje*)—promising to return again with more twelve years later. One is left with the interesting question: Did the innovation of the Rongkor and Lodzong in the eighteenth century precipitate the formation of a new and complex local system of value and exchange among the Subansiri peoples?

Ritual and Identity at the Border

There is no doubt that the payment of compensatory goods was of importance from the tribal point of view for a number of related reasons. But in terms of ritual practice, the Tibetans themselves considered the actual yak sacrifice and oath-swearing the most effective component of the Lodzong ceremonies for halting the violence. They thought so precisely because these were viewed as "Lopa" or barbarian customs that would have the most binding influence over them. The Tibetan attribution of these Lodzong practices to tribal origins appears justified in the light of comparative ethnography; tribal people to the south commonly tie sacrificial animals to erect posts and decorated wooden sacrificial structures, invoke the gods as witness, smear blood to mark a pact, divide up the carcass and distribute it, believe that the gods will avenge any breach, and so on. Yet in reality, throughout the Tibetan borderlands in particular, live animal sacrifice was practiced and was never such a clear-cut marker of otherness as opposed to Tibetanness.

Tibetan Buddhist sources often proclaim that live animal sacrifice came to an end when Tibet was "civilized" by Buddhism in "the distant past." Doctrinally, at least, imported Indic Buddhist ethics would not tolerate the use of live animals, and various mock substitutes were introduced for use in a class of uniquely Tibetan Buddhist sacrifice rituals. Yet the role of ethics here is perhaps much less important than a major shift in power relations that occurred: "The banning of animal sacrifices was historically in Tibet the sign of Tibetan Buddhist dominance over local pre-Buddhist deity cults . . . and the lama approaches the local deities through the universalistic procedures of Tantric ritual."[81] The fact that the twentieth-century Tibetan Buddhist state had to sponsor and participate by way of its own innovations in a live animal sacrifice is a good example of the expediency of ritual modes of statecraft. It echoes another ancient circumstance, the Sino-Tibetan treaty oaths of the eighth and ninth centuries, when sacrificial animals were killed and Tibetan participants anointed their lips with the blood. R. A. Stein has recently shown that the Tibetans were complying with Chinese custom during these ceremonies, although their own royal cult of the period did, of course, use animal sacrifice.[82] Many ethnic Tibetan communities, particularly in borderland areas, continued to perform their own live yak and other animal sacrifices, also in connection with oath-swearing, well into the twentieth century.[83] This feature of their common social history is one that Tibetan Buddhists most often prefer not to acknowledge but to project onto and identify strongly with the so-called primitive, barbarian, or uncivilized others with whom they were sometimes forced to deal.

The contradictions and resultant tensions between real aspects of Tibetan life, especially the taking of life through hunting, domestic butchery, social violence, and local sacrifices, and the expectations of introduced Buddhist moral discourses is a constant and time-honored theme in Tibetan society. I have already demonstrated how, from an individual pilgrim's view, the ravine circuit itself is precisely about addressing such contradictions and tensions and providing a ritual solution to them. This tension, and issues of self-definition and identity that flow from it, can become amplified in the borderland areas, where ethnic self and other confront each other directly in various interactions. This amplification is particularly pronounced in popular yet geographically peripheral pilgrimage venues, where representational distinctions of ethnic identity can be most forcefully drawn out and reiterated within the context of certain organized forms and structures like the Lodzong.

Part IV

✦

LOCAL LIVES

10

✦ ✦ ✦ ✦

Complex Identities and Local Rituals

In this and the final chapter, I will consider the lives of the local populations that were permanently settled around Pure Crystal Mountain during the middle of this century. My primary concern is to outline and discuss ways local lives were influenced by residence at a cult mountain site that was of pan-Tibetan ritual importance, as well as how the residents played a role in the maintenance of the mountain's traditions. Here I will begin by analyzing the construction of various local identities and will consider some of the community rituals that were related to both the mountain and the Tsariwa themselves. Certain annual community ceremonies will be shown to form important linkages between the Tantric cult, local mountain worship, and the interests of the state. In chapter 11, I give a short account of Tibetan social organization, human ecology and economy, and administration in the Tsari communities, and investigate the vicissitudes of everyday life relative to the particular status of the area as a sacred sanctuary, its many pilgrim visitors, and its borderland location.

Although many anthropological works about a particular place commence with descriptions of the local physical setting and its human residents, I have intentionally reserved this material until the end. This stylistic inversion is justified partly on the grounds of another type of inversion. Tsari was an unusual place compared to other small Tibetan mountain districts, in that it regularly experienced major population inversions. From early summer through to autumn each year the place was temporarily but consistently colonized by a large and diverse population of outsiders, the pilgrims. And every twelve years it experienced a massive influx for several months during the Rongkor. Thus, these outside ritual users annually outnumbered the estimated five to six hundred Tsariwa living in small communities around the mountain during the 1940s and 1950s.[1] In addition, most of the complex cult of Pure Crystal Mountain was historically generated and periodically reconstituted by agents external to the region. Even the communities of Tantric meditators, whose ritual lineage ancestors originally "founded" the mountain, were by the very nature of their practice only itinerant visitors there. Because Tsariwa life and the local environment were significantly defined in terms of, and influenced by, most aspects of the mountain cult's content, history, and dynamics, one can appreciate little about them without having first understood the overall cult traditions in some detail. However, none of these considerations should be taken to mean that the Tsariwa were unimportant or insignificant in relation to the mountain cult and its ritual institutions. Indeed, in some respects they figured quite prominently in terms of their identities, the regular rituals, and a host of service roles concerning the staging of pilgrimages, some of which have already been briefly mentioned in previous chapters.

Constructions of Local Identity

How did the Tibetans living around Pure Crystal Mountain define themselves both as a group and in relation to others, how did they represent this identity to others, and how were they, in turn, represented by others? For the local Tibetans, all levels of their identity were bound up with the cultural definitions of the place they lived in. This fact itself seems to hold true in all other parts of the Tibetan world and in South Asia generally. As already indicated in the discussion of the Rongkor procession, the construction of Tibetan identities is uniquely bound to locality, usually natal or residential place, and in Tibetan society generally, kinship names are replaced by household and village names as terms of designation.[2]

Children of Saints?

Tsariwa, or "Ones from Tsari," is the local collective identity term. All those who use it define themselves in relation to their birth and residence place at Tsari by means of increasingly smaller units of the microgeography of the region. For present purposes I am only going to consider the gross divisions customarily employed. There are roughly two of these: persons who live in the upper, northern valleys around the mountain, especially from the Phödzo Sumdo-Chikchar area in the east around to the Yümé-Yütö area in the west; and those who live southeast in the *rong* area at Lo Mikyimdün or Seven Households village. This division takes account of altitude and ecology and the lifestyle possibilities they dictate; relative proximity to the mountain and its major shrines and retreat places (Chikchar and Yümé); and proximity to the tribal populations. Thus, one can see that Lo Mikyimdün village area was in a zone of its own compared to all the other Tsari communities (see fig. 8.1). This division is reflected in the more formal administrative boundaries for the region (which I discuss in chapter 11), although administration was also historically constituted partly by way of sectarian claims, the distribution of power between the government Dzong (administrative centres), and ritual restrictions relating to modes of production.

The origins of the Tsariwa, presently impossible to trace for lack of sources, are probably quite diverse. At least in the twentieth century, the high incidence of persons with hereditary, annual *mibog* ("human-lease") obligations to estates in distant places reflects a history of inbound migration to the district.[3] In addition, quite a few Tsariwa know that some of their ancestors were originally pilgrims to the area who decided to stay and settle and eventually married into the communities. All available historical sources indicate that permanent lay communities have existed around Pure Crystal Mountain for at least the last three or four centuries. The Tsariwa from the upper valleys have their own commonly held ideas concerning the origins of the lay communities there, for example:

> In the distant past, only meditators lived in Yümé. But gradually some Tantric masters had children together with women, and most of the people are descendents of male and female yoga practitioners. It is similar in the east of Tsari, how the people came to settle there and develop villages.[4]

Similarly: "Tsari was a place originally meant only for meditators, and then slowly villages grew because the meditators, male and female, started getting married and having children. And so the Tsariwa are by breeding very religious people, the offspring of meditators and saints."[5]

Whatever the case, their representations of their own identity are tied closely to the site's history as a place of Tantric ritual importance. The upper valley peoples are also unequivocal about their being of Tibetan (Phöpa) ethnic origin—for a good reason as I will now explain.

Children of Barbarians?

The identity representations associated with the Tsari peoples who inhabited the lower border village of Lo Mikyimdün were more complex than those of the "highlanders." From the point of view of biological descent, there appears to have been a long history of mixed marriages or liaisons between Tibetans and neighboring tribal peoples in the village. The villagers here are known to have at times purchased Tinglo tribal children as slaves and employed tribal youths as laborers, some of whom later became part of the community. They also allowed visiting tribal traders to stay in the village overnight, a practice not followed in other parts of the borderlands.[6] In the 1950s there were Tibetan families, mixed marriage Tibetan-tribal families, and Tibetanized Khalo tribal families all living in the village. In addition, as I mentioned in chapter 8, the residents' lifestyle and appearance in terms of dress, accoutrements, architecture, crops, and in some cases physical features resembled something of a hybrid between those of highland Tibetans and tribal peoples in the eyes of visiting pilgrims, a fact also commented on by the few Europeans who visited the site in this century.[7] Many of the inhabitants could speak both Tibetan and some tribal dialects.

On the basis of local knowledge, the highland Tsariwa and Char people rationally classified the *rong* dwellers around Lo Mikyimdün in the east as being more "Tibetan" or more Phöpa than Lopa, in other words partly "tribalized Tibetans," while those living around Lung, Dakshing, and Charmé in the southwest were considered more Lopa than Phöpa, being partly "Tibetanized tribals." However, the outsiders who visited as pilgrims frequently referred to the people in Lo Mikyimdün as Lopa because of their general appearance and their residence at the border, and partly because of the name of the place, a point I will return to shortly. *Lopa* is, as I have noted, a very pejorative term signifying "barbarian" or "savage" to Tibetans. D. Y. Yuthok, a Lhasa aristocrat, gives a typical description of how the Lopa at Tsari were seen by people from Central Tibet and other regions:

> The area around the holy mountain was inhabited by a primitive race of people called the Lobas. Though they officially were subjects of the Tibetan government and were nominally Buddhists . . . [in] many ways they were uncivilized and undisciplined. They did not wear any clothes except a small piece of cloth large enough to cover their sex organs. The Loba men always carried knives as well as bows and poisoned arrows. They are said to eat insects.[8]

The stereotype of Lopaness in most Tibetan accounts usually includes references to such things as nudity; sexual openness; the propensity to violence; lack of personal hygiene and particularly strong body odor; love of dancing; the practice of slavery; the consumption of exotic foods like worms, insects, frogs, lizards, and monkeys; the practice of incest; animal sacrifice; and the indiscriminate killing of living things.[9] In general, this stereotyping is the stuff that "high cultural" superiority in relation to preliterate, materially simple societies is made of and would not be at all out of place in European colonial discourse of the eighteenth and nineteenth centuries.

Many Lo Mikyimdün residents took strong exception to being called Lopa, for they were Tibetans as far as they were concerned. This sensitivity of identity was known to the other Tsariwa, who would sometimes tease the people of Lo Mikyimdün, saying "Hey, you Lopa!" to which they would jokingly reply, "Hey, you beggar (*trangpo*)!" referring to the upper valley dwellers' winter alms-collecting tours.[10] The jokes, and the sensitive and potentially embarrassing issues of ethnic and cultural identities that underlie them, continue up to the present day.

To avoid the stigma of Lopaness, the Lo Mikyimdün people took pains to point out their Tibetanness to outsiders such as pilgrims. One traditional strategy, remembered by a pilgrim visitor to the village, was to claim that the name Lo Mikyimdün actually meant "Seven Households to the South" and not "Seven Households of Lo" because of a misunderstanding of the spoken words. This misunderstanding is possible because the Tibetan word for "south" (spelled *lho*) and the abbreviated form of the name Lopa as Lo (spelled *klo*) are pronounced virtually the same. Michael Aris has pointed out an interesting modern usage of exactly the same shift. In relation to the Tibetan designation of borderland populations called Lopa within the "nationality" (*minzu*) label system of Chinese state-attributed ethnic identities, he notes "Their name is written *lHo-pa*, "Southerner," by the Chinese, apparently since the traditional spelling carries the pejorative sense of "barbarian" in Tibetan."[11] As for this strategy in relation to the area of Lo Mikyimdün, it is known to have been named Lowo (spelled *klo-bo*, as in "barbarian") already in the fifteenth century, and this spelling has been consistently used for rendering the name Lo Mikyimdün from the early eighteenth century to the present in local Tibetan documents.[12] The traditional variant spellings of the name are even more telling as to outsider perceptions of the place. A Tibetan pilgrim-author who visited the area in 1919–20 used a spelling that reads "There Are Lopa Households" (*klo mi'i khyim 'dugs*), which is pronounced almost the same as Lo Mikyimdün by most Tibetans.[13]

Eschewing the identity of Lopa at Tsari was not just done because the term itself is derogatory; in some cases it was clearly considered a matter of status and advantage to be identified as Tibetan, as the following account by a resident of Chikchar during the 1950s points out:

> There was a Lopa servant [a euphemism for "slave"] girl from one of the local households whom I knew. She ran away once and went to live with a Lopa man deep down in the *rong*, and they had many children together. I was the religious and lay official in Tsari at the time, so these Lopa used to say I was their relative, for obvious reasons. The Lopa used to say I was their ancestor! I also used to say that to them for a joke. But they always brought Lopa food like rice and maize to me when they came up to trade. My real relatives over in Char were disgusted with me for having relations with Lopa, and even for joking that we were related. It was not the thing to do, they were embarrassed by it. For the Lopa's part, it was to their advantage to be able to say, "We have relatives in Tibet," because when there were fights and rivalries they would be left alone as the others were scared of the possible Tibetan government reprisals if they harmed them. So it helped them to pretend this.[14]

These identities of Tsariwa as Lopa were indigenous ethnic classifications, some of the markers that were generic for southern borderland peoples and of long historical standing. But another set of identity markers was applied to the people of Tsari, and those in Lo Mikyimdün in particular, and these were the basis for local rituals performed by pilgrim visitors and were also compounded with the identity of Lopa on other occasions.

Divine Persons?

During the 1950s, some of the laypeople around Tsari, particularly those of Lo Mikyimdün, were identified by outsiders as embodiments or incarnations of divine beings of one type or another. Such identities have a long and changing history at Tsari, and several rituals and many beliefs came to be based on them. I will briefly trace their development in order to appreciate the particular representations of persons and place found in later times.

The occurrence of this type of identity can be traced back to the visionary definition of the total environment of Tsari as a maṇḍala palace in one form or another by earlier Tibetan lamas who were Tantric practitioners. For example, in a fourteenth-century lama's account, aspects of the natural environment are represented as emanations of the Tantric initiatory goddesses of the maṇḍala: "As there are pure manifestations of the sky-goers as people of all kinds, and animals, various beasts of prey, and game animals, one should not cause harm, and should generate a positive view toward everything [at Tsari], because one cannot know just how they will appear."[15]

Ancient and later popular Tibetan beliefs about the sensitivity of nature deities and their environments to human activities are well documented. Such Buddhist statements as we have here represent an aspect of the colonization of these traditions by the lamas and of their eventual ethicization in Buddhist terms. Other related claims about Tsari were regularly made. In 1464, a lama visiting Tsari dreamed of being welcomed by a southern tribesman, whom he surmised to be the local protective deity known as the Tsari Shingkyong. And a sixteenth-century lama had visions of local protective deities that resembled Lopa warriors, with animal skin hats and leaves covering their genitals.[16] Lamas also claim to have met with local women at Tsari whom they recognized as female sky-goers, and so on. Later practitioners who visited Tsari and were familiar with such claims interpreted their own meetings with Tsariwa on the basis of them. For example, a Bhutanese cleric on pilgrimage to the area in the eighteenth century had an exchange with a party of Lopa men and women, after which he reflected, "[A]ny men and women you see in the place of Tsāri need to be thought of as divine heroes (*pawo*) and amazons (*pamo*)."[17] Claims such as these recur in Tibetan sources on Tsari right up to the present day. Tibetan assumptions and ideas about the ontological continuities between persons and places and theories of embodiment as they are expressed in Tibetan Tantra allow for human residents to be divine beings as a natural feature of a *né* such as Pure Crystal Mountain.

In an early-nineteenth-century lama's account of the area, the local inhabitants are specifically related to the divine retinue of the maṇḍala palace and its landscape architecture: "In Pure Crystal Mountain there dwells a divine assembly of two thousand eight hundred. In every rock mountain, lake, and tree of its outer environs there live innumerable divine heroes and sky-goers. The men and women who live here are a lineage of divine heroes and sky-goers.[18]

At about this time the general representation of Tsariwa in relation to the landscape maṇḍala palace begins to be specifically applied to the peoples in the *rong* around Lo Mikyimdün in the genre of guidebook literature:

> There is a village that suppresses the Lopa called Lo Mikyimdün. Here a human lineage of divine heroes and amazons, who originate in the twenty-four Tantric sites, are said to take birth. Even their population is exactly sixty-two [like the number of deities in the Khorlo Dompa maṇḍala].[19]

And, in a well-known Tibetan geography of the world from the early nineteenth century: "In that [place] known as Tsari Maṇḍala Plain, there are such things as households that are called Lo Mikyadeng [i.e., Mikyimdün], and they are said to have sky-goers in a succession of human descendants, who are known as the *né* guardian sky-goers of Tsari.[20]

By the nineteenth century, the identity of the Lo Mikyimdün people was firmly related to the local protective deities of Tsari, and the village was seen as a sort of front-line defense of the landscape maṇḍala against the non-Tibetanized tribes to the south.[21] This view fits with the general landscape architecture of the maṇḍala in its lower regions, as it is around its outer base that the classes of guardian or protective deities dwell, defending the perimeter against subversion. The quite specific identity the people in this hitherto little-known border settlement gained during the period is undoubtedly related to the growing importance of the place as the main staging point for the popular Rongkor procession at this time. These identities of local people from Lo Mikyimdün became expressed in relations between Tsaṛiwa and visitors to the area, both in terms of attitudes and in ritual forms.

How Can You Be Sure Who's Divine?

Many pilgrims who visited Lo Mikyimdün performed a particular ritual in the village.[22] Three brief but recent accounts of this ritual present it respectively from the point of view of the pilgrims who performed it, from that of the villagers themselves and in the eyes of upper valley Tsariwa. A Lhasa aristocrat on pilgrimage there recalls:

> The pilgrims who visited Seven Households begged food from the inhabitants following a long-standing custom. It was said that a living deity dwelt in the locality who was always ready to give a spiritual or physical boon depending on the prayer of the pilgrim. There was only one hitch: no one knew where she stayed and no one could recognize her. It was said that she gave the blessings through food begged from the inhabitants living there, but even the families in this village did not know when and how the deity blessed the food. In the hope that the food they gave to the beggars had been blessed by the deity and that they would also receive a blessing, the villagers gave generously to the begging pilgrims. Inspired by this tradition, the pilgrims did not want to miss the opportunity to get this immense spiritual and worldly blessing. So with their begging bowls they went to as many houses in the village as they could. They had firm faith that somehow at one of the houses they would receive some food that had been blessed by the deity. It is strange that although the villagers never knew from which house, theirs or another, the blessed food had come, still they too believed in the legend and always gave food to the begging pilgrims. In our case we sent the servants with bowls to beg from every single household and warned them not to skip even one. . . . They had brought a variety of foods. . . . [A]ll of this was cooked together and was distributed equally between the family members, servants and even the animals. We never did know just who the deity was.[23]

A local resident of Lo Mikyimdün remembers these type of pilgrims passing through his village:

> When they arrived in our valley, although they had the status of Lhasa aristocrats, they had to go begging there in our village asking for "radishes, pots of yogurt, a little barley flour, a little butter"—like that. If you ask why it was good to beg there, well, at the time there were always some divine heroes of the male lineage and amazons of the female lineage, and you could never be sure that those two were not standing at the door of the households. Because this was so, they each did the rounds of every household door to get all the food of the divine heroes and amazons. Well, because of that, although they were government aristocrats they were compelled to beg in that way. The people of our valley told them, "We are not Lopa. We are pure Tibetans." That valley of ours was the border ravine. Because that was so they probably thought, "They are Lopa," but we were really of pure Tibetan stock.[24]

Finally, a resident of Chikchar in upper Tsari saw it as follows:

> All the pilgrims went to each house to beg something from the villagers. What they gave was just something like a potato or an onion, but maybe that had empowerment (*chinlab*), because you never knew who might be the divine hero or amazon. The people of Lo Mikyimdün always kept giving to the pilgrims, just small things like a potato or so, but they didn't mind giving because everyone considered them divine, so they liked that![25]

The ritual involved a play on identities at several levels; it briefly transposed subordinate and superordinate groups, and it allowed for the invocation of various distinctions. Potentially, both parties—pilgrims and villagers—stood to gain. The pilgrims believed they got sacred power from the food obtained by thorough ritual technique and felt the "faithful" villagers were being benevolent towards them. The villagers had a feeling they gained status by having other, often high-ranking, persons begging from them and treating them as though they might be divine. They also gained a unique opportunity to represent their own borderland identities to peoples from the center and other upland parts of Tibet. It was an opportunity to resist the collection of often pejorative identity markers applied to them by others.

The Field-protector's Fierce Human Retinue

Although called Lopa by many, the people of Lo Mikyimdün were for the most part Tibetan or Tibetanized to some significant extent and were Buddhists, or at least nominally Buddhist in the case of tribal settlers. But the peoples in all the territory south of the village area were considered to be true Lopa by the Tsariwa. The Lopa groups already mentioned, who had seasonal contacts and reasonable relations with the local Tibetans, were also represented by themselves and others as having a type of divine identity. According to the Tsariwa, their nearby tribal neighbors were, or at least considered themselves to be, the human retinue or subjects of the dark, lion-faced local protective deity of the mountain, who was commonly referred to as the Tsari Shingkyong. There are other Tibetan borderland precedents for such representations of eastern Himalayan highland populations. René de Nebesky-Wojkowitz has shown how the costumes and accoutrements in the iconography of various classes of Tibetan protective deities are the same as those for southern tribal peoples, including the Lopa.[26] An identical type of representation is used to characterize the Dagpa people of far eastern Bhutan, who are held to be the human retinue of the deity Jomo Remati.[27]

Unlike the fairly benevolent Buddhist identity that the Lo Mikyimdün people enjoyed, the Lopa as retinue of the Tsari Shingkyong were considered fierce and barbaric. The entourages of many Tibetan mountain gods are represented as warring, hunting hordes disturbing the peace of the innocent at the slightest provocation, and this picture fitted well with Tibetan perceptions of Lopaness. Tibetan sources that identify Tsari with sites like charnel grounds in the Indian Tantric texts are careful to equate the local deities who are described as gathering in such places with the Tibetan local protectors at Tsari. Such assimilations have always been an important aspect of legitimizing the *néri* mountains as Tibetan Tantric cult places, as well as providing a fundamental linkage to local mountain cults for their incorporation into the formal, textually mediated systems of Buddhism and Bön. This syncretism is quite clear in the *néri* cult. A lama from Tsari who had regular contacts with tribal people to the south reflected on the way they related to the Tsari Shingkyong compared with the local Tibetans:

> They used to worship the Shingkyong quite often; they didn't know about any other Tibetan religion. They worshiped the Shingkyong wherever they could, that was their

main interest. They did a very different Shingkyong ritual from us. When the Lopa did it, their ritual priest, like in the photos you have [see figure 8.4], got a large male or female yak; the bigger the offering the better it was. Then they chanted, "I make offerings to the Shingkyong . . . ," and so on, and at first just pretended to cut the animal, to sacrifice it. After this mental worship they really did stab it and kill it, with the priest leading the way. Then they cut the animal up and took the parts of the body away with them. Even if they could not make a large offering, they would just crush an egg as a sacrifice. They always sacrificed living things, harmed them. There was a tree where the Lopa and the Tibetans believed the Shingkyong lived, down on the Rongkor route. It was called Dakshing, or maybe Takshing. That was a Lopa dialect name for the place, not a Tibetan one. The Tibetans called it Ngampa Tratrok ("Awe-inspiring Screams"), the charnel ground that is mentioned in the Tantras.[28]

In general, the Tibetan descriptions conform to the tribal ethnographies. The last point is significant as these types of potentially violent deities are depicted as dwelling in certain trees at charnel grounds in the Tantras. Like the typical tribal warrior, the dark, lion-faced Tsari Shingkyong also sports a lance, a bow, and a quiver of arrows.[29] The lama's further comments are revealing as to how Tibetans understood this violent identity relating to the deity and how they used it to explain tribal behavior within the context of their own practices and beliefs:

The Lopa considered themselves the subjects of the Shingkyong. While we Tibetans were not allowed to hunt, or even shout or spit in certain holy areas, the Lopa went on hunting and killing wild animals, and usually nothing happened to them [by way of the deity's retribution], so maybe they were the Shingkyong's retinue, that is what we believed. The Lopa themselves used to say, "We are the Shingkyong's retinue." Sometimes at Tsari, if people dreamed about Lopa, that was taken as a sign that they must perform worship of the Shingkyong.

There are many types of representations of person in Tibetan culture that invoke various nonhuman or semidivine identities. But these identities, like all representations in general, are never subscribed to in a monolithic fashion by those who share the same worldview. They are debated, accepted, or rejected. This was certainly the case for identities associated with the peoples of Tsari, as is clear from the recent memoir of a visit to the region by a high-ranking Gelukpa cleric: "This was the most famous place of pilgrimage in Tibet, for it is said to be the palace of the deity Cakrasamvara [i.e. Khorlo Dompa]. . . . Some say that the natives of Tsari are guardian spirits; but I think they are simply primitive people.[30]

Servants and Keepers of the Né

Another important aspect of Tsariwa identity was a complex perception of themselves as servants of the *né* or keepers of the *né*, an idea that outsiders also shared about them. This may be related to the concept that the local people where somehow assimilated to the guardian deities of the place. But in everyday life for the Tsariwa, this idea actually translated as an identity based on various kinds of works and services that members of the local communities performed to maintain the mountain cult and its pilgrimage traditions. It should be stressed here that this identity does not imply purely voluntary services or even worship in this context, although there was a degree of that involved. The identity of servants or keepers of the *né* entailed productive activities and ritual obligations, both of which formed part of the overall economy and were rotated and discharged by full members of the village community. This aspect of local identity derived from a set of concepts and designations including *néshab*, or "service to the *né*"; *tsulpa*, the name of the pilgrims' resthouse (*tsulkang*) keepers, which carries the sense of one with a "duty," "responsibility," or even "custom;" *chölé*, or "religious work"; and *longkhen*, meaning something between "beggar" and "solicitor of donations." I will limit the discussion here to annual village ritual obligations involving *chölé* and will describe service works and "begging" in chapter 11. An interesting aspect of village ritual at Tsari is the link it formed between the state and the local communities by way of the worship of the protective deities of the mountain.

The Cult of Protective Deities

The Tibetan protective deities are so called because they are supposed to protect religion, its practitioners, and the sites they use and occupy from all manner of problems, harm, and obstructions. However, as Nebesky-Wojkowitz demonstrated, the label "protective" is merely a convention under which a complex cult with a staggering number of deities, practices, and purposes is subsumed.[31] In general, the cult of protective deities is an area of blurred distinctions in Tibetan religion, with so many exceptions that it defies rigid classification—in large part because of the multiple identities and ambivalent natures of many of the deities themselves, created through the historical process of assimilation of autochthons into systematized Buddhism and Bön.

As natural centers (as opposed to monastic shrine rooms) of the cult of protective deities, *néri* came to function as popular and important sites in Tibetan religious life where the beliefs, orientations, and practices of both local and universal cults were combined. At Tsari, the worship of the mountain's protective deities was a domain of mutual ritual interest for all parties concerned. Like their tribal neighbors, Tibetans frequently approached the Tsari Shingkyong and other protective deities at the site. But they did so through the medium of Tantric Buddhist rituals from the monastic cult (*cham*, *kangso*, *torma*, etc.) at certain times and with popular folk ritual forms (*sang*, *lungta*, *mo*, etc.) at others, depending on both context and the status and ritual knowledge of the practitioners involved. Because the main protective deities of Tsari and the attitudes and rituals associated with them are crucial for understanding the social linkages implicit in their worship at the mountain, I will introduce them briefly here.

There were many protective deities located at Tsari, but their importance, particular meanings, and worship varied widely, being dependent on their class, specific history, and location (*né*), sectarian interests, and wider popularity in a pan-sectarian/public context. I shall focus only on the two most prominent here. The goddess Dorje Yüdrönma, or "Adamantine Lamp of Turquoise," has her *né* on the northeast slopes of the mountain, and her main shrine was the Zimkhang temple in Chikchar village. She was worshiped in regular village life and in annual community festivals at Tsari. However, as I noted in chapter 6, she also had the status of a Tantric sky-goer and was closely linked to the activities of meditators in the retreat centers of Chikchar. In this respect, she can be seem as an emanation of the meditation deities. Her Tantric status derives from her history of being subdued and converted by a lama hero who opened Tsari, and becoming his ritual sexual consort. In this context she is recognized as having had a prior secret Tantric identity as Lhenchik Kyéma, which equated her with the concept of *sahajā*, the "innate woman," in highest yoga Tantra theory. The Tibetan claim that this goddess was an embodiment of the *sahajā* (itself a technically problematic claim) on Tibetan soil, resident or manifest at Tsari, was already advanced by lamas in the twelfth century in order to justify the identity of the mountain as a site of Tantric ritual frequently mentioned in the Indian texts. This claim was a leading cause for a long-running controversy among scholars from several Buddhist sects over the status of Tsari and other *néri* in Tibetan sacred geography.[32] It also reveals another mechanism for assimilating important Tibetan autochthonic deities and their cult places into a new form of Tibetan Tantrism.

Apart from these local lay and Tantric significations, Dorje Yüdrönma was also a focus of much wider and popular Tibetan interest, both as a deity frequently consulted in divination (*mo*) performed by lamas and as a type of countrywide protector of Tibet. In the latter role, she was seen as leader of the important Tenma Chunyi group of Buddhist mountain deities worshiped within the Nyingmapa, Kagyüpa, and Gelukpa sects alike. The Tenma Chunyi appear to have been important mountain deities prior to the development of Tibetan Tantra and their assimilation into its later cult. In this capacity as "Mistress of All Tenma Goddesses in the Tibetan Realm," Dorje Yüdrönma attracted the attention of the Gelukpa sect and state.[33] Some of the most prominent visionary Gelukpa lamas of the seventeenth and eighteenth century, such as the Fifth Dalai Lama and Lelung Shepé Dorje, who also had connections with the cult of Tsari, composed worship rituals for her during the period when the Rongkor procession was begun at Tsari.

The most important of all protective deities at Pure Crystal Mountain was the Tsari Shingkyong, or "Field-protector," mentioned earlier in relation to the identity of tribal peoples and their rituals. This god is also known as Shingkyong Kunga Shonu, Shingkyong Senge Dongchen, or "Lion-faced Field Protector," and Shingkyong Yabyum.[34] This last epithet signifies a male and female pair (*chamdre*), who are lion-headed with human bodies, and this is how they are commonly represented at Tsari in the icons of the local shrine and in the performance of ritual dances (*cham*). The main shrine of the Tsari Shingkyong was located at Yümé, but all Tsariwa and many pilgrims worshiped this deity, as did those participating in the monastic cult of various sects. His territorial range was believed extensive beyond the mountain, and he manifested in various ways (in dreams, visions, "self-produced" images in rocks, etc.) to the local people and the public in general. The male is often represented as a dark, menacing, and potentially violent figure who inspired great fear and respect. All kinds of ritual breach, on pilgrimage and in daily affairs around the mountain, which were believed to result in mundane problems, illness, and even death, were his domain. He was also a bestower of prosperity and power. He was worshiped daily by many Tsariwa with *sang* and prayer or petition, and in annual festivals. A Tsariwa now in exile in Europe characterized the local community's relationship with the deity as follows:

> The Shingkyong has come to know us and our families for generations, and if we don't worship him, then he will get upset and perhaps punish us. If we worship him, it is very good for our fortunes, and difficulties are cleared. Sometimes in festivals here in Switzerland we read prayers for the Shingkyong, and sometimes when you have a *mo* divination done, the result is that you have to worship the Shingkyong, so it is still important even though we are now far away from Tsari.[35]

In all the above respects, the Tsari Shingkyong is typical of local Tibetan mountain gods (*yüllha* and *shidak*), and ritual approaches to him are those of the pan-Tibetan cult of local mountain worship. Yet the Tantric texts of the monastic cult related to the *néri* are clear about his "real" identity:

> The field-protector of the great vaporous realm of Khachö is large, black, and irresistibly terrible, with the face of a lion, violent and frightful; his lower part radiates a dark luster. . . . His own splendor is the dance of the great, glorious Heruka, whose emanation is visible as the body of the great field-protector.[36]

He is none other than the emanation of the highest Tantric meditation deity of the mountain, Khorlo Dompa (or Heruka), and the female Shingkyong in turn is assimilated to the female lion-headed sky-goer goddess of the Tantric cult, Sengdongma (Sanskrit: Siṃhamukhā) and is thus an emanation of Dorje Pagmo.

I have deliberately exposed the different and overlapping identities, levels of meaning, and ritual significations of these popular and complex protective deities at the mountain because it is by way of them and their worship that many different interests become focused together: those of the lay villager and community, the pilgrim, the monastic cult, the Tantric meditator and lama, and the state. The most interesting expression of these combined interests at Tsari was the cycle of annual village festivals. The most important of these events were funded by the Lhasa government, staged by the villagers as a annual ritual obligation, presided over by the local monks and lamas, and performed in conjunction with the regulation of ritual time and space for pilgrimage on the mountain.

The "Great Religious Work" of Yümé

One aspect of the notion of Tsariwa identity as servants or keepers of the *né* was their active role in staging village-based festivals of worship for the gods and goddesses of the mountain. This activity could be described as *chölé*, or "religious work," in Tibetan, and in fact the name of the main example of a Tsari village festival I will describe here is Chölé Chenmo, or the "Great Religious Work." There is hardly a small mountain community in ethnic Tibetan areas that does not have an annual festival involving worship of the local mountain or territorial gods and a short, intensive period of ritual and social gathering of some form or other. These are the sort of events I referred to briefly in chapter 3 where I discussed the local type of mountain cult in relation to the *néri* type. The larger villages at Tsari—Yümé, Chikchar, and Lo Mikyimdün—all had such rituals. These included an annual deployment of *lungta* and a *sang* offering to the local mountain god of each community at some high spot, followed by a short festival, the annual *tsechu* offerings, and the celebration of the New Year (*losar*) according to the style found in many Tibetan village communities. In addition, the three main villages of Tsari staged rituals dedicated to worship of the Buddhist protective deities of the mountain and to the *né* itself and used this worship as an occasion for a community-wide social celebration, thus combining distinctly religious and secular dimensions.

For the most part, the latter type of community ritual at Tsari coincided with the critical points in the annual cycle of Tantric practice and popular pilgrimage around the mountain. They were staged in: Yümé and Chikchar at the time of "opening the doors to the *né*" (*négo chewa*) just prior to the spring advance circuit (Ngakor) procession of the upper mountain; at Chikchar for the opening of the middle circuit (Shungkor) and the resthouses for the public summer pilgrimage season on the upper mountain, and its closure (*négo dam*) again in the autumn; in Lo Mikyimdün and Tsari Tsokar for the opening and closing of pilgrimage seasons; and in Chikchar immediately following the completion of the Rephu yoga exercises in midwinter. Although quite different in detail, these rituals shared several common features: They all marked spacial and temporal transitions in relation to the use of the mountain and its associated *né*; they included the worship of the main protectors of the mountain—Dorje Yüdrönma and Tsari Shingkyong—in the form of specific ritual dances (*cham*) and other offerings and prayers; and they incorporated local traditions in the form of narrative folk dance (*dro*), songs (*lu*), jokes (*zhé*), and oratory such as proverbs (*pé*), often performed in a friendly competitive spirit and accompanied by feasting, beer drinking, and merrymaking. In addition, all major festivals that related directly to the opening and closing of the *né* were sponsored by the state. A good example is the Yümé Chölé Chenmo, the first such festival in the local calendar.

Organization and Sponsorship

The Chölé Chenmo was the major annual festival in the western administrative subdistrict of Tsari Nub. Although it was staged in the remote village of Yümé, during living memory it also involved the full participation of all the residents of Chösam village and the resthouse-keeper families of Gönporong that lay in between them. Thus, up to several hundred persons could be involved. Being only about ten kilometers apart as the crow flies, Yümé and Chösam were separated by the high Ribpa La pass (4900 m) and were geographically quite isolated and ecologically distinct. During the 1940s and 1950s the two communities shared many interconnections due to marriage, migration, and economic activities. Although Chösam was the larger village and located at a key juncture on the main pilgrimage and travel route to central Tsari, it lacked any religious institutions. The Chölé Chenmo was staged, and probably originated, in more remote Yümé, where there was a temple built on an important holy site, a community of Drigungpa monks, and a long history of being one of the two main Tantric retreat centers of the mountain. The ritual took place in the second week of the third Tibetan month (approximately late April) and lasted seven days, allowing enough time to prepare for departure on the advance circuit procession, which began soon afterward in Chikchar on the nineteenth day of the month.

As was common throughout central Tibet prior to Chinese reforms, the basic social unit in a village was the household as a named, ranked entity, whose members shared a common tax obligation either to the local estates for land they used or to the central government, and who also shared periodic ritual obligations to the village collective. The communities of Tsari were characterized by two types of full member status households, the *trekang*, or "tax-paying households," and the *tsulkang*, or "rest-house-keeper households" (the term also referred to the actual resthouses). I will discuss the system further in chapter 11. Staging of the Chölé Chenmo was a rotating responsibility among the *trekang* households of both Yümé and Chösam villages. In the 1950s the duty was circulated annually among thirteen of the *trekang* households in both villages, who were designated *depa* (literally "in charge") when they assumed the role. For each year there were always two *depa* households who were involved; every year a new one joined the pair and the one that had just supervised the event retired. Together this working unit was known as the *depa sarnying*, or "old and new in charge," with the old *depa* taking the leading role. The sharing was necessary in part because preparations were labor intensive, and the local *trekang* did not always have a full labor complement on hand for various reasons. The system also ensured the continuity of local responsibility for worship and service to the mountain that the ritual represented, as was also symbolically attested during the proceedings.

In addition to the labor time involved, the main preparations required the procuring of materials; the construction of large, specialized ritual cakes; the erection of ceremonial tents and stagings; the preparation of dance costumes and accoutrements, large quantities of festival foods, and freshly brewed barley beer; and the selection of the best candidates to perform in certain aspects of the lay ceremonial. For the monastic aspects of the ceremony the *depa* had to supply materials and labor to the Yümé Tsuglagkang, as the temple was called, and its small compliment of five Drigungpa monks. While the actual labor involved in annually staging Chölé Chenmo was rotated among the *trekang* as a contribution to the collective tax obligation, the burden of sponsoring the festival was not. In this respect the system differed markedly from the performance of such village rituals in many other Tibetan-speaking communities, where it was the rotation of and even competition over actual sponsorship that was important and that partly defined membership in the village corporation, status ranking in certain cases, and other potential benefits.[37]

The expenditure component of the major annual village ritual was completely absent at Tsari, because the event was supported by the Lhasa government. The different government Dzong that jointly administered Tsari district—Kurab Namgyel Dzong and Kyemdong Dzong—were charged with granting an annual, fixed allotment of grain to the *depa* households involved each year by way of meeting the full costs for the ritual services.[38] Arrangements were made for the grain to be supplied by government-controlled estates and the private Yabshi estate of Nang Dzong in the neighboring districts of Dakpo, Kyemdong, Lawanang, and Nyel, and the *depa* households with the appropriate authorization collected it themselves. The same system operated in the east of Tsari also, although in modified form, because the tax status of the *trekang* and other conditions there were different. In Lo Mikyimdün, for instance, if a *trekang* was able and wanted to assume regular responsibility for the staging of the large Metog Chöpa ritual and festival that marked the "closing the doors of the *né*" every autumn in the east, they were exempted from the annual taxes due to the Dzong for as long as they performed the duty. The so-called Metog Chöpa *trekang* of Lo Mikyimdün could continue with this arrangement for as long as they were able to discharge the obligation, and it could change hands due to altered circumstances at times. The overall result was the same in both the western and eastern versions of the system.

Outline of Performance

In order to avoid repeating a mass of detail on standard ritual and ceremonial procedures already well attested in other studies, I will limit myself here to a very brief overview of Chölé Chenmo, pausing only over significant pieces of local variations:

Day One: General preparations were well underway. Two very large cakelike replicas, each about one meter in height, were fashioned to represent the two most potent aspects of the *né* landscape, the main summit of Pure Crystal Mountain (Dakpa Sheri) and the sacred lake of Turquoise Lake Palace (Phodrang Yumtso). Paired and gendered mountain and lake form the ideal Tibetan sacred landscape, and here the mountain represented the male deity and the lake the female. The replica of the mountain was decorated with a pair of male and female snow lion figures, one on each side of the peak. In the center were affixed specific symbolic ornamenting devices (*gyentrö*) used for finishing regular ritual cakes (*torma*). The replica of the lake was shaped like a wide volcanic cone, with a depression in the center like the bowl of the lake itself. On the outer sides of the form were placed two female snow lion figures. The materials used for the bulk of the images included *tu* (a rich, sweet food made from cheese mixed with butter and unrefined sugar), and butter and barley flour. The two large images were built on wooden platforms with handles, such that they could be transported by teams of four bearers during the ceremony. These images were keep next to the altar in the main shrine room for most of the week where they absorbed empowerment (*chinlab*) during the course of various rituals. Other sacrificial cakes were also made for offering to the meditation deities and protectors, and for driving out evil forces. All this extended over several days.

Day Two: The *depa*, who had brewed fresh barley beer or *chang*, took the finest and most potent "first brew" (*changphu*) to the temple and poured a large quantity into a ritual cauldron in the shrine room. Outside the temple songs, dances, and a procession were performed by a troupe of young men and boys chosen by the *depa sarnying*. In the troupe seven young men represent the *pawo*, or "divine heroes," and seven boys played the part of *pamo*, or "divine amazons," symbolizing the pairs of Tantric sky-goer deities who inhabit the sublime landscape maṇḍala palace of Pure Crystal Mountain. Males had to take the role of the *pamo*, as up until the last day of the festival women were forbidden to enter within the low perimeter wall surrounding the Yümé Tsuglagkang, the great sacred rock of Khandro Bumde ("Community of One Hundred Thousand Sky-goers") that is Yümé's main power place and the circumambulation path that encompasses them both. They could, however, easily view the action over the wall. The divine heroes wore round yellow ceremonial hats (*bokto*) and a series of five different coloured sashes interwoven across their chests (representing the five sky-goer families), and long ceremonial swords (*tripadam*) hung from their belts. The divine amazons wore long, folded skirts, silken shoulder capes, and five-paneled tiaras, and each carried a ritual bell and small double-sided hand drum. Headed by a pair of guides playing large monastic cymbals and a pole-drum respectively, the seven couples performed a slow, clockwise procession around the ritual ground, the temple, and the sacred rock of Khandro Bumde, during which they danced with symbolic postures and played their ritual instruments. The procession was followed up by a bearer carrying burning incense. In the temple the beer was offered in a special service to the Tantric sky-goers and "mothers" who inhabit the mountain, along with prayers. The beer, thus empowered, was later drunk by the villagers.

Day Three: The *depa* fed all the assembled villagers with tea, special barley dough balls, and broth. After this the Yümé Chagchen Lama, the ritual specialist charged with leading the advance circuit procession to open the pilgrimage route on the upper mountain (see chapter 7), began chanting the ritual formulae (*mani*) that accompanied the rite. The assembled villagers joined him in this chanting exercise, which signified that the Chagchen Lama and his company of local pilgrim-assistants would soon go to start opening the snowbound pilgrimage trail.

Days Four and Five: Largely a repeat of Day Three.

Day Six: The large, now empowered images of Pure Crystal Mountain and Turquoise Lake Palace were carried from the temple to one of the houses of Yümé used for staging the event. Members of the main or "old" Chölé Chenmo *depa* household ceremonially transferred the annual responsibility for the worship of the *néri* and staging of the ritual to the members of the "new," just recruited *depa* household by handing over the large images of mountain and lake to them. The rich, sweet material of the images was later shared equally among and eaten by all the villagers. In the house a party was staged during which the divine heroes and amazons were feasted. The divine heroes were served the first brew beer by finely dressed women adorned with their best jewelry, called the "beer-serving mothers" (*ama changma*). The divine heroes, for their part, sang various songs. A figure with an ornamented bamboo stick, the "good man" (*mizang*), was present, he performed folk dance and helped keep the beat for the singing.

Day Seven: Ritual dances (*cham*) were performed by the monks in the courtyard of the temple. These included the ubiquitous Black Hat dance (Shanak *cham*) and the Shingkyong Yabyum dance, in which the chief male and female protectors of Tsari appear as dark human figures with lion heads, as they do in the temple icons and in their liturgical descriptions.[39] This was a very popular dance, and it was also performed at all major rituals concerning the Tsari pilgrimages, such as the Lodzong and the closing ceremonies for the upper mountain. It was always accompanied by two figures costumed as monkeys who cavorted around, played the role of jokers, and were supposed to control the spectators.[40] The monks performed the "casting the ritual cakes" (*torgya*) ceremony for driving off evil forces, after which the divine heroes let off a salvo of gunfire into the air from their matchlock rifles. At the festival ground in front of the temple, the divine heroes and amazons danced. The divine heroes amused the crowd, gesturing with their long swords, and sang proverbs and other special songs associated with Chölé Chenmo.[41] A long night of village feasting, drinking, song, and dance in the Yümé pilgrims' resthouse rounded off the event.

The Local Mountain Cult Writ Large

Like all major rituals at Tsari, Chölé Chenmo has its roots in the Tantric cult and the agency of yogins and lamas, but it has become modified well beyond those origins, subject to the vicissitudes of history. Yümé and nearby Yütö were the original center of development for Tantric retreats at Tsari, predating the importance of Chikchar but not outlasting it. It is said that the original meaning of Chölé Chenmo was to mark the end of the winter meditation retreat by yogins in the Yümé area and to worship the Tantric sky-goers. However, since any vital retreat tradition at Yümé fell into more or less complete decline from the nineteenth century onward, this significance has long been redundant in relation to the event. At least a part of the proceedings, the procession of divine heroes and amazons around the main sacred boulder of Khandro Bumde, appears to hark back to the narrative of the very first Tantric yogins visiting the site (see chapter 5), at which time a ranked assembly of such divine figures appeared to them at the same boulder and then were absorbed into it. This history of Chölé Chenmo, from Tantric retreat ritual to worship of the mountain and its gods both in relation to pilgrimage traditions and as occasion for secular social unification, reflects completely the gradual transition of the ritual status of Pure Crystal Mountain from an exclusively Tantric one to a popular and public cult. The same comments apply equally to the other annual village rituals around the mountain, and I have already shown in chapter 6 how the Tantric Rephu exercise at Chikchar was following this course. A consequence of the importance the Chölé Chenmo came to assume in Yümé-Chösam is that the annual summer worship of the local mountain god and the associated community festival had been reduced to a very minor affair of one day in the 1950s and was not well attended by comparison.

There were no doubt many dimensions of social intercourse operating during Chölé Chenmo, when the two separate communities came together to share the rituals and celebrations. The details of liaisons, arguments, business deals, and gossip are now more or less lost to memory. One thing does seem to be clear from the various accounts: the general lack of competitiveness, displays of status, and devices indicating ranking that are often present in such festivals. Those who received any special attention were in fact the persons who acted the parts of the divine figures, and the *depa* families usually got modest gifts of thanks from the participants on the final day. The absence of any locally based sponsorship obligation no doubt plays a role here, as it removed one of the most common avenues through which privilege was expressed in practice (seating orders, distribution of ritual materials, access to ritual space, and so on). Nonetheless, once again women were graphically reminded that female access to ritual space around the mountain could never be taken for granted.

If any group could be seen to have benefited, it might have been the absent state, as principal sponsor or donor. Government sponsorship of Chölé Chenmo and similar events, has to be viewed of course, within the economy of the Tsari district as a whole, which was a marked variant on that found in other parts of Central Tibet (see chapter 11). However, the ultimate reasons for it were the government's concern that the annual worship of the cult of chief local protective deities be carefully maintained at a site that was of pan-Tibetan importance. It was important not just because many Tibetans went there as pilgrims; Tsari was a place the Gelukpa state had become increasingly bound up with over the recent centuries, and its deities were recognized as being extremely potent and potentially determinative of the religiopolitical fortunes of the regime and its supporters. This same concern informed part of the Lhasa state's involvement in a host of other regular ritual practices and institutions concerning its relationship to the forces of the nonhuman world, although most of these were monastically based in large Gelukpa monasteries or focused on Lhasa itself as the seat of government. I will have occasion to discuss other examples of this state concern manifest around the mountain in the following chapter.

In addition to contributing a regular, general offering to the local protective gods and the archetype deities by way of sponsoring these Tsari village rituals, the state also ensured that the annual use of the great *néri* by all manner of persons was sanctioned by propitiation at the most critical points in the year—the opening and closing of access to the ritual space of the mountain. As an inheritance from the days of Tantric ritual dominance of the site, these festivals served, in any case, as temporal markers dividing the use of the mountain's space between an open lay and public period over the summer and a closed esoteric period over the winter. There had certainly been trouble at the site in the past concerning ritual boundaries that had affected members of the Lhasa regime itself (see chapter 7), and the quite capricious character of the Tibetan mountain gods was no less a background concern of the government than it was of most ordinary Tibetan villagers, such as the people of Yümé and Chösam themselves. The pervasive motto of all those concerned with the mountain was: Handle With Care! In this respect the state's interests and involvement by way of the Tsariwa and their annual festivals seems to be a clear case of the local cult writ large, which is something one could definitely not say of the government's role in the Tsari Rongkor Chenmo procession or support of the rest-house system by comparison. The resultant ritual regulation of space and time at Tsari was not unlike many annual ceremonial openings and closures of community territory found throughout the Tibetan cultural zone, in which the local mountain and territorial gods receive worship. Most such community ceremonies are, however, explicitly associated with the access to, use, and maintenance of local domestic resources (grazing, firewood, gathering, hunting, and so on), not just control of entry.[42] *Néri* and their potential powers were also a resource that had to be carefully controlled in traditional Tibet.

The fact of government sponsorship of their main annual festivals was seen by the Tsariwa not as state generosity but as the basis for an obligation that defined them as "Ones from Tsari" and that they were for the most part happy to fulfill. The Tsariwa gained their own measure of religious and secular advantages out of the arrangement, but it also served to bind them to a continuity of identity that was incidentally of ongoing benefit for the state. Such occasions as Chölé Chenmo were bound up with and reiterated the Tsariwa's own local identity as the mountain's special inhabitants, servants, and keepers. The dances, processions, and so forth represented to the community the already established notion of the mountain's powerful divine hosts—the retinue of the meditation deities and the ambivalent Shingkyong couple—being within their very midst, while the impressive (and reportedly tasty) images of the great mountain and lake *né* showed the home that they in particular were each responsible for as community members and that was a source of embodied sacred energy.

Néshab, or "service to the *né*," at Tsari, in the form of ritual obligations performed as "religious works," entailed traditional ideas of both *shabtog* and *shabten*. *Shabtog* means "services rendered to superiors," the superiors in this case being both the *né* itself and the Tibetan government; *shabten* means "property given by the government in compensation for service." Although the latter term usually applied to the holding of estates by officials who served the government, it was also applicable to the context of Tsari, as aside from the compensation of grain or tax suspension in exchange for performing rituals, the Tsariwa received various other forms of annual compensation or payments from the government for additional forms of service around the mountain. It was this compensation, rather than access to the use of land, the productive basis on which most Tibetan peasants depended, that enabled the Tsariwa to make their living.

Mostly, domestic life at Tsari was not a celebration, and occasions like Chölé Chenmo represented exceptional annual high points for the peoples of the local communities. Daily life and subsistence around the mountain was in fact a complex and often hard-to-balance equation for the lay population. The existence of popular pilgrimages there seems to have made life around Pure Crystal Mountain possible and enhanced it in various ways. Even the different dimensions of identity in relation to the *néri* that the Tsariwa subscribed to or were given proved to be of economic value in certain ways. However, the various ritual prohibitions and service duties the inhabitants had to maintain narrowed their domestic options in many respects, as I will show in the final chapter.

11

Culture, Nature, and Economy around a Holy Mountain

> The mountain around which the Short Pilgrimage ran was an 18,000' peak called Takpa Shiri. Its choice as a holy place seemed to me an excellent example of human economy. If it had remained profane, life would have been on a far lower level. Sanctification was the greatest asset it possessed.

This perspicacious observation by F. M. Bailey, the British colonial spy who visited Tsari in 1913, captures in essence what a larger volume of social, cultural, and ecological data now reveal to us about Tibetan domestic life around Pure Crystal Mountain; people lived there because of its sanctity, not in spite of it.[1] In the following overview of the social organization, economy, and ecology of the local communities of Tsari, I will relate their particular features to the status of the area as a holy sanctuary, the presence of its many pilgrim visitors, and its borderland location. The analysis raises general questions about the relationship between culture, nature, and society in premodern Tibet, as the material provides a particular example of a productive cultural response to apparent environmental limitations. It may also inform some longer term social patterns evident around the mountain, particularly trends in local population drift occurring throughout this century.

The Tsari district was unique compared with the immediate environs of many other major *néri* sites in Tibet in that it maintained a sizable and permanently settled domestic population. Well-known pilgrimage mountains such as Tise, Amnye Machen, or Nyanchen Tanglha were often uninhabited or used only occasionally by a few itinerant religious practitioners and nomadic herders. There are both cultural and ecological factors behind this difference. For one thing, the local environment of Tsari has a high rainfall and rich ecosystem that supports domestic life in ways that were not possible at sites up on the high plateau proper. In addition, its lay population became established and grew in relation to the development there of Tibet's largest and most popular mountain pilgrimages, and these events came to serve as an economic basis for the long-term survival of local communities. But the villages of Tsari cannot be compared to those communities that so often gather around famous pilgrimage shrines and holy sites the world over and that are sustained by the so-called pilgrimage economy based on providing private accommodation, guiding, ritual services, entertainment, the sale of sacred and mundane paraphernalia, and the like. There was a very minor element of such activity at Tsari, but in general, due of the nature of the ritual and the fact that the site comprised an entire and complex landscape rather than one nucleated center or single shrine, the pilgrims did not stay; they moved on through. Furthermore, sacred objects and substances associated with the site were natural and commonplace, free to be collected within ritual limits. Thus, they were not sold or exchanged (in return for "donations") like the multitude of empowered objects associated with great lamas and shrines sought by pilgrims interacting with the well-established monastic cult throughout Tibet. Tsari did have a pilgrimage economy, but not of this type. It was characterized instead by a complex system of institutionalized service and a high degree of diversity, determined in part by the area's particular status as a holy landscape. I shall turn first to the attitude toward the natural environment itself, as a context for domestic life.

Religious Environmental Restrictions

Crucial for understanding all local social organization and economy at Tsari is the existence there of various religious environmental restrictions. These related to the definition of the total environment as a divine embodiment and abode of numerous powerful deities. These restrictions and the beliefs on which they were based were taken by the Tsariwa and other Tibetans as the primary justification for major modifications to the traditional Tibetan patterns of production and exploitation of natural resources existing in the area.

I have already shown in the previous chapters that all life and the material substance of the local environment were considered sacred or divine in various ways. These beliefs, originally introduced by lamas and élite clerics, became incorporated into popular perceptions of the mountain and its environs. More important, these beliefs came to serve as the basis of later administrative policies that the Lhasa government often stringently applied to the area. Up to and during the 1950s, there was a local ban on all cultivation for agriculture and a prohibition of hunting or killing of any living thing around the mountain. The clearing of any land for pasture development by burning scrub and forest was also forbidden, as was the pollution of lakes and springs. In addition, localized restrictions applied to the village areas. No domestic pigs or chickens were allowed to be kept as they disturbed and dug up the holy ground and were considered unclean animals; no local butchery of livestock was permitted; and at the site of Chikchar, all sewing of clothing and manufacture of local handicrafts was forbidden within the precincts of the valley, although any goods so made outside could be brought back there for use, sale, or trade. These restrictions applied to the whole upper mountain and its adjacent valleys with their settlements and lands right up to the summits of the surrounding passes, the only exception being the lower *rong* area to the east around the village of Lo Mikyimdün, as this area was considered to lie just outside the sphere of the holy sanctuary. Upper valley residents were also permitted to maintain very small kitchen gardens with a few vegetables alongside their houses.

Taken together, all these regulations imposed severe limitations on economic possibilities that were not experienced, or not at least to the same degree, by other Tibetan rural communities. The ban on community agriculture at Tsari itself appears to have been unique in Tibet. It represented the most serious impediment to the local economy, at least on the face of it; I shall take up this question again toward the end of the chapter.

The exact history of these environmental restrictions and their institutionalization prior to the nineteenth century remains vague, but the cultural precedents for them are certainly longstanding. Records of lamas attempting to ban the hunting of wild animals in the area date back to the thirteenth century, and in chapter 10 I have already cited statements from the same period advocating the protection of game animals at the site on the basis of Tantric theories of divine embodiment.[2] Since the "Pandit" explorer Kinthup's visit to Tsari in 1883–84 and up to the Chinese occupation in 1959 no cultivation or hunting was permitted within the district.[3] During the twentieth century at least, the restrictions were the subject of administrative concern. Officials from the government Dzong at Kurab Namgyel and Kyemdong checked periodically that they were being observed and were able to punish offenders who violated then. Someone caught hunting on the mountain, for example, could be fined heavily, but also, as a rule, would be severely beaten by the officials at the Dzong as an example to others.[4] This latter action, which could lead to disability or eventually even death through lack of treatment of injuries, served as a particularly strong incentive for local peoples not to break the restrictions. In general, the social limits placed on domestic practices such as hunting, which are often attributed to adherence to traditional ethics and religious beliefs in Tibet, have to also be seen in the context of the potentially brutal exercise of premodern local authority.

As was also common throughout Tibet, both resident and visiting lamas supplemented the power of civil authorities by preaching to the local villages about maintaining religious environmental restrictions. A record of one such event at Tsari survives from the early nineteenth century and suggests that the villagers were indeed liable to disregard the restrictions in order to survive, as a lama noted on his departure from the area after a stay of over a year there:

> You, faithful male and female patrons
> Of this empowered ground, the great *né* of Tsāri;
> Do not feed yourselves by hunting birds and game animals![5]

It is no surprise that the lama's plea began with the time-honored theme of giving up hunting. Hunting was something that no amount of laws, threatened punishments, or grim images of hell could eliminate from Tibetan rural communities, and it was usually (and quite easily) pursued in secret. Several elderly men from the upper villages admitted hunting, but only outside the restricted area in the forested valleys to the south in order to trap musk deer. With luck, it was possible to trap four or five animals per week during the winter. The musk pods obtained were both a valuable trade item and one demanded by government officials in Lhasa as a special form of annual tax. Hunting was openly practiced around Lo Mikyimdün where the ban did not apply, and the Subansiri tribes hunted every autumn on the southern flanks of the mountain.[6]

Further reinforcement for such restrictions manifested at the local level. The Tsari village headmen were attentive in general to ensure there were no obvious or gross violations of the restrictions, as that would reflect badly on their own reputations and that of the village as a whole in the eyes of both the secular and religious authorities. In addition to all this human persuasion, the Tsariwa, like most Tibetans, did believe they would fall foul of the local gods of the country if they set about disturbing the environment without taking particular care. At the very least, the wrath of the local gods always served as a post facto explanation for any misfortune that occurred after they had done so. Whatever beliefs they may have held or fears of authority they might have harbored, during the twentieth century the environmental prohibitions appear to have been generally obeyed within the specified area by the local community and by pilgrims. This fact was observed by Western visitors to the upper valleys, most of whom also noted the localized abundance and tameness of wild animal and bird species there.[7] There was even a certain sense of community pride about living in a nature sanctuary, and the Tsariwa have a song that celebrates the area around the western settlement as an ideal refuge for traditionally persecuted game:

In Yütö and Yümé at Tsari,
When there are deer they are happy,
As they have no enemies whatsoever outside,
And grass and water are plentiful within.[8]

None of the individual religious environmental restrictions at Tsari is without precedent in premodern Tibetan society, and many are found at other holy places or even in different Asian Buddhist contexts. It is rather their large scale, their wide variety, and the high degree of their institutionalization around such a remote site as Pure Crystal Mountain that makes them noteworthy. While their origins may lie in the history of the site as a Buddhist retreat center and the agency of certain lamas, this fact does not explain the later interests that the Lhasa state took in maintaining the restrictions. The Tibetan Buddhist state's administrative concern with the restrictions had little or nothing to do with a Buddhist ethic of nonviolence and karmic consequences, which are purely individual in scope. They were informed instead by a complex syncretic Tibetan religious attitude to the natural world combining Tantric theory, folk beliefs about nature, and astrologically mediated concerns with maintaining prosperity and power.

The Tibetan Tantric understanding of the embodiment of divinity in the physical world, for example in the landscape maṇḍala parallels in certain respects and articulates with common folk attitudes toward nature. The powerful protective gods and inhabitants of the mountain maṇḍala of the *néri* cult, as emanations of the meditation deities, are ever vigilant of transgressions of local ritual limits and sensitive to disturbance of their physical abodes. Thus ploughing, hunting, burning, disturbing the ground, and so on are all considered acts bound to incur their wrath, resulting in accidents, illness, bad fortune, hostile weather, and the like. But in any community folk tradition the same could be said of the local *yüllha*, *shidak*, *lu*, or *sadak* deities in the natural world, who may be similarly upset by the hunting of the animals they own or use as mounts, the pollution of the waters they dwell in, or the breaking the surface of the soil under which they reside by people building houses, ploughing for crops, collecting stones and plants, making fire-pits in pastoral encampments and so on. These and many more mundane actions must be continually ritually addressed in domestic life to ensure both continued individual and community prosperity, luck, and power (although the chance of inadvertent offense remains ever present).

None of these correspondences are surprising, as the Tantric protectors are in many cases assimilated autochthons who brought their local personalities and habits with them into the Tibetan version of the maṇḍala world-system. This syncretism forms the basis for general state concerns about the maintenance of large-scale restrictions at Tsari, and the consequences of disturbance of the powerful divine inhabitants and environment there were seen as having potentially far-reaching effects on the prosperity of Tibet. Apart from the general level of administrative control that the state maintained, a good example of this concern was manifested during astrologically critical years in the life of each incumbent Dalai Lama. At these times more than any other, government officials went to Tsari and made scrupulous checks on the observance of local environmental regulations, threatening village headmen with the worst if the rules were violated in any way. Such years were known variously as *lokar* ("astrologically [critical] year") or *lokeg* ("obstacle/misfortune year"), and fell on the thirteenth year and thereafter at twelve-year intervals throughout a Dalai Lama's life.[9] They were years during which the person of the incumbent Dalai Lama, and thus the stability of the religious polity as a whole, were particularly vulnerable to evil influences and misfortunes, such as were believed to result from any provocation of the powerful gods of the realm or environmental disharmony at places like Tsari.

At the local level, the Tsariwa and other Tibetans certainly justified the particular social order and economy that developed at the mountain in terms of these environmental restrictions and their maintenance and the beliefs that lay behind them. However, as I shall argue later, they perhaps represent a uniquely Tibetan cultural solution to a problem posed by certain local ecological conditions. In the face of these limits, cultural or ecological, the Tsariwa enjoyed a partial compensation in the form of pilgrimage-related work, and they modified their economy in whatever ways they could in order to make a sustainable living there.

Economy and Society

The district of Tsari had certain unique features when compared with other types of Tibetan rural communities described in the anthropological literature, such as the agricultural villages (*shingpa/drongpa*) of the Tibetan valley systems, the remote nomadic pastoral communities (*drokpa*) of the uplands, the mixed agropastoral (*samadrok*) settlements, and the trading centers occurring throughout the region.[10] Most pre-1959 Tibetan rural economies were based predominantly on the settled cultivation of crops, primarily barley, or pastoral nomadism with yak, yak-cattle hybrids, sheep, and goats, or a varying mixture of both modes of production. Hunting and other harvesting strategies often supplemented the nomad economy and, to a variable extent, those of other village communities, whose inhabitants also turned to crafts, petty trading, and laboring. In some cases, long-distance internal trading cycles were also involved, but these were often related to exchanges of the products of pastoral nomadism with those of settled agriculture and were necessitated by the remoteness of pastoral communities from populated markets.

The household (or tenthold), as the basic unit of traditional Tibetan social organization, was formed largely around both shared, hereditary access to productive lands and the discharge of the tax obligations that entailed. Taxation was related to productive units, that is, to land area under cultivation or grazing, and head of livestock, while there were also certain per capita taxes on persons. Tax obligations and payments usually took the form of supplying produce or cash, and in addition providing many different forms of corvée labor, such as road maintenance or the supply of transport animals for government business, and performing military service. In pre-1959 Tibet the functioning and maintenance of the entire state infrastructure, the large organized monastic institutions, and the estates of the landed aristocracy were all directly dependent on these forms of taxation being levied in every community. Life at Tsari in the 1950s followed many of these patterns found in other types of Tibetan rural communities, but they were applied there in a particular combination and in modified forms. The main features that differentiated Tsari from other places were the predominant role played by specialized service activities and the high level of economic diversification that the majority of households attempted to maintain in order to ensure both viability and continuity.

Administration and Community Structure

During the 1950s the Tsari District had an estimated population of five to six hundred persons. It was grouped predominantly within extended family household units in four main village communities (Yümé, Chösam, Chikchar, and Lo Mikyimdün) and three minor settlements (Domtsen, Yarab, and Phödzo Sumdo). There were also small monastic and retreat communities at Yümé and Chikchar and a nunnery near Lo Mikyimdün. Various other localities around the mountain were only seasonally occupied or used by resthouse keepers, meditators, pilgrims, or local pastoralists.

Although the district was small in total area and population compared to many others in Tibet, it came under a complex civil and religious administration. Tsari fell within the area of Central Tibet (Ü), being located right at its southern margins. It was subject to the authority of the Lhasa government by way of the system of regional Dzong, or administrative centers, several of which were located in neighboring districts. At the district level there were three divisions: Tsari Nub, or "Western Tsari"; Tsari Shar, or "Eastern Tsari"; and the Lo Mikyimdün–Tsari Tsokar area (see figure 8.1). Each division had different administrative regimes. In relation to the central government, all three fell under the overall control of Kurab Namgyel Dzong, located in the Drulung valley of Dakpo to the north.[11] The Dzong had interests in collecting taxes; control of access to grazing land; law enforcement and defense; the transmission of various government decrees from Lhasa; and their execution in the districts, for example, the policing of religious environmental restrictions. Tsari Nub also fell under the religious administration of the Drigung sect, who had some historical rights over certain religious sites and lands in the area. Tsari Shar and Lo Mikyimdün fell under the religious administration of the Sangnag Chöling Drukpa of Char, who maintained the temple and retreat center at Chikchar, oversaw affairs at Tsari Tsokar, and enjoyed some rights over certain lands and persons. Accordingly, many of the people in these districts identified themselves as either Drigung or Drukpa. In addition, the area of Lo Mikyimdün had another level of government control, mainly involving certain tax obligations, imposed on it through Kyemdong Dzong located not far to the north at the Kongpo-Dakpo border.

The interface between central government interests at Tsari and each community was maintained via the village headman. This person communicated with the Dzong and the monasteries when needed, as well as acting as intermediary between them and the local households. He (for they were always men) represented the interests of all the main village households, as well as those of the Dzong, by ensuring that taxation dues were paid; that festivals, religious ceremonies, and service duties were conducted as per tradition or contract; that government decrees were communicated and observed, and that disputes were referred to higher authorities. In return for these services he received a modest annual payment of grain from the Dzong. The local headmen were either called *chimi* ("leader") or *thumi* (literally "representative"), and their "deputies" were called *thuntsob*; the terminology reflected the fact that they were usually elected by each village rather than appointed from outside. In principle, such positions were supposed to change every two to three years, and candidacy depended on one's reputation for being a "strong man," someone who could organize and direct people to do things when need be, and work effectively with external officials. There were variations in this system. For example, in the 1950s Lo Mikyimdün rotated the position of headman every few years among its seven main tax-paying households, and at Chikchar the Sangnag Chöling Drukpa, who often cooperated with Lhasa in running affairs at Tsari, assigned the job to the senior cleric at their retreat center there on the sudden death of the former representative. All the senior heads of the main full member status households worked closely with the headman as a group or council for decision-making and organization at the level of the village as a whole.

Two Types of Household

As mentioned briefly in chapter 10, the most basic unit of social organization at Tsari was the household, and the local villages were composed of two primary types of household. The full village member status households were the *trekang*, or "tax-paying households," and the *tsulkang*, or "resthouse-keeper households." A *trekang* was essentially a taxed production unit whose members shared a common tax obligation to external authorities and landowners and shared periodic ritual and labor obligations to the village collective. A *tsulkang* was a service unit whose members formed a labor pool and shared in undertaking certain government contracts. An important point is that *trekang* households could also hold the status of *tsulkang* simultaneously, and the distinctions between them were often blurred in practice. The *trekang* households tended to be more prosperous, and they could act as a *tsulkang* in addition because they could marshal the resources required for successfully discharging both sets of obligations the two entailed. The shared and hereditary rights of settlement, access to pastures, and tax obligations for their use were mainly what constituted the *trekang* as a household unit throughout the upper districts, while Lo Mikyimdün *trekang* shared additional obligations because they cultivated fields as well. All the *trekang* within each administrative district were treated as a corporate tax entity by the government; thus, the *trekang* households of each village area paid their annual taxes together as a group. Exactly how these taxes were assembled within the village system as a whole was the collective concern of the village headmen and households. Those households with *tsulkang* status were exempt from certain taxes to the village, such as corvée duties, rotating ritual services, and so on.

While the households were defined and organized around the Central Tibetan system of economic and administrative interests, quite often in reality they were roughly based on an extended family whose members were either domiciled within the same dwelling or in adjacent houses, although there were many exceptions to this situation. In quite a few instances the households were named after either specific local place names or institutions with which they were somehow historically associated. For example, the principal *tsulkang* households often had the names of the particular pilgrim's resthouse that they traditionally operated, and other leading *trekang* households had the same names as the various *létsen*, or "functionaries," who originally were workers and patrons representing the earlier Tantric meditation retreat centers throughout the area. The members of a *trekang* were called *trelpa* and were headed or represented by the *trelpé apha*, or senior male taxpayers, while those of a *tsulkang* were known as *tsulpa*.

These two types of named households formed a kind of upper level of Tsari society. A second, lower strata was composed of other families and individuals who were generally poorer and did not have full rights in the village. They were in some ways equivalent to those usually designated *düdchung* in Central Tibetan agricultural communities: small families who held no rights over the use of local land and thus mainly constituted a labor pool for the full member households. In such capacities at Tsari, they were often referred to as "tax helpers" (*trerok*), because they assisted the tax-paying households in meeting their annual tax obligations at times of high labor demand. Their local residence was a matter of consent by the villagers, and due to labor shortages settlers were usually not rejected. Mobile *düdchung*-type persons in Central Tibet had the *mibog*, or "human lease," tax status, requiring a modest annual payment ("lease fee") back to the original estate to which they had been attached. Many persons at Tsari, including members of both the main household types and poorer laboring families, had *mibog* obligations, suggesting inward migration of generally lower status individuals from other areas over a long period.[12] The differences in wealth and status between the principal households and the poorer families seems related to the antiquity of their arrival and establishment as much as to their changing fortunes.

Because the area was subject to strict religious environmental restrictions, the productive possibilities involving local land and resources open to the upper valley Tsariwa were mainly confined to limited pastoralism. Thus, much of the local population were never tied to productive lands in the same way or to the same extent as in many other parts of Tibet. They were more often tied instead, or as well, to service roles. Aside from the staging of annual rituals already mentioned, these roles related to the servicing of pilgrimages and took a number of forms: the specific duties of the *tsulpa* or resthouse keepers; the obligation of corvée transportation for pilgrimage in specific cases; and a host of other minor labor obligations, such as the performance of temporary military service during the Rongkor Chenmo, and so on.

The Pilgrimage Resthouse System

Many Tibetans who made pilgrimage visits at Tsari prior to 1959 remember the Tsariwa primarily as the *tsulpa* or keepers of a system of resthouses spread around Pure Crystal Mountain and further throughout the district. The role of *tsulpa* was another important aspect of the notion of Tsariwa identity as servants or keepers of the *né*. The local inhabitants were being referred to as *tsulpa* in accounts of pilgrimage several centuries ago; however, not all the Tsariwa were *tsulpa* in the 1950s, and the designation only applied to specific households. The term *tsulkang* itself appears to be a local usage applied to both the resthouses and the service households that ran them. Local etymologies suggest that *tsulpa* carries the notion of a duty or responsibility. In general, *tsultrim* means "discipline" in the sense of religious behavior. *Tsulkang* were temporary lodgings for persons who, as pilgrims, were committed to religious behavior during their ritual journeys, unlike ordinary inns or caravanserai where drinking liquor, gambling, sex, and brawling might be found. This sense parallels the Sanskrit *dharmaśālā*, the common term used for pilgrimage resthouses in North India.

The resthouses appear to have always been related to systems of official administration of the mountain. The early establishment of resthouses at Tsari can be dated to the mid–fourteenth century, as one of the administrative provisions made by the Pagmo Drupa hegemony in Central Tibet under the rule of Changchub Gyeltsen (1302–1364).[13] The system eventually came to be administered mainly by the Lhasa government and partly by the two resident sects, as was the case during the 1950s. At that time there were sixteen *tsulkang* in the two main divisions of Tsari, plus two more at Tsari Tsokar operated by Lo Mikyimdün and a peripheral one at Drupchuka in Dakpo, which—although outside the official district boundary to the northwest—was widely regarded as the first *tsulkang* on the Tsari pilgrimages due to legendary events that took place there when the *néri* was first opened.[14] Considering only the *tsulkang* located directly around the mountain in Tsari Nub and Tsari Shar (see figure 6.1), six were substantial houselike dwellings with multiple rooms (at Chösam, Chikchar Uri, Domtsang, Gönporong, Yümé, and Ribpa La), while the remaining ten (at Domtsen, Phödzo Sumdo, Lawa Phuk, Mipa, Tama Lamgo, Phodrang Yumtso (two), Tagtsang, Chaktha Treng, and Sinmo Nering) were smaller, or more in the order of well-made huts if located high on the upper slopes. Each district maintained one of the two small resthouses located at Phodrang Yumtso, which fell right on the district boundary. These two classes of larger and smaller resthouses were treated as two distinct levels of the system, as I will show. Overall, the Drigungpa of western Tsari loosely administered all the resthouses on the mountain that fell within Tsari Nub, and the Sangnag Chöling Drukpa all those within Tsari Shar and Lo Mikyimdün.

For the sects' part, this usually only entailed checking that reliable and capable *tsulpa* households were taking care of every site during each season, and ensuring that maintenance repairs where carried out when needed. The actual material support of all aspects of the resthouse system came from the government itself.

While Tsariwa state that the system of *tsulkang* was technically neither a compulsory duty nor a tax obligation for them, the government and the sects always sought to ensure that local households had continuous participation in the system. In terms of achieving an overall economy of organization and operation, the authorities were in fact dependent on the Tsariwa's local labor to maintain the resthouses. The villagers in turn were dependent on the benefits that operating *tsulkang* brought them in order to survive economically, because of the way the local environmental restrictions narrowed their options. The responsibility of maintaining a resthouse was formalized in a contract between the Lhasa government, transacted via the Dzong, and individual households, who gained the status of *tsulkang* once they undertook the duty. These service contracts lasted a minimum of three years, in principle, but in the case of the large *tsulkang* in particular, they were maintained intergenerationally. Thus, in the most developed form of the system, one can speak of named households being tied to a service role for which their members shared hereditary responsibilities. In general, the contracts for the smaller resthouses tended to be less stable and changed hands occasionally. While the large resthouses were either in or near villages, and the keepers could combine their duties with annual domestic life more easily, the smaller sites were more remote and were accessed and used only over the summer, and their contracts gave fewer benefits to the keepers in relation to the work involved.

As a basic payment for their annual work, all *tsulkang* households received a barley grain allotment. The fixed grain payments had originally been established by the decree of a former Dalai Lama, and the incumbent Dalai Lama's office in Lhasa administered the system through neighboring Dzong and government estates. As with the payment for ritual services discussed in chapter 10, barley grain was the important currency, as it was not grown in Tsari but nevertheless formed the favored staple component of diet there, as it did throughout the rest of Tibet. The households keeping large resthouses received twenty-five government *bo* measures (approximately 330 kg) of grain per year, while those maintaining smaller resthouses received exactly half that amount.[15] The households had to collect the grain themselves from government estates in the neighboring districts of Dakpo, Nyel, and Kongpo, as designated by the Dzong. For example, the *tsulpa* from Tsari Nub went during each winter or spring to the estates of Nyel district to the west, near Lhuntse Dzong, collected their grain, and had much of it processed into roasted flour (*tsampa*) before returning home. This latter step was necessary, as mills were very difficult to maintain at Tsari due to the annual flooding of the mountain streams, and most milling was done outside the district.

In addition to the grain payment, those who ran the large resthouses were allotted free grazing rights to nearby pastures while they held the contract. In general, only limited grazing rights were allocated to any one *trekang* household at Tsari, for which they had to pay annual taxes. If a *tsulkang* household did not have much livestock of its own, it could rent this surplus pasture to other villagers in return for butter and cheese, or sometimes labor services, by personal agreement. A final form of compensation for which all the *tsulkang* households were eligible was the receipt of a *longyig*, or official "begging permit," on which I will have more to say later. In addition to these basic payments, other materials were also supplied to enable the running of the resthouses up to a certain standard. Various domestic utensils, such as metal cauldrons for boiling water, and an annual supply of brick tea were provided by the Dzong for serving on special occasions, such as pilgrimage visits by government officers and high lamas. Some resthouses were given religious icons, such as Buddha statues, for use in shrine rooms where pilgrims could worship.

The large resthouses also got three or four head of livestock, usually *dzomo* (female yak-cow hybrids) and a male animal, which they grazed around the resthouses on the pasture allotments. These were intended for supplying milk to make fresh yogurt to give to pilgrims during the season, while the household could use any surplus itself. All such permanent material supplies did not become the property of the household but were on loan to them while they were contract holders. If a *tsulkang* contract changed hands for any reason, all such items and animals that were registered as having been given by the Dzong for that resthouse had to be transferred to the new contract holders, and any deficiencies made up. Reasonable exceptions were made, however, for *tsulkang* livestock proven to have fallen prey to natural causes, such as disease, old age, or heavy snowfall, and the Dzong arranged for replacements in legitimate cases. If a retiring household could not or would not transfer all the *tsulkang* assets it was liable for, then it could not resign its contract obligations, and the matter would have to be dealt with by the authorities.

The large *tsulkang* were run for most of the year like regular households. The actual work of the *tsulpa* at the smaller, more remote sites consisted of opening the resthouses in the late spring and making them weatherproof again after the winter snows. During the four or five months of the annual pilgrimage season, keepers had to stay in daily residence and maintain a supply of firewood for pilgrims to cook with, keep large copper pots of water hot for the visitors, clean the quarters, and ensure there were lamps to burn at night. If pilgrims were sick or had accidents, they would assist them. Apart from the supply of a little yogurt in summer at certain resthouses, no food was provided by the *tsulpa* except by separate personal request and payment. The only other exception was for the visits of government officials and highly ranked clerics and aristocrats who held *lamyig*, or "travel permits," allowing requisition of corvée labor and services, and whose arrival the Dzong had given notice of in advance. The keepers, as members of a *tsulkang* household, were not directly liable for any form of corvée labor duties in relation to their status. They were, however, expected to give *lamyig*-holding pilgrims special treatment, feed them with meat and other luxury foods not commonly consumed at Tsari, and reserve the best rooms for them while they passed through. In general, some experienced keepers recited oral guides to pilgrims, a few literate ones had written copies on hand also, and local stories and anecdotes were often told. Quite often pilgrims did give a small donation or gift to the *tsulpa* in appreciation for their services. After a good season a hospitable and efficient keeper could come away with a tidy store of small gifts in cash and kind. Some *tsulpa* say pilgrims gave them presents so as to earn merit, as they believed these local residents had a semidivine or higher status identity because they lived up near the mountain's summit for long periods.[16]

For Tsariwa, the *tsulkang* duty offered obvious advantages in the context of an agriculture-free and limited pastoral and harvesting economy. Yet overall the work was quite labor-intensive, and running each resthouse could place different (although somewhat predictable) annual demands on the household labor pool. These demands varied according to the size, distance from household domiciles, and volume of pilgrims who regularly lodged at any particular site. In addition to these specific operating conditions, *tsulkang* contract holders had to ensure they had the available labor power every year, which had to be calculated in relation to changing household sizes and economic conditions. Some example will illustrate how this worked in practice.

One Chösam family who maintained a modest dairy herd on high pastures around northern Tsari, and did some trading, also held the contract for running the small resthouse at Phödzo Sumdo. This site was quite a distance to the east at the other end of the Tsari upper valley system. The family constituted a *trekang* household because of the amount of pasture they held grazing rights for, which entailed various annual tax obligations, including corvée labor. They found their labor pool was regularly overextended to a degree not compensated for by the benefits derived from *tsulkang* operation. They were forced to retire from the *tsulkang* contract and concentrate on herding and other activities and obligations instead. Another son was born, and some years later, with more labor power and under improving economic fortunes, they took over one of the two small *tsulkang* at Phodrang Yumtso from which another household had been forced to retire. In contrast, the household that ran the large resthouse at Gönporong prospered during the same period. It was comprised of three families (actually three generations) living in the same large domestic complex right at the site of the resthouse itself. This spot was located on the route between two other large resthouses at Yümé and Ribpa La, all within an easy day's walk. Thus, it was not the only possible overnight lodging for pilgrims and was seldom crowded. Yet it gained all the benefits due a large *tsulkang*, including pasture rights. Ample wood and water were also close at hand. With these favorable conditions, the household was able to maintain other economic activities because its labor pool remained large and not unduly dispersed, and it even employed laborers from poorer families to extend its interests when necessary. On the other hand, different large resthouses, such as Chösam, were difficult to run because of high numbers of visitors. Nearly all pilgrims and officials began and ended their journeys to Tsari in Chösam village and thus stayed in that resthouse at least twice.

Overall, the fact that *tsulkang* operation was labor intensive tended to limit the exploitation of other seasonal possibilities for economic diversification in the area, particularly summer herding, as well as the ability to fulfill heavy corvée obligations that fell due over the pilgrimage season. If *tsulkang* households lost able members and did not have the resources to recruit outside labor, they quickly ran into difficulties. Even collecting the annual grain payment could mean a long trip out of the district, which had to be compensated for in other ways by combining it with trading, and so on. Yet regular resthouse service was in many ways just as attractive to Tsariwa as any of the other options open to them, and households took and kept *tsulkang* contracts whenever they could manage to do so.

Economic Diversity of Tax Households

There were only eighteen possible resthouse contracts in the Tsari district, and most *trekang* households and poorer families had to engage in other economic activities in order to sustain and reproduce themselves. Most *tsulkang*, in fact, also had to diversify. The easiest avenue for doing so in the upper valley area was herding and dairy production, as these were permitted activities. They were common in Lo Mikyimdün also, as the Tsokar area had good high pastures. Maintaining herding at a viable level required sufficient grazing access to local pasture, which was allocated by the two government Dzong. To a much lesser extent, grazing rights were leased from the Sangnag Chöling Drukpa and the Drigungpa around Yümé, who held certain rights over areas of land, as well as from neighboring estates in Dakpo. Grazing rights were monopolized by the *trekang* households. In the 1950s the number of *trekang* in relation to local populations in each main settlement zone was (all figures are estimates only):

1. Tsari Nub: Yümé area, population 100, 6–7 *trekang*; Chösam area, population 120, 12 *trekang*.
2. Tsari Shar: Chikchar-Domtsen area, population 80, 10 *trekang*.
3. Lo Mikyimdün area, population 250–300, 7 *trekang*.

There was no typical *trekang*, as they varied in size, status, and wealth, all of which changed over time. *Trekang* were compounded more often with *tsulkang* in the upper valley area, while in Lo Mikyimdün they tended to be more prosperous and drew from the large pool of settler labor there. To give an overall impression of the annual productive cycle of most *trekang* in the village system, I will briefly discuss their involvement in a number of primary areas, including: pastoralism; wood and handicraft work; trading; and, finally, specialized forms of taxation. (Although various minor harvesting strategies were locally practiced, along with limited cultivation of crops around Lo Mikyimdün, I will not consider them here.)[17]

Pastoralism

Although the status of *trekang* as taxpayers was based mainly on access to land for pastoralism, this form of production was itself limited in scope at Tsari. Tsari meadows were lush, often even boggy, and had a wide species diversity due of good rainfall. But the types of pasture most suited to high-yielding dairy stock were on the whole more scattered and limited. Hay needed to be made (cut and dried) from long grass growing along forest margins in many cases. The possibility for building up very large, mobile, and highly productive herds like those of successful nomads of the northern plateau did not exist at Tsari, where herds were often only around thirty to forty animals at most. Pastoralism was important at Tsari but was always limited to a more modest scope, so as a main household income it required supplementing with secondary activities. Nonetheless, pastoral operations served both as the basis for substantial annual taxes—a head tax due on each milking animal, assessed every year by the Dzong officials—and as the source for major tax payments demanded in the form of butter.[18] The actual products of pastoralism, butter and cheese, were valuable in that they were the only substantial item that the Tsariwa actually produced themselves, with the exception of a few handicrafts. After domestic requirements and tax payments, any surplus butter and cheese were traded with neighboring districts in exchange for vital grain supplies that could not be locally grown. Among upland Tibetans who knew the religious traditions of Tsari well, the Tsariwa's butter and cheese were considered special compared to ordinary dairy foods, as they were natural derivatives of the empowered environment around Pure Crystal Mountain.

Pastoral practice at Tsari required certain household members to live in tents at high pasture areas remote from the village for up to four or five months, from late spring to early autumn. The division of pastoral labor followed the usual Tibetan pattern: all herding and dairy production was done solely by women, with the help of children where possible (laborers were occasionally recruited also); men butchered and tended beasts of burden. While not directly concerned with pastoralism, most men did care for livestock in the form of pack yaks, mules, and horses. These animals required pasturing, but this was done in the valleys; they were only used to provide transport for pilgrims, corvée obligations, and for annual trading trips.

The only aspect of pastoralism that involved local men was butchery, and then often in only a minor role due to religious sensibilities. Relatively few stock were butchered annually in the upper valleys for domestic consumption, but certain large resthouses with frequent visits from government officials and high-status pilgrims butchered more animals than usual to accommodate their dietary demands. None of the butchering was done by the Tsariwa themselves. For example, in Tsari Nub during the 1950s, a hereditary family of butchers from Dakpo or other low-status families from Nyel were employed and called in to butcher stock, so that the Tsariwa would not have to incur the burden of sin this action involved. Actual ritual restrictions on butchering that existed earlier in this century had more or less died out by the 1940s because they became impractical. These restrictions dictated that all livestock for slaughter in the western areas had to be taken to Dawatang, or "Moon Plateau," near Yütö, and butchered only there. This stricture related to a tradition of conceiving the entire local landscape centered on the Yümé area as the hypostatic body of the leading Tantric meditation goddess of the mountain, Dorje Pagmo. Topographical features around the valley were systematically identified with her body parts. While the centrally located and main meditation cave in the area, Zilchen Sangwé Phuk, was the site of her genitals, her breasts were two hills at Yütö, and above them at Dawatang itself lay her face and mouth.[19] Butchery there with the fresh blood flowing into the local ground was said to please the goddess, who also symbolically accepted meat in her formal Tantric worship. By the early decades of this century the Yütö settlement itself was abandoned in the wake of general population drift to the east, and so the fate of an increasingly impractical ritual restriction on domestic life was sealed.

The actual system of pastoralism at Tsari resembled in many respects a modified form of the *samadrok* mixed agropastoralism found throughout Tibet. For most Tibetan *samadrok* communities, the pastoral component was itself secondary to a related agricultural base and settlement with which the former maintained close links and exchanges.[20] However, such was never the case at Tsari because cultivation was either banned or, where it existed in the *rong* area, was of secondary or minor importance compared to other activities. Thus, Tsari pastoralism was a complement to a range of other activities in the household economy, including, in some cases, the *tsulkang* contracts.

Bamboo and Handicraft Work

The harvesting, processing, and trading of bamboo and bamboo goods occupied quite a number of local households at all status levels. Certain types of bamboo from Tsari already had a widely acknowledged ritual status, and in general the cane also represented a rare but useful domestic material on the plateau to the north. The Tsariwa harvested narrow canes from the lower valley and *rong* areas, or obtained the massive tubelike tropical bamboo stems through trade with tribal peoples to the south. There were two aspects to the local bamboo economy: the harvest and sale of raw canes, and the manufacture of domestic items. A traditional working song entitled "Explaining the Bamboo of Tsari," sung rhythmically by persons engaged in bamboo work, describes the first type of practice well:

> If you don't know about the growth of sprouting bamboo,
> When bamboo grows it sprouts in the interior of Tsari.
> If you don't know about the harvest of reaped bamboo,
> When bamboo is to be harvested, reap it with your little right hand!
> If you don't know about the collection of gathered bamboo,
> When bamboo is to be collected, gather it with your little left hand!
> If you don't know about the chopping of cut bamboo,
> When bamboo is to be chopped, cut it with a gold hatchet!
> If you don't know about the fastening of bound bamboo,
> When bamboo is to be fastened, bind it with multicolored string!
> If you don't know about the pulling of hauled bamboo,
> When bamboo is to be pulled, haul it with a small black yak!
> If you don't know about the selling of sold bamboo,
> When bamboo is to be sold, sell it in the Lhasa markets!
> If you don't know about the fixing of a set price,
> Make it three *sang* and two *zho* for each cane![21]

While men harvested and sold or traded raw cane, it was mainly the women of Tsari who made a wide variety of domestic wares from the local cane. Laborers were often recruited into households to assist in this work, as the profits to be gained were good. The range of locally produced caneware and bamboo items included: strainers of all shapes and sizes for water, teamaking, cheesemaking and papermaking; churns; boxes and baskets, both open and with fitted lids; backpacks and work baskets; winnowing trays; and baby cribs. These were taken to large markets or communities throughout Central Tibet during the winter trading expeditions for cash sale or trade.[22] Both bamboo products and raw cane were also demanded by certain Dzong as part of annual tax payments, and the Lo Mikyimdün *trekang*, for instance, had to supply a special type of churn for papermaking each year to the officials at

Kyemdong. It should be noted that the actual sale of cane and bamboo products was itself not taxed directly by the authorities. This was also the case with trading profits, hunting, and other activities. There was no efficient way for the premodern state, which maintained only a low level of personnel, to audit all such economic activities. Instead the government, and by extension the Gelukpa monasteries, ensured that they got their own requirements of certain goods and services by requesting these directly in the form of special taxes.

Trading

The success of both the pastoral and bamboo components of any household economy at Tsari was dependent on outbound trading trips. When pastoralism, resthouse work, and pilgrimage labor came to an end in the autumn, trading generally occupied the able adult members of most households, together with all available transport animals. The trips could take anywhere from two to four months to accomplish. The trading practices of the Tsariwa had two main dimensions: exchanging locally made products for those of adjacent communities intended for local consumption (e.g., bamboo, butter, and cheese for grain); and acting as go-betweens for the long-distance transfer of goods between Subansiri tribal populations and Central Tibetan markets. The accessibility of Tsari from the Subansiri basin was only feasible for loaded tribal trading parties throughout the winter, when the trails were drier and bridges did not get washed out in the *rong*. Therefore, both dimensions of trade could be combined during the same period of the year when household labor was more freely available. As it was, poor laborers were recruited by most *trekang* to assist on trading trips so that domiciles were not emptied of all able adults over winter.

The exchange of local Tibetan produce constituted the necessary aspect of Tsari trade, and not just because all staple foods needed to be imported. Due to their location in a dead-end mountainous area of the borderland, through which even east-west transit was often better avoided, the Tsariwa were always obliged to travel out to connect with other Tibetan communities, main markets, and routes. This situation was similar to that faced by most upland Tibetan nomadic pastoral communities. But the Tsariwa's border location was a compensation for this relative isolation, as they could also profitably exploit the long-distance tribal-Tibetan trading interface. The annual trading expeditions also efficiently combined a third aspect by incorporating on their return leg visits to the government estates that gave the grain payments due for the services of the resthouse keepers and festival organizers.

Both local trade of produce and long-distance tribal-Tibetan trade were based on long-term, carefully cultivated trading partnerships between households and other parties. Tsariwa households had agricultural trading partner households in Dakpo and other surrounding districts with whom they made annual exchanges. Households in the border villages of Lo Mikyimdün and Yümé had regular trade relations with tribal families living in the upper Subansiri. For the most part it was only in Lhasa, in the large public market areas, that they sold and exchanged goods with unknown or little-known partners. The social dimension of Tsariwa-tribal trading partnerships was one of the most positive types of interchanges that existed between the two populations. Contrary to the practice in other Tibetan border settlements, especially in areas further to the east, tribal traders were permitted to reside overnight in the Tsari border villages. These villages maintained small resthouses built for the tribal traders to stay in during their winter visits. They were essential, as the Subansiri peoples found it extremely cold in the Tibetan areas, even though villages like Lo Mikyimdün were well below the altitude at which most Tibetan communities dwelt. In Yümé, for example, this trade lodge was called the "Lopa house" (*lokang*), and it was one of the contract obligations of the Yümé *tsulkang* to supply firewood to its users over the winter. Trading partner friendships with tribal peoples often served the Tsariwa well in times of trouble. For example, in the case of an abduction of Tibetan children from Yümé by lower dwelling Nishi peoples, the higher dwelling Dakshing Lopa trading families were able to rescue the children and return them safely to their Tibetan friends. When many of the Tsariwa escaped down into the Subansiri basin, fleeing advancing Chinese troops in 1959, they were sheltered by tribal trading partners and later were assisted by them during their onward journeys to the Indian plains.

Tsari was one of a number of important trade conduits for the steady exchange of goods and materials (but seldom people and ideas) between highland Tibetan and the lowland Tibeto-Burman speaking populations that existed along the entire southeastern borderlands between Monyül in the west and Dzayül (the Mekong River gorges) in the east. There was a marked similarity in the content of this trade throughout the entire zone. In the light of earlier records, the actual content of cross-border trade at Tsari as it existed in the 1950s appears little different from what it was several centuries earlier, with the exception of a few modern items. The Tsariwa accepted traditional Tibetan medical ingredients (including musk pod, bear's gall, stag's horn, dried crabs), madder vine (a dye-stuff), animal skins (including deer, monkey, leopard, and occasionally bear and tiger), rice, maize, millet, buckwheat, chilies, and high-grade cane for weaving from the Subansiri traders. Many of these things could be sold directly for cash to dealers in Lhasa and fetched a good price, while a portion of them were also reserved to make specialized tax payments demanded by the government.[23] In Lhasa and other Central Tibetan markets, the Tsariwa traded bamboo wares and purchased with cash the items that were sought after by the tribal traders, including Tibetan woolen cloth and blankets, Tibetan copper pots, smaller aluminium pots from Calcutta, needles, metal tools and utensils, salt, long Tibetan swords, and occasionally Tibetan ritual instruments (metal bells and cymbals).

By the late 1950s, Indian salt, numerous other manufactured goods, and the beginnings of a cash economy had started to find their way into the formerly remote Subansiri basin, hard upon the heels of the Indian government's rapid administrative push into the area. This activity not only began to undermine the region's dependence on goods from Tibet but was set to overshadow the local intertribal value system for barter, in which Tibetan trade goods (especially long swords and ritual bells) figured prominently, both as units of abstract value and as a form of currency.[24] However, before the Tsariwa had a chance to feel these disadvantageous effects, the Chinese occupation of 1959 abruptly halted the long-established cross-border trading patterns at Tsari and elsewhere along the Himalayan divide. If the trade had continued, it is certain that some items at least, including all the rare animal products, would still find a ready market in contemporary Tibet, just as they did for centuries prior to Chinese colonialism.

Corvée Pilgrimage Service

The other major area of activity of the *trekang* was that of discharging their annual collective tax obligations. While even the poorest subsistence dwellers at Tsari had individual taxes to pay, in the form of *mibog* payments or other minor contributions, the *trekang* households shouldered the heaviest burden of annual taxes in any village. *Trekang* often met whatever individual tax payments (in cash and kind only) able members of poor families had in return for their labor services in all aspects of the economy throughout the year. As in the rest of Central Tibet, there were two forms of tax payment due from the *trekang* at Tsari: those made in kind or cash; and those discharged with corvée services. As I have already noted various payments in kind and cash, it is mainly corvée services that is of concern here.

Corvée service differed between the upper valley villages and Lo Mikyimdün. The latter area paid heavier taxes in kind in general, because of its location outside the zone of environmental restrictions and its history of settlement, and because it had access to a range of special products from trade, agriculture, and harvesting. Lo Mikyimdün *trekang*, in fact, had tax obligations to three different external authorities: the government Dzong at Kurab Namgyel, the Dzong at Kyemdong, and the Drukpa of Sangnag Chöling.[25] Another difference was that the upper villages had most of the *tsulkang* households and had no land under cultivation and had to live within the other environmental restrictions. The upper village *trekang* tended to have more corvée obligations and contributions to make to the upkeep of the local monasteries.[26] Although there were quite different corvée obligations at Tsari, resembling those in other parts of Tibet, I will discuss only those related to the main annual pilgrimages and the cult of the mountain in general.[27]

Apart from the obligations to contribute labor to the annual ritual cycle already discussed in chapter 10, each *trekang* was liable for numerous other services related to the pilgrimages and the maintenance of the mountain cult. These included repairing pilgrimage trails and bridges, repairing temples and shrines, performing militia duty and support roles for the Lodzong and Rongkor Chenmo, and doing corvée pilgrimage service. Judging from the published accounts, the performance of a corvée pilgrimage service obligation was a unique variant of the traditional taxation system, one that appears to have been practiced only at Tsari. The main obligation was to carry baggage for important pilgrims who visited Tsari and performed the popular Shungkor circuit. This service only applied to pilgrimage parties who were holders of official *lamyig*, or "travel permits," although that potentially covered a wide range of persons, including high government ministers, Lhasa officials and aristocrats, highly ranked incarnate lamas, and senior clerics.

Pilgrimage was clearly no journey for official business, and apart from the highest rank visitors who could issue their own *lamyig* as they pleased, most other holders got them from the neighboring Dzong or from Sangnag Chöling. They stopped en route to the mountain at such places and met with the local officials and dignitaries, who were often known or related to them in some way. This practice was clearly an unorthodox, though perhaps not uncommon, type of extension of the normal corvée transport system intended for government business. This fact was quite apparent to the Tsariwa, who had no choice but to fulfill their hereditary tax obligations without question and who, like most traditionally minded Tibetans, would continue to display a high level of deference to their social superiors unless extremely provoked. For the ordinary Tsariwa, the performance of physically demanding corvée portage (*ula*) around the rugged alpine trails of the Shungkor was not a welcome obligation. And it was one that could be made worse by the occasional high-handed behavior of the *lamyig* holders, and the knowledge that at other times they were paid and treated well to do the same work by wealthy pilgrims who employed them as private porters.

If a *lamyig* holder was about to arrive at Tsari, messengers were usually sent ahead by the Dzong to give the villagers advance warning. The permits usually requested all three standard forms of corvée—riding mounts (*tawu*), pack animals (*kema*), and porters (*ula*), the former two being used as far as Chikchar or Mikyimdün and the latter employed on the high altitude circuits themselves where animals could not travel. The headman, his deputy, or the senior *trekang* members, whoever was present, would select candidates for the corvée service. Riding mounts were usually provided on a rotating basis among the *trekang*, while the selection of porters was usually done by the drawing of lots. Often, if possible, laborers would be used as substitutes by *trekang* members to do the unpleasant work of *ula*. The *trekang* of Tsari Shar were responsible for providing pilgrimage porters from Chikchar up to the subdistrict boundary at the resthouses of Phodrang Yumtso. From there porters from the *trekang* of Tsari Nub who had arrived in advance took over and carried through to the completion of the pilgrimage at Chösam. The east Tsari porters usually returned home on the shortest route, using the high altitude Tsekor, or "peak circuit" described in chapter 6.

As mentioned, in addition to performing pilgrimage as a tax obligation, some Tsariwa also acted as hired porters. A more interesting case of paid local pilgrimage work was that of substitution pilgrimages, a practice not uncommon at other popular sites in Tibet.[28] Performing the Shungkor on behalf of wealthy, elderly, and infirm or "busy" clients, hired pilgrims were paid in "offerings" of cash by the clients, who thereby gained a share of the merits for the ritual. Their employees duly transferred the merits, as was commonly accepted practice in popular Tibetan Buddhism, of the ritual journey by rededicating them to their clients.

The corvée pilgrimage system at Tsari, like most corvée obligations in general, placed high and often unpredictable demands on the able-bodied household labor pool, or at least required the redirection of other resources in the household economy if substitute laborers were employed. Moreover, it was a demand effective at short notice, and fairly rapid mobilization of both persons and animals over the entire pilgrimage season had to be counted on by the *trekang* collective in each village. For this reason and because of the net drain on the households that such work represented, all pilgrimage labor, including both obligatory *trekang* duties and voluntary *tsulkang* contracts, was not gender specific, unlike most other areas of rural economic activity in traditional Tibet. Both men and women performed all pilgrimage work equally, with the exception that women could not act as porters or keep resthouses within the upper exclusion zone.

Necessary Compensations

I have now presented the main facets of the traditional local economy around the pilgrimage place of Pure Crystal Mountain. It operated within a range of limiting cultural and geographical factors, including religious restrictions of access to resources and their use, tax obligations, and the relatively remote location. The local response to these limits was largely to attempt to maintain economic diversity at the household level. A common theme emerges when considering the particular dynamics of space and time attendant on all aspects of household activity—the obligatory *trekang*, the voluntary *tsulkang*, and the necessarily diverse pastoralism, craft work, trade, and other practices: the critical role of labor availability. Household labor shortage in village economies was a widespread feature of premodern Tibet, although the reasons for it varied from one place to another.[29] Added to the usual factors of local climatic patterns and intensity of productive methods common in other areas, labor availability at Tsari was also specifically related to the cultural definitions of the place as a holy sanctuary and pilgrimage venue. Institutionalized pilgrimage work obviously provided necessities for local survival, especially grain supplies, but the maintenance of the mountain cult as a whole checked the potential of households significantly, and the standard of village life was, while never impoverished, maintained at a very modest to low level in the long term. Given the specific conditions that prevailed there in the 1950s, it is doubtful whether the district could have supported any more inhabitants at a sustainable level than it already did.

Apart from the compensating strategies of the households just discussed, the recognition of the various limits placed on domestic life at Tsari manifested in other particular ways. One was a special dispensation permitted by the state itself, giving Tsari households the official right to go on annual begging tours. Another was the practice of slave keeping. Both these aspects of local economy represent potentially embarrassing cultural memories of traditional prediaspora life for the contemporary exile population, although, when viewed in both the specific local and the Tibetwide context, there is nothing particularly unusual about either of them.

The issuing of official "begging permits" (*longyig*) to the villagers of Tsari was a clear indication that the Lhasa state itself recognized the constraints that existed for successful domestic life at Tsari as a holy place. Tsariwa consider that it was done specifically because they were not allowed to grow staple crops in the area. The practice of officially sanctioned begging existed at the turn of the century, but there is no indication of when it begun. *Longyig* were issued directly by the Kashag, or cabinet, in Lhasa, and marked with its official seal. They permitted the holders to beg or solicit any kind of donations throughout the territories controlled by the Central Tibetan state. These begging permits were clearly not intended by the government as a type of social safety net to aid the poorest members of the community. They had to be "earned," and only the *trekang* and *tsulkang* households of Tsari who successfully discharged their duties were eligible to receive and use them. Although this was the criterion imposed, in practice it was not the case. In the small communities of Tsari, where everybody knew each other and social and material differences were not very marked, members of the poorest families outside of the full member village households regularly got access to *longyig*. For example, if they were used as laborers to help collect the annual barley grant due from an estate for *tsulkang* services, or on long-distance trading trips, they might borrow a *longyig* if it was not needed and go off separately to beg in other districts.

From the close of the pilgrimage season up to the next spring opening, Tsariwa could make short or long begging tours, often combined with trading trips, over a wide area of the country. They ranged from Darjeeling and Tawang to the west, up to western Tibet (Tsang) and Lhasa, through Kongpo and Powo to the east, and as far as Dartsemdo (Tachienlu) on the Sichuan border.[30] On these tours they sought and were given food staples and various items for trading, including weapons, ritual implements and instruments, and live animals, as well as cash. The trade items were usually exchanged to obtain staple food supplies for domestic provisions and to discharge some of the various tax obligations.

Begging was widespread in traditional Tibet, and there were many kinds of beggars. At one extreme there were those living in abject poverty, who were perceived as miserable and unfortunate beings. There were also a class of mobile religious figures and mendicants (bards, hermits, professional pilgrims, exorcists, and so on) who sought alms on their wanderings, and who mostly enjoyed a higher status than the down and out. In general, giving to beggars of all types was viewed positively as a compassionate and meritorious activity. At Tsari, begging was related to local identity in various ways. Tsariwa saw themselves as a certain type of beggar ("solicitors of donations," according to the modern Tsariwa) defined by the particular circumstances in their sacred homeland, rather than as socially outcast or unproductive persons. They were generally viewed this way by the outsiders who knew something of the popular cult of Pure Crystal Mountain. At times they could play on the popular beliefs about them being divine incarnations, and so on. However, as life in rural Tibet often involved a struggle to make ends meet, not everyone maintained a charitable view of their activities:

> All the Tsariwa used to come to our villages in Kongpo to beg. They would bring small rocks, bits of plants, water, and other substances and say that they were very precious and powerful as they came from the Tsari mountain. So you had to prostrate before them three times, and then they would collect lots of offerings that people gave. Then they would move off through the whole of Kongpo begging like that. I think they were lazy! Some Kongpo folk used to joke about the begging: If you had a neighbour or relative who was always asking you for something or other, you would say they were like a Tsariwa![31]

The practice of Tsariwa begging was often dependent upon a performative dimension that invoked their own identity as inhabitants of the famous holy mountain and aspects of the powerful landscape they lived in. The former keeper of the Ribpa La *tsulkang* recalled one such style of performance, in which the miraculous female deer's central antler (*shamo üra*) that appeared at the time of each Rongkor Chenmo (see chapter 8) was brought into play as a prop to supplement the *longyig*:

> These antlers had great empowerment and were very auspicious. Sometimes when Tsariwa went on begging tours they would just travel from place to place with these antlers, show them to people, and explain the miracle of it. They could also tell many amazing stories about the mountain. They did go to different places with these things and got donations by begging.[32]

Other Tsariwa begged without the *longyig* and depended entirely on this type of performance, using important relics in the mountain's cult. The *tsulkang* at Gönporong, for example, possessed what were said to be the shoes and walking stick of the saint Kyewo Yeshé Dorje, who first opened the mountain for circumambulation. They would take these regularly to government estates in Dakpo and empower the residents with them. In return they received gifts of grain from the estates. All such begging is perhaps not too dissimilar from the activities that earned a livelihood for the class of wandering Tibetan storytellers and bards generally called *manipa*. Begging Tsariwa increased their chances of success by visiting persons or families they knew to be ex-pilgrims, especially wealthy ones, and by going to areas where the local population was known to be well represented on the Rongkor Chenmo and annual pilgrimages, and who were more inclined to be interested and sympathetic as donors. By all accounts, begging tours were a successful means for supplementing income.

The other compensatory measure, this time a less frequent and informal one, was the keeping of domestic slaves as an additional source of household labor. The local term for "slave" was *nyomi*, literally "human commodity," although often persons who had been purchased by a household were referred to euphemistically as "servants" (*yogpo*). All known slaves at Tsari were Subansiri tribal peoples and were kept mainly in Lo Mikyimdün and Chikchar. The Tibetan practice of keeping neighboring tribal peoples in slavery was common in the first half of this century throughout the southern and eastern borderlands, from Dzayül to Sikkim.[33] Tibetans also recruited tribal labor on a seasonal basis in Dakpo and Kongpo just to the north and east of Tsari.[34] The Subansiri tribes themselves kept slaves to boost their household labor forces and provided slaves to the Tsariwa when required.[35] Both young tribal girls and boys were available as slaves, and the only record of the exact prices charged by tribal dealers at Tsari comes from earlier this century: "At Migyitün they also sell slaves to the Tibetans who cost 45 sangs (about Rs. 75)."[36] In the 1940s and 1950s, the local acquisition of tribal slave labor was sometimes done in barter deals for the Tibetan ritual instruments so highly valued by the Subansiri tribes. A young tribal boy could be traded for a Tibetan bell of fine quality with ritual formulae cast into it.[37]

Young tribal children were preferable to adolescents and adults, being less likely to try and escape, as they often did at Tsari.[38] Once a slave had been completely purchased, he or she received no wages for any work they did but lived as "servants" as part of the extended family in the household. Tribal children could, if they did not run away, eventually become fully Tibetanized as a result.

Culture and Nature

From the Tibetan point of view, the critical limiting factor in the local economy—no staple agriculture—was determined by certain representations and social facts. The place was a Tantric holy mountain; therefore, cultivation was forbidden because it upset the divine inhabitants. But was agriculture there even possible? The simple answer is: No. The whole traditional Tibetan religious position and the complex nonagriculture economy it justified has to be seen as a productive cultural response to what from a modern scientific perspective are specific ecological and biological limits of nature.

When Chinese Communist troops and settlers arrived at Tsari in 1960, they asked the villagers who had not gone into exile why they did not cultivate any crops in this apparently fertile environment. The answer they received was predictable; the area was a great holy place and farming was forbidden on religious grounds because it disturbed the powerful deities and their environment. Furthermore, growing crops was against all known traditions, and even if they did cultivate, it would not work, and there was a historical explanation: When the great Tantric magician Padmasambhava first came to open the mountain, he hid the fruits of all foods that grew there, so that pilgrims who visited in the future would not get distracted from their serious religious practice by them. The Chinese response was to form the Tibetan villagers into household work gangs to clear, dig, and plough fields, fertilize them, and plant grain crops. All such attempted cropping failed. Wheat and barley grew tall, leafy stalks but set no grain at all. It was the same with the local walnut trees, which bore only the most vestigial and inedible bitter nuts. Only roots and leafy vegetables could be grown, as had always been done by the Tsariwa in their small kitchen gardens in the past. The new colonial occupants of Tsari were forced to import all their own staples, which they supplemented by hunting the abundant and semitame wildlife throughout the area. They eventually abandoned all parts of the upper valleys and became established only at Lo Mikyimdün, where potatoes (a tuber crop) grow well. The situation has remained basically the same at Tsari up to the time of this writing.

The few European visitors to the district this century were all either highly trained observers (that is, spies, as were Bailey and Moreshead) or botanists and ecologists (for example, Frank Ludlow and George Sherriff, Francis Kingdom Ward). They left substantial notes on the area's climate, geology and geography, and flora and fauna.[39] All mention the unique microclimate and vegetation around the mountain compared with the adjacent Tibetan districts. There are an exceptionally high rainfall and cloud cover (a fact often noted in Tibetan sources also) and very cold winters in the area. Apart from possible climatic effects, the lack of fruiting in locally grown domestic crops is also suggestive of other inhibiting physical factors, such as a critical trace element deficiency in the soils. Proper scientific testing and analysis would be needed to establish the exact causes of local fruiting failure. Many Tibetans remain convinced by traditional explanations.

The particular cultural logics that ordered local people's lives at Tsari developed because of the way in which some fundamental material constraints were interpreted and adapted to in the context of a traditional Tibetan Buddhist worldview. They may form the basis for the only type of settled and sustainable preindustrial lifestyle pattern possible in the area, that is, one dependent on the existence of something like a major pilgrimage cult around Pure Crystal Mountain.

Epilogue

> When the Chinese first came in the 1950s some of their officers and officials asked us, "Since there is no farming here, no cultivation, how do you make your living?" They also asked why we didn't farm or cultivate; at the time they were very polite, not saying much, just listening. We Tsariwa answered that it was a great power place, and that we just lived our lives by begging much of the time, which was true. So the Chinese told us they would change things such that we wouldn't have to beg any more. Many Tsariwa were very happy to hear this, for they were naive and innocent.
>
> —SG

At the time of the Chinese occupation of Tibet in 1959, many of the religious and lay inhabitants of Tsari fled from the area and went into exile. Families were divided, and many remain so today; and the local Tibetan population is depleted. Those Tsariwa who stayed and survived suffered both hardship and humiliation at times as they faced the effects of great political turbulence and irrelevant and fluctuating policies emanating from a source far more distant than any that had ever ruled over their lives. Monasteries and shrines in the area were looted and razed. All pilgrimages around the mountain were banned for over two decades.

In recent years a few temples and shrines have been rebuilt or restored, and local power places are being openly worshiped once again at Tsari, as they are at other Tibetan *néri* mountains. Annual pilgrimages have been revived, but only those on the main middle circuit, on the women's circuit, and to the nearby sacred lake of Tsari Tsokar. Modest numbers of pilgrims from other parts of Tibet or visiting from exile now make these ritual journeys each summer. The tradition of Tantric retreats has not been openly reestablished.

Nowadays, a gravel road runs down the course of the Tsari River valley, along part of the former pilgrimage route. It provides strategic access to a Chinese military base on the disputed Sino-Indian border just below the village of Lo Mikyimdün. Logging trucks also use it to haul timber cut from forests along the mountain's flanks. Wild animals have virtually disappeared; most have now been shot or trapped. Soldiers and hunters patrolling the upper mountain relieve themselves without concern for polluting its sacred slopes. The advantages promised by the arrival of the Chinese colonial version of modernity, such as public schools and clinics, have failed to materialize. There is still no cultivation in the upper valleys, although, as far as I am aware, no one living at Tsari today has to beg.

Tibetan Word List

Phonetic Form and Tibetan Spelling

ama changma a ma chang ma
amdo a mdo
amdo sharkog a mdo shar khog
amnye machen a myes rma chen
apho rinpoché a pho rin po che
atre a krad

barawa gyeltsen palzangpo 'ba' ra ba rgyal mtshan dpal bzang po
bardo tranglam bar do 'phrang lam
barkor bar skor
bepa yumtso sbal pa g.yu mtsho
beyül sbas yul
bhusuku bhu su ku
bimbi la 'bi 'bi la
bo 'bo
bokto 'bog tho
bön bon
bonga nakpo bong nga nag po
bongbu lamtso bong bu bla mtsho
bongnak bong nag
bönkyong bon skyong
bönpo bon po
bumpa bum pa
butsa bu tsha

cha bya
cha chögyel pelzang bya chos rgyal dpal bzang
cha rinchen bya rin chen
chagchen lama phyag chen bla ma
chagkor dribjhong phyag skor sgrib 'byong
chagtse phyag 'tshal
chagya chenpo phyag rgya chen po
chakberong lcags sbal rong
chaktha treng lcags thag 'phrang
chaktha trengo lcags thag 'phrang sgo
cham 'cham
chamdre lcam dral
champarong byams pa rong
chana dorje phyag na rdo rje
chang chang
changchub gyeltsen byang chub rgyal mtshan
changma chang ma
changphu chang phud
changsem byang sems
changsem karpo byang sems dkar po
changsem marpo byang sems dmar po
changtang byang thang
changüri byang dbu ri
chaphurgang bya 'phur sgang
char byar
char chekhapa bya 'chad kha pa
char la char la or phyag [rgya chen po] la
charlo bya klo
charmé bya smad
chartsa gunbu dbyar tswa dgun bu
chatrim bca' khrims

chayül bya yul
chayülpa bya yul pa
chebu lopa gcer bu klo pa
chedrak bye brag
chena spyan snga
chi phyi
chibpön chibs dpon
chikchar cig car
chikchar marpo cig car dmar po
chikchar pelgi nakjong cig car dpal gyi nags ljongs
chikchar pelgi naktrod cig car dpal gyi nags khrod
chimi spyi mi
chin byin
chingyilab byin gyis brlabs
chinlab byin brlabs
chö chos
chö pelchen chöyé chos dpal chen chos yes
chöd gcod
chödong mchod sdong
chödrog chos grogs
chödze mchod rdzas
choga cho ga
chöki gönpo chos kyi mgon po
chöki lama chos kyi bla ma
chokrab mchog rab
chöku dewa chenpo chos sku bde ba chen po
chökyong chos skyong
chölam chablam spyod lam chab lam
chölé chos las
chölé chenmo chos las chen mo
chongyé 'phyong rgyas
chongshi cong zhi
chöpa mchod pa
chösam chos zam
chösamdong chos zam gdong
chöshé chos gzhas
chöten mchod rten
chöyingpa chos dbyings pa
chu bcud
chu drowa drölwa chu 'gro ba sgrol ba
chulen bcud len
chum karpo lcum dkar po
chumdong chenpo lcum sdong chen po
chumik nakpo chu mig nag po
chumphu chu mo phug
chure chu ras
chuwori chu bo ri

dak 'dag
daklha gampo dwags lha sgam po
daknang dag snang
dakpa dag pa
dakpa khachö dag pa mkha' spyod
dakpa khachörishi dag pa mkha' spyod ri bzhi
dakpa sheri dag pa shel ri
dakpa tsari thugpa dag pa tsa ri'i thugs pa
dakpashri (*dakpa sheri*) dag pa shri
dakpo dwags po
dakpo drumpa dwags po bhruṃ pa
dakpo lhaje dwags po lha rje
dakpo tratsang dwags po grwa tshang
dakshing dag zhing
dalai lama tā la'i bla ma
damchen dorje legpa dam can rdo rje legs pa
damchen la dam can la
dangra dwangs rwa
daö shonu zla 'od gzhon nu
dartsemdo dar rtse mdo
demchok bde mchog
densa gdan sa
densatilpa gdan sa thil pa
depa sde pa
depa sarnying sde pa gsar rnying
depa shung sde pa gzhung
depön sde dpon
desee tsangpa sde srid gtsang pa
deu chönchung lde'u chos 'byung
deuyak lagang lde'u g.yag la sgang
dik sdig
dik drib sdig sgrib
dikpa karnak sdig pa dkar nag
dilgo khyentse dil mgo mkhyen brtse
dompa 'dom pa
domsum rabye sdom gsum rab dbye
domtree dom mkhris
domtsang dom tshang
domtsen rdo mtshan

dongmo chuluk ldong mo chu bslugs (or slu gu)
dongrag gong og sdong rag gong 'og
dordzin rdor 'dzin
doring rdo ring
doring pandita rdo ring paṇḍita
dorje rdo rje
dorje chang rdo rje 'chang
dorje drak rdo rje brag
dorje dzinpa rdo rje 'dzin pa
dorje jigjay rdo rje 'jigs byed
dorje legpa rdo rje legs pa
dorje neljorma rdo rje rnal 'byor ma
dorje pagmo rdo rje phag mo
dorje pagmo denyishel rdo rje phag mo bden gnyis zhal
dorje phuk rdo rje phug
dorje rawa rdo rje ra ba
dorje sempa rdo rje sems pa
dorje yudrönma rdo rje g.yu sgron ma
drablha dgra lha
drakchen drag can
drakburwa brag 'bur ba
dre bre
drepung 'bras spungs
drib grib or sgrib
dribnyi sgrib gnyis
drigung 'bri gung
drigung kyabgön 'bri gung skyab mgon
drigung lingpa 'bri gung gling pa
drigung phowa chenmo 'bri gung 'pho ba chen mo
drigungpa 'bri gung pa
drigungthel 'bri gung mthil
drilbu dril bu
dro bro
drokpa 'brog pa
drölma la sgrol ma la
drölma lamtso sgrol ma bla mtsho
drongpa grong pa
druk 'brug
druk ralung 'brug ra lung
drukchen 'brug chen
drukchen ngawang chögyel 'brug chen ngag dbang chos rgyal
drukchuma drug cu ma
drukpa 'brug pa
drukpa sang 'brug pa gsang [sngags chos gling]
drukpa togden 'brug pa rtog ldan
drukpé lamtso 'brug pa'i bla mtsho
drulung gru lung
drum grum
druma gru ma
drumalung gru ma lung
drungkor drung 'khor
drupchuka sgrub chu kha
drupde sgrub sde
düdchung dud chung
düdgön lamtso bdud mgon bla mtsho
düdgön nakpo bdud mgon nag po
dukhor wangchen dus 'khor dbang chen
dulwa 'dul ba
dünjom rinpoché bdud 'joms rin po che
dütsenma dus mtshan ma
dzambuling 'dzam bu gling
dzayül rdza yul
dzogrim rdzogs rim
dzokchen pema rigdzin rdzogs chen padma rig 'dzin
dzokchen nyingthik rdzogs chen snying thig
dzomo mdzo mo
dzong rdzong
dzongpön rdzong dpon

ekajaṭī e ka dzā ṭi
eyül e yul

gabshi tenzin penjor dga' bzhi bstan 'dzin dpal 'byor
gampo sgam po
gampopa sgam po pa
ganden dga' ldan
ganden phodrang dga' ldan pho brang
gangshak gangs gshag
gangten gangs brtan
gar 'gar
gardampa 'gar dam pa
gardampa chödingpa 'gar dam pa chos sdings pa
gayo la dga' yo la
gekhod ge khod
gelong dge slong

gelukpa dge lugs pa
gendün chöphel dge 'dun chos 'phel
genyen dge bsnyen
gesar ge sar
go la sgo la
gomchen sgom chen
gomtha sgom thag
gönpo trakshe mgon po traḳsad
gönporong mgon po rong
göpa rgod pa
gowoche mgo bo che
guru rinpoché gu ru rin po che
gya rgya
gyabkor rgyab bskor
gyama rgya ma
gyare rgya ras
gyare mikraphuk rgya ras mig ra phug
gyarepa rgya ras pa
gyelrab salwé melong rgyal rabs gsal ba'i me long
gyelwa götsangpa rgyal ba rgod tshang pa
gyelwang kunga penjor rgyal dbang kun dga' dpal 'byor
gyentrö rgyan spros
gyergom chenpo gyer sgom chen po
gyergom nyipa gyer sgom gnyis pa
gyergom shigpo gyer sgom zhig po
gyergon tsultrim senge gyer sgom tshul khrims seng ge

heruka he ru ka

jalandhara dzā landha ra
jamyang chöki trakpa 'jam dbyangs chos kyi grags pa
jel mjal
jelwa mjal ba
jhang byang
jigjay 'jigs byed
jigten gönpo 'jig rten mgon po
jindag sbyin bdag
jinpa sbyin pa
jokhang jo khang
jomo kharak jo mo kha rag
jowo tempa la jo bo them pa la

kagyü bka' brgyud
kagyü lamtso bka' brgyud bla mtsho
kagyüpa bka' brgyud pa
kalā dungtso ka lā dung mtsho
kalon bka' blon
kangso bskang gso
kangyog rkang mgyogs
kardogtang dkar rdog thang
kargong dkar gong or mkhar gong
karmapa karma pa
karmapa mikyöd dorje karma pa mi skyod rdo rje
karmapa rangchung dorje karma pa rang 'byung rdo rje
karmapa rolpaé dorje karma pa rol pa'i rdo rje
karmapa wangchuk dorje karma pa dbang phyug rdo rje
kashag bka' shag
kawa karpo kha ba dkar po
kema khal ma
khachö mkha' spyod
khachö wangmo mkha' spyod dbang mo
khachö wangpo mkha' spyod dbang po
khachöma mkha' spyod ma
khachöpa mkha' spyod pa
khachöri mkha' spyod ri
khachöri dorje phuk mkha' spyod ri rdo rje phug
khachörishi mkha' spyod ri bzhi
khadingdrak mkha' lding brag
khalo kha klo
kham khams
khampa khams pa
khandro mkha' 'gro
khandro bumde mkha' 'gro 'bum sde
khandro doénying phuk mkha' 'gro rdo'i snying phug
khandro lapuk mkha' 'gro la phug
khandro sanglam mkha' 'gro gsang lam
khandro trütso mkha' 'gro 'khrus mtsho
khandro tsogshong mkha' 'gro tshogs gzhong
khandroma mkha' 'gro ma
kharak kha rag
khargyug la mkhar rgyugs la
khélang khas blangs
khorlo 'khor lo

khorlo dompa 'khor lo sdom pa
kongbu shetö rkong bu shel stod
kongmo la gong mo la
kongpo rkong po
kongpo bönri rkong po bon ri
kor skor
kor duchenmo skor dus chen mo
korwa skor ba
ku sku
kula sku bla
kulha thogyel sku lha thog rgyal
kunga rinchen kun dga' rin chen
kunga shonu kun dga' gzhon nu
kunkhyen kun mkhyen
kunyer sku gnyer
kurab namgyel dzong sku rabs rnam rgyal rdzong
kutö sku stod
kyébu dampa skyes bu dam pa
kyemdong rkyem sdong
kyemen skye dman
kyemengi korwa skye dman gyi skor ba
kyepo yedor skye po ye rdor
kyewo skye bo
kyewo yeshé dorje skye bo ye shes rdo rje
kyimlha khyim lha
kyiphuk skyid phug
kyo kogang skyo kho gangs
kyobchen la skyobs chen la
kyobchen phuk skyobs chen phug
kyogo?
kyopa jigten sumgi gönpo skyob pa 'jig rten gsum gyi mgon po
kyudo skyus mdo
kyunang dkyud nang

la bla
la né bla gnas
labchi la phyi
ladakh la dwags
lado bla rdo
laghi la ghi
lagu lungu la dgu lung gdu
lakha la kha
lalo kla klo
lama bla ma
lamtso bla mtsho
lamyig lam yig
langdun glang mdun
lashing bla shing
latsee gla rtsi
lawa phuk la wa phug
lawagyal la bar rgyal
lawanang la bar nang
lawapa la wa pa
lé las
léki drib las kyi sgrib
lelung shepé dorje sle lung bzhad pa'i rdo rje
létsen las tshan
létsengye las tshan brgyad
lhalu lha klu
lhamo samdong lha mo zam gdong
lhamorong lha mo rong
lhanyer lha gnyer
lhapa lha pa
lhasa lha sa
lhatsogdu lha tshogs 'du
lhenchik kyéma lhan cig skyes ma
lhokha lho kha
lhundrupding lhun grub sdings
lhungidrup lhun gyi grub
lhuntse dzong lhun rtse rdzong
ling repa gling ras pa
linga ling ga
lingchen gling chen
lingchen repa gling chen ras pa
lo mikyimdün klo mi khyim bdun
lobsang chödzom blo bzang chos 'dzom
lobsang döndup drölma blo bzang don grub sgrol ma
lodag klo bdag
lodrö gyatso blo gros rgya mtsho
lodzong klo rdzong
lokag klo 'gag
lokang klo khang
lokar lo skar
lokeg lo skeg or lo skag
lonag klo nags
longkhen slong mkhan
longyig slong yig
lopa klo pa or glo pa

lopa khatra klo pa kha khra
lorepa lo ras pa
loro lo ro
losar lo gsar
losum chogsum lo gsum phyogs gsum
lowo klo bo or glo bo
loyül klo yul
lu 1. klu; 2. glu; 3. lus
ludud dorje klu bdud rdo rje
lugyel wangdrak klu rgyal dbang brag
luki drib lus kyi drib
lung 1. rlung; 2. klung
lungdu lopa klung du klo pa
lungta rlung rta

machen ma chen
machen lawa phuk ma chen la wa phug
madakdro ma dag 'gro
mangshi rmang gzhi
mani mạ ni
mani kambum mạ ni bka' 'bum
manipa mạ ni pa
markay mar khal
marnag rakta dmar nag rakta
marpa mar pa
martsöd dmar btsod
mé smad
melong dorje me long rdo rje
menjong sman ljongs
mérongwa smad rong ba
metog chöpa me tog mchod pa
mibog mi bogs
migöd mi rgod
mikra phuk mig ra phug
mikyimdün lopa mi khyim bdun klo pa
mila repa mi la ras pa
milaé gurbum mi la'i mgur 'bum
milam rmi lam
mipa mi lpags
miparong mi lpags rong
mipham lodrö mi pham blo gros
mitsangpa mi gtsang pa
mizang mi bzang
mo mo
molha mo lha
mon mon
mönlam chenmo smon lam chen mo
monyül mon yul

nabza masöl na bza' ma gsol
nak ngag
namgyel drölma rnam rgyal sgrol ma
namkha phuk nam mkha' phug
nang nang
nang dzong nang rdzong
nangtra snang khrar
naro chödruk na ro chos drug
né gnas
né pema köd gnas padma bkod
né tsachenpo gnas rtsa chen po
néchen gnas chen
néchok gnas mchog
nédakpa gnas dag pa
nédampa gnas dam pa
nédo gnas rdo
nédrog gnas grogs
négo chewa gnas sgo phye ba
négo dam gnas sgo bsdams
néjel gnas mjal
néki chinlab gnas kyi byin brlabs
néki logyü gnas kyi lo rgyus
nékor gnas skor
neljorpa rnal 'byor pa
néri gnas ri
nésa gnas sa
néshab gnas zhabs
néshé gnas bshad
nézang gnas bzang
ngakor snga skor
ngampa tratrok rngam pa sgra sgrogs
ngangkyel ngang skyal
ngari mnga' ris
ngawang chögyel ngag dbang chos rgyal
ngawang norbu ngag dbang nor bu
ngenchö brngan mchod
ngulsang dngul srang
ngor ngor
norburi nor bu ri
norje repa ngor rje ras pa
nyanchen tanglha gnyan chen thang lha
nyarong nyag rong
nyel gnyal

nyenpa gnyan pa
nyephu snye phu
nyingmapa rnying ma pa
nyö gnyos
nyö lhanangpa gnyos lha nang pa
nyöchenpo gyelwa lhanangpa gnyos chen po rgyal ba lha nang pa
nyöki dokchel gnyos kyi rdo gcal
nyomi nyo mi
nyötön gnyos ston
nyugtsig smyug tshigs

olkha 'ol kha
ömbar yumtso 'od 'bar g.yu mtsho
ömbartso 'od 'bar mtsho
orgyen rinpoché o rgyan rin po che
orgyenpa rinchenpal o rgyan pa rin chen dpal

pagmo phag mo
pagmo drupa phag mo gru pa
pagmo sangphuk phag mo gsang phug
pagsam wangpo dpag bsam dbang po
pagsha la phag sha la
pamo dpa' mo
pamo la dpa' mo la
panchen lama paṇ chen bla ma
paro spa gro
parparong parpa rong
pawo dpa' bo
pawo la dpa' bo la
pawongkha pha bong kha
pé dpe
péden pad gdan
pelchen chöyé dpal chen chos yes
pema karpo padma dkar po
pema khatang padma bka' thang
phayül chikpa pha yul gcig pa
phö domtsenchen bod rdo mtshan can
phodrang pho brang
phodrang chenpo yumtso pho brang chen po g.yu mtsho
phodrang kyomotso pho brang skyog mo mtsho
phodrang ütse pho brang dbu rtse
phodrang yumtso pho brang g.yu mtsho
phödzo sumdo bod rdzogs gsum mdo
phökhasum bod kha sum
pholha pho lha
phölung bod klung
phoma lhakhab pho ma lha khab
phöpa bod pa
phuglha phug lha
phurparong phur pa rong
pökyapa spos skya pa
pökyapa senge rinchen spo skya pa seng ge rin chen
potala po ta la
powo spo bo

rabné rab gnas
ralung ra lung
ralungthel ra lung thil
rangchung rang 'byung
rechung nyengyü ras chung snyan brgyud
rechungpa ras chung pa
relcha ral cha
relpaé chalug ral pa'i cha lugs
rephu ras phud
ribpa la rib pa la or ri pa la
rimdro rim gro
rinchenbum rin chen 'bum
rinphuk rin phug
riwa drukse ri ba 'brug gsas
riwo shānti ri bo shānti
rong rong
rongkor chenmo rong skor chen mo
rukel ru khal

sabtra sa bkra or sa khra
sachö sa spyod
sadak sa bdag
sakya pandita sa skya paṇḍita
sakyapa sa skya pa
samadrok sa ma 'brog
samdong zam gdong
samten pelwa bsam gtan dpal ba
samyé bsam yas
sang 1. gsang; 2. bsangs; 3. srang
sangchab gsang chab
sangna bsangs sna
sangnag chöling gsang sngags chos gling
sangnag sarma gsang sngags gsar ma
sangphu gsang phu

sangye gyatso sangs rgyas rgya mtsho
sangye möpa sangs rgyas mos pa
sangye tönpa tsöndrü senge sangs rgyas ston pa brtson 'grus seng ge
saog sa 'og
saogchö sa 'og spyod
sarma yangdzö gsar ma yang mdzod
sarmarong gsar ma rong
sarmawa gsar ma ba
sasum sa gsum
satrel sa khral
sengdongma seng gdong ma
senge dongchen seng ge'i gdong can
senge lodrö seng ge blo gros
senmogong sen mo gong
sera se ra
serpangma ser spang ma
shabkar zhabs dkar
shabten zhabs rten
shabtog zhabs tog
shadur bya dur
shakam la sha skam la
shakya rinchen shakya rin chen
shamali sha ma li
shamarpa chöpel yeshé zhwa dmar pa chos dpal ye shes
shamarpa khachö wangpo zhwa dmar pa mkha' spyod dbang po
shamarpa lama zhwa dmar pa bla ma
shamarpa trakpa senge zhwa dmar pa grags pa seng ge
shambhala sham bha la
shamo sha mo
shanak cham zhwa nag 'cham
shang tselpa zhang tshal pa
shangpa shang pa
shangü la sha ngus la
shar dungri shar gdung ri
shawa ripa sha ba ri pa
shawapa shar ba pa
shérab drilburi shes rab dril bu ri
shérab gyatso shes rab rgya mtsho
shibmo tratrig zhib mo khrag khrig
shidak gzhi bdag
shijay zhi byed
shikha gzhis ka
shingiköpa zhing gi bkod pa
shingkham zhing khams
shingkyong zhing skyong
shingkyong torma zhing skyong gtor ma
shingkyong yabyum zhing skyong yab yum
shingpa zhing pa
shingtri gyelpo shing khri rgyal po
shinje gyelpo gshin rje rgyal po
sho sho
shokag sho bkag
sholnyer zhol gnyer
shugpa shug pa
shugseb shug gseb
shungkor gzhung skor
si sri
sinbumtang sri 'bum thang
sindhura sindhu ra
sinmo nering srin mo ne'u ring
sog srog
soglu srog blu
sokyewo so skye bo
sönam bsod nams
sönam gyeltsen bsod nams rgyal mtshan
sönamki tsog bsod nams kyi tshogs
songtsen gampo srong btsan sgam po
sung gsung
sungdüd srung mdud

tag dorje stag rdo rje
taglung stag lung
tagtsang stag tshang
tagtsangrong stag tshang rong
tagyugtang rta rgyug thang
takar la rta dkar la
takshing stag shing or bdag shing?
tama lamgo stag ma la mgo
tango rta mgo
targo rta mgo
tashi bkra shis
tashi dargye bkra shis dar rgyas
tashi gomang bkra shis sgo mang
tashi lhunpo bkra shis lhun po
tashi thongmön bkra shis mthong smon
tashijong bkra shis ljongs
tawang rta dbang
tawu rta 'u

ten rten
tendrel rten 'brel
tenkhar rten mkhar
tenma chunyi brtan (or bstan) ma bcu gnyis
tenzin penjor bstan 'dzin dpal 'byor
terma gter ma
teura lte'u ra
thab dorjeri thabs rdo rje ri
thab shérab sungjuk ümari thabs shes rab zung 'jug dbu ma ri
thama mtha' ma
thangthong gyelpo thang stong rgyal po
tharpagyen thar pa rgyan
thigle thig le
thimphu thim phu
thug thugs
thukpa thug pa
thumi 'thus mi
thuntsob 'thus 'tshob
tinglo gting klo
tingshag ting shags
tise ti se
tö stod
tö druk stod 'brug
tokden tsariwa rtog ldan tsa ri ba
tongdröl mthong grol
tongpön stong dpon
tönpa shenrab ston pa gshen rab
torgya gtor rgyag
torma gtor ma
trakpa chungné grags pa 'byung gnas
trakshe lamtso trakṣad bla mtsho
trangka ṭang ka
trangpo sprang po
tranre 'gran ras
traor bra 'or
traorpa chöwa trakpa bra 'or pa chos 'bar grags pa
trehor tre hor
trekang khral khang
trelpa khral pa
trelpé apha khral pa'i a pha
trelten khral rten
trerok khral grogs
trigugchen gri gug can
tringpo 'bring po
trinley tsoshi 'phrin las mtsho bzhi
tripadam gri dpa' dam
tripön khri dpon
trön sgron
trön karutra sgron ka ru brag
trü khrus
tsa rtsa
tsādra rinchendrak tsā 'dra rin chen brag
tsalung rtsa rlung
tsalung thigle rtsa rlung thig le
tsampa rtsam pa
tsang gtsang
tsang nyön heruka gtsang smyon he ru ka
tsangnag phukpa thukje senge rtsang nag phug pa thugs rje seng ge
tsangpa gyare gtsang pa rgya ras
tsangpa gyare yeshé dorje gtsang pa rgya ras ye shes rdo rje
tsangpo gtsang po
tsari tsa ri *or* rtsa ri *or* tswa ri *or* rtswa ri
tsari kyingkortang tsari'i dkyil 'khor thang
tsari machen tsari ma chen
tsari mendzong tsa ri sman rdzongs
tsari nub tsa ri nub
tsari nyingma tsa ri rnying ma
tsari nyipa tsa ri gnyis pa
tsari rechen tsa ri ras chen
tsari sarma tsa ri gsar ma
tsari shar tsa ri shar
tsari tsagong tsa ri tsa gong
tsari tsagong parvata tsari rtswa gong parbata
tsari tsokar tsa ri mtsho dkar
tsāritra tsā ri tra (*also* tsa ri tra)
tsariwa tsa ri ba
tsarong tsa rong
tse tshe
tsechu tshe bcu
tsechug rtse phyug
tsedrung rtse drung
tsekor rtse skor
tselpa tshal pa
tselpa tokden tshal pa rtogs ldan
tsenchen mtshan can
tsendug btsan dug

tsenpo btsan po
tsethar tshe thar
tsog tshogs
tsogchö chenmo tshogs mchod chen mo
tsogchö sertreng tshogs mchod ser sbreng
tsogi khorlo tshogs kyi 'khor lo
tsokar mtsho dkar
tsongkhapa tsong kha pa
tsuglagkang gtsug lag khang
tsulkang tshul khang
tsulpa tshul pa
tsultrim tshul khrims
tu thud
tumoéme gtum mo'i me

ü dbus
ula 'u la
umā u mā
uma dbu ma
umdze kari dbu mdzad dkar ri?
uphang dbu 'phang
üra dbus rwa
üri dbu ri
üri[pa] dbu ri [pa]

wang dbang
wangchuk chenpo dbang phyug chen po
wanglag dbang lag
wangtang dbang thang

yabshi shikha yab gzhis gzhis ka
yabyum yab yum
yabzang g.ya' bzangs
yakdro g.yag bro
yakdzi dawa trakpa g.yag rdzi zla ba grags pa
yanlag yan lag
yarab g.yag rabs
yarlung yar klung
yasor ya sor
yeshé dorje ye shes rdo rje
yid yid
yidam yi dam
yogpo g.yog po
yondak yon bdag
yüllha yul lha
yümé yul smad
yümé charok yul smad bya rog
yumtso g.yu mtsho
yütö yul stod

zangdok pelri zangs mdog dpal ri
zanglung zangs lung
zangzang nering zangs zangs ne ring
zen gzan
zhé gzhas
zho zho
zilchen sangwé phuk zil chen gsang ba'i phug
zimkhang gzim khang

Notes

1. Introduction

1. ZhKN:500–501. I have used my own translations of the autobiography of Shabkawa Tsogdruk Rangdröl (1781–1851) throughout, although readers may want to compare the fine translation recently published by Ricard (1994).

2. For general reviews, see Bernbaum (1987), Dowman (1988), Ekvall (1964), Large-Blondeau (1960), Macdonald (1985), Ngawang Dak-pa (1987), Stablein (1978), and Waddell (1895). The "classic" ethnographic work is that of Jest (1975, 1985), although it focuses mainly on the local pilgrimage activities of a small Tibetan-speaking population within Nepal. In contrast, Ekvall and Downs (1987) interviewed many pilgrims from all areas of Tibet but performed no actual fieldwork and discussed no single, major site. Studies by anthropologists have recently increased (see n. 3). More comprehensive literary and historical studies include those by Dowman (1981), Ferrari (1958), Huber (1990, 1994b, 1994c, 1995), Kapstein (1997), Macdonald (1975, 1979, 1981, 1990), Snellgrove (1979), and Tucci (1971). Related materials are found in Aziz (1975, 1987), Bernbaum (1980), Brauen-Dolma (1985), Buffetrille (1994c), and Kaschewsky (1982).

3. Recent forums for this growing research include the volume edited by A. W. Macdonald (1997), the *Tibet Journal* special issue "Powerful Places and Spaces in Tibetan Religious Culture" (19:2–4, 1994 and 20:1, 1995), edited by T. Huber, and the panel "Pilgrimage and Sacred Geography" initiated by H. Diemberger and L. Epstein at the Sixth conference of the International Association for Tibetan Studies in 1992, and subsequent publication of papers read there in Kværne (1994). See, in addition, Buffetrille (1993, 1994a), Cech (1992), Diemberger (1993), Huber (1994a), and Karmay (1992).

4. Several studies of pilgrimage to major Tibetan mountain sites appeared just as this book was going to press. They represent, in part, a welcome departure from the general trends mentioned herein; see Buffetrille (1996, 1997) and Ramble (1997).

5. For example, Turner (1973, 1974; Turner and Turner 1978).

6. Some of these are listed in Eade and Sallnow (1991:4–5); see also Birnbaum (1984:10) on China.

7. Berg (1994:16), who is quoting Sallnow (1987:8).

2. Tibetan Pilgrimage

1. There is no Tibetan category that corresponds well to either "ritual" or "rite," and no detailed classification of practices either, but see Blondeau and Karmay (1988), Macdonald (1987a), and Tucci (1980) for useful discussions. The whole concept of "ritual" as a modern analytical category has recently been subject to an interesting critical review by Bell (1992).

2. For example, see Blondeau (1990) and Blondeau and Karmay (1988), Beyer (1973), and Samuel (1993), respectively.

3. In Tibetan sources there is no clear classification of pilgrimage (*nékor*) as a type of ritual or rite. It can be subsumed under the standard textual formula: "to perform prostration, offering and circumambulation" (*phyag mchod dang skor-ba byed-pa*), therefore being distinct from *chöpa* (Sanskrit: *pūjā*). According to definitions and etymologies it is not strictly a type of *choga* (Sanskrit: *vidhi*) (see Blondeau and Karmay 1988:124–25; Tucci 1980:114–15); however, in colloquial usage we find it said that "[p]ilgrimage is the *choga* of the laity" (*gnas-skor 'jig-rten-gyi cho-ga yin*) (Jest 1975:353). Depending on the motivations and goals of the participants, it can also be viewed as a type of *rimdro* ("apotropaic ritual/rite"), where the purpose is reparatory or preventive and concerned with benefits in this life, yet according to the religious élite it also earns one merit and better future rebirths, and is therefore soteriological.

4. The cult of the reliquary shrine (*stūpa*), as expressed in texts like the *Mahāparinirvāṇa-sūtra*, and the notion of the immanence in the world of an enlightened Buddha or saint after their final nirvāṇa (see Ray, 1994:chaps. 10–11; Schopen, 1987) appear to have provided much of the basis for early Indian Buddhist pilgrimage. In certain respects, later Tibetan pilgrimages can be viewed as elaborate developments of these ideas.

5. See the interesting essay by Lichter and Epstein (1983) on complex Tibetan understandings of causality and the tendency to gloss them under single Buddhist rubrics such as karma.

6. What follows is discussed in greater detail in Huber (1994c); see also the discussion of Ekvall and Downs (1987:24–8, chap. 9).

7. See Cech (1993:41–43) and Schwartz (1994:227).

8. See A. Macdonald (1971:especially 298–309) and Stein (1972:202–3).

9. See March (1977:94), Karmay (1987), Nebesky-Wojkowitz (1956:481–83), and Stein (1972:226–29).

10. See Aziz (1978a:253), Stein (1972:227–28), and Tucci (1980:187–89).

11. Compare Snellgrove, "empowerment (adhṣṭhāṇa) . . . byin-gyis-brlabs-pa = pervaded by grace" (1987:634) and Beyer, who uses "empowering" for the same term (1973:525). Martin has "charisma" for *chinlab* when referring to transmission of teaching between persons (1994b:27, n.101). The commonly used translation "blessing," coined in the nineteenth century by Christian missionary lexicographers with the intention of translating the Bible, hardly captures the range of meanings of *chinlab* in popular thought and rituals like pilgrimage (Huber 1994c: 41–42).

12. Mumford (1989:97).

13. See Fourteenth Dalai Lama (1990b:140).

14. Geshé Ngawang Dhargyey (interview, 1987).

15. For a range of examples, see Buffetrille (1993:103–4 and 1997:111 on *nédo*), Dowman (1988:102, 212), Jest (1975:366), Johnson and Moran (1989:42, 45–46), Mumford (1989: 97), Pranavananda (1983:12, 50, 127 n., 132), and Waddell (1895:309–10, 320). Such *né* materials are used in a variety of ways for protection, healing, purification, restoring vitality, promoting the fertility and health of farm animals, and so on. In addition, the value of collected

né substances is such that they are bought, sold, and traded among Tibetans. I should make it clear that such substances are not classified as relics by Tibetans, although a relic itself may be the *ten* or "support" on which a *né* is based. Martin has discussed classification of Tibetan relics and makes the distinction that "in Tibet, the emphasis of the relic cult was less on the wonder working power of relics and more on the miraculous nature of the relics in and of themselves." (1992:183). The opposite is true of *né* substances, which are mundane materials with "enhanced" properties. They are believed to have the power with practical application, hence their exchange value.

16. See Sangren (1993).

17. See Samuel (1993:260), Ström (1995:208), Gold (1988:146), and Anon. (1986b:4–5).

18. YNyZh:3b–4a, *Lus kyi sgrib pa sbyong phyir phyag 'tshal dang skor ba*. Variations on this common formulation appear to have been introduced into Tibet during the eleventh to twelfth centuries, being mentioned, for instance, in the teachings of the Indian Buddhist yogin Phadampa Sangyé (d. 1117/8): *Phyag 'tshal bskor bas lus kyi sdig pa 'dag* (Kaschewsky 1973:179).

19. Fourteenth Dalai Lama (1990b:132); my italics.

20. For example, see Naquin and Yü on physical hardship and expiation in Chinese pilgrimage (1992:20).

21. See Lalou (1959:27) and Karmay (1975: 205–6).

22. *Phyi pa'i phyi gtsang, nang pa'i nang gtsang* (see Stablein 1978:22).

23. See Sax (1991:13). The standard encyclopedia definition of "Tibetan Pilgrimage" (Bernbaum 1987:351) erroneously associates this Indian imagery of heat and burning with popular Tibetan pilgrimage. The idea of an internal fire is, of course, found in some higher level Tibetan Buddhist rituals based on Indian sources. If any parallel Indic conception is to be sought for notions of internal transformation in popular pilgrimage in Tibet, it must surely be that of *abhiṣeka*.

24. Anon. (1986a:75).

25. See Grapard's comments on Japanese Buddhist mountain pilgrimages: "It is well known that pilgrims coming back from sacred spaces were regarded with awe: common people saluted them, made offerings, even tried to touch them" (1982:207).

26. See Diemberger (1994), Mumford (1989), Ortner (1978), Schicklgruber (1992), as well as Chophel (1983:3, 9, 10, 12, 21), Nebesky-Wojkowitz (1956: 307, 388–9), and Tucci (1980:173, 201).

27. For examples, see Buffetrille (1994b:84), Jest (1975:356, pl. 105), Hedin (1909:195), and Dowman (1988:102).

28. White and black stones associated with moral assessments are pervasive, for example in Tibetan images of reckoning in hell: "Before the fearsome judge [the Lord of Death], a demon holds the scales on which are weighed the sins and virtues of each new arrival. These are envisaged as a pile of white stones for virtues and another of black stones for sins" (Lichter and Epstein 1983:235); see Buffetrille (1997:99–100). A related pilgrimage phenomenon in Tibet is the pilgrim's passage through narrow caves or traverse of dangerous trails (e.g., across cliff faces or along precipitous mountain ridges) which are called *bardo tranglam*, "narrow path of the intermediate state [between death and rebirth]." The implication being that the virtuous need not fear, and that a successful passage during pilgrimage will mean a successful transit of the intermediate state also, rather than a fall to hell.

29. As found in the work of the so-called ethnosociological movement from Chicago and those they have inspired; for example, Daniel (1984), Inden and Nicholas (1977), Marriott (1976), Marriott and Inden (1977), and Sax (1990).

3. The Cult of Pilgrimage Mountains in Tibet

1. A reliable body of Western language sources and scholarship on Tibet's *néri* type mountains is now developing. See for example, on Amnye Machen: Buffetrille (1994c, 1997); on Kawa Karpo: Bacot (1909), Large-Blondeau (1960), Rock (1947); on Kongpo Bönri: Cech (1992), Hanna (1994), Karmay (1992), Ramble (1997); on Labchi: Huber (1994a, 1997), Macdonald (1990); on Nyanchen Tanglha: Kaschewsky (1990); on Tise: Huber (1990), Huber and Rigzan (1995), Loseries (1990), Norbu and Prats (1989); on Tsari: Huber (1990, 1992, 1994b), Martin (1988), Sørensen (1990), Stein (1988a), and a frequently cited work by De Rossi Filibeck (1990), which contains many errors. Contrasted to this material, in popular writings and documentary accounts the only Tibetan *néri* to be accorded more than a passing interest is Tise, better known as Mount Kailash or Kailāsa, about which a veritable shelf-full of books and articles has been written. Most non-Tibetans therefore tend to view Tise as the archetypal and most important (and in some cases the only!) sacred mountain for Tibetan peoples. For materials concerning the Western "cult" of Mount Kailash, see Allen (1982) and Snelling (1990).

2. Nebesky-Wojkowitz (1956:406).

3. Kværne (1987:498). I use the term here cautiously, fully acknowledging its historical origins and usage (Lopez 1996).

4. See Karmay for an excellent discussion of the deities involved (1996:66–73).

5. Karmay (1994a:117; see Karmay 1995 and Karmay 1996: 60, which adds the important point that the same mountains can function for both cults). Karmay's brief account of a local Tibetan mountain ritual during 1985 in Amdo confirms the continued existence of practices observed earlier this century throughout the same general area (Schröder 1952:63–68; Stubel 1958:33–34; see Tucci 1966:153, 192–93). Some cautions are perhaps in order in relation to recent research on what have been called "Tibetan" mountain cults. First, the social context in which present-day cults survive is very dynamic. For example, my own ethnographic observations during 1996 in Karmay's 1985 field site suggests that the mountain cult he described is already declining in significance and vigor and being modified in the face of many local changes stimulated by Chinese colonialism and modernity. Second, most recent fieldwork on local mountain cults has been conducted not in Tibet proper at all but in communities located on the very periphery of ethnographic Tibet (in Bhutan, northern Nepal, and Ladakh), where quite different social and historical conditions have prevailed in both the long and short term (see the interesting studies in Blondeau and Steinkellner 1996; Diemberger 1994; and Pommaret 1994; Diemberger and Hazod 1994 is something of an exception). Given this situation, it is no surprise that such a great diversity of forms of local mountain worship have emerged in these studies. Until much more research is done in the vast area *between* Ladakh and extreme eastern Amdo and related to the studies already carried out in peripheral locations, it is perhaps premature to discuss the "Tibetan" mountain cult(s) with any certainty. In addition, it can be noted that almost every feature of the mountain cults already studied can also be found in those known from Mongolia. Yet Tibetanists have tended to ignore this rich data and its comparative historical and ethnographic significance, particularly relevant in the case of Amdo.

6. Karmay (1994a:119).

7. Karmay (1994a: 119). Despite having the utmost respect for Karmay's scholarship, I find his discussion here of "national identity" and the local mountain cult somewhat problematic. Aside from the anachronism of applying the modern political concept and identity referent of "nation" to the complexity of both premodern and later colonized ethnographic Tibet, this discussion overlooks one of the primary features of local mountain cult ritual that is both ethnographically and textually evident: The identities that are involved in such rituals

are most often entirely parochial, and the unique relationship of each small community and territory with its own mountain deities certainly serves to generate and reinforce many local distinctions, as opposed to common panregional identities. Moreover, even in particular ritual contexts, while Tibetan mountain cults are commonly held to integrate community, they also reiterate strong internal identity distinctions within the community between males and females, clerical and lay institutions, and elite and subordinate members of social units. The "individual patriots" produced by the local mountain cult in Karmay's discussion are none other than elite, lay males prone to protracted feuding with their Tibetan neighbors who, in turn, dwell under and worship their own local mountain.

8. See, for example, Kleeman (1994).

9. See Beckwith (1987:9–10), where further sources are listed.

10. For examples of the wide range of different contexts in which the mandala was applied in South and East Asia, see Grapard (1982), Gutschow (1982), Kölver (1976), Lansing (1991), Martin (1994b), Macdonald (1997), Mus (1978), Tambiah (1976), Tsuda (1978), and Tucci (1970).

11. See, for instance, Martin (1994a).

12. See Kirkland (1982) and Karmay (1996).

13. To borrow Grapard's (1982:209) phrase from the Japanese context.

14. See Karmay (1975:198), Huber (1990), and Kaschewsky (1990), respectively.

15. As witnessed in the long tradition of Sakyapa-Kagyüpa sacred geography polemics originating in Sakya Pandita's *Domsum rabye*, for full details and sources on which see Huber (1990).

16. Macdonald (1990:207).

17. Tambiah (1976:103). In a general discussion of Tibetan notions of place Stein (1972: 41–44) had earlier alluded to what Tambiah is suggesting here.

18. For an example of such vicissitudes at the *néri* site of Labchi, see Huber (1997).

19. Stein (1990:341, n.106).

20. See Naquin and Yü (1992) and Birnbaum (1984:10).

21. Grapard (1982) and Mammitzsch (1997).

22. Samuel (1994:704–5).

23. Examples are given in Huber (1990).

24. In between the initial visions and later circumambulations and processions, the mountain landscapes were, of course, ritually marked out, being magically imprinted and impregnated in various ways by the acts of the Tantric superheroes described in the narratives of the opening of the sites (for examples of these, see chapter 5).

25. See, for instance, Sallnow (1987) and Bastien (1978).

26. See, respectively, Samuel (1993:160–61), who takes inspiration from D. Walker, and Epstein and Peng (1994), who follow E. V. Daniel.

27. Stein (1990:225–46) has noted the ancient Chinese conceptions of sacred mountains as works of architecture and the later influence of representations of the Indian Buddhist cosmic mountain Sumeru in China (246–72). It is easily possible that these ways of thinking arrived in Tibet from China and Central Asia long before the Tibetans themselves systematically transferred Buddhism to their land from North India. Almost every ideal conception of space and place found in early Tibetan documents and the later folk religion has parallels in earlier Chinese precedents, and in Central, East, and Southeast Asian historical and ethnographic materials.

28. See, for instance, Aris (1990), Buffetrille (1994a), and Ramble (1997).

29. See Macdonald (1990) and Samuel (1993: 196, 217–22).

30. Indeed, as an aspect of the transformation of a worldview this de-linking of space and locality is an example that prefigures in various ways a more thoroughgoing "delocalization"

of categories of space and time, which is a later hallmark of worldview transition related to the advent of modernity (Giddens 1990).

31. On, Japan, see Reader (1988), and on Tibet, see Huber (1990) and Jest (1975:354–56) for examples relating to Tsari and Tise, respectively.

32. For other examples, see Jest (1975:368, n.166). Here one can contrast the fixed and regular appointment of such ritual timing with that of the more fluid and individual timing related to astrology and divination so common in ancient and popular Tibetan traditions.

33. For instance, at the *néri* Nyanchen Tanglha and its lake "partner" Namtso, "during the year of the sheep, the god of that great peak, and minor gods of nearby mountains, congregate for a year-long sojourn in the lake" (Ekvall and Downs 1987:104); while at Tsari each monkey year the Tibetan protective deities known as Tenma Chunyi are all said to assemble; and at Tise during the horse year the three chief animal-faced sky-goer goddesses of the Khorlo Dompa Tantra system are believed to be present.

34. See, for example, Keyes (1975) on Thailand.

35. Ekvall and Downs (1987:144–54); their comments are based on individual interviews with diverse refugee pilgrims living in exile rather than any in-depth study of a single major tradition or site.

36. Eade and Sallnow (1991:3).

4. Cosmodrama and Architectonics of Landscape

1. KZ II:170.

2. See U.S. Army Map Service (1954), Series U502, map NH 46–15, Kyimdong Dzong. Scale: 1:250,000.

3. Bauman (1992:162).

4. See Karmay (1975:202–7, 1986) and Stein (1971).

5. Tucci (1932, 1989), Stein (1972–74, 1995), Iyanaga (1985), Macdonald (1990), and Davidson (1991), and see Allen (1984).

6. On the "cut-and-paste" origins of the supreme yoga Tantras and the borrowing of their *pīṭha* cult from Śaiva sources by their Buddhist compilers, see Sanderson (1990, 1994).

7. Huber (1990).

8. PK I:2b–4a.

9. KZ I:2a–b.

10. See, for example, GRCh:7a–10b, and the Sakyapa texts in Davidson (1991:205–7).

11. Davidson has noted the scheme's origins in the eighth-century *Sarvatathāgata-tattvasaṃgraha* (1991:230, n.16). The entry *sa-gsum* in BGTsh, 3:2911 reads: "The three [regions] above the earth (*sa bla*), on the surface of the earth (*sa steng*), and beneath the earth (*sa 'og*)."

12. Examples of icons of the maṇḍala with charnel grounds are found in Pal (1984:pls. 11, 31, 34); see icons of Dorje Pagmo also surrounded by the charnel grounds (pls. 15, 16); iconographical details are given in Tucci (1989:chap. 1), Chandra (1987:7–34), and Tsuda (1978:215–28).

13. *Mkha' spyod kyi gnas brgyad; sa spyod kyi gnas brgyad; sa 'og spyod kyi gnas brgyad*. These three realms are sometimes referred to as *khecara* (or *Khecaratva*), *bhūcara* (or *gocara*), and *nāgaloka* (or *bhūgarbha*), respectively, in the Sanskirt sources.

14. Discussions of how this arrangement applies to the maṇḍala in iconographic and meditational terms are found in Tsuda (1978) and in Lokesh Chandra's preface to Kazi Dawa Samdup (1978). My interest here is purely in terms of describing Tibetan conceptions of cosmic and geographic space.

15. *'Khor lo sdom pa'i thugs kyi gnas*.

16. If an early twentieth-century Drigungpa text is to be believed, the scheme was designed by Jigten Gönpo in the twelfth century after intensive study of the Tantras; see SLG: 17b.

17. This scheme contradicts the full version of the *tribhuvana* arrangement for the subjugation narrative found in GRCh:8a–10b, as Tise is reckoned a *sachö* site and Labchi a *khachö* site. A prayer to Labchi invokes it as *gnas mchog dag pa mkha' spyod la phyi gangs*; see SLG:73a. It is perhaps rather a product of Jigten Gönpo's meditative experience of sky-goers from the three sites than a derivation of *tribhuvana*.

18. See, for example, ZhKN: chaps. 10, 11, 13 or TsMN:chaps. 6–12.

19. YNyZh:3a–3b. This is a sophisticated statement invoking old notions of Tibetan geographical space sloping down from the high (*tö*) west to the low (*mé*) east. It cleverly describes the nature of each of the three pilgrimages in terms of parochial notions of regional character. That is, in the twelve-yearly events, mostly locals went to Tise, Central Tibetans had to make a very long journey to Labchi (due to their faith in religion), and easterners made the long, hard journey around Tsari, advised by their lamas that it was the best way to cleanse sins. The statement also details the basic Khorlo Dompa geography of Tibet in terms of its localized deities.

20. *Khachöma* translates the Sanskrit *khecarī*, and similarly the goddesses active in the *sachö* realm are *sachöma* (*bhūcarī*) and in the *saogchö* realm are *saogchöma* (*pātālacarī*). The three are depicted in Essen and Tingo (1989: 179, pl. 112). Tibetan sky-goers, particularly as goddesses, are derived from the complex *ḍākinī* figures of Indian Tantric traditions, on which see the general study by Herrmann-Pfandt (1992). However, one should be aware that at the level of popular cult and belief, Tibetans define sky-goers in ways not attested in the Indian Tantric texts.

21. Matthieu Ricard (personal communication, 1992) identifies *khachö* specifically as the Dhūmatāla Buddhafield of Dorje Neljorma (with whom Dorje Pagmo is interchangeable). Dhūmatāla appears to mean "vaporous state" or "smoky state," according to the Tibetan sources (e.g., ZhKKS:1b; see Monier-Williams, *A Sanskrit-English Dictionary*, 518), and is also a geographical location in the Swat Valley (northwest Pakistan) identified with the Tantric site of Uḍḍiyāna (Tucci 1971:397 n.1, 399 n.4; GGL:340).

22. ZhKN:488.

23. ZhKN:489.

24. For example, the most common prayer to the mountain opens with the line: "Glorious Tsaritra, *khachö* pure abode" (*gnas dag pa mkha' spyod dpal gyi tsa ri tra*).

25. See Kathog Situ's list of his 1919 visit, GJLY:365, l. 1–2.

26. See, for example, Willis (1985:315–18) and Tsuda (1978:215–21).

27. Ricard (1994:442 n.1).

28. PK I:18a.

29. SG, interview.

30. Ricard (1994:442 n.1).

31. The basic scheme for the Tsari *dorje* landscape was first applied by the Fourth Karmapa Rolpaé Dorje (1340–1383) (HKK I:379, l.4). For the fully developed scheme see KZ I: 5b and TKNY: 80–81.

32. Tsari Tsokar was a popular pilgrimage destination in the area, second only to the various circuits of Pure Crystal Mountain itself. It was opened and developed as a place of meditation and pilgrimage later than the other sites of Tsari Nyingma and Tsari Sarma. This was first begun by the Fourth Karmapa Rolpaé Dorje, who established both residence and meditation facilities there (see PK I:14a; KGT II:969; HKK I:378–80). After visiting the site to circumambulate its sacred lake, the Eighth Karmapa Mikyöd Dorje (1507–1554) established a residence at Tsokar (HKK II:50). Further development of the site is credited to the Ninth Karmapa Wangchuk Dorje (1556–1603) during his extensive tour of the Tsari area in about

1595 (HKK II:202–3). Tsokar came to be considered an important part of the whole pilgrimage system of the Tsari district and, prior to 1959, a small temple and meditation retreat sites existed there. The villagers of Lo Mikyimdün maintained the *tsulkang* or pilgrim resthouses at Tsokar, celebrated its annual ritual opening and closing ceremonies, and used the site for summer grazing. Accounts of Tsokar are found in TKNY, TsNY II:32, Ward (1941:chapt. 9) and Yuthok (1990:96–97).

Tsari Sarma and Tashijong are little known, closely related sites just on the Tibetan side of the main Himalayan divide, adjacent to the upper Siyom River catchment (see figure 8.1). They are historically important examples of a number of replicas—"branches" (*yanlag*) or "divisions" (*chedrak*) in Tibetan—of Pure Crystal Mountain which were propagated over the centuries due to the mountain's great prestige as a holy place (see the study of other such sites in Huber 1990). Thus, in the biography of the Third Shamarpa Chöpel Yeshé (1406–1452), Tashijong is described as being "a new division of the *né* of glorious Tsāritra" (HKK, I:488, l.6). The area was apparently opened during the early fourteenth century by Tharpagyen (*alias* Kumārarāja) (1266–1343), the main disciple of Melong Dorje (1243–?1303) (Roerich 1979:197–200), both of whom were active at times along the south eastern Tibetan borderlands. Tharpagyen in particular was an important transmitter of the Dzokchen Nyingthik lineage, passing it on to such figures as the Third Karmapa Rangchung Dorje (1284–1339)—who himself visited Tsari in 1313 and was active at Pure Crystal Mountain and Tashijong (HKK I: 204, l.7–205, l.4)—and to the First Shamarpa Trakpa Senge (1283–1349) (Roerich 1979: 199, 529, 696). Thereafter, the early Shamarpa lamas took up the tradition of meditating at Tharpagyen's new holy place. The Second Shamarpa Khachö Wangpo (1350–1405) spent time at Tsari Sarma (KGT II:985), and also authored the earliest surviving visionary account of the Tsari region (see TsNY I). The Third Shamarpa, who was very active throughout the greater Tsari area, established monastic foundations at both Tsari Sarma (Rinphuk) and Tashijong (KGT II: 1086–87; HKK I:496, l.5). The Fourth Shamarpa, who was known as "patron [*yondak*] of Tsari," and the fifth incarnation also practiced there (KGT II:1118; BDT 7:499, 504). In a nineteenth-century guidebook both Tsari Sarma and Tashijong were still regarded as Khorlo Dompa cult places (KZ I:27b). The precise details of popular pilgrimage at both sites remain unclear and require further study. Both the Sherriff and Ludlow and Kingdom-Ward expeditions visited the area and made brief observations on the pilgrimages there (see Fletcher 1975: 174; Ward 1941:120).

33. PK I:26a; on the temple-founding, PK III:578–590.

34. With a stone image of the goddess in the earth under the temple foundations, a bronze image of her inside on the surface, and a sublime rainbow-body image in the sky above, SP and SG (interviews); and see the comments of Stein's informant in 1954 (Stein 1988a:40 n. 84).

35. Here I am thinking of the three-level array of the twenty-four internal *nāḍī* and *pīṭha* in the meditator's psychic body. Stein has already suggested a similar correspondence with the three *cakra* (heart, neck, and top of the head), in the body (1988a:40).

36. KZ I:6a.

37. KZ I:18a.

38. KZ I:26b.

39. KZ I:15b.

40. PK I:9b.

41. For example, some sets of four are listed in PK I: 16a–17a.

42. KZ I:23a.

43. *Mtsho 'di nyid dpal 'khor lo sdom pa'i dkyil 'khor du gzigs te nang du byon.*

44. PTY, chap. 12. Images of pure crystal reliquary shrines, often with mountainlike proportions, are mentioned in important Mahāyāna texts, such as the *Saddharma-puṇḍarīka-sūtra* (Kern

1909:147, 149, 231–37). The motif of the crystal mountain in the Tibetan Gesar epic and its associations with European traditions, such as the Glasberg, has been noted by Hummel (1971).

45. PK I:7b.

46. PK I:7b.

47. See, for example, Rhie and Thurman (1991: 382) and Snellgrove (1987, 2:pl. 37).

48. KZ I: 15a.

49. TsLY I:3a; and see the descriptions in TsLY II.

50. For Tibetan paintings of this and the other seven types of *chöten*, see BT:pls. 107–14. On the iconography of *tashi gomang* shrines representing the mountain palace paradise of Zangdok Pelri, see Montmollin (1992).

51. TsLY I:4a–b; and see here also the arrangement of deities given in the account of the setting up of the palace of Dakpa Khachö at Tsari in the Gesar epic, MGY:499.

52. KZ II:186.

53. See the accounts in Roerich (1979:601), Könchog Gyaltsen (1988:21, 36), and PK I: 9a–b, 27b.

54. Könchog Gyaltsen (1988:36).

55. ND, interview.

56. DPN:1042–43.

57. For early examples, see the *Mani Kambum* (twelfth cent.) as quoted in Gyatso (1989: 38); the *Deu Chönchung* (twelfth cent.) in Karmay (1994b:412); the *Milaé Gurbum* (late fifteenth cent.) in MGB: 416; and later examples in GRCh:70b and Wylie (1962:2). The notion of mountains as crystal monoliths is also found in Bönpo religious geographies (Karmay 1975: 173).

58. Gyatso (1989) and her essay in Reynolds et al. (1986:32–33); Aris (1979); and Stutchbury (1994).

5. History and Prayer as Map

1. BTP:264. This proverb is also revealing in that it shows that distinctions such as those between "pilgrims" and "tourists" at places of pilgrimage are not just an analytical concern of contemporary anthropologists but a traditional Tibetan one as well.

2. For example, below the standard Tibetan prayer to Tsari that forms the inscription on the rear of the painted-scroll image of Pure Crystal Mountain (figure 4.3) is written: "If this [image] is seen or [prayer] heard by any sentient beings, they will become liberated from misfortunes [and] bad rebirths!" (*'di sems can gang gis mthong 'am thos na ngan song rkyen ngan las sgrol bar gyur cig*). Similarly, when the mountain is described in the Gesar epic, it is said "to purify karmic defilement when seen"; TsMDz:68.

3. Huber (1992), Aziz (1975, 1978b), and Schwartzberg (1994).

4. Stoddard ventures that Gendün Chöphel (1903–1951) was probably the first Tibetan to produce a modern map of the globe in 1937, and he was involved in hot debate with Tibetan intellectuals of his day who argued for the traditional view that the world was flat and not round (1988:469). Ford notes that even in the 1950s the most highly ranked officials and military commanders of the Lhasa government relied on local oral maps and simple traditional drawn maps, hence were desperate to obtain modern cartographic maps from foreigners for planning an effective defense against the invading Chinese army (1957:61).

5. Despite an often clipped colloquial style, Pema Karpo was a gifted author. His little guide to Tsari, written around 1570–75, is a classic example of the later "synthetic" style of longer Tibetan pilgrimage guidebooks. Based on the skeleton of his verse eulogy (see PK II), it is a pastiche of prayer, polemic, cosmology, esoteric ritual instruction, Tantric Buddhist

geography, anecdote, narrative history, and more, some from his own hand but much of it cut and pasted from earlier sources.

6. See my translation (ff. 23b–24a) for his narrative of Tsangpa Gyare's victory over the evil frog of Tsari, the subject of a ritual dance (*cham*) called *chöshé* performed during Bhutanese annual festivals (BZhC, Aris 1980b:46).

7. See, for example, DPN:1037–40.

8. See, for instance, KZ I:15–73, KZ II:169–94, and, for an oral example, TsNY III.

9. See, for example, TsSD I, TsSD II (being *The Great Oath Prayer of Tsari* partially translated herein), and TsNgJ.

10. When doing fieldwork on Tsari in 1991 and 1992, I already knew the Tibetan text well from translating it, and I remembered parts by heart. I was able to recognize, initially to my surprise, that my informants often lapsed into quotations from the text when telling stories and giving explanations.

11. At the same time, of course, Pema Karpo is continually transferring status to members of his own Drukpa lineage at the expense of the figures from the Gelukpa, Drigungpa, Tselpa, and others, who—according to him—make mistakes, fail, precipitate calamities, and can be downright nasty by comparison.

12. The translation is based on PK I:18a–29a or ff. 241–63, and PK Ia:42–77. Folio numbers given in brackets are for the 1973 edition (PK I). Extra words and phrases inserted in the translation for the sake of meaning and style are enclosed in brackets; English glosses on certain important place names follow the Tibetan form enclosed in parentheses. My notes to the translation are limited to identifying places, persons, and traditions important to the history, cult, and geography of the area.

13. Char, the district immediately to the west of Tsari, has been a center important for the Tibetan Drukpa sect since the time of Pema Karpo (Huber 1992:11–15) and for the development of religious and domestic affairs at Tsari up until 1959.

14. An interlinear annotation in the fourteenth-century history *Gyalrab Salwé Melong* discusses Padmasambhava temporarily leaving Samyé and going to the Tibetan border areas, where it is said "he took up residence in Tsa-ri." (Sørensen 1994:369 n.1202).

15. On this figure, see Tibetan "Lwa-wa-pa/La-ba-pa," and Sanskrit "Kambala/Kambalapa" in Templeman (1983:33–36, n.126) and Dowman (1985:179–85).

16. See Dowman (1985:222–28); but see "Kusulu" in Nālandā Translation Committee (1982:xxix, 202, 230).

17. *Parpa*, or *parpa-ta* in full, probably refers to a type of leech or worm (see BGTsh, 2: 1615) in the jungle and gorge country to the south of the mountain, and is not to be confused with *par-pa-ta*, the "horned cumin" (*Hypecoum leptocarpum* or *H. erectum*), a medicial herb.

18. On this incident, see Kaschewsky (1971:131).

19. The "lineage" here refers to the eight subsects of the Kagyü lineage that originated from Pagmo Drupa (1110–1170) and his disciples. These subsects, particularly the Drukpa, Drigungpa, and Tselpa, dominate the early religious history of Tsari.

20. The Nyötön of Nyel (a district of Lhokha just to the west of Tsari) is listed as one of Rechungpa's disciples in Roerich (1979:273). His name indicates he came from Traor, the site of one of the "six communities of Nyel" of later fame, among which the place of Nangtra (or Ngangkyel) mentioned here is also counted; see Petech (1973:41–42, n.13).

21. Or "Lūipa/Lū-yi-pa"; see Templeman (1983:8–10) and Dowman (1985:33–38). His liturgy for realizing the Khorlo Dompa maṇḍala, which became popular in Tibet, is being referred to here.

22. The text gives his name as Daö Shonu, but I have substituted the more widely known form Gampopa throughout for ease of recognition. Gampopa's role here is apparently linked with Marpa's well-known prophecy to Mila Repa, written in the late-fifteenth-century biog-

raphy by Tsang Nyön Heruka (1452–1507) and ostensibly spoken in the eleventh century: "Adjacent to each other in the east there remain the great sacred places, Devikoti and Tsari. The time to open them has not yet come. In the future your spiritual descendants will establish themselves there" (translation in Lhalungpa 1977:94).

23. This is Daklha Gampo, the district north of Tsari, on which see Ferrari (1958:121 n. 204) and Wylie (1962:94).

24. Use of the name Tsari Tsagong to refer to the mountain appears already in Sakya Pandita's (1182–1251) *Domsum rabye* (DS:33b), composed around 1232. The "superior herb" here could be one of a number of Tibetan Tantric alchemical herbs—including *ludud dorje* and *lingchen*—found on the mountain, which I discuss in chapter 6.

25. Yeshé Dorje was the ordination name of Char Chekhapa (1101–1175), a disciple of Rechungpa, Shawapa, and Gampopa (Daö Shonu), who came from Loro, a district southwest of Tsari. He was also known as Kyepo Yedor (Roerich 1979:273–6, 462) and is not to be confused with Tsangpa Gyare Yeshé Dorje (1161–1211), who arrived later. See the brief but earlier (1446) account of Kyewo's visit in LHR:228.

26. Or Drulung, Drum, and Drumalung in other sources; it leads north of Tsari into the Tsangpo valley and is one of the routes by which Central Tibetans visited the Tsari area as pilgrims. It was the site of the Kurab Namgyel Dzong, which administered the Tsari district for the Lhasa authorities.

27. The white alchemical stone (*chongshi*) consists of deposits or concretions of lime or calcite used in medical and alchemical preparations and collected by both yogins and pilgrims; see MM:46 and the entries in BGTsh, 1:735–36.

28. According to KG, the following prayer was sung by Tsariwa when they passed around a large brass bowl of beer at certain local festivals.

29. This site is the main sacred lake at Tsari, south of Dakpa Sheri peak. See the description in Bailey (1957:208).

30. Also described as "the Lake of Sindhura, which is like a long-handled ladle" by Tibetans. It contains the important ritual substance known as *sindhura* (or *sindūra* in Sanskrit), a type of ochre resembling minium, suspended in its waters. *Sindhura* is discussed in chapter 6.

31. Or "giant ling," which the Tsariwa describe as a tall species of herb resembling a wild onion or garlic, on which see chapter 6.

32. The opposition of "spittle for smashing demons" and a potent Buddhist alchemical herb here is interesting and suggestive in the light of a Bönpo narrative concerning the origins of Tibetan purification rituals and medicinal plants presented by Karmay (1975:204–6). In that source the goddess sprinkles her ambrosial spittle down to earth because of the great pollution caused by the actions of demons, and this causes medicinal herbs and other things to come into being. These include the white grouse ("medicinal bird"), *chongshi* (the medicinal stone), the purifying and medicinal lake water and mountain snows of the ideal holy place, and so on, all of which are also celebrated at Tsari in both Buddhist Tantric and popular traditions. Our author appears to be putting down the Bön tradition here.

33. These are Nyö Lhanangpa (1164–1224) founder of the Lhapa subsect of the Kagyü lineage, Gardampa Chödingpa (b. 1180), and Chö Pelchen Chöyé, also known as Norje Repa; see Roerich (1979:601–4).

34. So called as here three routes crossing high passes leading to the west, north, and east of Tibet all meet, and the ancient name for this part of the Tsari valley was Phö or "Tibet," the same name used in other sources as a broader geographical referent. Pilgrim access from southern Tibet was via the Char La (5060 m) to the west, from Central Tibet via the Kongmo La (5335 m) to the north, and from Kongpo, Kyemdong, and eastern areas via the Bimbi La (4785 m) to the east.

35. The peak of Jomo Kharak is located in Central Tibet some 150 kilometer from Tsari

and was an important early meditation and retreat site, especially for the Tselpa Kagyü lineage (DTM:138; Dowman 1984: 117, 330). The point here is that Tsangpa Gyare traveled from there to meet his rivals at Tsari in one day, using the yogic paranormal power of "swift-footedness" (*kangyog*).

36. Ling Repa (1128–1188) was the teacher and lineage "father" of Tsangpa Gyare. See the brief but earlier (1446) account of Tsangpa Gyare's visit in LHR:652.

37. Yümé, including most western areas of Pure Crystal Mountain, became the principal center of Drigungpa activities and administration at Tsari, and these little dialogues are intended to show how their acquisition was due to the benevolence of the saint from the Drukpa sect, the same sect as that of our author.

38. An important mountain goddess of the Tenma Chunyi group. On her iconography and role at Tsari, see Nebesky-Wojkowitz (1956:190–91, 222) and Huber (1990:147).

39. Nineteenth-century oral traditions at Tsari maintained that yak living on the upper pilgrimage routes of the mountain were tended by the goddess (Burrard 1915:335). This was still the case in the 1950s, and the tradition partly reflects local practices. During the twentieth century no local herders actively used these areas for pasturage, but feral yak inhabited the place. These animals had the ritual status of *tsethar*, "freed life," or *soglu*, "ransomed life," being those once marked for slaughter but then set free to live out their days in peace on the mountain. This practice was prescribed by lamas and physicians for certain pilgrims who wished to counter the bad consequences of actions that angered a range of deities and spirit powers believed to cause physical and mental illness. These yak were tended in the summer by the pilgrimage resthouse keepers, who offered yoghurt made from their milk to pilgrims in imitation of the story of Tsangpa Gyare and the goddess given in the text that follows.

40. Nebesky-Wojkowitz asserts that this deity at Tsari is a member of the Genyen class of ancient mountain gods (1956:222). He was worshiped among the Gelukpa since the seventeenth century (e.g., Tohoku University 1953: no. 5625 (75); SBK: 335) and still is among the Tibetan Drukpa (PDB: 23a–b). The close similarities of this event with the conversion narrative of one of the guardian deities of the Bhutanese Drukpa should be noted, as one finds that Tsangpa Gyare's own clan descendent "Kun-dga' Seng-ge is said to have subdued and converted the *dGe-bsnyen Chen-po* Jag-pa Me-len and turned him into the 'protector' *Srog-bdag* gShan-pa dMar-po" (Aris 1979:176).

41. Tsariwa say that pilgrims collect a substance here called *kargong*, a kind of white mineral or soapstone that is used medicinally; see MM: 54 and the Tibetan and Chinese entries in BGTsh, 1:53.

42. According to his biography, Pema Karpo built his temple enshrining the famous Dorje Pagmo image in Chikchar after he received this prophecy. While excavating the foundations for it, he discovered "Nyö's paving-stone" with an image of the goddess on it (PK III: 597). The temple is named after the symbolism of the Dorje Pagmo icon that possesses two faces, that of a woman with a vestigial one of a sow behind her ear. The temple is described in TsNY II:29–30.

43. There are two Gyergom mentioned in the chapter on Pagmo Drupa's disciples in the *Deb ther sngon po*. This is Gyergom Chenpo (1090–1171), the founder of Gyama monastery and a disciple of Chayülpa (1075–1138), the founder of Chayül monastery west of Tsari (Roerich 1979: 314–315, 565–66). On Gyergom Nyipa see n.46.

44. This 5090-meter pass was often used by southern Tibetan pilgrims to connect western Tsari and the neighboring district of Char.

45. The Kyu River flows down from Takar pass into Char, and so lies just outside the ritual sphere of the Pure Crystal Mountain maṇḍala.

46. Gyergom Tsultrim Senge (1144–1204) alias Gyergom Nyipa established the Shugseb monastery in Nyephu in 1181, thus founding the little-known Shugseb Kagyü lineage, which

followed the system of Shijay; see BGTsh, 1: 385. Samten Pelwa (1291–1366) was the Tselpa Tokden, also known as Tokden Tsariwa, responsible for sending out the hermits. He founded the monastery of Lhundrupding at Tsari; see DTM: 140–44 and Roerich (1979:885).

47. This is Sangye Tönpa Tsöndrü Senge (1219?–1290?), the seventh Shangpa Kagyü hierarch and holder of the Chöd lineage; see Roerich (1979:743–46).

48. Gyelwa Götsangpa (1189–1258) founded the Tö Druk tradition. Much of the following account about him is also found in Roerich (1979:683).

49. This goddess is Kākāsyā, one of the eight wrathful guardians of the Khorlo Dompa maṇḍala, stationed at the eastern gate.

50. On Üripa alias Lorepa (1187–1250) and his nephew Tsari Rechen alias Tsariwa, see Roerich (1979: 672–76).

51. Tag Dorje was a fourteenth-century king of Kyemdong in the Tsangpo valley between Dakpo and Kongpo. He patronized early temple building at Tsari (GJLY: 365–66) and the meditation community there (PK V:303a–b). Kyemdong remained an important source of patronage for practitioners at the mountain. Later Kyemdong became the site of a Lhasa government Dzong that partially administered Tsari district. Ralungthel was the administrative center of the House of Gya and the Drukpa lineage, located in Tsang.

52. On Pökyapa Senge Rinchen (1242–1297 or 1258–1313?), abbot of Ralung, see Roerich (1979:671) and Smith (1969:33). On the events here see also PK V: 605–6, and the earlier (1466) LHR:663, which refers to him as Senge Lodrö: "Because he was offered the *né* by the *shidak* of Tsari Chikchar he dispatched meditators and that is how the entrance to the *né* was opened."

53. This is a play on words. Tsangpa Gyare and his religious successors, who also opened the mountain, belonged to the Gya (spelled *rgya*) clan of Ralung. The clan name has the same spelling and pronunciation as the species of *gya* antelope (Saiga tatarica).

54. The prayer is known to me in four versions: a partial recitation by Drölma, which I recorded in Dehra Dun in 1991; a full recitation by several Tsariwa, recorded in India by Könchog Gyaltsen and printed privately as a small booklet in about 1975 (TsSD II); a full recitation by Yümé Chagchen Pema Tenzin, recorded in Tibet by Trinley Mingyur and Döndrup Tsering and published recently in Lhasa (TsSD I); and a heavily abbreviated printed version dating at least from the first decade of the twentieth century, if not earlier (TsSD III).

55. The great Tibetan Buddhist reformer Tsongkhapa is reputed to have chanted these seven lines in response to the local sky-goers' punishment for his doubts at Tsari (see Pema Karpo's narrative, f.19a). They were chanted by pilgrims who visited Tsari, and it was traditional to memorize the verses. The first three lines of it are sung by all the monks at the Drukpa monastery of Sangnag Chöling whenever they eat traditional *thukpa* broth, at which time they substitute "I offer this to . . ." for the words "I pray to . . .". The full seven lines form the inscription on the rear of painted-scroll images of Pure Crystal Mountain, such as figure 4.3.

56. It can be chanted when entering the sphere of the Tsari maṇḍala near Phö Domtsechen, in imitation of Kyewo Yeshé Dorje's petition during the opening drama. It was used to commence local seasonal rituals. In particular, this verse and the entire prayer were recited by Tsariwa when the mountain was ritually opened each year during the third Tibetan month, on which see chapter 7.

57. TsSD I: 1,3, TsSD II:1–2, 8; only minor variations exist between them, which I have edited according to my own discretion. It should be noted that the content of the prayer is also somewhat ecumenical, for although the Kagyü lineage is mentioned in the opening sections quoted here, many of the deities, saints, and sites featured in the main body of the prayer are those of common interest to all Tibetan sects oriented toward the "new Tantras" (*sangnag sarma*).

58. A good example is found in NTshN.

59. See Huber (1994a, 1997) on the related site of Labchi.
60. KZ I:6a–b, 8a–b; KZ II:172.
61. Yuthok (1990:93–94).
62. SG, interview.
63. PK I:11b.
64. Huber (1990, 1994a).
65. YTN:107b–108a. This is only a provisional translation of the passage, the latter part of which is grammatically problematic. Nevertheless, it provides clear evidence of the point I am trying to make here.

6. A Tantric Environment

1. See Huber (1990).
2. I asked for etymologies from most of my informants as a matter of course, but see the early textual discussions in TsLY I:293–94 or 7a–b and PK I:5b.
3. The names Tsari, Tsaritra, and Tsari Tsagong appear already in Sakya Pandita's (1182–1251) *Domsum rabye* (DS:33b), composed around 1232.
4. One of Pema Karpo's methods for this practice in the Khorlo Dompa system is briefly described in Beyer (1973:73–74).
5. For examples, see Ehrhard (1994:8–9, 20) on Né Pema Köd, Huber (1990:152–55) on Tsādra Rinchendrak, Huber and Rigzin (1995:14) on Tise, and Stein (1988a:40–41) on Tsari.
6. See TsMDz, particularly chap. 21–22. The story reminds one of an episode in another Asian epic long known in Tibet, the *Rāmāyaṇa*, and the monkey hero Hanuman's mission to secure vital medicinal herbs from a Himalayan mountain.
7. See Bourdieu, whose discussion of the concept entails the convertibility of forms of symbolic capital, such as prestige and renown, back into economic capital (1977:171–83).
8. Much of what one finds in various chronicles and biographies is already described in Pema Karpo's account translated in chapter 5. Although several schools of the Kagyü lineage, including the Drigungpa, Shugsebpa, Karmapa, Drukpa, and Tselpa, were well established at the mountain during different periods, the site was always patronized by individual Nyingmapa meditators (e.g., Dudjom Rinpoche 1991: 570–71, 784, 802, 819; TsLY I) as well as by Gelukpa practitioners since the time of Tsongkhapa (1357–1419). But Tsari was virtually never visited by Sakyapa Tantrists, even though they also shared a strong interest in the Khorlo Dompa system of Tantric practice, along with the other Sarmawa schools. At least some reasons for this nonparticipation lie in the long tradition of Sakyapa-Kagyüpa sacred geography polemics (for details, see Huber 1990). Followers of Bön (especially from eastern Tibet) performed the popular pilgrimages at Tsari, such as the Rongkor Chenmo (see chapter 8), and the site was recommended to Tantra practitioners in certain Bönpo texts as a place at which to gain special powers (SMB:14).
9. Roerich (1979:885); and see DTM: 140–41.
10. Roerich (1979:579, 603). Much of the story of this community at Tsari remains unknown. The clichéd Drigungpa scheme for the colonization of the three famous Khorlo Dompa *néri* mountains has been outlined by Petech (1978) and Huber (1997:242) and is applied to Tsari in various Tibetan sources. The three dispatches of hermits to Tsari mentioned in the sources were orchestrated by Drigungpa Jigten Gönpo (1143–1217), ostensibly at the behest of his teacher Pagmo Drupa (1110–1170). The first party dispatched to Tsari comprised eighty hermits, followed by a second with nine hundred hermits in the early years of the thirteenth century (SLG:21a–25b; GRCh:46b–49b; DTM:125; and PK I:22b). The third and

final party, with the exaggerated figure of over fifty-five thousand members, included a yogin named Kyo Kogang (GRCh:49b). It was led to Tsari by the *Dordzin* Gowoche in either 1215 or 1217 (SLG:25b reports that the final dispatches occurred in Jigten Gönpo's seventy-fourth year, but gives this as *shing-mo-phag* or 1215 rather than *me-glang* or 1217). This colonization of Tsari coincided with a period of religious and political expansion by the Drigungpa throughout Tibet, and by the time of the second dispatch the sect had already established its interests at Daklha Gampo, immediately north of the mountain (Roerich 1979:571). After a period of decline in the fifteenth century, the Drigungpa gave new impetus to their centers at places in the borderlands, such as Tsari and other *néri*, especially after Kunga Rinchen (1475–1527) came to the seat; see Könchog Gyaltsen (1986:107) and Petech (1978:321).

11. Shakabpa (1984:82). Changchub Gyeltsen has numerous such administrative innovations attributed to him; however, because of the complexity of the accounts of his life and times (see van der Kuijp 1991), other historical testimonies will need to be sought before such claims can be firmly established.

12. Some historical background to the establishment of a Drukpa power base around the mountain needs to be outlined: Tsari district itself does not appear in the Tibetan sources as a distinct political or administrative unit until later in the Ganden Podrang period, under the system of Dzong (administrative centers). Prior to that it was probably, if at all (since it lacked settled, tax-paying inhabitants), treated as an extension of one or other of the adjacent regions such as Char, Dakpo, and Nyel. The region of Char, along with Dakpo, Nyel, Chayül, Loro, and Eyül, had ancient associations with the royal lineage of Yarlung, a branch of which ruled them as dependencies up until the thirteenth century. In the Yüan-Sakya period, these areas were included under the Hülegü appanage, but were separated sometime after the mid–thirteenth century. They then came under the control of the Cha clan, headed by Cha Rinchen (brother of Cha Chögyel Pelzang, middle to late thirteenth cent.) (Sørensen 1994:472–73 nn. 1778, 1785; 477 n. 1814, 480 n. 1836; Petech 1990:89). The Cha clan heads usually became the myriarchs (*tripön*) of these districts up to the end of Pagmo Drupa rule (Roerich 1979: 1087–90; Tucci 1949:613–614, 647–648). The early alliances between local rulers, successive state(s), and religious interests in the area are still unclear, although doubtless complex. A very early monastery was founded at Chayül by Chayülpa (1075–1138), although it was burnt down during the 1285 Drigungpa-Ilkhanid raid on Chayül and then reestablished in 1291 under Yüan patronage (Roerich 1979:289, 303). The local foundations of Yabzang, Gyama, and Teura can also be mentioned (Petech 1990:56–57, 89). Links between local rulers and important Drukpa lamas appear to begin with Orgyenpa Rinchenpal (1230–1293) and his priest-patron relationship with Cha Rinchen (Roerich 1979:1088). By the fifteenth century, the Drukpa became more closely associated with the Cha, as Jamyang Chöki Trakpa (1478–1523), a son of the prince of Cha, was chosen as the third Drukchen incarnation. Although recognized as Drukchen by the Druk family of Ralung, he was never given power over the traditional monasteries and estates of his incarnation lineage. Instead, the Cha ruler, the important *tripön* and Kagyüpa patron Tashi Dargye, had Tashi Thongmön monastery built for his young son. The monastery and its estates, however, failed to come under the control of subsequent Drukchen incarnates, as the next rebirth, Pema Karpo, was born out of the Cha family to a minor aristocratic house in Kongpo instead. Perma Karpo did regularly visit Tashi Thongmön to teach, but he founded his own seat in Charmé not far to the east and directly adjacent to Tsari, establishing the monastery of Sangnag Chöling there under the patronage of the local ruler (*depa*) of Cha (Smith 1968:2–3). After the protracted Drukpa quarrel over choosing Pema Karpo's rightful incarnation, the *desee* Tsangpa backed the prince of Chongyé's son, Pagsam Wangpo (1593–1641). As fifth Drukchen, he gained control of Sangnag Chöling, and it became the seat of the Drukchen lineage of the so-called Northern Drukpa up until 1959. The monastery was an important center of religious scholarship for the Tibetan Drukpa,

and its incumbents continued to play a large role in developing and maintaining the cult of Pure Crystal Mountain.

13. For Tibetan historical accounts of Chikchar, see KZI:12a–13a, KZII:173–4, DPN:1041, GJLY:362 5, Yuthok (1990:94); for Western descriptions, see Burrard (1915:335), Bailey (1957:199–202), and Ward (1941:87).

14. Namkhai Norbu Dewang (1967: 270/286).

15. *Gnas chen tsā ri tra la / sgrub pa lo gsum byas pas / sgrub g.yog mang po mi dgos / ma dang mkha' 'gros chog gi*. See Namkhai Norbu Dewang (1967: 290/298) on sGrub-gnas Shel-dkar-phug.

16. On this practice in Tibet, see Evans-Wentz (1935:158–59) and Snellgrove (1987:292–94).

17. On the complex meaning of the term *changsem* in Buddhist Tantric ritual, see Snellgrove (1959, p. 1:25–27).

18. Details of a version of the *tsalung* practice are available in English translation in Geshe Kelsang Gyatso (1982).

19. The Chure involved the practitioners wrapping their naked bodies in wet cotton sheets outdoors during the winter, and then having to dry these using only their body heat. David-Neel gives a poor account of Chure, making it seem more like sport than serious ritual (1965: 163 4), see Evans-Wentz (1935:158–59). An interesting account of Rephu in contemporary Ladakh by yogins in the same Drukpa practice lineage that existed at Tsari is given by Crook (1994). Such practices are clearly of Indian origin, and were already advocated in the Dharmaśāstra literature; for example, the *Manu-smṛti* mentions that those in the *vanaprastha* ("hermit" or "forest dweller") *āśrama* should wear wet clothing in winter so as to generate "ascetic heat" (*tapas*) (6.23–24, translation in Doniger 1991).

20. The Tibetan calender differs from the Western one in important respects that make it difficult to give precise equivalent months here for the staging of rituals. Richardson observes:

> The Tibetan year contains twelve lunar months, each of thirty days which necessitates the insertion of an intercalary month every three years to keep in line with the solar year. Thus the Tibetan first month . . . may fall any time between February and March of the western calendar. In each month the first, eighth and fifteenth days are specially devoted to religious observance. (1993:9).

I have indicated approximate western months throughout after each Tibetan month. The reader will notice that the Tibetan days for the staging of rituals conform most often to the pattern mentioned here.

21. They represented the meditation sites and temples of Densa, Göpa, Üri, Zimkhang, Lawa Phuk, and Sinbumtang, and the stewards from the Chikchar *drupde* and Chikchar temple also attended. Originally all these posts were held by meditators (not monks), and only later were lay retreat assistants appointed as a separate rank. Some Tsariwa explain this shift in terms of a decline in the retreat practices of the past, as a result of which yogins went to live with local women, have children, and reenter lay social life. A biography of Gyelwang Kunga Penjor (1428–1476) mentions that in about 1460, when visiting the meditation cave of Tsari Machen above Chikchar, he was welcomed by the "thirteen *letsen*" (BDT, 8: 263). In general, the *letsen* served under a religious administrator known as *dordzin* (i.e., *dorje dzinpa*), who was normally a Tantric teacher. *Dordzin* is the term used in later historical sources to designate the local Drigungpa and Drukpa administrators at the related Khorlo Dompa holy mountains of Labchi and Tise (Aris 1986: 168, n.70; Huber and Rigzin 1995: 15; Huber 1997:242). The earliest occurrence of the term associated with the site of Chikchar that I am aware of is in the biography of the Second Drukchen Ngawang Chögyel (1464–1540) (see BDT 8:520).

22. There are a variety of popular and esoteric songs that mention the role of the sky-goers associated with Pure Crystal Mountain as "beer-serving maids" (*changma*) (some of these songs are discussed in chapter 7, and hereafter in the case of the Sixth Dalai Lama). Other

Dorje Yudrönma rituals involve virgin, prepubescent girls or boys playing the role of or approaching the goddess. In the Yudrönma mirror divination technique, the diviner invokes the goddess and then uses a well-appointed young girl or boy to look into the divination mirror and report the visions they see in it. The divination mirror is one of the accoutrements of the goddess, who will only accept a virgin child to gaze on it (Dorje Tseten 1994: 117).

23. *Cig car sri 'bum thang la/seng ge khri mchog sbam po/khri steng de ru bzhugs pa/nga tsho'i dpal ldan 'brug pa.* In this song on the superior yogic practice of the Drukpa meditators, the lion's throne referred to is the seat of the Buddha, that is, attaining Buddhahood.

24. ZhKN:490.

25. *Da lta'i skabs 'dir bskyid pa'i glu zhig len/da lta'i skabs 'dir dga' ba'i bro zhig brdung/mtshan ldan bla ma rgyal ba kun gyi dngos/rang sems gdod ma'i dbyings su shar ba la/rnal 'byor nyams bsangs dga' bar byas lags so.* This is one example of a collection of over twenty songs that might have been used here, and many more were improvised.

26. Apart from this source (see the translation in chapter 5), there exist very general or vague references to early yoginīs visiting the Tsari area, but not the upper mountain; see Dowman (1980: 104, 1984: 139), Allione (1986: 125), and Roerich (1979: 885). Some of these isolated haigiographical accounts must be treated with due caution, since they may merely be attempts to glorify the figures they present by associating their names with such a famous Tantric site—moreover, one that appears to have excluded "ordinary" womens' entry for many centuries.

27. See BNG:f. 147, 3–4. Barawa had an established lineage connection with Tsari through his teacher Drakburwa (alias Rinchenbum), who had also practiced at the mountain and whose brother was the Chöki Lama of Tsari (Roerich 1979:894–95).

28. Bailey (1914a:11).

29. Bailey (1914a:69).

30. On celibacy observed during the mystic heat and other *tsalung* practices, Evans-Wentz notes, "The yogin must also observe the strictest sexual continence, for it is chiefly upon the *yogically* transmitted sex energy that proficiency in *Tummo* depends" (1935:157–58); he also comments on maintaining chastity in the precepts for Mahm̃udrā and Naro Chödruk ("Naropa's Six Yogas") practitioners (72, 79, 81, 86). R. Mayer has noted that the Drukpa Tokden practitioners, such as those at Chikchar, "are unusual in that they are all fully ordained *gelong*; their asceticism is an intensification of the monks' discipline, rather like the *Dhutañgas* of the Theravāda tradition. Togdens are not meant to ever speak to women (nowadays, they have to, but only to give teachings)" (personal communication, 1994). See Ray (1994:446) on *dhutaguna*-type vows among Tibetan Kagyüpa yogins.

31. See, for example, Roerich (1979:650) on Taglung monastery, Sakya and Emery (1990: 62) on Ngor monastery, and Waddell (1895) on the Jokhang temple in Lhasa.

32. In a proclamation circulated to Tibetan government Dzong, the "loitering" of women near the buildings was forbidden; see Carrasco (1959:94). Certain restrictions on women still apply at government Dzong in contemporary Bhutan.

33. See Paul (1985).

34. Knowledge of Tibetan practices such as mystic heat yoga was circulated in the West by way of earlier travel accounts that portrayed Tibet as a land of magic and mystery (e.g., David-Neel 1965). While aspects of the Western fantasy of Tibetan religious life, such as levitation and walking through walls, are now regularly dismissed by contemporary Tibetan lamas and teachers, the practice of mystic heat yoga has been put forward by them for scientific verification and analysis; see Fourteenth Dalai Lama (1990a).

35. One commonly recounted is the story of Ümdze Kari, a former supervisor of the Chikchar *drupde* with a great fondness for drinking beer. He would go into the village to consume ale in the winter, but as was the rule he had to return to the retreat center each

night. Sometimes he was too drunk to reach home and would fall asleep in the deep snow on the side of the trail. In the mornings villagers would find large patches of snow melted back to the bare ground along the path. They knew that this was where the Ümdze, a yogin proficient in mystic heat yoga, had spent the night.

36. SG, interview.

37. KZ I:22b.

38. KZ II:186.

39. KZ I:25b.

40. Using Tibetan literary materials, Stein (1988a:37–49) has investigated a complex of representations and rituals concerning the hypostatic body of Dorje Pagmo in landscape at Tsari and other sites, while Ehrhard (1994) has given further examples of landscape bodies at Né Pema Köd, a place just to the east of Tsari. One might compare Stein's comments and questions (40) with some of the Tibetan beliefs given herein, as well as Bäumer's (1991) comments on Kashmir Śaivism. The landscape body of Dorje Pagmo at Tsari also figures in domestic traditions, which I will discuss in chapter 11.

41. PK I:15b. The entry *Sindhura* in a nineteenth-century Materia Medica asserts: "It is produced [within the body] at the time of [attaining] Tantric paranormal powers, and its equivalent appears on some lake shores and within rock clefts at holy places such as Tsari and Mu-li-ting" (MM:60).

42. Dorje Tseten (1994:115).

43. In the biography of Doring Pandita his son Gabshi Tenzin Penjor (b.1760), an aristocratic layman, records that he extracted a large quantity of *sindhura* powder from a lake on Pure Crystal Mountain in 1794 (DPN:1043). It is well know to Tibetans that he encountered many difficulties in his later life, some apparently connected with the mountain; see my notes on him and his family in chapter 7.

44. On the Dorje Pagmo Secret Cave (Pagmo Sangphuk), see KZ II:180.

45. *Cordyceps sinensis* (DTsM:177–78). Fruits from the *shamali* tree (*smilax chinensis / Bombax malabaricum*) were also collected at Tsari for the treatment of hemorrhoids; see BGTsh 3:2839.

46. Or *Codonopsis convolvulacea*, a photograph of which is found in Fletcher (1975:342); see the comprehensive references concerning Tibetan knowledge about the plant in Martin (1988: 352 n.26), and a traditional drawing of it in MM:201.

47. I have used the translation of Martin (1988:349–57) here, adapting it slightly to conform to the style used in the present work. This song has been analyzed in detail by Martin (1988) and further elaborated on by Sørensen (1988, 1990).

48. See KZ III for the contents and preparation of these ritual pills.

49. *Ja phra'i nang la blug pas/klu bdud rdo rje zil pa/'di nas bzhes gang bzhes dang/ngan song myong dgos min 'dug*. The image of *ludud dorje* has also been used explicitly by Tsariwa in exile as a symbol of their local identity and homeland. An image of the plant together with Pure Crystal Mountain and Turquoise Lake Palace forms the logo of the recently constituted Tsari Welfare Association in Switzerland (Sud-si tsa-ri'i skyid-sdug).

50. See, for example, Yuthok (1990:98) and David-Neel (1988:69–70, 167 n.2).

51. What is called *khandro lapuk* at Tsari is in fact not a radish or root but a tall species of wild alpine rhubarb *Rheum noloile*. The thick, succulent stem is cut and peeled (thus resembling a large white radish) when young, and the pith is eaten. It is also known as *chum karpo*, or "white rhubarb," and *chumdong chenpo*, or "large-stemmed rhubard," and regarded as a medicinal herb by Tibetans (BGTsh, 1:298,768; DTsM:211; MM:147).

52. Under *gling*, Das, *Tibetan-English Dictionary*, 257, has: "*gliṇ darbha, kuśa* a kind of sacred grass"; however, neither of the grasses known as *darbha* (*Saccharum cylindricum*) and *kuśa* (*Poa cynosuroides*) in India matches the Tibetan descriptions I have for *lingchen*, which is more like a wild leek or onion. The name appears closely related to those applied to plants producing

reeds or canes, such as the sixteenth-century usage *gling-rtswa-shing* (KGT II:1173), or *gling-bu'i shing* (BGTsh, 1:424). Lingchen is also valued by the Tsariwa as a domestic food when it is young, and cooked in stews. When old it is collected and dried, then cooked with barley flour and fed to cattle in the winter.

53. See, for example, Tucci (1980:158). This type of limestone or calcite is very highly rated as a rejuvenative elixir by yogins; see MM:46.

54. Tsari is, as far as I know, unique in the Tibetan context for its detailed ritual itinerary. But there are parallel esoteric Buddhist developments that treat natural mountain landscapes as maṇḍala by ritual journey in Japan—see Grapard (1982)—and that prescribe the ritual ascent of "human-made mountain" maṇḍala, such as Barabuḍur—for which see Wayman (1981).

55. PK I:30a–31a; and see the brief summary by Stein (1988a:40).

56. Usually abbreviated as *kha sbyor yan lag bdun ldan* in the texts.

57. Or *mchog gi dngos grub* also *parama-siddhi*, *mahāmudrā-siddhi*, or "resultant-time *mahāmudrā*" (*'bras dus kyi phyag chen*).

7. Popular Short Pilgrimages

1. Gyelwang Kunga Penjor (1428–1476), quoted in PK I:32b.

2. The Shungkor is the only one of the mountain's ritual itineraries that non-Tibetans are known to have performed. The Pandit explorer named Kinthup circumambulated it in 1883–84 (Burrard 1915:335), the British spy F. M. Bailey in 1913 (1914a:11–12, 68–71, 127–29; 1957:205–11), and the British botanist G. Sherriff in 1936 (Fletcher 1975:109–12). They give us mainly geographical descriptions, with virtually no mention of the variant Ngakor or Kyemengi Korwa routes.

3. My informants report about seven hundred to a thousand pilgrims attending in the 1940s and 1950s, and Bailey (1914a:11) about two thousand in 1913.

4. SG, interview.

5. TTT:15.

6. *Gnas dag pa mkha' spyod dpal gyi tsā ri tra / bka' brgyud bla ma rnams dang yi dam lha / mkha' 'gro chos skyong rnams la gsol ba 'debs / las ngan sdig sgrib dag par byin gyis brlobs / rkyen ngan bar chad zhi bar mdzad pa dang / mchog dang mthun mong dngos grub stsal du gsol.*

7. *Rtsa ri drag po'i gnas la / ma phebs zhu rgyu min 'dug / zhabs la smyug ma'i tsher ma / ma gzugs byas nas phebs shig.*

8. See Bailey (1957:200).

9. Pilgrim's walking sticks, called *chüber* in Tsari dialect, were made primarily of juniper (*shugpa*) wood, and the top was carved into a point with a round waist cut below it like the top of a flagpole, just below which was tied a tassel of yak hair dyed red.

10. SG, interview.

11. While original Tsari bamboo was prized in Bhutan, there was also a separate local cult of "Tsari" bamboo there. My informants Mynak Tulku and Kunzang Tengye say that the site of Chumphu near Paro is recognized by Bhutanese as the "second Tsari" (Tsari Nyipa), and that pilgrims also collect the bamboo there and regard it in the same manner as the traditions I am detailing here; see also Huber (1990:145, n.47).

12. Geshé Ngawang Dhargyey told me that in Kham during the 1950s, strings of Tsari bamboo nodes were worn as general protective charms. This practice continues in Tibet and Bhutan today and among the exile Tsariwa.

13. The Tibetan painted scroll of Pure Crystal Mountain (figure 4.3) depicts pilgrims at either side of the summit departing from the completed middle circuit with bundles of bamboo canes on their shoulders.

14. Olschak and Wangyal give a contents analysis of a bronze image of Padmasambhava; it contains "small bags filled with . . . earth from the holy mountain *Tsa-ri*. . . . Between the bags were bamboo ear-rings from *Tsa-ri*" (1987:8). SG (interview) reports that when large monasteries in Tibet planned to construct major *chöten* or images, they would send to Tsari for bamboo, soil, and water for use in their fabrication and empowerment. For example, the catalog of the contents of the Fifth Dalai Lama's burial shrine records that earth and other items from Tsari were deposited in it (CHD:610).

15. Around the main site where empowered bamboo grows, Deuyak Lagang near Yümé, the soil is believed to contain *chinlab* because the blood of an enlightened being was spilled there and soaked into it in the past. A Tibetan guide to the southeastern *néri* of Kawa Karpo, which is also represented as a maṇḍala palace of Khorlo Dompa and Dorje Pagmo, comments: "Il y a les arbres essences de vie des Dâkinî: ce sont tous les bambous qui poussent là." Quoted in Large-Blondeau (1960:237).

16. *Tsa ri rtse nas skor yod / smyug ma rong nas brag yod / ma dang mkha' 'gro'i byin rlabs / smyug ma'i tshig la zhugs yod.*

17. *Tsa ri rtse'i nas skor yod / smyug ma rong nas bcad yod / nga la rdo rje phag mos / bka' chad gnang don mi 'dug.* See Sørensen (1990:137).

18. TW (interview) relates:

> I collected many pieces of empowered bamboo on the ravine circuit at Tsari, and gave it all away to my grateful friends at home as they could not make the trip. Years later, after Tibet and Tsari were closed by the Chinese, I thought of getting a small bamboo back from my friends, as I had kept none myself. But not one would part with any, even when I offered to buy it back for a tidy sum; they said it was far too precious.

19. *Tsa ri rtse nas skor yod / smyug ma rong nas blangs yod / tsa ri skor bas lag rtags / smyug ma'i tshig gsum phul chog.*

20. Tibetan text in Tucci (1966:33).

21. BMZh:72. The other verses are identical in form, but have a "Chinese fruit-tree" and a "willow in Lhasa" as their subjects. This entire song could be interpreted as dance instructions.

22. Tibetan text in Das (1972: app. 10); see there his comments on the subject of the song; also 50.

23. Stein (1988a:42).

24. Stein (1972:225).

25. Tucci: "By the parents who have been so gracious (with me), I have been sent to visit the holy places; on the head I wear the hat with visor called skal-bzang, and in the hands I have the cane-stick with three knots" (1966:50).

26. My analysis here adds further weight to the point made eloquently by Martin (1988) in relation to another song about Tsari: Philologists trained in the Indological or Buddhological context who work with Tibetan textual sources may "get the translation right," but they can often fail to recognize the universe of Tibetan cultural meanings associated with certain combinations of apparently mundane references.

27. The ranking gained from the number of circuits performed was not arbitrary, and various catalogs or enumerations are found in the guidebooks to Tsari. See, for example, TsLY I:302–3 or 11b–12a; PK I:32a–b; KZ I:28b–29b. Similar systems apply at sites such as Tise (Huber and Rigzin 1995: 27–28, Johnson and Moran 1989:121, Kawaguchi 1909:167–68), with thirteen circuits being the ideal number at many *néri* (thirteen being an ideal number for Tibetans in any case).

28. Marriott and Inden (1977), Marriott (1976).

29. DPN:1043. The practice of throwing valuable offerings into lakes is also reported from northern Tibet (Bower 1976:102–3).

30. In much the same way, no traditionally minded Tibetan would dare to steal the gold and precious materials deposited in a *tenkhar* shrine on a mountain (Tucci 1966:189).

31. See Tucci (1980:200). Karmay (1991) has noted that this ritual logic of gift or exchange is very ancient in Tibet, predating the thorough introduction of Indic religious systems, and in the case of the "ransom" (*lü*, spelled *glud*) rituals practiced during the period of the Tibetan Empire (seventh-ninth centuries), it most often focused on mountain deities.

32. Compare the concern for excrement here with the beliefs and practices relating to the Dalai Lama's bodily excretions in Sherring (1974:251), remembering that such highly ranked lamas are also considered to be *né*. In 1883–84 the explorer Kinthup already reported, "On the journey to Tsāri by this [middle circuit] route, no one is allowed to spit even, and the halting places are kept exceedingly clean" (Burrard 1915:335). In general Tibetan tradition, urinating on the hearth, in wells, and in ponds is considered bad as it upsets deities resident in these places, which can result in illness for the person.

33. A more detailed discussion of women's exclusion from the upper mountain has been presented elsewhere (Huber 1994b), and I refer interested readers to that.

34. Filippi (1971:143). In 1883–84 the explorer named Kinthup (Burrard 1915:335) and in 1913 the British spy F. M. Bailey (1914a:70; 1957:201, 205) both made careful observations on the subject of women's exclusion.

35. Jäschke, *A Tibetan-English Dictionary*, has "*gom-pa bdun 'bor-ba* . . . to make seven steps, as a ceremony, which may also be counted equivalent to a religious pilgrimage, the actual performance of which is not possible" (73).

36. It is instructive to compare this recent Tibetan preservation of traditional gendered space under Chinese colonialism with the study made recently by Charlene Mackley in Amdo (1994).

37. On the social significance of *kyemen* and other colloquial Tibetan gender terminology, see Aziz (1989:79–82).

38. DPN:1042–43.

39. SG, interview.

40. See the account of such an alternative pilgrimage to Tsari Tsokar by a twentieth-century woman aristocrat, whose party included several other women (Yuthok 1990:89–102). Note that although detailing the three main circuits of Pure Crystal Mountain, she never once mentions the exclusion of women. Tsari Tsokar was a popular pilgrimage destination in the area, on which see note 32 of chapter 4.

41. Reported in Burrard (1915:335).

42. Doring was one of the five highly ranked *depön* families in the aristocracy (Petech 1973: 50–64). This account apparently refers to the Doring *Kalön* Gabshi Tenzin Penjor (b. 1760) who, together with his younger sister Lobsang Döndüp Drölma, who was a nun, his wife, Namgyel Drölma, and daughter, Lobsang Chödzom, performed the pilgrimage in 1794 (DPN: 1042). He maintained close personal connections with the Eighth Drukchen, who was very active at Tsari, and who wrote various important works about the mountain and its pilgrimage traditions.

43. "Apha," "Tashi," SG, and SP (interviews).

44. Filippi (1971:143).

45. There may be some confusion of identities in the oral sources; however, the Doring family appears to have been obliged to contribute to the maintenance of the Tsari pilgrimages. It is known that both Doring Kalön Tenzin Penjor and his wife fared very badly in political scandals surrounding the Gorkhali invasion and the role of the Sharmapa lama in it during the late eigh-

teenth century. Doring was involved in bitter public scandal again in 1805–6 over his son's appointment to the cabinet (Petech 1973:56–60). Various oral guides mention either a resthouse or a cave at certain points on the pilgrimage routes where the Doring family had to provide a measure of parched barley flour, or a cup of beer or curd to each pilgrim who passed. In addition, some say that the Doring estate payed an annual tax of a hundred lambs at Tsari in the seventh Tibetan month. A Bhutanese map of the Tsari Rongkor Chenmo circuit kept at Tango monastery near Thimphu shows a thatched hut near the end of the route in Charmé. It is labeled the "Doring resthouse of Char River spur" (*bya chu sgang rdo ring tshugs* (>*tshul*) *khang*), and a similar hut as well as a tent are depicted on another Tibetan map of Tsari (see figure 8.6) and labeled "resthouse above the Char River" (*bya chu gong tshul khang*) (Huber 1992:17). However, in 1883–84 Kinthup reported that a Tibetan government fine of supplying curd to every pilgrim high up on the Shungkor route was imposed on the "Dakpu Dungpa" because his daughter crossed the Drölma La and was killed (Burrard 1915:335). Kinthup must be referring to the Dakpo Drumpa, the leading aristocratic family of Dakpo to the north of Tsari who were established in Lhasa. The Doring and Drumpa names have perhaps become confused in the oral traditions, but both families seem to have paid different fines around the mountain.

46. See also lay Tibetan statements such as "The female Tibetans are descendants of the She-ogress, hence the impetuous, violent, witchlike nature of women" (Miller 1980:160) or the descriptions of the "unworthy qualities" of women as jealousy, wickedness, always doing what is not good or acceptable, unreliability, hypocrisy, and so on, noted in Chophel (1983: 83–86).

47. For some compelling parallels between these Tibetan narratives and Hindu material, see Sax on the story of Rupkund and women's exclusion from the upper sections of the Rāj Jāt pilgrimage of Nandadevi in the Garhwal Himalaya (1991:94–97).

48. SG, interview.

49. In addition to the seven steps being considered a proxy pilgrimage (see n.35), it is interesting to compare the seven steps here, as they are linked to the ending of a stage of rebirth, with a narrative element in the classical biographies of the Buddha; immediately after his birth the Buddha takes seven steps to the north, and states, "This is my last rebirth" (Thomas 1949:31). None of my informants made this link, but the similarity is striking.

50. "Nawang," interview.

51. SG, interview.

52. "Pema," interview.

53. See, for example, Gyatso (1989).

54. On Mahāyāna Buddhism, see Paul (1985).

55. Here, for instance, one can think of the Buddha being born "cleanly" through his mother's side to avoid the polluting effects of her birth canal and vulva (note that this can also be interpreted as a "perfect" birth devoid of the usual physical stresses and suffering of vaginal birth); the female genitals as the physical conduit through which all beings are reintroduced back into an ultimately unsatisfactory cyclic existence (*saṃsāra*); as well as the presentation of some alternative world-systems, or Buddhafields, as being so pure they contain no women in them.

56. A famous tenth-century Tibetan Buddhist ordinance attacks the "village tantrists" for being "[i]mprisoned in the dirt of the five kinds of sensual objects and women" (Karmay 1980:153). In Tibet during 1987 I observed that no women were permitted to enter the main protectors' temple at Ganden monastery; there were signs to this effect over the door, and many women pilgrims waited outside while their male companions entered for worship. I was told by a monk that it is because women are polluted and might upset the protectors that they are excluded. A Tibetan explanation for this exclusion relating to menstruation and pollution (*drib*) is found in Chophel (1983:12).

57. In relation to my findings on women's exclusion, Heather Stoddard has advanced an interesting theory to explain the origins of the practice (personal communication, 1995). She proposes that the partial anticlockwise circumambulation route of the women's circuit could be seen as a relic of a "feminine" lefthanded circumambulation (*apradakṣiṇā*) of the Khorlo Dompa maṇḍala, associated with the "left-handed etiquette" implicit in the dynamic structures and practices of the Mother division of highest yoga Tantras. She asserts, "[I]n the majority of mandalas, and in everyday outward practice, this 'left-circling' has practically been effaced." The only mention of this "left-handed etiquette" in relation to Tibetan pilgrimage I myself have come across is in a pilgrimage guide for the well-known *néri* of Shar Dungri in Amdo Sharkog, which was inscribed on the wall of a small Sakyapa monastery at the mountain's base, and which I hand-copied in 1996. It mentions that the site is an abode of Khorlo Dompa for Buddhists, and that circumambulations there are either "right-handed circuits in the manner of the Father [division of highest yoga] Tantra and left-handed in the manner of the Mother [division of highest yoga] Tantra" (*pha rgyud ltar g.yas skor dang / ma rgyud ltar g.yon skor*). The complete lack of any mention of "left-circling" in current Tibetan evidence relating to women's exclusion at Tsari may well be a testimony to the antiquity of the effacement of such practices around the mountain. Based on the few concrete historical references available (see chapter 6), I still think that the exclusions from the upper pilgrimage circuits originally related to the bans on women from the Tantric retreat centers, these being extended to make the area of certain retreat caves on the upper mountain out of bounds to women during the summer.

58. Recent Tibetan visitors to Tsari report that since the mountain reopened for pilgrimage, Tibetan nuns have several times attempted to defy the ban on women performing the middle circuit but have been stopped from doing so by their pilgrimage parties. Such contemporary examples of resistance must also be seen in the new context of changing Tibetan lives, which have been influenced by Chinese occupation, the conditions of exile, and increasing contact with other cultures and worldviews.

59. See, for example, Sperber (1995) on the Hindukush and Huber (1994b:363–64) on Japan.

60. See Diemberger (1994), Karmay (1994a, 1995), and Mackley (1994:88 n. 19), who notes that even physical violence is used against women to enforce ritual exclusion. In general, the local mountain cults provide occasions for intense celebrations of masculinity and the symbols of male power, usually including public displays of male prowess in handling weapons and horses and in oratory.

61. For examples, see Berglie (1980:41) on the gods of Mount Targo, Macdonald (1985:9) on the local gods of Halasé hill, Nebesky-Wojkowitz (1956:473) on the deities of mountain springs, and Tucci (1966:188, 190–91) on the great sensitivity of *pholha*, *phuglha*, and *kyimlha* deities to various contacts with women.

62. However, there is a general Tibetan belief in the possibility of sex change because an infant's sex is not necessarily fixed just after birth. For instance, there are various rituals involving naming and the use of charms to prevent newborn boys turning into girls, see Aziz (1988:28) and Chophel (1983:4).

63. See, for example, Gyatso (1989:145 n. 59) and Karma Lekshe Tsomo (1989:122–23).

64. See Huber (1994b:363–64).

8. Barbarian Tributes and Great Processions

1. Ekvall and Downs (1987:54). The monkey year is said to be chosen primarily because it is astrologically auspicious, being the birth year of the saint Padmasambhava and associated with the birth of the Buddha at Lumbini (TsNY II:7); or is the year when all the leading protective deities gather at the mountain; or is the year of Tsangpa Gyare's opening of the

site (BGTsh, 2:2183), the monkey year of 1188—calculated from the dates and events given in PK Ia:nya-ta, BGTsh, 3:3225, and PK IV:241.

2. All my informants give this figure for the 1944 and 1956 events, while other sources indicate similar or even higher numbers during the nineteenth and early twentieth century; See Bailey (1957:200), Nebesky-Wojkowitz (1956:406), Wylie (1962:36), Yuthok (1990: 90), and ZhKN:501.

3. See, in particular, Betts (1949), Dalton (1872), Duff-Sutherland-Dunbar (1915), Elwin (1956, 1959), Fürer-Haimendorf (1948, 1955, 1962, 1967, 1982, 1990), Graham Bower (1953), Shukla (1959), and Stonor (1952).

4. The origins of such oaths of nonmolestation (and of course the attacks that entailed them) date back at least to the early fifteenth century. A sixteenth-century biography of the Third Shamarpa Chöpel Yeshé (1406–1452) records that after he attempted to convert local tribal peoples (*lopa*) at Tsari to Buddhism, he received the "promise" (*khélang*) from them not to harm pilgrims at the site (KGT II:1096–67).

5. Petech (1973: see index under Tsa-ri) notes they came from positions such as fourth rank Tsechug (Dalai Lama's private treasurer), fifth rank Lhanyer (Lhasa municipal head), fifth rank Sholnyer (Zhol dependency magistrate), and sixth rank Chibpön (master and controller of horse and stud).

6. The amount and composition of the troops varied from one great ravine circuit to the next, depending on the state of Tibetan-tribal relations in the area. Bailey records two hundred regulars from garrisons in southeastern Tibet dispatched for the 1908 event (1914a:10); this strong force came in the wake of a 1906 war with tribes around Tsari. Less than one hundred troops were sent on the disastrous 1944 event, when several hundred pilgrims were killed by tribals. Therefore, twice as many well-armed troops were sent in 1956.

7. See MGY:492–500 for a full written version.

8. For descriptions, see Bailey (1914a:18–19), Nebesky-Wojkowitz (1956:407–8), and Yuthok (1990:90). Ludlow's informants identified the "Morang Loba" as the group to the south of Tsari attacking the Pachakshiri inhabitants on the Tibetan-controlled territory of the Lhalu family estates in 1937 (1940:6).

9. One Tibetan oral etymology of this term is "border Lopa," meaning "next to" or "facing" (*kha*) Tibet—see BGTsh, 1:186: "Lopa who live in the upper parts of Loyül." It remains a question as to how this local name related to the nineteenth-century term *lopa khatra*, which can be translated "striped-mouth/face Lopa," possibly referring to the Aka tribe just west of Subansiri in the Kameng district. Fuchs indicates that Aka means "painted," as they paint their faces with black marks (1973:199); see also Aris (1976:628 n. 66). On *lopa khatra* and related terms used in relation to tribes at Tsari, see KGT II:1096, l.15, Das (1970:123), Wylie (1962:36), and ZhKN:479, and to groups north of the Brahmaputra in general, Wylie (1962:178 n.583) and LPhG:32a.

10. *Tsendug*, which is also called *bonga nakpo* or *bongnak*, is the black aconite (*Aconitum ferox Wall/balfourii Stapf* and *Aconitum ferox/spicatum*); see Parfionovitch et al. (1992: 75, 231, 233).

11. This headpiece, called the *podom* in Assam, is worn by the Apa Tani, "Dafla," and "Hill Miri," and although each group has a specialized method of fastening it, the superficial appearance is very similar (Chowdhury 1991:120). This hairstyle contrasts with the long loose or cropped hair worn by Tibetanized tribes living closer to the Tibetan villages, and together the range of hair styles and headgear reported is indicative of the variety of groups attending.

12. On the tribal use of tally sticks, see Nebesky-Wojkowitz (1956:408) and Fürer-Haimendorf (1967:63).

13. For example, at the 1956 Lodzong, four *rukel* (approximately 100 kg) of salt was given (SG, interview). This large quantity reflects the high value placed on salt by the tribes of the upper Subansiri basin, who had no local or easy access to the substance. The area lay in the

middle of the Himalayan salt divide, being remote from both the main salt trade of the Indian plains to the south and the Tibetan plateau to the north.

14. Concerning the payment of beads at Tsari, Duff-Sutherland-Dunbar noted that already by the turn of the century products from the industrialized West had entered the bargaining process as "the Tibetan benevolences . . . of (imitation) turquoise necklaces, and strings of the blue porcelain beads commonly worn by the Abors, Galongs, and the peoples of the Subansiri Valley. . . . [T]he [imitation turquoise] beads are made in Birmingham, or Germany, and find their way to Tsari through Calcutta, Darjeeling, and Lha-sa"(1915:6, n. 1).

15. Only ritual bells (*drilbu*) and small cymbals (*tingshag*), both with sacred syllables (mantra) cast on them, were acceptable to the tribal chiefs at the Lodzong. Such items were highly valued and sought after, although not for use as instruments (see chapter 9). The possession and exchange of Tibetan bells were widely related to status ranking in the Apa Tani, "Dafla," and "Hill Miri" societies; see Fürer-Haimendorf (1955:198–200, 1982:54, 57, 85).

16. Note that some informants insist the image was of Dorje Pagmo, the chief Tantric goddess of the mountain. GJLY: 366, l.1 describes this special oath-image as a *terma*, or "hidden treasure" discovered by Tsangpa Gyare, one of the original lama heroes who opened the mountain. Hugh Richardson also mentions that texts were placed on top of the gate (personal communication, 1989). The details given in Dorje Tseten (1992:9) are incorrect.

17. ZhKN describes the same sacrifice in 1812: "[The two yaks] were laid down after being tied up, and were set upon by many Lopa of the barbarous borderland who lunged at them with long and short swords, and cut off their legs and the like, their flesh and hide while they were still alive, then carried it off" (479). It is instructive to compare these Tibetan descriptions with notes on Apa Tani sacrifices by Fürer-Haimendorf (1955:88,120).

18. Nebesky-Wojkowitz mentions the use of the sacrificial yak's bloody hide in the oath-swearing (1956:407), but none of my informants confirmed this, suggesting it may have been the case in 1932 or earlier. One should note that the use of the bloody sacrificial yak hide, the marking with blood, and the eating of raw meat are all reported for an East Tibetan oath-swearing ritual (Duncan 1964:193).

19. This *cham*, in which both Kunga Shonu and his female partner are portrayed in human form with lion faces (BSNg:39–43), is still performed at the Sangnag Chöling monastery in exile, in Darjeeling, India.

20. Bailey (1914a:11;1957:201) mentions such speculation at the turn of the century.

21. Decisions of Tibetan social allotment were often decided with dice; see Carrasco (1959:51) and Henderson (1964:1103).

22. Informants report that some parties of aristocratic pilgrims had up to ten servants or porters per person. The performance of corvée porterage on the great ravine circuit was bitterly resented by those who had to do it. On corvée transportation entitlements and obligations in Tibet, see Carrasco (1959:90–91), Cassinelli and Ekvall (1969:250–52), and Goldstein (1971a;1989:4–5). Corvée transport took many forms, but at Tsari it appears to be unique in that it was demanded and provided specifically for certain pilgrimages.

23. Such tribal thefts from pilgrims were already documented at the turn of this century (Duff-Sutherland-Dunbar 1915:5–6).

24. See Bailey (1914a:11).

25. ZhKN:482.

26. *Khams pa rong skor a krad za mkhan.*

27. Combe (1926:127).

28. KPT, interview.

29. ZhKN:489.

30. SP and SG, interviews.

31. For example, on commitment, a lover might declare his or her circumstances and

ability to begin a relationship or marriage and then make a reference to the solemn commitment required for the venture: "I do not dwell with beloved father, I do not dwell with beloved mother; Beloved sweetheart I have no parents. Shall we circumambulate Tsari." (Duncan 1961:37; see Sørensen 1990:122). On the importance of parents and their respect: "If I were on my own, I would go to Tsaritra. If I [have to] leave my elderly parents, what's the use of Tsaritra? (*nga rang gcig pu yin na/rtsa ri tra la phyin pa/pha ma rgan rgon bzhag na/rtsa ri tra yis gar yong*)"; (see an almost identical Khampa song about Né Pema Köd; Namkhai Norbu Dewang 1967:259/274); and: "Put Pure Crystal Mountain foremost, and keep the mountain ranges in mind. Put your parents foremost, and keep your relatives in mind (*dag pa shel ri gtso byas/ri la ri brgyud dran byung/drin can pha mas gtso byas/nye la nye brgyud dran byung*)." On the mendicant giving up the family: "If attached to his kind parents, a yogin is mistaken. Having thought to repay one's kind parents, go to circumambulate the power place of Tsari" (PD: f. 50a–51a).

32. Aziz (1987:257).

33. Here it is interesting to compare the sentiments of the Buddhist *kaihogyo* practitioners of the grueling mountain marathon at Mt. Hiei; "If you do this [pilgrimage], there is nothing that cannot be accomplished" (Stevens 1988:133).

34. TW, interview.

35. Gombo's comments on a Tibetan pilgrimage to Bodh Gaya (1985:239–40) and Prindle's on the Hindu Dudh Kunda pilgrimage (cited in Macdonald 1985:13 n.14) are relevant in this context.

36. From the poem "dPal skad kyi ka bshad," published in 1936 (my translation from the French in Stoddard 1985:176).

37. *Gnas rtsa ri bskor ba'i chos grogs red/bya gong mo bsad pa'i sdig grogs red.* There may, in fact, be more to this song than a sentiment of solidarity. At the end of the great ravine circuit, many pilgrims were starving. In order to exit Tsari district after the event, some had to cross the Kongmo La pass, known for its white grouse (*bya gong mo*), which are sometimes considered sacred due to their vegetarian habits and their ancient associations with purity and healing (see Karmay 1975:205). It is possible that hunting the birds for food there inspired this song. The Khampas sing the praises of the white grouse who live near the high mountain passes (Namkhai Norbu Dewang 1967:258/272).

38. See Norbu (1994) and Huber (1991) for critical views.

39. Burrard (1915, p. 1:171) and Huber and Rigzin (1995:29). Compare to Mongol Buddhist beliefs on the number of pilgrimage circuits performed around the great Chinese Buddhist sacred mountain of Wu-t'ai Shan (Gilmour 1883:161).

40. Here one cannot resist mentioning the Khampa brigand encountered by Kawaguchi (1909:173) on pilgrimage at the *néri* of Tise, who sought purification not only for his past murders but also for any others he might perform in future lives as well!

41. SG. interview. See ZhKN:482.

42. ND and TW, interviews; See Grapard's comments on Japanese Buddhist mountain pilgrimages: "It is well known that pilgrims coming back from sacred spaces were regarded with awe: common people saluted them, made offerings, even tried to touch them" (1982:207).

43. Yuthok (1990:90).

44. See Bacot on Kawa Karpo (1909:20–22).

45. See, for instance, Aziz (1987:256), Demiéville (1973), Lagerwey (1992:319–20), and Sax (1992).

46. Schopen (1987).

9. Statecraft and Status in Contested Territory

1. *Chos srid gnyis 'brel* (Goldstein 1989:2).
2. For example, Samuel (1993).
3. See Tambiah (1976) and Inden (1990).
4. Inden (1990:267).
5. Samuel (1993).
6. Foucault (1979, 1980).
7. Bourdieu (1977).
8. Bell (1992).
9. Bell (1992:130).
10. Bell (1992:170; 196).
11. Various oral accounts from Tsariwa mention that it was started by the saints Padmasambhava (eighth cent.) or Thangthong Gyelpo (b. 1385), while others credit Sönam Gyeltsen (fourteenth cent.) (TsNY III:4), Gesar (MGY:498–99), or Tsangpa Gyare (1161–1211) (BGTsh, 2:2183).
12. TsNY III:5.
13. See Smith (1982:53–56).
14. A "revealed treasure" guidebook to Tsari confirms that it was being performed every twelve years (*lo bcu gnyis la rong skor che ba'o.*) toward the middle of the eighteenth century (TsLY I:12a–b).
15. See Ishihama (1993) and Richardson (1993:7).
16. Macdonald (1987b:10–11).
17. Kaschewsky (1971:131).
18. DPN:1043–44.
19. See SLG:406–7 and chaps 5 and 7 herein.
20. Willis (1985:308–11).
21. See, for example, De Rossi-Filibeck (1988:96).
22. See Huber (1990:149–51).
23. See Huber (1997:244).
24. The oral sources all agree that a Dalai Lama's mother was somehow involved—either that she was the initial patron or that the event was staged to commemorate her death—but they conflict as to whether it was the mother of the Fifth, Sixth, or Seventh incarnation. No textual source has so far established which, if any, was involved. One could note here that the Tsogchö Chenmo ritual in Lhasa was founded in the same period by the regent Sangye Gyatso to commemorate the death of the Fifth Dalai Lama.
25. See Ehrhard (1994).
26. The tour of Tsari is described in LLN:447–70.
27. Karmay (1988:29).
28. For the Fifth Dalai Lama see SBK:48 (22); for Lelung see SBK:326 (pa), 328 (pi), 335 (29, 31), 339 (yu), 340 (shu, su). The Seventh Dalai Lama also composed texts on the local deities at the request of the people of Tsari (SBK:70, no. 87).
29. See Martin (1988) and Sørensen (1990:113–42) on the song. See DLSN:50–51 and Aris (1988:188–89) on the biography.
30. Smith (1970:16–18).
31. The classic examples are the visits of the saint Thangtong Gyelpo (b. 1385) to Tsari (TGN:124, 143–52; Gyatso 1986:98–100) and of the Third Karmapa Rangchung Dorje (1284–1339); See also Ehrhard (1994:6–7).
32. See Ekvall and Downs (1987:157), whose informants for the Rongkor Chenmo expressed the same sentiments.

33. Bell (1992:196).
34. Carrasco (1959:123) and Goldstein (1989:2).
35. Karsten (1983:118).
36. Goldstein (1989:17).
37. Petech (1973:17).
38. Goldstein (1973:445).
39. Compare the photographs of élite Tibetan maṇḍala tent arrangements in Tsarong (1990:4, 82) and Normanton (1988:126–27).
40. Cohn (1990:44).
41. Sax (1991:202–3).
42. Bell (1992:196).
43. See Tambiah (1985:327–30).
44. SG, interview. On Tsarong, see Goldstein (1989:66,165, pl.21), Petech (1973:137–38), and Spence (1991).
45. On his 1900 visit to the area, see DL13A:339b; DL13B:98–99.
46. The date is as yet unknown. He was still in government at the time of the 1932 Rongkor, but the date of his procession could have also been 1920, when he was commander-in-chief of the Tibetan army or, less likely, 1944. It is known that he gave a large, "well-used" map of southern Tibet, partly depicting Tsari, the western section of the Rongkor, and the Lonag tribal areas (see figure 8.6), to the British diplomat Hugh Richardson as a gift at Lhasa during 1944 (Hugh Richardson, personal communication, 1989; see Huber 1992 for a complete study of this document).
47. TTT:9–10.
48. See Norbu (1994).
49. These products included madder vine or *martsöd* (*Rubia cordifolia*), used to produce dye for monk's robes at the major Gelukpa monasteries; musk (*latsee*); bear's gall (*domtree*); and bog orchid roots (*wanglag*), which were all rare and expensive medicinal ingredients and items of profitable onward trade; various types of subtropical animal skins (monkey, tiger, leopard, deer, etc.); and rice.
50. Norbu (1994:191–92).
51. See Sax (1991:202).
52. Katia Buffetrille (personal communication, 1992).
53. On this organization, see Goldstein (1989:27–31).
54. See Turner (1973, 1974) and Turner and Turner (1978).
55. Prior to 1950, notably Fürer-Haimendorf (1948, 1955, 1962, 1967, 1982, 1990) in 1944–45, and Betts (1949; Graham Bower, 1953) in 1946–48; but see also Dalton (1872), Elwin (1956, 1959), Shukla (1959), and Stonor (1952).
56. Fürer-Haimendorf (1948:244).
57. Bailey (1914a:19; 1957:209–11, 218).
58. This situation was clearly the case, despite modern Tibetan claims to the contrary. A Nyarong Khampa informant of Duff-Sutherland-Dunbar who performed the Shungkor circuit at around the turn of the century reported: "The top of the Trema-la [i.e., Drölma La] is the boundary between Tibet and the Lopa country. To carry out the Tsari pilgrimage, the devout traveller must go round the mountain, a four days' progress, involving a two days' journey through Loba country. The sacred way runs high up on the mountain side and does not dip into the valley below" (1915:5). This territorial claim was enforced..Another informant performing the Shungkor circuit reported robbery and murder of pilgrims in his party by tribals along the southern section of the route (Duff-Sutherland-Dunbar 1915:5).
59. Bailey (1914a:19).
60. Bailey (1957:218–19), Fürer-Haimendorf (1955:157–60), and Ludlow (1938:7).

61. This massacre also has to be seen in the light of ongoing raiding and subsequent Tibetan government military actions against the same tribes to the south of Tsari in the 1930s; Ludlow (1940:4).

62. Fürer-Haimendorf (1955: chap. 14).

63. Elwin (1956, n.p.).

64. Richardson (1984:282; see 117).

65. See Bailey (1914a, 1957) and Morshead (1914).

66. Lamb (1966, 2:322–23).

67. Lamb (1966, 2:537).

68. Goldstein (1989:417).

69. Richardson (1984:230) and Woodman (1969:239, map 19).

70. Jäschke, *Tibetan-English dictionary*, 469.

71. *Concise Oxford Dictionary*, 1145.

72. For some examples, see Burrard (1915:178), Fürer-Haimendorf (1955:181–82, 230), Lamb (1966, 2:310–11), Waddell (1905:439 n. 3), and Ward (1938:616).

73. See Pemberton (1835:80–81), Mackenzie (1884:27–46), and Gait (1905:364–365).

74. Gait (1905:364–365) and Fürer-Haimendorf (1955:182).

75. Fürer-Haimendorf (1967:62) and Betts (1949:151).

76. Fürer-Haimendorf (1962:128).

77. See Fürer-Haimendorf (1955:88, 120, 144, 154–55; 1967:64, 69) and Shukla (1959: 86–88).

78. Fürer-Haimendorf (1967:70).

79. Fürer-Haimendorf (1962:52–53). These tribal values associated with Tibetan bells in the Subansiri where already known in the mid–nineteenth century (Dalton 1872:36–37).

80. Fürer-Haimendorf (1967:72).

81. Samuel (1994:704).

82. Stein (1988b), Stein (1972:200), and Tucci (1980:230–31, 239).

83. See, for example, Asboe (1936), Diemberger (1991:140 n. 14), (Duncan 1964:193), Nebesky-Wojkowitz (1956:237, 241, 427), Stein (1972:200), Stubel (1958:35), and Tsering (1985:206).

10. Complex Identities and Local Rituals

1. All population figures given in this study are only estimates based on the memories of exile Tsariwa for the 1950s period. About 170 people from the upper valley villages went into exile in 1959, with less than that number remaining behind. Lo Mikyimdün and its environs had a population approximately equal to the whole upper valley zone.

2. See Aziz (1974:30).

3. Hereditary *mibog* status was common in communities controlled by the Lhasa government, and allowed for peasants to move between estates provided that they continued to pay an annual cash fee to their original estate lord; see Goldstein (1971b).

4. SP, interview.

5. "Drolma," interview.

6. Bailey (1914a:19–20).

7. See Bailey (1914a:69; 1945:123) and Ludlow (1938:9).

8. Yuthok (1990:90).

9. See also Aris (1986:81 n. 70), Duff-Sutherland-Dunbar (1915:3), Ehrhard (1994:6–7), Gyatso (1986:99), Karmay (1992:530), Nebesky-Wojkowitz (1956:407–8), and Wallace (1980:64).

10. SG, interview.

11. Aris (1980a:9).

12. For a fifteenth-century spelling of Lowo see GBJ:441, l.5–6. An early eighteenth-century spelling of Lo Mikyimdün is found in LLN:466.

13. GJLY:366.

14. SG, interview.

15. KZI:17a–b. This idea of divine embodiment may have been borrowed from well-known Indian sites of the Khorlo Dompa cult; see, for example, the thirteenth-century Tibetan accounts of Uḍḍiyāṇa in Swat Valley (Tucci 1940) and more recent Tibetan ones inspired by them (GGL:340–42).

16. See GBJ:438, l.2–4 and PK III:449, respectively.

17. YTN:104b, apparently paraphrasing an earlier statement by Gyelwang Kunga Penjor (1428–1476); see GBJ:440, l.2–3.

18. ZhKN:489.

19. KZ II:175.

20. See Wylie for Tibetan text (1962:36).

21. This particular designation of the area goes back earlier, and the cave of Padmasambhava there was called "suppressor of the Lopa" in the early eighteenth century (LLN:466). The whole idea of the suppression of the Lopa to the south of Tsari is found in the fifteenth-century activities there of Thangthong Gyelpo (Gyatso 1986:91).

22. It is highly likely that the ritual outlined here and the beliefs it is based on derive from the account of the thirteenth-century pilgrimage of Orgyenpa Rinchenpal (1230–1293) to Uḍḍiyana (Swat Valley), which says: "Among the women of the town there is one who is said to be a *yoginī*. Since it is difficult to recognise her, I took food from the hands of all women of the town and by eating it I surely got spiritual perfection from them" (Tucci 1971: 400). This source for the Tsari ritual is hardly surprising, since Orgyenpa was an early and important teacher in the Drukpa Kagyü lineage, and one finds Pema Karpo using many references to the Tibetan Uḍḍiyana traditions throughout his works on Tsari.

23. Yuthok (1990: 96–97).

24. TTT:28–29.

25. SG, interview.

26. Nebesky-Wojkowitz (1956:8–11).

27. See Aris (1986:82 n.95).

28. SG, interview.

29. The material on charnel grounds is dealt with in more detail in Huber (1990). On the Shingkyong's weapons see Nebesky-Wojkowitz (1956:65).

30. Wallace (1980:64).

31. Nebesky-Wojkowitz (1956).

32. See Huber (1990).

33. PDB:22a; see Nebesky-Wojkowitz (1956:95, 190–93, 222).

34. See ZhKGT; ZhKKS; BSNg:39–43; PDB:18a; MGY:499, and Nebesky-Wojkowitz (1956:65–66).

35. NT, interview.

36. ZhKKS:1b–2b.

37. For example, Aziz (1978a:250–51) and Clarke (1991).

38. Approximately several hundred kilograms of grain were allotted, together with more modest supplies of tea and butter. Any additional materials required had to be contributed by the *depa* household themselves (RD, interview).

39. See BSNg:39–43.

40. The monkey is particularly associated with Tsari in popular discourse. There were species of monkey found in the forests to the south, but not within Tibetan territory on the

mountain itself. Some Tibetans link the fact of the Rongkor Chenmo performance every monkey year with the presence of monkeys there, while others are emphatic that Tsari is the area of origin for the Tibetan race, following popular anthropogenic myths featuring a divine monkey ancestor, on which see Martin (1994b:76–81). A recent "monkey-year" edition of the Tibetan Buddhist magazine *Bod ljongs nang bstan* (1992:1), published in Lhasa, was dedicated to pilgrimage literature on Tsari. Its front cover features a modern painting of Pure Crystal Mountain, entirely secular compared to traditional icons, in which a pair of monkeys sport in the bamboo at the mountain's base.

41. These songs are now sometimes performed in exile as a display of the particular culture and identity of the Tsari diaspora community.

42. See, for example, Diemberger (1994:145–46), March (1977:90–93), and Ramble (1995:88–89).

11. Culture, Nature, and Economy around a Holy Mountain

1. Bailey (1957:205).

2. Roerich (1979:200).

3. See Burrard (1915:335), and for the twentieth century, Bailey (1914a:10, 68), Ludlow (1938:9), Morshead (1914:7), and Ward (1941:81).

4. Compare to Denma Locho Rinpochey (1994:86), Duncan (1964:67, 233), and Stubel (1958:59).

5. ZhKN:512.

6. See the comments in Huber (1991).

7. See Bailey (1914a:11–12, 68), Burrard (1915:335), Ludlow (1938:9), and Ward (1936:390, 1941:82–89).

8. *Tsa ri yul stod yul smad / sha ba yin na dga' la / phyi la dgra yang min 'dug / nang du rtsa chu 'dzom pa.*

9. See, for instance, Chophel (1983:32) and Cassinelli and Ekvall (1969:261).

10. For a useful overview of the anthropological literature on Tibetan communities and the types occurring, see Samuel (1993).

11. This had been the case since early this century at least; see Bailey (1957:201–2) and Ward (1936:403).

12. *Mibog* holders at Tsari paid mainly to different government and monastic estates in the surrounding districts of Lhokha, Dakpo, and Kongpo. The amount of these payments varied greatly among individuals. Annual cash payments of five to fifteen *sang* were common, representing the normal range found in Central Tibet (see Goldstein 1971b:530–31; Aziz 1978a: 71), but others were extreme (see n. 18 hereafter). Bamboo canes, yogurt, butter, and other products were sometimes requested by Tsari *mibog* owners.

13. Shakabpa (1984:82).

14. Much of the resthouse network described here was already in place by the late eighteenth century; see DPN:1040–44. A long-established resthouse at Yütö was closed in the 1930s when the village was abandoned.

15. The *bo* was a volume unit for dry grain, varying from about twelve to fifteen kilograms. (Goldstein 1971a:8 n.10).

16. SP, interview.

17. There was no religious restriction on wild plant harvesting. Tsariwa households collected a medicinal bog orchid root, *wanglag*; various alpine scrubs and flowers dried and mixed for use in ritual fumigation, *sangna* ("mixed incense"); and other herbs. These were used for tax payments or sold at markets such as Lhasa.

18. The tax imposed on each milking animal throughout the three districts was one *markay*

(approximately three kg) of butter per year payable to Kurab Namgyel Dzong. There was also a minor tax of meat due to the Dzong (NT, interview). Many villagers had annual per capita taxes due the Sangnag Chöling Drukpa and Kyemdong Dzong, payable in butter at the rate per person of seven to eight *markay* and twelve *markay*, respectively (TD, interview; TTT: 23). This tax burden became crippling for many Tsari households in the 1950s due to high inflation of the *markay* unit, which changed in value from twenty *sang* in 1950 to three hundred *sang* by 1958 (Goldstein 1971a:12).

19. The details are given in local guidebooks and the oral tradition, but the scheme was first recorded in the sixteenth century (PK I:25b, 28a); see also Stein (1988a:40–41) and Ehrhard (1994).

20. Goldstein (1971a:2–3), Cassinelli and Ekvall (1969:265), and Ekvall (1968:21).

21. BMZh1, 2:413–14. One *sang* equals ten *zho*; in 1950, one *bo* measure (see n.15) of grain was valued at about twenty *sang* (Goldstein 1971a:11 n.12).

22. For example, the best large baskets sold for about ten *trangka*, and small for five *trangka*, in the Lhasa markets during the 1940s and 1950s (SP, interview). One *trangka* (coin) equaled four *sang* in 1950, at which time there were five Tibetan *sang* to the Indian rupee (Shakabpa 1984:334). On this trade from Tsari to Lhasa at the turn of the century, see Waddell (1905: 439 n.2).

23. For example, just for the *trekang* of Lo Mikyimdün, these taxes annually included: musk pods and bear's gall directly to officials in Lhasa (SP, interview); a large quantity of rice and animal hides to Kyemdong Dzong; one hundred yak-loads of madder vine for dying monks' robes in the large Gelukpa monasteries of Ganden, Sera, and Drepung around Lhasa; and over one hundred lengths of cotton each of five *dompa* (one *dompa* equals approximately 1.7 m) for use as prayer flags to Kurab Namgyel Dzong (TTT:20–23).

24. Fürer-Haimendorf (1962:52).

25. Bailey noted that this three-way obligation existed at the turn of the century (1914a: 10). It continued until the 1950s (TTT:20–23).

26. Certain families had hereditary tax obligations to the religious estates of the Drigungpa and the Drukpa, as well as local pasture leases from them. They discharged these by directly supporting the local monasteries. They gave butter and barely flour to feed the monks, repaired the buildings, and, in Yümé, fed and housed about ten soldiers who were stationed there every winter to protect the temple against tribal attacks. (TD and NT, interviews).

27. Many forms of corvée were not different from those common in other Tibetan villages that formed parts of the government transportation network. For example, raw materials for papermaking were regularly carried by corvée from Chayül Dzong to Chösam, from where the Tsariwa had to deliver them to Kyemdong Dzong.

28. On Tibetan substitution pilgrimages in Lhasa, see Waddell (1895:319), and at the *néri* of Tise, see Hedin (1909:202).

29. Compare, for example, Aziz (1978a:102–8) on a village in western Tibet.

30. SG, SP, and ND, interviews; TTT:20–24, Bailey (1914a:10), and Ludlow (1940:16).

31. "Dorje," interview.

32. SG, interview.

33. See Bailey (1945:89, 93, 118–19; 1957:219), Bell (1924:78–79), Carrasco (1959: 47, 56, 63, 68), Duff-Sutherland-Dunbar (1915:8), Fletcher (1975:188), Gorer (1984:36, 43–44, 127), Hanbury-Tracey (1938:25), and Ward (1941:121).

34. See Ludlow (1940:6), Kingdom-Ward (1990:181), and Ward (1941:121–22, 126–27).

35. See Fürer-Haimendorf (1955).

36. Bailey (1914a:33, 19; 1957:219); see the Tibetan price for a tribal slave in neighboring Dakpo noted by Ludlow (1940:6).

37. SG, interview.

38. TTT:35–36.

39. Bailey (1914a, 1914b, 1957), Morshead (1914), Fletcher (1975), Ludlow (1938, 1940), Ludlow and Sherrif (1937), Ward (1936, 1941, 1947), and large collections of their botanical and zoological specimens, unpublished fieldnotes, diaries, and photographs in British herbaria, museums, archives, and private collections. Some of these materials can be located at the India Office Library and Records (London), the Royal Geographic Society (London), the Natural History Museum (London), Royal Botanic Gardens (Kew), Royal Botanic Gardens (Edinburgh), and the National Library of Scotland (Edinburgh).

Bibliography

Tibetan Language Sources and Abbreviations

Note: Tibetan sources are arranged in alphabetical order of the abbreviations used in the notes. Phonetic equivalents of Tibetan author names and a brief description of each Tibetan title (in brackets) are given as required.

BDT Khetsun Sangpo (mKhas-btsun bZang-po). *Biographical Dictionary of Tibet and Tibetan Buddhism.* Vols. 7 and 8. Dharamsala, 1977 and 1981.

BGTsh *Bod rgya tshig mdzod chen mo* [Tibetan-Chinese Dictionary]. 3 vols. Beijing, 1985.

BMZh *Bod kyi dmangs gzhas* [Tibetan Folk Songs]. Lhasa, 1990.

BNG Barawa Gyeltsen Palzangpo ('Ba'-ra-ba rGyal-mtshan dPal-bzang-po, 1310–1391). *Rje bstun 'ba' ra ba rgyal mtshan dpal bzang po'i rnam thar mgur 'bum dang bcas pa* [Biography and Collected Songs of Barawa Gyeltsen Palzangpo]. In *The rnam thar and mgur 'bum of 'ba'-ra-ba with his sgrub a ñams su blaṅ ba'i lag len dgos 'dod 'byuṅ ba'i gter mdzod.* New Delhi, 1976. Ff. 1–443.

BSNg *Bod gsang sngags chos gling sprel zla tshes bcu'i gar 'cham gyi rtsa tshig* [Manual of Ritual Dances Peformed at the Tibetan Monastery of Sangnag Chöling]. Cursive MS, 50 pp. N.p., n.d.

BT Rigzin Dorje (Rig-'dzin rDo-rje) et al. *Bod kyi thang kha* [Tibetan Painted Scrolls]. Lhasa, 1984.

BTP *Bod kyi gtam dpe phyogs bsgrigs* [Compilation of Tibetan Proverbs]. Lhasa, 1990.

BZhC Dasho Nagpel (Drag-shos Nag-'phel). *'Brug gzhung 'cham gyi bshad pa* [Explanation of Bhutanese Ritual Dances]. Thimphu, 1971(?).

CHD Desi Sangye Gyatso (sDe-srid Sangs-rgyas rGya-mtsho, 1653–1705). *Mchod sdong 'dzam gling rgyan gcig rten gtsug lag khang dang bcas pa'i dkar chag* [Account of the Burial Shrine of the Fifth Dalai Lama]. Xining, 1990.

DL13A Phurchog Jampa Tsultrim (Phur-lcog Byams-pa Tshul-khrims. *Lhar bcas srid zhi 'am gtsug rgyan gong sa rgyal ba'i dbang po bka' drin mtshungs med sku phreng bcu gsum pa chen po'i rnam par thar pa rgya mtsho lta bu las mdo tsam brjod pa ngo mtshar rin po che'i 'phreng ba* [Biography of the Thirteenth Dalai Lama (1876–1933)]. 2 vols. Zhol Par-khang Woodcut, 1940.

DL13B *Bod kyi lo rgyus rig gnas dpyad gzhi'i rgyu cha bdams bsgrigs, 2 (Tā la'i bla ma sku phreng bcu gsum pa thub bstan rgya mtsho'i dgung tshig)* [Biography of the Thirteenth Dalai Lama (1876–1933)]. Lhasa, 1989.

DLSN Ngawang Lhundrup Dargye (Ngag-dbang lHun-grub Dar-rgyas). *Tshang dbyangs rgya mtsho'i gsang rnam* [The Secret Biography of the Sixth Dalai Lama (1683–1706), 1757]. Lhasa, 1981.

DPN Tenzin Penjor (bsTan-'dzin dPal-'byor, b. 1760). *Rdo ring Paṇḍita'i rnam thar*, smad-cha [Biography of the Tibetan Nobleman Doring Pandita, pt. 2, written 1806]. Chengdu, 1986.

DS Sakya Pandita Kunga Gyeltsen (Sa-skya Paṇḍita Kun-dga' rGyal-mtshan, 1182–1251). *Sdom pa gsum gyi rab tu dbye ba'i bstan bcos* [Treatise on the Discrimination of the Three Vows, c. 1232]. In *Sa-skya-pa'i-bka'-'bum*, vol. 5. Tokyo, 1968. Pp. 297.1.1–320.4.5 (Na, ff. 1a–48b, 5).

DTM Tselpa Kunga Dorje (Tshal-pa Kun-dga' rDo-rje, 1309–1364). *Deb ther dmar po* [Religious History of Tibet written 1346–1363]. Beijing, 1981.

DTsM Karma Chöphel (Karma Chos-'phel). *Bdud rtsi sman gyi 'khrungs dpe legs bshad nor bu'i phreng mdzes* [Manual of Tibetan Medicinal Plants]. Lhasa, 1993.

GBJ Sonam Chogden (bSod-nams mChog-ldan). *Dpal ldan bla ma dam pa'i mdzad pa rmad du byung ba'i bcu'i tshul du gsal bar ston pa ngo mtshar bdud rtsi'i thig pa* [Biography of Gyelwang Kunga Penjor (1428–1476)]. In *bKa' brgyud gser 'phreṅ rgyas pa. The rDzoṅ-Khul Tradition*, vol. 2. Darjeeling, 1982. Ff.389–499.

GGL Gendün Chöphel (dGe-'dun Chos-'phel, 1903–1951). *Rgya gar gyi gnas chen khag la bgrod pa'i lam yig* [Guidebook for Travel to the Buddhist Holy Places of India, expanded version c. 1945]. In *Dge 'dun chos 'phel gyi gsung rtsom*, vol. 3 Compiled by Hor-khang bSod-nams dPal-'bar et al. Lhasa, 1990 (Gangs-can Rig-mdzod, 12). Pp. 311–51.

GJLY Kathog Situ Chöki Gyatso (Kaḥ-thog Si-tu Chos-kyi rGya-mtsho, 1880–1925). *Gangs ljongs dbus gtsang gnas skor lam yig nor bu zla shel gyi se mo do* [Account of a Pilgrimage around Central Tibet from 1918 to 1920]. Tashijong, 1972.

GRCh Tenzin Chöki Lodrö (bsTan-'dzin Chos-kyi Blo-gros, 1869–1906). *Gangs ri chen po ti se dang mtsho chen ma dros pa bcas kyi sngon byung gi lo rgyus mdor bsdus su brjod pa'i rab byed shel dkar me long* [Historical Account and Guidebook for the Holy Places of Mount Tise (Kailash) and Lake Mapam (Manasarovar), 1896]. In *Dpal 'khor lo sdom pa'i sku yi gnas gangs ri ti se dang gsung gi gnas la phyi gangs kyi ra gnyis kyi gnas yig*. Delhi, 1983. Ff. 25–246.

HKK Situ Panchen Chöki Chungné (Si-tu Pan-chen Chos-kyi 'Byung-gnas, 1699/1700–1774) and Belo Tsewang Kunkyab ('Be-lo Tshe-dbang Kun-khyab, b. 1718). *Bsgrub rgyud karma kam tshang brgyud pa rin po che'i rnam par thar pa rab 'byams nor bu zla ba chu shel gyi phreng ba* [History of the Karma Kagyüpa Sect of Tibetan Buddhism, 1775]. 2 vols. New Delhi, 1972.

KGT Pawo Tsuglag Drengwa (dPa'-bo gTsug-lag Phreng-ba, 1504–1566). *Dam pa'i chos kyi 'khor lo bsgyur ba rnams kyi byung ba gsal bar byed pa mkhas pa'i dga' ston* [History of Buddhism in Tibet and Surrounding Countries, written 1545–1564]. 2 vols. Beijing, 1986.

KZ I Kunzig Chöki Nangwa (Kun-gzigs Chos-kyi sNang-ba, 1768–1822). *Tsā ri tra ye shes kyi 'khor lo'i gnas kyi ngo mtshar cha shas tsam gsal bar brjod pa'i yi ge skal ldan dga' bskyed dad pa'i nyin byed 'char ba* [Detailed Guidebook to the Holy Place of Tsari (Early nineteenth Century)]. In *The Collected Works (gsuṅ 'bum) of H. H. the Eighth rGyal-dbaṅ 'Brug-chen of the Northern 'Brug-pa, Kun-gzigs-chos-kyi-snaṅ-ba* (1768–1822), vol. 4. Rewalsar, 1985. Pp. 15–73.

KZ II Kunzig Chöki Nangwa (Kun-gzigs Chos-kyi sNang-ba, 1768–1822). *Gnas chen tsā ri tra'i gnas yig nyung ngu tsam bkod pa'i gsal 'debs* [Concise Pilgrim's Guide to the Holy Place of Tsari (Early nineteenth Century)]. In *The Collected Works (gsuṅ 'bum) of H. H. the Eighth rGyal-dbaṅ 'Brug-chen of the Northern 'Brug-pa, Kun-gzigs-chos-kyi-snaṅ-ba* (1768–1822), vol. 2. Rewalsar, 1985. Pp. 169–94.

KZ III Kunzig Chöki Nangwa (Kun-gzigs Chos-kyi sNang-ba, 1768–1822). *Dam rdzas myong grol chen po 'ja' 'od ril bu'i dkar chag /ngo mtshar kun dga' bskyed pa'i bdud rtsi* [Manual of Ingredients for the Relic Pellets Called "Rainbow Light"]. In *The Collected Works (gSuṅ 'bum) of H. H. the*

Eighth rGyal-dbaṅ 'Brug-chen of the Northern 'Brug-pa, Kun-gzigs-chos-kyi-snaṅ-ba (1768–1822), vol. 4. Rewalsar, 1985. Ff. 141–48.

LHR Tatsag Tsewangyel (rTa-tshag Tshe-dbang-rgyal). *Dam pa'i chos kyi byung ba'i legs bshad lho rong chos 'byung ngam rta tshag chos 'byung zhes rtsom pa'i yul ming du chags pa'i ngo mtshar zhing dkon pa'i dpe khyad par can* [History of the Kagyüpa Lineage of Tibetan Buddhism, written 1446–1451]. Xining, 1994 (Gangs-can Rig-mdzod, 26).

LLN Lelung Jedrung Shepé Dorje (Sle-lung rJe-drung bZhad-pa'i rDo-rje, b. 1697). *Rig pa 'dzin pa blo bzang 'phrin las kyi rtogs pa brjod pa skal bzang dga' ston* [Biography of the Tibetan Incarnate Lama Lelung Shepé Dorje]. In *The Collected Works of Sle-lung rJe-drung bZhad-pa'i rDo-rje*, vol. 1. Leh, 1985.

LPhG Jigme Lingpa ('Jigs-med Gling-pa, 1728–1791). *Lho phyogs rgya gar gyi gtam brtag pa brgyad kyi me long* [Tibetan Account of India 1789]. In *The Collected Works of Kun-mkhyen 'Jigs-med Gling-pa*, vol. 4. Gangtok, 1972. Pp. 62–82.

MGB Tsang Nyön Heruka (gTsang-smyon He-ru-ka *alias* Rus-pa'i rGyan-can, 1452–1507). *Mi la'i mgur 'bum* [Collected Songs of the Tibetan Saint Mila Repa (1040–1123), 1488]. Gangtok, 1983.

MGY *Gling rje ge sar rgyal po'i rtogs brjod/mon gling g.yul 'gyed dri za'i rgyud mang* [Episode of the Gesar Epic, the Lord of Ling's Campaign Against the Rulers of Mon]. Chengdu, 1982.

MM Jampé Dorje ('Jam-dpal rDo-rje). *An Illustrated Tibeto-Mongolian Materia Medica of Ayurveda*. New Delhi, 1971.

NTshN Tsetrul Thubten Gyeltsen (rTse-sprul Thub-bstan rGyal-mtshan). "Gnam mtsho'i gnas bshad dad pa'i chu rgyun [Guidebook for the Holy Place of Lake Namtso]." *Bod ljongs nang bstan* 1/1991:10–27.

PD Pema Döndrup (Padma Don-grub, 1668–1744). *Bdag bya btang ras pa padma don grub kyi chos byas 'tshul dang thob 'tshul dang bka' ba spyad 'tshul rnams* [Autobiography of Pema Döndrup with Account of a Pilgrimage to Tsari (Early eighteenth Century)]. In *Autobiographies of Three Spiritual Masters of Kutang*. Thimphu, 1979. Ff. 1–143.

PDB *Dpal ldan 'brug pa'i rgyun gyi thugs dam rtsa gsum bstan srung dam can rgya mtsho'i mchod bstod gtor bsngos phrin bcol gyi rim pa yid bzhin nor bu dbang gi rgyal po'i phreng ba srid zhi'i dgra las rnam rgyal* [Manual of Rituals for Worship of the Protective Deities of the Drukpa Kagyü Sect]. Woodcut, 63 pp. N.d., n.p. 1979.

PK I Pema Karpo (Padma dKar-po, 1527–1592). *Gnas chen tsa ri tra'i ngo mtshar snang pad dkar legs bshad* [Guidebook to the Holy Place of Tsari, written c. 1570–1575]. In *Collected Works (gSuṅ-'bum) of Kun-mkhyen Padma-dkar-po*, vol. 4. Darjeeling, 1973. Ff. 207–74.

PK Ia Pema Karpo (Padma dKar-po, 1527–1592). *Gnas chen tsa ri tra'i ngo mtshar snang pad dkar legs bshad* [Guidebook to the Holy Place of Tsari, written c. 1570–1575]. Darjeeling, 1982.

PK II Pema Karpo (Padma dKar-po, 1527–1592). *Tsa ri tra zhes pa'i gnas la bstod pas pad dkar legs bshad* [Verse Eulogy to the Holy Place of Tsari]. In *Collected Works (gSuṅ-'bum) of Kun-mkhyen Padma-dkar-po*, vol. 9. Darjeeling, 1973. Ff. 532–35.

PK III *Sems dpa' chen po padma dkar po'i rnam thar thugs rje chen po'i zlo gar* [Biography of the Tibetan Scholar Pema Karpo (1527–1592)]. In *bKa' brgyud gser 'phreṅ rgyas pa: The rDzoṅ-khul Tradition*, vol. 3. Darjeeling, 1982. Ff. 367–616.

PK IV Pema Karpo (Padma dKar-po, 1527–1592). *'Gro ba'i mgon po gtsang pa rgya ras pa'i rnam par thar pa ngo mtshar ngang pa'i rlabs 'phreng* [Biography of the Tibetan Buddhist Saint Tsangpa Gyare (1161–1211)]. In *bKa' brgyud gser 'phreṅ rgyas pa: The rDzoṅ-khul Tradition*, vol. 2. Darjeeling, 1982. Ff. 193–329.

PK V Pema Karpo (Padma dKar-po, 1527–1592). *Chos 'byung bstan pa'i padma rgyas pa'i nyin byed* [Tibetan History of Buddhism, written 1575–1580] (*Tibetan Chronicle of Padma-dkar-po*). New Delhi, 1968 (Śata-Piṭaka Series 75).

PTY Orgyen Lingpa (O-rgyan Gling-pa, 1329–1367). *O rgyan gu ru padma 'byung gnas kyi skyes rabs rnam par thar pa rgyas par bkod pa padma bka' thang yig* ["Revealed Treasure" Biography of the Indian Buddhist Saint Padmasambhava, excavated 1352]. Rewalsar, 1985.

SBK *Gsung 'bum dkar chag* [Catalog of Collected Works of Authors from the Gelukpa Sect of Tibetan Buddhism]. Lhasa, 1990.

SLG Tenzin Chöki Lodrö (bs Tan-'dzin Chos-kyi Blo-gros, 1869–1906). *Gsang lam sgrub pa'i gnas chen nyer bzhi'i ya gyal gau dā wa ri 'am / 'brog la phyi gangs kyi ra ba'i sngon byung gi tshul las tsam pa'i gtam gyi rab tu phyed pa nyung ngu rnam gsal* [Historical Account and Guidebook for the Holy Place of Labchi, 1901]. In *Dpal 'khor lo sdom pa'i sku yi gnas gangs ri ti se dang gsung gi gnas la phyi gangs ra gnyis kyi gnas yig*. Delhi, 1983. Ff. 261–402.

SMB Kyungkar Menri Lobpön Tenzin Namdak (Khyung-dkar sMan-ri Slob-dpon bsTan-'dzin rNam-dag). *Bod yul gnas kyi lam yig gsal ba'i dmigs bu* [Modern Pilgrimage Guidebook to Bön Holy Places in Tibet]. Dolanji, 1983.

TGN Gyumed Dechen ('Gyur-med bDe-chen, b. 1540). *Dpal grub pa'i dbang phyug brtson 'grus bzang po'i rnam par thar pa kun gsal nor bu'i me long* [Biography of the Tibetan Buddhist Saint Thangtong Gyelpo (b. 1385)]. Beijing, 1982.

TKNY Tenzin Zangpo (bsTan-'dzin bZang-po). *Tsa ri tra ye shes kyi 'khor lo'i lta ba mtsho dkar sprul pa'i pho brang gi gnas yig gsal ba'i sgron me* [Modern Pilgrimage Guidebook for Tsari Tsokar]. In *Bod kyi gnas yig bdams bsgrigs*, edited by Tshe-ring dPal-'byor. Xining, 1995 (Gangs-can Rig-mdzod, 8). Pp. 63–134.

TsLY I Namchak Tsasum Lingpa (gNam-lcags rTsa-gsum Gling-pa). *Yon tan rtsa ri'i lam yig gsal ba'i sgron me'i mthong ba don ldan 'dzam gling gyas bzhag du grags pa* ["Revealed Treasure" Guidebook to Tsari (Mid–eighteenth Century)]. In *gNam lcags rtsa gsum gling pa'i zab gter*. N.p. 1989. Vol. 9 (Ta). Ff. 281–306.

TsLY II Daö Nyingpo (Zla-'od sNying-po). *Khyon dag pa ye she kyi 'khor lo tsa ri tra'i lam yig indra ni la'i do shal* [Account of a Pilgrimage to Tsari (Late eighteenth Century?)]. Cursive MS, 28ff. Nepal-German Manuscript Preservation Project Collection, Kathmandu, microfilm reel no. 18/10, running no.L204.

TsMDz *Gling ge sar rgyal po'i sgrung / tsa ri sman rdzongs* [Episode of the Gesar Epic, the "Tsari Medicinal Herb Dispatch"]. Xining, 1990.

TsMN Götsang Repa Natsog Rangdröl (rGod-tshang Ras-pa sNa-tshogs Rang-grol, 1494–1570). *Gtsaṅ smyon he ru ka phyogs thams cad las rnam par rgyal ba'i rnam thar rdo rje theg pa'i gsal byed nyi ma'i snying po* [Biography of the Tibetan Buddhist Saint Tsang Nyön Heruka (1452–1507), written 1547]. In *The Life of the Saint of gTsaṅ*. New Delhi, 1969.

TsNgJ Jamgön Kongtrul Lodrö Thayé ('Jam-mgon Kong-sprul Blo-gros mTha'-yas, 1813–1899). *Dpal gyi tsā ri tra'i bsngags brjod mdor bsdus dpyid kyi pho nya'i mgrin dbyans* [Verse Eulogy to Tsari (Late nineteenth Century)]. In *Rgya-chen bKa'-mdzod. A Collection of Writings of 'Jam-mgon Koṅ-sprul Blo-gros-mtha'-yas*, vol. 11. Paro, 1975. Ff. 461–66.

TsNY I Khachö Wangpo (mKha'-spyod dBang-po, 1350–1405). *Tsa ri tra byin legs kyi gnas yig* [Visionary Guidebook to Tsari (Late fourteenth Century)]. In *The Collected Writings (Gsung-'bum) of the Second Zhwa-dmar mKha'-spyod-dbaṅ-po*, vol. 4. Gangtok, 1978. Ff. 83–100.

TsNY II Chogra Chöki Senge (Cog-grwa Chos-kyi Seng-ge). "Gnas mchog tsa ri tra'i gnas yig shel dkar me long [Guidebook to the Holy Place of Tsari]." *Bod ljongs nang bstan* 1/1992: 6–48.

TsNY III Lobpön Sonam Sangpo (Slob-dpon bSod-nams bZang-po). *Rtsa ri gnas yig* [Oral Guide to the Holy Place of Tsari]. Cursive MS, 5 pp. Recorded by Tsering Dorje. Oral History Archives, Library of Tibetan Works and Archives, Dharamsala, c. 1982.

TsSD I Yümé Chagchen Pema Tenzin (Yul-smad Phyag-chen Padma bs Tan-'dzin). "Tsa ri'i gsol 'debs bro mo che ["The Great Oath" Prayer to the Holy Place of Tsari]." *Bod ljongs nang bstan* 1/1992: 1–3.

TsSD II *Gnas chen tsā ri tra'i gsol 'debs* [Prayer to the Holy Place of Tsari]. Privately printed pamphlet of oral traditions, 9 pp. Recorded by Drigung Khenpo Könchog Gyaltsen, India, c. 1975.

TsSD III *Rtsa ri'i gsol 'debs* [Prayer to the Holy Place of Tsari (pre-1904 origin)]. In *Gnas yig bzhugso*. Manuscript Wadd 99 (1–6), Collection Staatsbibliothek zu Berlin. Ff. 14a, l.3–17a.

TTT Tsari Tsulpa Trashila (rTsa-ri Tshul-pa bKra-shis-lags). *Gnas chen rtsa ri bskor ba dang bskor lugs klo rdzong gnang lugs sogs kreb 'khor sgra bcug gnang ba phebs rgyur zhus pa gsham gsal* [Oral Account of Tsari, Its Pilgrimage Traditions, and the Lopa Tribute Ceremony]. Cursive MS, 41 pp. Recorded for Oral History Archives, Library of Tibetan Works and Archives, Dharamsala, 1987.

YNyZh Drigung Kyabgön Chetsang Rinpoché ('Bri-gung sKyabs-mgon Che-tshang Rin-po-che, b. 1946). *Yul nyer bzhi'i gnas mchog gangs dkar ti se'i gsol 'debs byin rlabs kyi chu rgyun* [Prayer and Explanation of Pilgrimage to Mount Tise (Kailash) and Tibetan Néri Mountains]. Printed MS, 4ff. India, 1990.

YTN Jamyang Gyeltsen ('Jam-dbyangs rGyal-mtshan). *Khyab bdag rdo rje 'chang ngag dbang yon tan mtha' yas kyi gsang gsum mi zad rgyan gyi 'khor lor rnam par rol ba'i rtogs pa brjod pa skal bzang mos pa'i pad mo rgyas byed ye shes 'od stong 'phro ba'i nyi ma* [Biography of Yönten Thayé (1724–1784), Thirteenth Head Abbot of Bhutan]. In *Collected Works of Yon-tan mTha'-yas*, vol. 1. Dodeda, 1975. Text ā, ff. 1–136.

ZhKGT *Zhing skyong chen po kun dga' gzhon nu'i mchod pa'i cho ga dpa' bo rnam par rol pa'i dga' ston*. Woodcut, 18ff. Printed at Rumthek Monastery, Sikkim, 1972.

ZhKKS Tsewang Norbu (Tshe-dbang nor-bu). *Tsa ri zhing skyong gyis bskang so sdus pa* [Worship Ritual for the Protective Deity of Tsari]. Cursive MS, 3ff. Tsari Domtsang Rong. Nepal-German Manuscript Preservation Project Collection, Kathmandu, microfilm reel no. E1831/11.

ZhKN Shabkawa Tsogdruk Rangdröl (Zhabs-dkar-ba Tshogs-drug Rang-grol, 1781–1851). *Snyigs dus 'gro ba yongs kyi skyabs mgon zhabs dkar rdo rje 'chang chen po'i rnam par thar pa rgyas par bshad pa skal bzang gdul bya thar 'dod rnams kyi re ba skong ba'i yid bzhin gyi nor bu bsam 'phel dbang gi rgyal po*, stod-cha [Autobiography of the Tibetan Yogin Shabkar, part 1, written 1837]. Xining, 1985.

European Language Sources

Allen, C. 1982. *A Mountain in Tibet. In Search for Mount Kailas and the Sources of the Great Rivers of India*. London, André Deutsch.

Allen, N. 1984. "The Thulung Myth of the Bhume Sites and some Indo-Tibetan Comparisons." In *Asian Highland Societies in Anthropological Perspective*, edited by C. von Fürer-Haimendorf. Delhi, Sterling. Pp. 168–82.

Allione, T. 1986. *Women of Wisdom*. London, Arkana.

Anon. 1986a. "His Holiness the Dalai Lama visits Ladakh." *Chö-yang: The Voice of Tibetan Religion and Culture* 1, 1: 73–75.

———. 1986b. "News Report: The Buddhist Event of the Century." *Tibetan Review* (January): 4–6.

Aris, M. 1976. " 'The Admonition of the Thunderbolt Cannon-ball' and Its Place in the Bhutanese New Year Festival." *Bulletin of the School of Oriental and African Studies* 39, 3: 601–35.

———. 1979. *Bhutan. The Early History of a Himalayan Kingdom*. Warminster, Aris & Phillips.

———. 1980a. "Notes on the History of the Mon-yul Corridor." In Aris and Aung San Suu Kyi 1980: 9–20.

———. 1980b. "Sacred Dances of Bhutan." *Natural History* 89 (March): 38–47.

———. 1986. *Sources for the History of Bhutan*. Wien, Arbeitskreis für Tibetische und Buddhistische Studien Universität Wien (Wiener Studien zur Tibetologie und Buddhismuskunde, 14).

———. 1988. *Hidden Treasures and Secret Lives*. Delhi, Motilal Banarsidass.

———. 1990. "Man and Nature in the Buddhist Himalayas." In *Himalayan Environment and Culture*, edited by N. K. Rustomji and C. Ramble. New Delhi, Indus. Pp. 85–101.

Aris, M., and Aung San Suu Kyi, eds. 1980. *Tibetan Studies in Honour of Hugh Richardson*. Warminster, Aris & Phillips.

Asboe, W. 1936. "Sacrifices in Western Tibet." *Man* 36: 75–6.

Aziz, B. N. 1974. "Some Notions about Descent and Residence in Tibetan Society." In *Contributions to the Anthropology of Nepal*, edited by C. von Fürer-Haimendorf. Warminster, Aris & Phillips. Pp. 23–39.

———. 1975. "Vitality at the Interface: Anthropological Explorations in the Eastern Himalayas." In *National Geographic Society, Research Reports—1975 Projects*. Washington, D.C., National Geographic Society. Pp. 67–83.

———. 1975. "Tibetan Manuscript Maps of Dingri Valley." *Canadian Cartographer* 20, 1: 28–38.

———. 1978a. *Tibetan Frontier Families*. New Delhi, Vikas.

———. 1978b. "Maps and the Mind." *Human Nature* 1, 8: 50–59.

———. 1987. "Personal Dimensions of the Sacred Journey: What Pilgrims Say." *Religious Studies* 23, 2: 247–61.

———. 1988. "Women in Tibetan Society and Tibetology." In Uebach and Panglung 1988: 25–34.

———. 1989. "Moving Towards a Sociology of Tibet." In *Feminine Ground: Essays on Women and Tibet*, edited by J. D. Willis. Ithaca, N.Y., Snow Lion. Pp. 76–95.

Aziz, B. N., and M. Kapstein, eds. 1985. *Soundings in Tibetan Civilization*. Delhi, Manohar.

Back, D. M. 1985. "Zu Einem Gedicht des VI. Dalai Lama." *Zeitschrift der Deutschen Morgenländischen Gesellschaft* 135, 2: 319–29.

Bacot, J., 1909. *Pèlerinage du Dokerla (Tibet Sud-oriental)*. Paris, Leroux.

Bailey, F. M. 1914a. *Report on an Exploration of the North-East Frontier, 1913*. Simla, Government Monotype Press.

———. 1914b. "Exploration of the Tsangpo or Upper Bramaputra." *Geographical Journal* 44, 4: 341–64.

———. 1945. *China–Tibet–Assam: A Journey, 1911*. London, Jonathan Cape.

———. 1957. *No Passport to Tibet*. London, Travel Book Club.

Bastien, J. W. 1978. *Mountain of the Condor: Metaphor and Ritual in an Andean Ayllu*. St. Paul, Minn., West.

Bauman, Z. 1992. *Mortality, Immortality and Other Life Strategies*. Cambridge, Polity Press.

Bäumer, B. 1991. "From Guhā to Ākāśa: The Mystical Cave in the Vedic and Śaiva Traditions." In *Concepts of Space Ancient and Modern*, edited by K. Vatsyayan. New Delhi, Abhinav. Pp. 105–22.

Beckwith, C. I. 1987. "The Tibetans in the Ordos and North China: Considerations on the Role of the Tibetan Empire in World History." In *Silver on Lapis: Tibetan Literary Culture and History*, edited by C. I. Beckwith. Bloomington, the Tibet Society. Pp. 3–11.

Bell, C. 1992. *Ritual Theory, Ritual Practice*. New York, Oxford University Press.

Bell, C. A. 1924. *Tibet, Past and Present*. Oxford, Clarendon Press.

Berg, E. 1994. "Journeys to the Holy Centre: The Study of Pilgrimage in Recent Himalayan Research." *European Bulletin of Himalayan Research* 6: 3–19.

Berglie, P-A. 1980. "Mount Targo and Lake Dangra: A Contribution to the Religious Geography of Tibet." In Aris and Aung San Suu Kyi 1980: 39–44.

Bernbaum, E. 1980. *The Way to Shambhala*. New York, Anchor Books.

———. 1987. "Tibetan Pilgrimage." In *The Encyclopedia of Religion*, edited by M. Eliade, vol. 11. New York, Macmillan. Pp. 351–53.

Betts, U. [Graham Bower]. 1949. "The Daflas of the Subansiri Area." *Journal of the Royal Central Asian Society* 36: 146–54.

Beyer, S. 1973. *The Cult of Tārā: Magic and Ritual in Tibet*. Berkeley, University of California Press.

Birnbaum, R. 1984. "Thoughts on Buddhist Mountain Traditions and Their Context." *Tang Studies* 2: 5–23.

Blondeau, A-M. and S. G. Karmay. 1988. " 'Le cerf à la vaste ramure': en guise d'introduction." *Essais sur la Rituel*. Vol. 1. Louvain-Paris, Peeters. Pp. 119–146.

———. 1990. "Questions préliminaires sur les rituels *mdos*." In *Tibet Civilisation et Société*. Paris, Éditions de la Fondation Singer-Polignac. Pp. 91–107.

Blondeau, A-M., and E. Steinkellner, eds. 1996. *Reflections on the Mountain: Essays on the History and Social Meaning of the Mountain Cult in Tibet and the Himalaya*. Wien, Verlag der Österreichischen Akademie der Wissenschaften.

Bourdieu, P. 1977. *Outline of a Theory of Practice*. Cambridge, Cambridge University Press.

Bower, H. 1976. *Diary of a Journey Across Tibet*. Kathmandu, Ratna Pustak.

Brauen-Dolma, M. 1985. "Millenarianism in Tibetan Religion." In Aziz and Kapstein 1985: 245–56.

Buffetrille, K. 1993. "Preliminary Remarks on a Sherpa Pilgrimage: The Pilgrimage to the Milk Lake in the District of Solu (Nepal)." In *The Anthropology of Nepal: From Tradition to Modernity*, edited by G. Toffin. Kathmandu, Centre culturel Français. Pp. 97–111.

———. 1994a. *The Halase-Maratika Caves (Eastern Nepal), A Sacred Place Claimed by Both Hindus and Buddhists*. Pondichéry, Institut Français de Pondichéry (Pondy Papers in Social Sciences, 16).

———. 1994b. "Révitalisation d'un lieu-saint bouddhique: les grottes de Halase-Maratika, Népal oriental (District de Khotang)." In Kværne 1994, 1: 81–94.

———. 1994c. "A Bonpo Pilgrimage Guide to Amnye Machen Mountain." *Lungta* 8: 20–24.

———. 1996. "Montagnes sacrées, lacs et grottes. Lieux de pélerinage dans le monde tibétain: traditions écrites, réalités vivantes." Doctoral dissertation, Université de Paris X, Nanterre.

———. 1997. "The Great Pilgrimage of A-myes rma-chen: Written Tradition, Living Realities." In Macdonald 1997: 75–132.

Burrard, S. G. (Supervisor). 1915. *Records of the Survey of India*. Vol. 8, pts. 1 and 2. *Exploration of Tibet and Neighbouring Regions, 1879–1892*. Dehra Dun, India, Office of the Trigonometrical Survey.

Carrasco, P. 1959. *Land and Polity in Tibet*. Seattle, University of Washington Press.

Cassinelli, C. W., and R. B. Ekvall. 1969. *A Tibetan Principality: The Political System of Sa sKya*. Ithaca, N.Y., Cornell University Press.

Cech, K. 1992. "A Religious Geography of Tibet According to the Bon Tradition." In Ihara and Yamaguchi 1992, 2: 387–92.

———. 1993. "The Social and Religious Identity of the Tibetan Bonpos." In *Anthropology of Tibet and the Himalaya*, edited by C. Ramble and M. Brauen. Zürich, Völkerkundemuseum der Universität Zürich. Pp. 39–48.

Chandra, L. 1987. Preface to Kazi Dawa Samdup. *Śrī-cakraśaṁvara-tantra. A Buddhist Tantra*. New Delhi, Aditya Prakashan. Pp. 7–34.

Chophel, N. 1983. *Folk Culture of Tibet*. Dharamsala, Library of Tibetan Works and Archives.

Chowdhury, J. N. 1991. "Pattern of Religion among Arunachal Tribes with Special Reference to the Adis." In *Religion and Society in the Himalayas*, edited by T. B. Subba and K. Datta. New Delhi, Gian. Pp. 116–34.

Clarke, G. E. 1991. "Nara (*na-rag*) in Yolmo: A Social History of Hell in Helembu." In *Tibetan History and Language. Studies Dedicated to Uray Géza on his Seventieth Birthday*, edited by E. Steinkellner. Wien, Arbeitskreis für Tibetische und Buddhistische Studien Universität Wien. (Wiener Studien zur Tibetologie und Buddhismuskunde, 26). Pp. 43–62.

Cohn, B. S. 1990. *An Anthropologist among the Historians and Other Essays*. Delhi, Oxford University Press.

Combe, G. A. 1926. *A Tibetan on Tibet*. London, T. Fisher Unwin.

Crook, J. 1994. "The Yogins of Ladakh." In *Himalayan Buddhist Studies. Environment, Resources, Society and Religious Life in Zangskar, Ladakh*, edited by J. Crook and H. Osmaston. Bristol, University of Bristol. Pp. 665–97.

Dalton, E. T. 1872. *Descriptive Ethnology of Bengal*. Calcutta, Office of the Superintendent of Government Printing.

Daniel, E. V. 1984. *Fluid Signs: Being a Person the Tamil Way*. Berkeley, University of California Press.

Das, S. C. 1902. *A Tibetan-English Dictionary*. Calcutta, Bengal Secretariat Book Depot.

———. 1970. *Journey to Lhasa and Central Tibet*. New Delhi (reprint edition), Manjusri.

———. 1972. *An Introduction to the Grammar of the Tibetan Language*. Delhi (reprint edition), Motilal Banarsidass.

David-Neel, A. 1965. *Magic and Mystery in Tibet*. New York, University Books (reprint edition).

———. 1988. *Tibetan Tale of Love and Magic*. Calcutta, Rupa (reprint edition).

Davidson, R. M. 1991. "Reflections on the Maheśvara Subjugation Myth: Indic Materials, Saskya-pa Apologetics, and the Birth of Heruka." *Journal of the International Association of Buddhist Studies* 14, 2: 197–235.

De Rossi Filibeck, E. 1988. "The Biography of Thar-pa'i rGyal-mchan." In Uebach and Panglung 1988: 95–98.

———. 1990. "A Guide-Book to Tsa-ri." In *Reflections on Tibetan Culture: Essays in Memory of Turrell V. Wylie*, edited by L. Epstein and R. F. Sherburne. Lewiston, N.Y., Edwin Mellon Press. Pp. 1–10.

Demiéville, P. 1973. "Le T'ai-chan ou Montagne du suicide." *Choix d'etudes sinologiques*. Leiden, E. J. Brill. Pp. 1–7.

Denma Locho Rinpochey. 1994. "My Life in the Land of Snows," *Chö-yang: The Voice of Tibetan Religion and Culture* 6: 84–104.

Diemberger, H. 1991. "Lhakama [*lha-bka'-ma*] and Khandroma [*mkha'-'gro-ma*]: The Sacred Ladies of the Beyul Khenbalung [*sbas-yul mKhan-pa-lung*]." In *Tibetan History and Language: Studies Dedicated to Uray Géza on his Seventieth Birthday*, edited by E. Steinkellner. Wien, Arbeitskreis für Tibetische und Buddhistische Studien Universität Wien. (Wiener Studien zur Tibetologie und Buddhismuskunde, 26). Pp. 137–53.

———. 1993. "Gangla Tshechu, Beyul Khenbalung: Pilgrimage to Hidden Valleys, Sacred Mountains and Springs of Life Water in Southern Tibet and Eastern Nepal." In *Anthropology of Tibet and the Himalaya*, edited by C. Ramble and M. Brauen. Zürich, Völkerkundemuseum der Universität Zürich. Pp. 60–72.

———. 1994. "Mountain-deities, Ancestral Bones and Sacred Weapons: Sacred Territory and Communal Identity in Eastern Nepal and Southern Tibet." In Kværne 1994. Vol. 1. Pp. 144–153.

Diemberger, H., and G. Hazod. 1994. "Traces of Ancient History and Myth in the South .Tibetan Landscape of Kharta and Phadrug." *Tibet Journal*. Special Issue: *Powerful Places and Spaces in Tibetan Religious Culture* 19,4: 23–45.

Doniger, W. 1991. *The Laws of Manu*. Harmondsworth, Penguin.

Dorje Tseten. 1992. "Sacred Sites of Tibet." *Chö-yang: The Voice of Tibetan Religion and Culture* 5: 2–9.

———. 1994. "Looking into the Future." *Chö-yang: The Voice of Tibetan Religion and Culture* 6: 111–118.

Dowman, K. 1980. *The Divine Madman: The Sublime Life and Songs of Drukpa Kunley*. Clearlake, Calif., Dawn Horse Press.

———. 1981. "A Buddhist Guide to the Power Places of the Kathmandu Valley." *Kailash: A Journal of Himalayan Studies*, 8, 3–4: 183–291.

———. 1984. *Sky Dancer*. London, Routledge and Kegan Paul.

———. 1985. *Masters of Mahāmudrā*. Albany, SUNY Press.

———. 1988. *The Power Places of Central Tibet: The Pilgrim's Guide*. London, Routledge and Kegan Paul.

Dudjom Rinpoche, Jikdrel Yeshe Dorje. 1991. *The Nyingma School of Tibetan Buddhism: Its Fundamentals and History*. Translated and edited by Gyurme Dorje and M. Kapstein. 2 vols. Boston, Wisdom.

Duff-Sutherland-Dunbar, G. 1915. *Abors and Galongs: Notes on Certain Hill Tribes of the Indo-Tibetan Border*. Calcutta, Asiatic Society (Memoirs of the Asiatic Society of Bengal, 5).

Duncan, M. H. 1961. *Love Songs and Proverbs of Tibet*. London, Mitre Press.

———. 1964. *Customs and Superstitions of the Tibetans*. London, Mitre Press.

Eade, J., & M. J. Sallnow. 1991. *Contesting the Sacred: The Anthropology of Christian Pilgrimage*. London, Routledge.

Ehrhard, F-K. 1994. "The Role of 'Treasure Discoverers' and Their Writings in the Search for Himalayan Sacred lands." *Tibet Journal*. Special Edition: *Powerful Places and Spaces in Tibetan Religious Culture* 19,3:3–20.

Ekvall, R. B. 1964. *Religious Observances in Tibet: Patterns and Function*. Chicago, University of Chicago Press.

———. 1968. *Fields on the Hoof: Nexus of Tibetan Nomadic Pastoralism*. New York, Holt, Rinehart & Winston.

Ekvall, R. B., and J. F. Downs. 1987. *Tibetan Pilgrimage*. Tokyo, Institute for the Study of Languages and Cultures of Asia and Africa.

Elwin, V. 1956. "The People of NEFA-II: In Subansiri." *Illustrated Weekly of India* 7,7 (October).

———. 1959. *India's North-East Frontier in the Nineteenth Century*. Oxford, Oxford University Press.

Epstein, L., and Peng Wenbin. 1994. "Ganja and Murdo: The Social Construction of Space at Two Tibetan Pilgrimage Sites in Eastern Tibet." *Tibet Journal*. Special Edition: *Powerful Places and Spaces in Tibetan Religious Culture* 19,2: 21–45.

Essen, G-W., and T. T. Tingo. 1989. *Die Götter des Himalaya. Buddhistische Kunst Tibets*. München, Prestel-Verlag.

Evans-Wentz, W. Y. 1935. *Tibetan Yoga and Secret Doctrines*. Oxford, Oxford University Press.

Ferrari, A. 1958. *mK'yen-brtse's Guide to the Holy Places of Central Tibet*. Roma, Istituto Italiano per il Medio ed Estremo Oriente (Serie Orientale Roma, 16).

Filippi, F. de, ed. 1971. *An Account of Tibet*. Taipei (reprint edition), Ch'eng Wen.

Fletcher, H. R. 1975. *A Quest of Flowers*. Edinburgh, Edinburgh University Press.

Ford, R. 1957. *Captured in Tibet*. London, George G. Harrap.

Foucault, M. 1979. *Discipline and Punish: The Birth of the Prison*. New York, Vintage Books.

———. 1980. *Power/Knowledge: Selected Interviews and Other Writings, 1972–1977*. Brighton, Eng., Harvester Press.

Fourteenth Dalai Lama. 1990a. *Freedom in Exile*. London, Harper Collins.

———. 1990b. *My Tibet*. Berkeley, University of California Press.

Fuchs, S. 1973. *The Aboriginal Tribes of India*. New York, St. Martin's Press.

Fürer-Haimendorf, C. von. 1948. "The Tribes of the Subansiri Region." *Journal of the Royal Central Asian Society* 35: 238–48.

———. 1955. *Himalayan Barbary*. London, John Murray.

———. 1962. *The Apa Tanis and Their Neighbours: A Primitive Civilization of the Eastern Himalayas*. London, Routledge & Kegan Paul.

———. 1967. *Morals and Merit. A Study of Values and Social Controls in South Asian Societies*. London, Weidenfeld & Nicolson.

———. 1982. *Highlanders of Arunachal Pradesh: Anthropological Research in North-East India*. Delhi, Vikas.

———. 1990. *Life among Indian Tribes: The Autobiography of an Anthropologist*. Delhi, Oxford University Press.

Gait, E. 1905. *A History of Assam*. 3rd rev. ed. Calcutta, Thacker, Spink.

Geshe Kelsang Gyatso. 1982. *Clear Light of Bliss: Mahamudra in Vajrayana Buddhism*. London, Wisdom.

Giddens, A. 1990. *The Consequences of Modernity*. Stanford, Stanford University Press.

Gilmour, J. 1883. *Among the Mongols*. New York, American Tract Society.

Gold, P. *Tibetan Pilgrimage*. Ithaca, N.Y., Snow Lion, 1988.

Goldstein, M. C. 1971a. "Taxation and the Structure of a Tibetan Village." *Central Asiatic Journal* 15, 1: 1–27.

———. 1971b. "Serfdom and Mobility: An Examination of the Institution of 'Human Lease' in Traditional Tibetan Society." *Journal of Asian Studies* 30, 3: 521–34.

Goldstein, M. C. 1973, "The Circulation of Estates in Tibet: Reincarnation, Land and Politics." *Journal of Asian Studies* 32, 3: 445–55.

———. 1989. *A History of Modern Tibet, 1913–1951: The Demise of the Lamaist State*. Berkeley, University of California Press.

———. 1994. "Change, Conflict and Continuity among a Community of Nomadic Pastoralists: A Case Study from Western Tibet, 1950–1990." In *Resistance and Reform in Tibet*, edited by R. Barnett and S. Akiner. London, Hurst. Pp. 76–111.

Gombo, U. 1985. "Belief in Karma and Its Social Ramifications in Saṁsāra." In Aziz and Kapstein 1985: 233–44

Gorer, G. 1984. *Himalayan Village: An Account of the Lepcha of Sikkim*. Gloucester, Eng. (reprint edition), Alan Sutton.

Graham Bower, U. [Betts]. 1953. *The Hidden Land*. London, John Murray.

Grapard, A. G. 1982. "Flying Mountains and Walkers of Emptiness: Towards a Definition of Sacred Space in Japanese Religions." *History of Religions* 21, 3: 195–221.

Gutschow, N. 1982. *Stadraum und Ritual der newarischen Städte in Kathmandu-Tal: Eine architecturanthropologische Untersuchung*. Stuttgart, Kohlhammer.

Gyatso, J. 1986. "Thang-stong rGyal-po, Father of the Tibetan Drama Tradition: The Bodhisattva as Artist." In *Zlos-gar*, edited by J. Norbu. Dharamsala, Library of Tibetan Works and Archives. Pp. 91–104.

———. 1989. "Down with the Demoness: Reflections on a Feminine Ground in Tibet." In *Feminine Ground. Essays on Women and Tibet*, edited by J. D. Willis. Ithaca, N.Y., Snow Lion. Pp. 33–51.

Hanbury-Tracy, J. 1938. *Black River of Tibet*. London, Frederick Muller.

Hanna, S. 1994. "Vast as the Sky: The Terma Tradition in Modern Tibet." In *Tantra and Popular Religion in Tibet*, edited by G. Samuel, H. Gregor, and E. Stutchbury. New Delhi, Aditya Prakashan. Pp. 1–13.

Hedin, S. 1909. *Trans-Himalaya*. Vol. 2. London, Macmillan.

Henderson, D. F. 1964. "Settlement of Homicide Disputes in Sakya (Tibet)." *American Anthropologist* 66, 5: 1099–1105.

Herrmann-Pfandt, A. 1992. *Ḍākinīs: Zur Stellung und Symbolik des Weiblichen im tantrischen Buddhismus*. Bonn, Indica et Tibetica Verlag.

Huber, T. 1990. "Where Exactly Are Cāritra, Devikoṭa and Himavat? A Sacred Geography Controversy and the Development of Tantric Buddhist Pilgrimage Sites in Tibet." *Kailash: A Journal of Himalayan Studies* 16, 3–4: 121–65.

———. 1991. "Traditional Environmental Protectionism in Tibet Reconsidered." *Tibet Journal* 16, 3: 63–77.

———. 1992. "A Tibetan Map of lHo-kha in the South-Eastern Himalayan Borderlands of Tibet." *Imago Mundi* 44: 1–15.

———. 1994a. "When What You See Is Not What You Get: Remarks on the Traditional Tibetan Presentation of Sacred Geography." In *Tantra and Popular Religion in Tibet*, edited by G. Samuel, H. Gregor, and E. Stutchbury. New Delhi, Aditya Prakashan. Pp. 39–52.

———. 1994b. "Why Can't Women Climb Pure Crystal Mountain? Remarks on Gender, Ritual and Space in Tibet." In Kværne 1994, 1: 350–371.

———. 1994c. "Putting the *gnas* back into *gnas-skor*: Rethinking Tibetan Buddhist Pilgrimage Practice." *Tibet Journal*. Special Edition: *Powerful Places and Spaces in Tibetan Religious Culture*. 19, 2: 23–60.

———. 1997. "A Guide to the La-phyi Mandala: History, Landscape and Ritual in South-Western Tibet." In Macdonald 1997: 233–86.

Huber, T., and Tsepak Rigzin. 1995. "A Tibetan Guide for Pilgrimage to Ti-se (Mount Kailash) and mTsho Ma-pham (Lake Manasarovar)." *Tibet Journal*. Special Edition: *Powerful Places and Spaces in Tibetan Religious Culture* 20, 1: 9–46.

Hummel, S. 1971. "The Motif of the Crystal Mountain in the Tibetan Gesar Epic." *History of Religions* 10, 3: 204–10.

Ihara, S., and Z. Yamaguchi, eds. 1992. *Tibetan Studies. Proceedings of the 5th Seminar of the International Association for Tibetan Studies, Narita, 1989*. 2 vols. Narita, Naritasan Shinshoji.

Inden, R. B. 1978. "Ritual, Authority, and Cyclic Time in Hindu Kingship." In *Kingship and Authority in South Asia*, edited by J. F. Richards. Madison, University of Wisconsin Press. Pp. 28–73.

———. 1990. *Imagining India*. Oxford, Basil Blackwell.

Inden, R. B., and R. W. Nicholas. 1977. *Kinship in Bengali Culture*. Chicago, University of Chicago Press.

Ishihama, Y. 1993. "On the Dissemination of the Belief in the Dalai Lama as a Manifestation of the Bodhisattva Avalokiteśvara." *Acta Asiatica* 64: 38–56.

Iyanaga Nobumi. 1985. "Récits de la soumission de Maheśvara par Trailokyavijaya—d'après les sources chinoises et japonaises." In *Tantric and Taoist Studies in Honour of R. A. Stein*, vol. 3, edited by M. Strickmann. Bruxelles, Institut belge des hautes etudes chinoises (Mélanges chinois et bouddhiques, 22). Pp. 633–745.

Jäschke, H. A. 1881. *A Tibetan-English Dictionary with Special Reference to the Prevailing Dialects*. London, Routledge & Kegan Paul.

Jest, C. 1975. *Dolpo. Communautés de langue tibétaine du Népal*. Paris, Editions du Centre National de la Recherche Scientifique.

———. 1985. *La turquoise de vie: un pèlerinage tibétain*. Paris, Métailié.

Johnson, R., and K. Moran. 1989. *The Sacred Mountain of Tibet: On Pilgrimage to Kailas*. Rochester, N.Y., Park Street Press.

Kapstein, M. 1997. "The Guide to the Crystal Peak." In *Religions of Tibet in Practice*, edited by D. S. Lopez, Jr., Princeton, Princeton University Press. Pp. 103–119.

Karma Lekshe Tsomo. 1989. "Tibetan Nuns and Nunneries." In *Feminine Ground: Essays on Women and Tibet*, edited by J. D. Willis. Ithaca, N.Y. Snow Lion. Pp. 118–34.

Karmay, S. G. 1975. "A General Introduction to the History and Doctrines of Bon." *Memoirs of the Research Department of the Toyo Bunko*, 33:171–218.

———. 1980. "The Ordinance of lHa Bla-ma Ye-shes-'od." In Aris and Aung San Suu Kyi 1980: 150–62.

———. 1986. "L'apparition du petit homme tête-noire (Creation et procreation des Tibétains selon un mythe indigène)." *Journal Asiatique* 274: 79–138.

———. 1987. "L'âme et la turquoise: un rituel tibétain." *Rituels himalayens*. (Numéro spécial de:) *l'Ethnographie* 100–101: 97–130.

———. 1988. *Secret Visions of the Fifth Dalai Lama.* London, Serindia.

———. 1991. "L'homme et le boeuf: le rituel de *glud* (*'rançon'*." *Journal Asiatique* 279: 327–81.

———. 1992. "A Pilgrimage to Kongpo Bon-ri." In Ihara and Yamaguchi 1992, 2: 527–39.

———. 1994a. "Mountain Cults and National Identity in Tibet." In *Resistance and Reform in Tibet*, edited by R. Barnett and S. Akiner. London, Hurst. Pp. 112–120.

———. 1994b. "The Origin Myths of the First King of Tibet as Revealed in the *Can-lnga*." In Kværne 1994, 1: 408–29.

———. 1995. "Les dieux des terroirs et les genévriers: un rituel tibétain de purification." *Journal Asiatique*, 283, 161–207.

———. 1996. "The Tibetan Cult of Mountain Deities and Its Political Significance." In Blondeau and Steinkellner: 59–75.

Karsten, J. 1983. "A note on the *ya sor* and the secular festivals following the *smon lam chen mo*." In *Contributions on Tibetan Language, History and Culture.* vol. 1, edited by E. Steinkellner and H. Tauscher. Wien, Arbeitskreis für Tibetische und Buddhistische Studien Universität Wien. Pp. 117–149.

Kaschewsky, R. 1971. *Das Leben des lamaistischen Heiligen Tsongkhapa Blo-bzaṅ-grags-pa* (1357–1419). 1. Teil. Wiesbaden, Harrassowitz (Asiatische Forschungen, 32).

———. 1973. "Die Lehrworte des Pha-dam-pa." In *Serta Tibeto-Mongolica: Festschrift für Walther Heissig zum 60. Geburtstag am 5.12.1973*, edited by R. Kaschewsky, K. Sagaster, and M. Weiers. Wiesbaden, Harrassowitz. Pp. 171–204.

———. 1982. "Zu einigen tibetischen Pilgerplätzen in Nepal." *Zentralasiatische Studien* 16: 427–42.

———. 1990. "Nyantschen Thanglha: Ein heiliger Berg Tibets." In *Die Heiligsten Berge der Welt*, edited by K. Gratzl. Graz, Verlag für Sammler. Pp. 119–27.

Kawaguchi, E. 1909. *Three Years in Tibet.* Madras, Theosophist Office.

Kazi Dawa Samdup. 1987. *Śrī-cakraśaṁvara-tantra: A Buddhist Tantra.* New Delhi, Aditya Prakashan.

Kern, H., trans. 1909. *The Saddharma-Pundarīka or The Lotus of the True Law.* Oxford, Clarendon Press (Sacred Books of the East, 21).

Keyes, C. F. 1975. "Buddhist Pilgrimage Centers and the Twelve-Year Cycle: Northern Thai Moral Order in Space and Time." *History of Religions* 15, 1: 71–89.

Kingdom-Ward, F. [Ward]. 1990. *Himalayan Enchantment.* Compiled and edited by J. Whitehead. London, Serindia.

Kirkland, J. R. 1982. "The Spirit of the Mountain: Myth and State in Pre-Buddhist Tibet." *History of Religions* 21, 3: 257–71.

Kleeman, T. F. 1994. "Mountain Deities in China: The Domestication of the Mountain God and the Subjugation of the Margins." *Journal of the American Oriental Society* 114, 2: 226–38.

Kölver, B. 1976. "A Ritual Map from Nepal." In *Folia rara: Wolfgang Voigt LXV. Diem natalem celebranti*, edited by H. Franke, W. Heissig, and W. Treue. Wiesbaden, Franz Steiner. Pp. 68–80.

Könchog Gyaltsen. 1986. *The Garland of Mahamudra Practices.* Ithaca, N.Y., Snow Lion.

———. 1988. *In Search of Stainless Ambrosia.* Ithaca, N.Y., Snow Lion.

Kuijp, L. W. J. van der 1991. "On the Life and Political Career of Ta'i-si-tu." In *Tibetan History and Language: Studies Dedicated to Uray Géza on his Seventieth Birthday*, edited by E. Steinkellner. Wien, Arbeitskreis für Tibetische und Buddhistische Studien Universität Wien (Wiener Studien zur Tibetologie und Buddhismuskunde, 26). Pp. 277–327.

Kværne, P. 1987. "Tibetan Religions." In *The Encyclopedia of Religion.*, edited by M. Eliade. Vol. 14. New York, Macmillan. Pp. 497–504.

Kværne, P., ed. 1994. Tibetan Studies. *Proceedings of the 6th Seminar of the International Association for Tibetan Studies, Fagernes 1992.* 2 vols. Oslo, Institute for Comparative Research in Human Culture.

Lagerwey, J. 1992. "The Pilgrimage to Wu-tang Shan." In *Pilgrims and Sacred Sites in China*, edited by S. Naquin and Chün-Fang Yü. Berkeley, University of California Press. Pp. 293–332.
Lalou, M. 1959. *Fiefs, Poisons et Guérissuers*. Paris, Société Asiatique (Manuscrits de Haut Asie Conservés a la Bibliothèque Nationale de Paris (Fonds Pelliot), 6).
Lamb, A. 1966. *The McMahon Line: A Study in the Relations between India, China and Tibet, 1904 to 1914*. 2 vols. London, Routledge & Kegan Paul.
Lansing, J. S. 1991. *Priests and Programmers. Technologies of Power in the Engineered Landscape of Bali*. Princeton, Princeton University Press.
Large-Blondeau, A-M. [Blondeau]. 1960. "Les pèlerinages tibétains." In *Les Pèlerinages*. Paris, Editions du Seuil (Collection Sources Orientale, 3). Pp. 199–246.
Lhalungpa, L. P. 1977. *The Life of Milarepa*. New York, E. P. Dutton.
Lichter, D., and L. Epstein. 1983. "Irony in Tibetan Notions of the Good Life." In *Karma. An Anthropological Inquiry*, edited by C. F. Keyes and E. V. Daniel. Berkeley, University of California Press. Pp. 223–59.
Lopez, D. 1996. " 'Lamaism' and the Disappearance of Tibet." *Comparative Studies in Society and History* 38, 1: 3–25.
Loseries, A. 1990. "Kailāsa-Der Heiligste Berg der Welt." In *Die Heiligsten Berge der Welt*, edited by K. Gratzl. Graz, Verlag für Sammler. Pp. 81–118.
Ludlow, F. 1938. "The Sources of the Subansiri and Siyom." *Himalayan Journal* 10: 1–21.
———. 1940. "Takpo and Kongbo, S. E. Tibet." *Himalayan Journal* 12: 1–16.
Ludlow, F., and G. Sherrif. 1937. "Expeditions. The Sources of the Subansiri and Siyom." *Himalayan Journal* 9: 144–47.
Macdonald, A. [Spanien]. 1971. "Une lecture des P.T. 1286, 1287, 1038, 1047 et 1290. Essai sur la formation et l'emploi des mythes politiques dans la religion royale de Sroṅ-bcan sgam-po." In *Études tibétaines dédiées à la mémoire de Marcelle Lalou*, edited by A. D. Spanien. Paris, Librairie d'Amerique et d'Orient. Pp. 190–389.
Macdonald, A. W. 1975. "A Little Read Guide to the Holy Places of Nepal." *Kailash: A Journal of Himalayan Studies* 3, 2: 89–144.
———. 1979. "A Tibetan Guide to Some of the Holy Places of the Dhaulagiri-Muktinath Area of Nepal." In *Studies in Pali and Buddhism*, edited by A. K. Narain. Delhi, B. R. Publishing. Pp. 243–253.
———. 1985. "Points of View on Halase, a Holy Place in East Nepal." *Tibet Journal* 10, 3: 1–13.
———. 1987a. "Avant propos." *Rituels himalayens*. (Numéro spécial de:) *l'Ethnographie* 100–101: 5–13.
———. 1987b. "Remarks on the Manipulation of Power and Authority in the High Himalaya." *Tibet Journal* 12, 1: 3–16.
———. 1990. "Hindu-isation, Buddha-isation, Then Lama-isation or: What Happened at La-phyi?" In *Indo-Tibetan Studies. Papers in Honour and Appreciation of Professor David L. Snellgrove's Contribution to Indo-Tibetan Studies*, edited by T. Skorupski. Tring, Eng., Institute of Buddhist Studies. Pp. 199–208.
Macdonald, A. W., ed. 1997. *Maṇḍala and Landscape*. New Delhi, D. K. Printworld.
Macdonald, A. W., and Dvags-po Rin-po-che. 1981. "Un guide peu lu des lieux-saints de Népal—II eme Partie." In *Tantric and Taoist Studies in Honour of R. A. Stein*, vol. 1, edited by M. Strickmann. Bruxelles, Institut Belge des Hautes Etudes Chinoises. Pp. 237–73.
Mackenzie, A. 1884. *The North-East Frontier of India*. Delhi (reprint edition 1979), Mittal.
Mackley, C. E. 1994. "Gendered Practices and the Inner Sanctum: The Reconstruction of Tibetan Sacred Space in 'China's Tibet.' " *Tibet Journal*. Special Edition: *Powerful Places and Spaces in Tibetan Religious Culture* 19, 2: 61–94.
Mammitzsch, U. 1997. "Maṇḍala and Landscape in Japan." In Macdonald 1997: 1–39.

March, K. S. 1977. "Of People and Naks: The Management and Meaning of High Altitude Herding among Contemporary Solu Sherpas." *Contributions to Nepalese Studies* 4, 2: 83–97.

Marriott, M. 1976. "Hindu Transactions: Diversity without Dualism." In *Transactions and Meaning*, edited by B. Kapferer. Philadelphia, Institute for the Study of Human Issues. Pp. 109–42.

Marriott, M., and R. Inden. 1977. "Toward an Ethnosociology of South Asian Caste Systems." In *The New Wind: Changing Identities in South Asia*, edited by K. A. David. The Hague, Mouton. Pp. 227–38.

Martin, D. 1988. "For Love or Religion? Another Look at a 'Love Song' by the Sixth Dalai Lama." *Zeitschrift der Deutschen Morgenländischen Gesellschaft* 138, 2: 349–63.

———. 1992. "Crystals and Images from Bodies, Hearts and Tongues from Fire: Points of Relic Controversy from Tibetan History." In Ihara and Yamaguchi 1992, 1: 183–96.

———. 1994a. "Tibet at the Center: A Historical Study of Some Tibetan Geographical Conceptions Based on Two Types of Country-lists Found in Bon Histories." In Kværne 1994, 1: 517–32.

———. 1994b. *Mandala Cosmogony: Human Body, Good Thought and the Revelation of the Secret Mother Tantras of Bon*. Wiesbaden, Harrassowitz Verlag.

Miller, B. D. 1980. "Views of Women's Roles in Buddhist Tibet." In *Studies in the History of Buddhism*, edited by A. K. Narain. Delhi, B. R. Publishing. Pp. 155–66.

Montmollin, M. de. 1992. "*bKra shis sgo mang* of Bhutan: On a Specific Tradition of Shrines and its Propagation in the Museum of Ethnography in Neuchâtel (Switzerland)." In Ihara and Yamaguchi 1992, 2:605–13.

Morshead, H. T. 1914. *Report on an Exploration on the North East Frontier, 1913*. Dehra Dun, Office of the Trigonometrical Survey.

Mumford, S. R. 1989. *Himalayan Dialogue: Tibetan Lamas and Gurung Shamans in Nepal*. Madison, University of Wisconsin Press.

Mus, P. 1978. *Barabadur*. New York, Arno Press.

Nālandā Translation Committee. 1982. *The Life of Marpa the Translator*. Boulder, Shambhala.

Namkhai Norbu Dewang. 1967. "Musical Tradition of the Tibetan People. Songs in Dance Measure." In *Orientalia Romana, Essays and Lectures*, 2. Roma, Instituto Italiano per il Medio ed Estremo Oriente. Pp. 207–347.

Naquin, S., and Chün-Fang Yü. 1992. "Introduction: Pilgrimage in China." In *Pilgrims and Sacred Sites in China*, edited by S. Naquin and Chün-Fang Yü. Berkeley, University of California Press. Pp. 1–38.

Nebesky-Wojkowitz, R. de. 1956. *Oracles and Demons of Tibet*. The Hague, Mouton.

Ngawang Dak-pa. 1987. "Les pèlerinages bouddhiques au Tibet." In *Histoire des pèlerinages non-chrétiens*. Paris, Hachette. Pp. 264–277.

Norbu, J. 1994. "The Tibetan Resistance Movement and the Role of the C.I.A." In *Resistance and Reform in Tibet*, edited by R. Barnett and S. Akiner. London, Hurst. Pp. 186–196.

Norbu, N., and R. Prats. 1989. *Gaṅs Ti se'i dkar c'ag: A Bon-po Story of the Sacred Mountain Ti-se and the Blue Lake Ma-phaṅ*. Roma, Instituto Italiano per il Medio ed Estremo Oriente.

Normanton, S. 1988. *Tibet. The Lost Civilisation*. London, Hamish Hamilton.

Olschak, B. C., and Geshé Thupten Wangyal. 1987. *Mystic Art of Ancient Tibet*. Boston, Shambhala.

Ortner, S. 1978. *Sherpas through Their Rituals*. Cambridge, Cambridge University Press.

Pal, P. 1984. *Tibetan Paintings*. London, Sotheby.

Parfionovitch, Y., F. Meyer, and Gyurme Dorje, eds. 1992. *Tibetan Medical Paintings: Illustrations of the Blue Beryl Treatise of Sangye Gyamtso (1653–1705)*, 2 vols. New York, Harry N. Abrams.

Paul, D. 1985. *Women in Buddhism: Images of the Feminine in Māhayāna Tradition*. Berkeley, Asian Humanities Press.

Pemberton, R. B. 1835. *Report on the Eastern Frontier of British India*. Gauhati (reprint edition 1966), Department of Historical and Antiquarian Studies in Assam.

Petech, L. 1973. *Aristocracy and Government in Tibet 1728–1959*. Roma, Instituto Italiano per il Medio ed Estremo Oriente. (Serie Orientale Roma 45).

———. 1978. "The 'Bri-guṅ-pa Sect in Western Tibet and Ladakh." In *Proceedings of the Csoma de Kórös Memorial Symposium Mátrafüred, Hungary, 24–30 September 1976*, edited by L. Ligeti. Budapest, Akadémiai Kiadó. Pp. 313–26.

———. 1990. *Central Tibet and the Mongols. The Yüan–Sa-skya Period of Tibetan History*. Roma Instituto Italiano per il Medio ed Estremo Oriente. (Serie Orientale Roma 65).

Pommaret, F. 1994. "Les fêtes aux divinités-montagnes *Phyva* au Bhoutan de l'est." In Kværne 1994, 2:660–669.

Pranavananda, S. 1983. *Kailās-Mānasarovar*. 2nd ed. New Delhi, Swami Pranavananda.

Ramble, C. 1995. "Gaining Ground: Representations of Territory in Bon and Tibetan Popular Tradition." *Tibet Journal*. Special Edition: *Powerful Places and Spaces in Tibetan Religious Culture* 20, 1: 82–123.

———. 1997. "The Creation of the Bon Mountain of Kongpo." In Macdonald 1997: 133–232.

Ray, R. 1994. *Buddhist Saints in India: A Study in Buddhist Values and Orientations*. New York, Oxford University Press.

Reader, I. 1988. "Miniaturization and Proliferation: A Study of Small-scale Pilgrimages in Japan." *Studies in Central and East Asian Religions* 1: 50–66.

Reinhard, J. 1978. "Khembalung: The Hidden Valley," *Kailash: A Journal of Himalayan Studies* 6, 1: 5–35.

Reynolds, V., et al. 1986. *Catalogue of the Newark Museum Tibetan Collection. Volume III: Sculpture and Painting*. Newark, Newark Museum.

Rhie, M. and R. A. F. Thurman. 1991. *Wisdom and Compassion: The Sacred Art of Tibet*. New York, Abrams.

Ricard, M., et al. 1994. *The Life of Shabkar: The Autobiography of a Tibetan Yogin*. Albany, SUNY Press.

Richardson, H. E. 1984. *Tibet and Its History*. 2nd. ed. Boston, Shambhala.

———. 1993. *Ceremonies of the Lhasa Year*. London, Serindia.

Rock, J. F. 1947. *The Ancient Na-khi Kingdom of Southwest China*. vol. 2. Cambridge, Harvard University Press.

Roerich, G. N. 1979. *The Blue Annals*. Delhi, Motilal Banarsidass.

Sakya, J., and J. Emery. 1990. *Princess in the Land of Snows*. Boston, Shambhala.

Sallnow, M. E. 1987. *Pilgrims of the Andes. Regional Cults in Cusco*. Washington, D.C., Smithsonian Institution Press.

Samuel, G. 1993. *Civilized Shamans: Buddhism in Tibetan Societies*. Washington, D.C., Smithsonian Institution.

———. 1994. "Tibet and the Southeast Asian Highlands: Rethinking the Intellectual Context of Tibetan Studies." In Kværne 1994, 2: 696–710.

Sanderson, A. 1990. "Evidence of the Textual Dependence of the Buddhist Yogānuttaratantras on the Tantric Śaiva Canon." Unpublished seminar paper delivered at Universität Hamburg, May 1990.

———. 1994. "Vajrayāna: Origins and Functions." in *Buddhism Into the Year 2000: International Conference Proceedings*, edited by Mettananda Bhikkhu. Bangkok and Los Angeles, Dhammakaya Foundation. Pp. 87–102.

Sangren, P. S. 1993. "Power and Transcendence in the Ma Tsu Pilgrimages of Taiwan." *American Ethnologist* 20, 3: 564–82.

Sax, W. S. 1990. "Village Daughter, Village goddess: Residence, Gender, and Politics in a Himalayan Pilgrimage." *American Ethnologist* 17, 3: 491–512.

———. 1991. *Mountain Goddess: Gender and Politics in a Himalayan Pilgrimage*. New York, Oxford University Press.

———. 1992. "Pilgrimage unto Death." In *To Strive and Not to Yield: Essays in Honour of Colin Brown*, edited by J. Veitch. Wellington, Victoria University of Wellington. Pp. 200–212.

Schicklgruber, C. 1992. "Grib: On the Significance of the Term in a Socio-religious Context." In Ihara and Yamaguchi 1992, 2:723–34.

Schopen, G. 1987. "Burial 'ad sanctos' and the Physical Presence of the Buddha in Early Indian Buddhism: A Study in the Archeology of Religion." *Religion* 17: 193–225.

Schröder, D. 1952. "Zur Religion der Tujen des Sininggebietes (Kukunor)." *Anthropos* 47, 1–2:1–79.

Schwartz, R. D. 1994. "The Anti-Splittist Campaign and Tibetan Political Consciousness." In *Resistance and Reform in Tibet*, edited by R. Barnett and S. Akiner. London, Hurst. Pp. 207–37.

Schwartzberg, J. E. 1994. "Cartography of Greater Tibet and Mongolia." In *The History of Cartography, vol. 2, 2: Cartography in the Traditional East and Southet Asian Societies*, edited by J. B. Harley and D. Woodward. Chicago, University of Chicago Press. Pp. 607–81.

Shakabpa, Tsepon W. D. 1984. *Tibet: A Political History*. New York, Potala.

Shakya, T. 1993. "Whither the Tsampa Eaters." *Himal* September–October: 8–11.

Sherring, C. A. 1974. *Western Tibet and the Indian Borderland*. Delhi (reprint edition), Cosmo.

Shukla, B. K. 1959. *The Daflas of the Subansiri Region*. Shillong, North-East Frontier Agency.

Smith, E. G. 1968. Foreward to *Tibetan Chronicle of Padma-dkar-po*, edited by L. Chandra. New Delhi, International Academy of Indian Culture (Śata-Piṭaka Series, 75). Pp. 1–8.

———. 1969. Preface to *The Life of the Saint of gTsaṅ*, edited by L. Chandra. New Delhi, International Academy of Indian Culture (Śata-Piṭaka Series, 79). Pp. 1–37.

———. 1970. Introduction to *Kongtrul's Encyclopaedia of Indo-Tibetan Culture*, edited by L. Chandra, New Delhi, International Academy of Indian Culture (Śata-Piṭaka Series, 80). Pp. 1–87.

Smith, J. Z. 1982. *Imagining Religion: From Babylon to Jonestown*. Chicago, University of Chicago Press.

Snellgrove, D. L. 1959. *The Hevajra Tantra. A Critical Study*. 2 pts. London, Oxford University Press.

———. 1979. "Places of Pilgrimage in Thag (Thakkhola)." *Kailash: A Journal of Himalayan Studies* 7, 2: 75–170.

———. 1987. *Indo-Tibetan Buddhism*. 2 vols. Boston, Shambhala.

Snelling, J. 1990. *The Sacred Mountain: Travellers and Pilgrims at Mount Kailas in Western Tibet and the Great Universal Symbol of the Sacred Mountain*. Rev. and Enl. ed. London, East-West.

Sørensen, P. K. 1988. "Tibetan Love Lyrics—The Love Songs of the Sixth Dalai Lama: An Annotated Critical Edition of Tshaṅ-dbyaṅ rGya-mtsho'i mGul-glu." *Indo-Iranian Journal* 31: 253–98.

———. 1990. *Divinity Secularized: An Inquiry into the Nature and Form of the Songs Ascribed to the Sixth Dalai Lama*. Wien, Arbeitskreis für Tibetische und Buddhistische Studien Universität Wien (Wiener Studien zur Tibetologie und Buddhismuskunde, 25).

———. 1994. *Tibetan Buddhist Historiography—The Mirror Illuminating the Royal Genealogies: An Annotated Translation of the XIVth Century Tibetan Chronicle, rGyal-rabs gsal-ba'i me-long*. Wiesbaden, Harrassowitz Verlag (Asiatiche Forschungen, 128).

Spence, H. 1991. "Tsarong II, The Hero of Chaksam, and the Modernisation Struggle in Tibet, 1912–1931." *Tibet Journal* 16, 1: 34–57.

Sperber, B. G. 1995. "Nature in the Kalasha Perception of Life." In *Asian Perceptions of Nature: A Critical Approach*, edited by O. Bruun and A. Kalland. Surrey, Eng., Curzon Press. Pp. 126–47.

Stablein, M. 1978. "Textual and Contextual Patterns of Tibetan Buddhist Pilgrimage in India." *Tibet Society Bulletin* 12: 7–38.

Stein, R. A. 1971. "Du récit au rituel dans les manuscrits tibétains de Touen-houang." in *Études tibétaines dédiées à la mémoire de Marcelle Lalou*, edited by A. Spanien. Paris, Librairie d'Amerique et d'Orient. Pp. 479–547.

———. 1972. *Tibetan Civilization.* Translated by J. F. Stapleton Driver. Stanford, Stanford University Press, 1972.

———. 1972–74. "Résumé des Cours." *Annuaire du Collège de France.* Paris. 1972, Pp. 499–510; 1973, pp. 463–70; 1974, Pp. 508–17.

———. 1988a. *Grottes-matrices et lieux-saints de la déesse en Asie orientale.* Paris, École Française d'Extrême-orient (Publications de l'École Française d'Extrême-orient, 151).

———. 1988b. "Les serments des traités sino-tibétaines (8e–9e siècles)." *T'oung Pao* 74: 119–38.

———. 1990. *The World in Miniature: Container Gardens and Dwellings in Far Eastern Thought.* Stanford, Stanford University Press.

———. 1995. "La soumission de Rudra et autres contes tantriques." *Journal Asiatique* 283, 1: 121–160.

Stevens, J. 1988. *The Marathon Monks of Mount Hiei.* Boston, Shambhala.

Stoddard, H. 1985. *Le Mendiant de L'Amdo.* Paris, Société d'Ethnographie (Recherches sur la Haute Asie, 9).

———. 1988. "The Long Life of rDo-sbis dGe-bšes Šes-rab rGya-mcho." In Uebach and Panglung 1988: 465–71.

Stonor, C. R. 1952. "The Sulung Tribe of the Assam Himalaya." *Anthropos* 47, 5–6: 947–62.

Ström, A. K. 1995. *The Quest for Grace. Identification and Cultural Continuity in the Tibetan Diaspora.* Oslo, Department and Museum of Anthropology, University of Oslo (Oslo Occasional Papers in Social Anthropology, 24).

Stubel, H. 1958. *The Mewu Fantzu: A Tibetan Tribe of Kansu.* New Haven, Human Relations Area Files Press.

Stutchbury, E. 1994. "Perceptions of Landscape in Khazha: 'Sacred' Geography and the Tibetan System of 'Geomancy.'" *Tibet Journal.* Special Edition: *Powerful Places and Spaces in Tibetan Religious Culture* 19, 4: 59–102.

Tambiah, S. J. 1976. *World Conqueror and World Renouncer: A Study of Buddhism and Polity in Thailand against a Historical Background.* Cambridge, Cambridge University Press.

———. 1985. *Culture, Thought and Social Action: An Anthropological Perspective.* Cambridge, Harvard University Press.

Templeman, D. 1983. *The Seven Instruction Lineages.* Dharamsala, Library of Tibetan Works and Archives.

Thomas, E. J. 1949. *The Life of the Buddha.* London, Kegan Paul.

Tohoku University. 1953. *A Catalogue of the Tohoku University Collection of Tibetan Works on Buddhism,* edited by Yensho Kanakura *et al.*, Sendai, Seminary of Indology Tohoku University.

Tsarong, D. N. 1990. *What Tibet Was: As Seen by a Native Photographer.* New Delhi, D. N. Tsarong.

Tsering, T. 1985. "Nag-roṅ mGon-po rNam-rgyal: A 19th century Khams-pa Warrior." In Aziz and Kapstein 1985: 196–214.

Tsuda, S. 1978. "A Critical Tantrism." *Memoirs of the Research Department of the Toyo Bunko* 36: 167–231.

Tucci, G. 1932. *Indo-Tibetica.* Vol.1. Rome, Reale Accademia d'Italia.

———. 1949. *Tibetan Painted Scrolls.* Vol.2. Roma, Libreria dello Stato.

———. 1966. *Tibetan Folk Songs.* Ascona, Switz., Artibus Asiae.

———. 1970. *The Theory and Practice of the Mandala.* New York, Samuel Weiser.

———. 1971. "Travels of Tibetan Pilgrims in the Swat Valley." In *Opera Minora.* Vol. 2. Roma, Università di Roma. Pp. 369–418.

———. 1980. *The Religions of Tibet.* Translated by G. Samuel. London, Routledge & Kegan Paul.

———. 1989. *The Temples of Western Tibet and Their Artistic Symbolism: Tsaparang.* (*Indo-Tibetica,* 3.2). Edited by L. Chandra. New Delhi, Aditya Prakashan.

Turner, V. W. 1973. "The Centre Out There: Pilgrim's Goal." *History of Religions* 12: 191–230.

———. 1974. "Pilgrimages as Social Processes." In *Dramas, Fields, and Metaphors: Symbolic Action in Human Society*. Ithaca, N. Y. Cornell University Press.

Turner, V. W., and E. Turner. 1978. *Image and Pilgrimage in Christian Culture*. New York, Columbia University Press.

Uebach, H., and J. Panglung, eds. 1988. *Tibetan Studies. Proceedings of the 4th Seminar of the International Association for Tibetan Studies, Schloss Hohenkammer-Munich, 1985*. München, Kommission für zentralasiatische Studien, Bayerische Akademie der Wissenschaften.

Waddell, L. A. 1895. *The Buddhism of Tibet or Lamaism*. Cambridge (reprint 1985), W. Heffer and Sons.

———. 1905. *Lhasa and Its Mysteries*. London, Methuen.

Wallace, A. B. trans. and ed. 1980. *The Life and Teachings of Geshé Rabten*. London, Allen & Unwin.

Ward, F. K. [Kingdom-Ward]. 1936. "Botanical and Geographical Explorations in Tibet, 1935." *Geographical Journal* 88, 5: 385–413.

———. 1938. "The Assam Himalaya: Travels in Balipara-1." *Journal of the Royal Central Asian Society* 25: 610–19.

———. 1941. *Assam Adventure*. London, Jonathan Cape.

———. 1947. "Tibet as a Grazing Land." *Geographical Journal* 110, 1–3: 60–75.

Wayman, A. 1981. "Reflections on the Theory of Barabuḍur as a *Maṇḍala*." In *Barabuḍur: History and Significance of a Buddhist Monument*, edited by L. O. Gomez and H. W. Woodward, Jr. Berkeley, Asian Humanities Press. Pp. 139–72.

Willis, J. D. 1985. "On the Nature of rNam-thar: Early dGe-lugs-pa *Siddha* Biographies." In Aziz and Kapstein 1985: 304–19.

Woodman, D. 1969. *Himalayan Frontiers: A Political Review of British, Chinese, Indian and Russian Rivalries*. London, Cresset Press.

Wylie, T. V. 1959. "A Standard System of Tibetan Transcription." *Harvard Journal of Asiatic Studies* 2: 261–67.

———. 1962. *The Geography of Tibet According to the 'Dzam-gling-rgyas-bshad*. Roma, Istituto Italiano per il Medio Ed Estremo Oriente (Serie Orientale Roma, 25).

Yuthok, D. Y. 1990. *House of the Turquoise Roof*. Ithaca, N.Y., Snow Lion.

Maps Consulted

1914. Part of the North-Eastern Frontier and Tibet. In Bailey 1914, 4: 428. (Scale: 1: 1,000,000.)

1938. Sources of the Subansiri and the Siyom. In Ludlow 1938. (Sketch map not to scale.)

1941. Tibet and the Eastern Tsang-po. In Ward 1941. (Scale: approximately 1 cm = 10 miles.)

1954. NH 46–15 Kyimdong Dzong. In Series U502, U.S. Army Map Service. (Scale 1: 250,000.)

1954. NH 46–14 Trigu Tsho. In Series L500, U.S. Army Map Service. (Scale: 1:250,000.)

1954. NH 46–13 Yamdrog Tsho. In Series L500, U.S. Army Map Service. (Scale: 1:250,000.)

1957. Takpo and Tsari. In Bailey 1957. (Scale: approximately 1.2 cm = 5 miles.)

Index

Tsari Nub, 105, 189, 201–2, 204–5, 209, 214
Tsari Nyingma, 47
Tsari Rechen, 70
Tsari River, 75, 91, 121, 131, 219
Tsari Sarma, 47, 238 n.32
Tsari Sarpa, 169
Tsari Shar, 201, 202, 204, 214
Tsari Shingkyong
  dwelling of, 143, 185
  Fifth Dalai Lama's vision of, 157
  identified with tribal peoples, 182, 184–85
  Khorlo Dompa as, 188
  names of, 139, 187
  as personification of Tsari's power, 125–26
  punishing ritual breach, 122–23, 187–88
  shrine of, 187
  worship of, 118, 185–88
Tsari Tsagong Parvata, 63
Tsari Tsokar, 47, 189
  administration of, 201–2
  Anglo-Tibetan negotiations over, 19
  history of, 237 n.32
  pilgrims' resthouse at, 204
  revival of pilgrimage to, 219
  women's pilgrimage to, 111, 121, 251 n.40
Tsāritra (Tsaritra), 43, 45, 64, 73, 76, 86, 109
Tsariwa
  as beggars, 5, 180, 186, 206, 215–17, 219
  collect tribute goods, 130, 137
  as descendents of yogins, 179
  as embodiments of deities, 181–84, 206–7, 260 n.15
  identity as Lopa, 179–82
  mibog status of, 178, 203
  as pilgrims' resthouse keepers, 186, 204–8
  population of, 177, 208, 219, 259 n.1
  as servants or keepers of the *né*, 185–86, 194–95, 204
  worship of Tsari Shingkyong, 185–88
  See also Tsari
Tsarong, 163
Tsekor, 93–96, 95 fig., 214
Tselpa, 61, 69–70, 85. *See also* Shang Tselpa
Tselpa Samten Pelwa, 84
Tso Karpo, 169
Tsogchö Chenmo, 156
Tsogchö Sertreng, 156
Tsongkhapa, 61–62, 72, 109, 156
tsulkang, 105, 186, 202–8. *See also* pilgrims' resthouses
tsulpa, 90, 105, 107, 112, 118, 186, 206
  meaning of, 203–4
  See also pilgrims' resthouses
Turner, Victor, 7–8
Turquoise Lake Palace
  disposal of weapons in, 118–19
  as maṇḍala palace, 52
  on pilgrimage to, 106, 111, 117–18
  pilgrims' resthouses at, 118, 204, 207, 214
  ritual replica of, 191–92
  wealth offering into, 118
  yogins visiting, 54, 65, 68, 94, 102, 117–18

Ü, 44, 128
Uḍḍiyana, 47, 52–53, 62
Uḍra, 83
Umā, 42
Üri, 85, 90
Üripa, 70

Vajrapāṇi, 40
Vajravārāhī. *See* Dorje Pagmo
Vimalamitra, 62

Wangchuk Chenpo, 42
Ward, Francis Kingdom, 218
weapons, 132–33
  of Arunachal tribes, 131, 135–36, 138, 144–45
  carried on pilgrimage, 109, 141–42, 145
  and masculinity, 119, 253 n.60
  as offerings to mountain gods, 24, 112
  of protective deity, 185
  ritual disposal of, 118–19
  as tax payment, 168
  as trade goods, 212
  as tribute goods, 138
  used in ritual, 24, 112, 192
wild animals and birds, 63, 180, 219
  antelope, as prophetic sign, 71
  Buddha manifest as deer, 148

Printed in the United States
843900001B

9 780195 120073